✦INDEPENDENCE✦

✦INDEPENDENCE✦

The Tangled Roots
of the American Revolution

✦

THOMAS P. SLAUGHTER

🏛 HILL AND WANG

A division of Farrar, Straus and Giroux New York

Hill and Wang
A division of Farrar, Straus and Giroux
18 West 18th Street, New York 10011

Copyright © 2014 by Thomas P. Slaughter
Maps copyright © 2014 by Jeffrey L. Ward
All rights reserved
Printed in the United States of America
First edition, 2014

Library of Congress Cataloging-in-Publication Data
Slaughter, Thomas P. (Thomas Paul)
    Independence : the tangled roots of the American Revolution / Thomas P.
Slaughter. — First edition.
        pages   cm
    Includes bibliographical references and index.
    ISBN 978-0-8090-5834-1 (hardcover)
    1. United States—History—Revolution, 1775–1783—Causes.   2. United
States—History—Colonial period, ca. 1600–1775.   I. Title.   II. Title :
Tangled roots of the American Revolution.

E210.S58 2014
973.3'11—dc23

                                                            2013034391

Designed by Abby Kagan

Hill and Wang books may be purchased for educational, business, or promotional
use. For information on bulk purchases, please contact the Macmillan Corporate and
Premium Sales Department at 1-800-221-7945, extension 5442, or write to
specialmarkets@macmillan.com.

www.fsgbooks.com
www.twitter.com/fsgbooks • www.facebook.com/fsgbooks

1   3   5   7   9   10   8   6   4   2

To
Jasmine and Moses (in alphabetical order)

To
Moses and Jasmine (in birth order)

To
both my children, with love

Why do wars or revolutions happen? We don't know. All we know is that for either of these to happen men must come together in a particular combination with everybody taking part, and we say that this is so because anything else is unimaginable, it has to be, it's a law.

—LEO TOLSTOY, *War and Peace*

CONTENTS

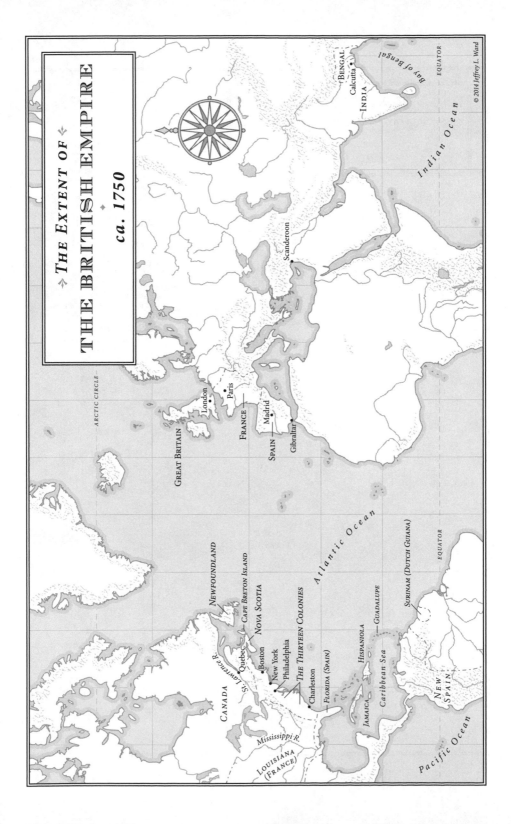

THE EXTENT OF
THE BRITISH EMPIRE
ca. 1750

© 2014 Jeffrey L. Ward

ARCTIC CIRCLE

GREAT BRITAIN
London
Paris
FRANCE
Madrid
SPAIN
Gibraltar

(BENGAL)
Calcutta
INDIA
Bay of Bengal
EQUATOR
Indian Ocean

Scanderoon

Atlantic Ocean

CANADA
St. Lawrence R.
Quebec
Boston
New York
Philadelphia
Charleston
THE THIRTEEN COLONIES
NOVA SCOTIA
CAPE BRETON ISLAND
NEWFOUNDLAND
FLORIDA (SPAIN)
Mississippi R.
LOUISIANA (FRANCE)

JAMAICA
HISPANIOLA
GUADALUPE
Caribbean Sea
SURINAM (DUTCH GUIANA)
NEW SPAIN
EQUATOR
Pacific Ocean

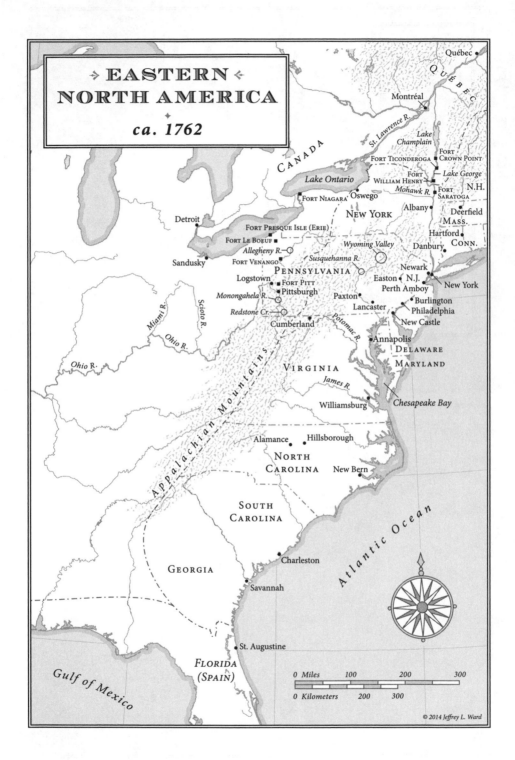

EASTERN
NORTH AMERICA
ca. 1762

Québec

QUÉBEC

Montréal

St. Lawrence R.

Lake
Champlain

CANADA

FORT TICONDEROGA

FORT
CROWN POINT

Lake George

FORT
WILLIAM HENRY

N.H.

Lake Ontario

Mohawk R.

FORT
SARATOGA

FORT NIAGARA

Oswego

Albany

Deerfield

Detroit

NEW YORK

MASS.

Hartford

CONN.

FORT PRESQUE ISLE (ERIE)

Danbury

FORT LE BOEUF

Allegheny R.

Wyoming Valley

Sandusky

FORT VENANGO

Susquehanna R.

Newark

Logstown

PENNSYLVANIA

Easton

N.J.

FORT PITT

Perth Amboy

New York

Miami R.

Scioto R.

Monongahela R.

Pittsburgh

Paxton

Burlington

Redstone Cr.

Lancaster

Philadelphia

Cumberland

New Castle

Potomac R.

Annapolis

Ohio R.

DELAWARE

Ohio R.

MARYLAND

VIRGINIA

James R.

Chesapeake Bay

Williamsburg

Appalachian Mountains

Alamance

Hillsborough

NORTH
CAROLINA

New Bern

SOUTH
CAROLINA

Atlantic Ocean

GEORGIA

Charleston

Savannah

St. Augustine

FLORIDA
(SPAIN)

Gulf of Mexico

0 Miles   100   200   300

0 Kilometers   200   300

© 2014 Jeffrey L. Ward

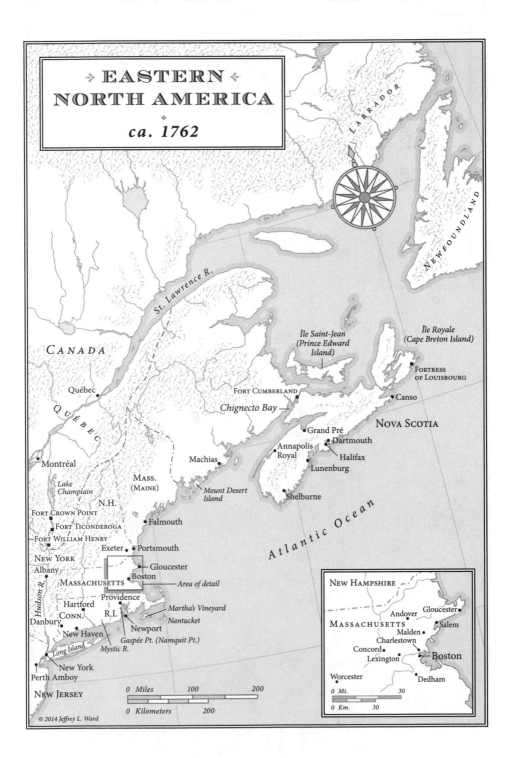

EASTERN
NORTH AMERICA
ca. 1762

LABRADOR

NEWFOUNDLAND

St. Lawrence R.

CANADA

QUÉBEC

Québec

Montréal

Lake Champlain

FORT CROWN POINT
FORT TICONDEROGA
FORT WILLIAM HENRY

NEW YORK
Albany

Hudson R.

MASSACHUSETTS

Hartford
Danbury
CONN.
New Haven
Long Island
New York
Perth Amboy

NEW JERSEY

MASS. (MAINE)

N.H.

Exeter
Portsmouth

Gloucester
Boston

Providence
R.I.
Newport
Gaspée Pt. (Namquit Pt.)
Mystic R.

Falmouth

Area of detail

Martha's Vineyard
Nantucket

Machias

Mount Desert Island

FORT CUMBERLAND
Chignecto Bay

Île Saint-Jean
(Prince Edward Island)

Île Royale
(Cape Breton Island)

FORTRESS OF LOUISBOURG

Canso

NOVA SCOTIA

Grand Pré
Annapolis Royal
Dartmouth
Halifax
Lunenburg

Shelburne

Atlantic Ocean

0 Miles   100   200
0 Kilometers   200

NEW HAMPSHIRE

MASSACHUSETTS

Andover   Gloucester
Salem
Malden
Charlestown
Concord
Lexington   Boston

Worcester   Dedham

0 Mi.   30
0 Km.   30

© 2014 Jeffrey L. Ward

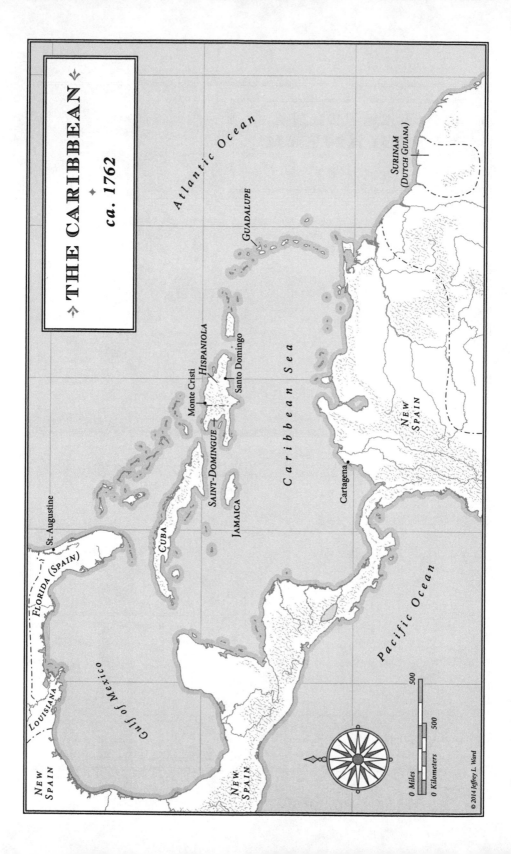

THE CARIBBEAN

ca. 1762

Atlantic Ocean

SURINAM
(DUTCH GUIANA)

GUADALUPE

HISPANIOLA

Monte Cristi

SAINT-DOMINGUE

Santo Domingo

Caribbean Sea

NEW
SPAIN

Cartagena

JAMAICA

CUBA

St. Augustine

FLORIDA (SPAIN)

LOUISIANA

Gulf of Mexico

Pacific Ocean

NEW
SPAIN

NEW
SPAIN

0 Miles   500

0 Kilometers   500

© 2014 Jeffrey L. Ward

PREFACE

"WHAT DO WE MEAN by the Revolution?" John Adams asked Thomas Jefferson rhetorically, after the two men had retired from public life. "The war? That was no part of the Revolution. It was only an effect and consequence of it. The Revolution was in the minds of the people, and this was effected from 1760 to 1775, in the course of fifteen years before a drop of blood was drawn at Lexington."

The Revolution had even deeper, more tangled roots than Adams unearthed for this letter. Disputes over sovereignty had begun in the seventeenth century with the very first charters on which the colonies based their claims; they continued as the colonists made treaties and waged war with Indians, skirted the Navigation Acts of 1651–1673, and then turned violently against British authority in Bacon's Rebellion in 1676 and the colonial uprisings associated with the Glorious Revolution of 1689. Conflicts of interest within the colonies, as much as between the colonies and the empire, showed that there were entrenched camps dedicated to certain fixed political principles long before 1760. At the same time, the expansion of global empires, the associated developments in international commerce, and changes in the colonies created new contexts for imperial politics.

Europeans immigrated to British North America to gain religious, economic, and political independence during the seventeenth and eighteenth centuries, and they built their freedom on the labor of slaves and on the land of Indians whose independence they stole. In London, meanwhile, kings and queens, imperial ministries, and members of

Parliament believed that the colonists harbored treasonous ambitions for independence from the very founding of the colonies, and they described them pejoratively as "independent," by which they meant chronically rebellious.

At the same time, the British North American colonists took great pride in what they experienced as true independence. To them, the term evoked courage, self-sufficiency, and devotion to family, parish, village, and God's higher law. They were committed to local relationships over distant ones and cast a suspicious eye on even their own colonial governments, which many of them considered remote and unrepresentative. They asserted this stubborn independence on spiritual grounds that encouraged them to be less respectful of hierarchy than their English contemporaries expected them to be.

The decision to emigrate, whether it was made on their own or imposed on them, expressed their independence from Europe, although not necessarily their desire to separate from it. But living at a distance from London made them more independent than they had been when they crossed the Atlantic. And neglect by the British ministers in charge of the colonies before 1750 nurtured this independence, which habits on both sides of the ocean entrenched. Then, as the colonies' domestic economies and population grew, as they geographically expanded and became ethnically heterogeneous, the colonists developed identities independent of the one that tethered them to the British Empire. Yet they continued to look as much backward as forward in time, and across the Atlantic as well as across the North American continent.

While Britain's relationship with its empire evolved, the theory of empire did not, and neither side fully grasped that misunderstandings both undermined and facilitated imperial governance. Colonists continued to strive for independence *within* the empire, while British administrators continued to believe that the colonists were aiming at independence *from* the empire. The tipping point came when a critical mass of colonists started to believe that they were *losing* their independence, while the imperial ministries were fighting to keep them from *becoming* independent. No one wanted change unless it was back to something they had lost, and both sides believed that the other was trying unilaterally to impose unwelcome change.

The rhetorical confusion is as much ours as theirs, but it does help to distinguish between independence and separation, for they were not the same in the minds of colonists before the late spring and summer of 1774. It is difficult to identify before then more than a handful of colonists who advocated separation from the British Empire, although many imagined that a separate nation would eventually arise organically in North America, given the colonies' economic and demographic growth, and that their descendants would conquer the continent. As late as April 1774, the worst case that John Adams could imagine was the *next* generation facing a war for separation. In a letter to his friend James Warren, written after the Boston Tea Party and before news of the Intolerable Acts reached North America, Adams offered his best guess about what the future held for the Anglo-American colonies.

> For my own Part, I am of the same opinion that I have been for many Years, that there is not Spirit enough on Either side to bring the Question to a compleat Decision—and that We shall oscilate like a Pendulum and fluctuate like the Ocean, for many Years to come, and never obtain a compleat Redress of American Grievances, nor submit to an absolute Establishment of Parliamentary Authority. But be trimming between both as we have been for ten Years past, for more Years to come than you and I shall live. Our Children, may see Revolutions and be concerned and active in effecting them of which we can form no Conception.

Despite all the strife during the previous century and especially during the previous decade, the imperial clock still ticked. Then, on April 19, 1775, about twenty miles from John Adams's home, the pendulum stopped. The Battles of Lexington and Concord completed the Revolution that Adams had not foreseen even one year earlier, and the Revolutionary War began.

In my telling, the story of American independence travels topically from New England to Nova Scotia, to the Caribbean and to Bengal, to New York and Pennsylvania, Virginia, and the Carolinas; it travels both ways across the Atlantic but focuses on the British North American colonies that revolted in 1775. The organization of chapters is not random, but I recognize that the story could be told from different vantage points, with Virginia rather than New England as the starting point, say, with Europe rather than the Nova Scotia borderlands, for the revolution began in different places and the colonists declared their independence at various times over 150 years. And I do not intend this to be a survey of British colonial America that pays equal attention to all places, people, and institutions. Religion comes up in these pages when religion matters to my narrative, for example, but there is a plethora of stories untold here that are true to events yet not directly connected to what I have written. There is more to say about Indians, slaves, women, sailors, ministers, courts, kings, parliament, loyalists, famous individuals from every walk of life, politicians, the Caribbean islands, Canada, and India, and I have done none of their stories complete justice. That is not because the stories are unimportant or less interesting than the one I am telling here, but because I wanted to stick with my central question: How did independence become revolutionary in British North America?

Although my story has one central theme, I do not propose that the Revolution had a single cause. Ambition, economy, greed, principles, ideology, imperial politics, social change and dissension, conflicting interregional interests, ideas, slavery, immigration, urbanization, ethnic hostility, and religion, among other factors, are all essential to the explanation. That being so, one runs the risk of incoherence, but I am conscious of how much I still must leave out on so many pages with so many themes and subplots. I am also aware that I do not define "independence" precisely at any point, or not any more than I already have in this preface. I try to be no more precise than the historical actors were, letting their meanings emerge from the contexts and usages, as I hope my interpretation does from the narrative. Wherever possible, and possibly to a fault, I have let them speak for themselves.

My decision to tell the story around the central theme of independence came rather late in the several decades that I have been teaching about the Revolution; it emerged cumulatively from the contemporary sources I use in my classes and lectures to illustrate the narrative. It is a term that was used repeatedly over time and across space by countless officials of the empire and by colonists. I find using their term preferable to applying my own or even to using one of their less fraught terms: "Freedom," "equality," or "liberty" would not have worked as well to communicate the core conflict that I describe.

Misunderstandings as much as disagreements, continuity as much as change, propelled events in colonial America, but war came unexpectedly in 1775. Self-interest and ideals dictated independence before rebellion declared it. The monarch, his ministers, most members of Parliament, and a large majority of the English public could no longer disregard the colonists' independence (lawlessness), and the colonists refused to surrender their independence (local sovereignty and personal freedom). In 1775, the long-standing British charge that the colonists were *"aiming at independance"* became true in every sense of the word for the first time.*

---

* Independance" was a common variant spelling, and "independancy" and "independency" were sometimes used as well. The quotation is from the *Providence Gazette*, May 12, 1765.

PART ONE

◆

Foundations

1

✦

BORDERLANDS

B Y THE SIXTEENTH CENTURY, both French and English fishermen were working the waters around Cape Breton, or Île Royale, today part of the Canadian province of Nova Scotia, and trading with the Abenaki and Micmac peoples who had lived and fished there for centuries.* Norse or Viking, possibly Irish, and other European fishermen and explorers had also frequented the region for hundreds of years. The Venetian explorer Giovanni Caboto, also known as John Cabot, passed that way in the fifteenth century; the English captain Charles Leigh recorded making landfall in 1597 along the Atlantic coast at a place whose first French name acknowledged his discovery, Havre à L'Anglois (English Harbor); and Samuel de Champlain at least passed it as he headed south.

By the early seventeenth century, the treacherous six-to-eight-week crossings of the Atlantic to these parts had already become part of maritime lore. "I have been to Canada seven times," wrote one French captain, "and I venture to state that the most favorable of those voyages gave me more white hairs than all those that I have made elsewhere. It is a continual torment for mind and body." Another Frenchman admitted his fear of sailing "over the unstable sea, every moment within two fingers of death [à deux doigts de la morte], as the saying goes." He was mindful of the "muttering, snorting, whistling, howling,

---

* King James I of England, who was also James VI of Scotland, named the province in 1621 as Nova Scotia (New Scotland) in honor of his native land.

storming, rumbling" seas that lifted the ships "aloft upon mountains of water, and thence down as it were into the most profound depths of the world." But the French and English kept coming for the fish, furs, land, adventure, independence, and wealth that they imagined awaiting them.

French explorers and fur traders founded Port Royal, a post on the Bay of Fundy coast of what we now call Nova Scotia, in 1605. That was less than two years before the first colonists landed at Jamestown, Virginia, establishing the first permanent English settlement in North America, and three years before the French founded another outpost at Quebec. And men from the two nations started fighting almost immediately. Virginia was nine hundred miles away from l'Acadie, as the French called their territory, but that was too close, and the continent of North America was too small, at nine million square miles, for the French and English to coexist peacefully. From the early 1600s through the middle of the eighteenth century, the islands and peninsulas of what we now call the Canadian Maritimes—New Brunswick, l'Acadie (Nova Scotia), Cape Breton Island, Île Saint-Jean (Prince Edward Island), and Placentia (Newfoundland)—were a borderland, the front line of conflict between the French and English in the New World.

The French abandoned Port Royal in 1607 rather than winter there. It was difficult to recruit traders and trappers, never mind settlers, and its promoters had to agree to some Huguenots (French Protestants) along with the Catholics, who said they would give it another try in 1610. Both groups survived only because the Micmacs suffered their presence, sustained them with trade, and created enduring connections based on intermarriage—all on the Indians' terms. Beginning in 1611, when the first two Jesuits arrived in New France, there were actually more conflicts between the missionaries and the men at the trading posts than either had with the Indians. During the winter of 1612–1613, when no supplies arrived from France, the trappers had to disperse to live with the Micmacs in their hunting camps. In the spring, a French ship removed the troublesome Jesuits and took them down the coast of what is now Maine to Mount Desert Island. There men under the command of Samuel Argall—an English pirate who had a commission from the governor of Jamestown to drive out the French—attacked and captured the Jesuits, and, in November 1613, with the help of a Jesuit guide, went on to plunder Port Royal. That effectively ended France's first settlement in the New World, but in 1608 the French explorer Samuel de Champlain had founded a settlement he called Quebec, on the St. Lawrence River, and so the French maintained footholds on the North American continent with their scattered outposts even after abandoning Port Royal to the English.

The French were colonizing North America at precisely the same time as the English were, and this was no coincidence: They did it to challenge the English and establish Catholic settlements in the face of English Protestant ones, and as one front line in the commercial and military warfare that punctuated the creation of the two empires competing with each other and with the Spanish and Dutch. At its peak in 1712, New France stretched from Newfoundland to the Rocky Mountains, and from Hudson Bay to the Gulf of Mexico, a vast territory divided into five colonies—Canada, Acadia, Hudson Bay, Newfoundland, and Louisiana. New France was always sparsely populated and financially modest in comparison to the English colonies on the mainland of North America.

In 1629, about seventy Scottish Presbyterians landed at the former Port Royal and established a trading mission. "We eat lobsters as big as little children," one of them raved, "plenty of salmons and salmon trouts, birds of strange and diverse kinds, hawks of all sorts, doves, turtles, pheasants, partridges, black birds, a kind also of hens, wild turkeys, cranes, herons, infinite store of geese, and three or four kinds of ducks, snipes, cormorants, and many sea fouls, whales, seals, castors [beavers], [and] otters." They, too, got along fine with the ever-flexible Micmac. Nonetheless, the Scottish enterprise failed and, in 1632, an Anglo-French treaty returned l'Acadie and Quebec to France.

The Micmacs, small bands and family groups rather than a unified tribe, were the principal Indian occupants of what is now Nova Scotia, and apparently they never numbered more than three thousand souls spread over the fifty thousand square miles that included what we now call New Brunswick, Prince Edward Island, and the southern part of Quebec's Gaspé Peninsula. They ranged in concert with the seasons. January brought them to the seacoast to fish for smelt and cod, and to hunt walruses and seals. In February and March they moved inland to hunt beaver, moose, and bear. From April through October, they were back at the seaside villages, where they gathered shellfish, lobster, crabs, and eels, as well as migratory wildfowl in the spring and fall;

between July and September they picked nuts, berries, and dry roots. As winter approached, they broke into smaller units to hunt and fish before beginning the annual cycle again in January.

Lines of authority in Micmac bands were vague and variable. Women gathered, cooked, and cared for children, who, unlike those of the European settlers, were not subject to corporal discipline. Men hunted and fished in season, and occasionally waged war on each other, on the Abenaki who lived south of them in what is now Maine, or on the French and English. They were not used to cooperating beyond the level of the band and so battled in small groups with limited aims and without coordinated strategy. They lived in an active spiritual world— surrounded by animal and human manitous (spirits), and ever conscious of their individual and collective *ginap* (spiritual power). Their shamans easily accepted and used Catholic artifacts—crosses and rosary beads—and adopted Catholic rituals like communion, with its wafers and holy water. The Catholic missionaries tolerated this syncretistic spirituality, realizing they could not expunge native ceremonies and beliefs. When Puritans came to these parts, however, they saw the lives of the Indians around them as being in sharp contrast with their own— with their Christian faith and their conflicted relationship to the earth-bound world, against which they were at constant war—against animals and plants, the native people, even their own inherent natures.

Micmac beliefs in the three souls of each being—the life soul, brain soul, and free soul—prepared them for the trinitarian concepts taught by the Catholic missionaries. They believed that the life soul dies when the body dies, that death of the brain soul leaves one witless, and that the free soul roams in life, in death, and in dreams. Unlike the Puritans, they accepted the natural world as it was, adapting themselves to its demands rather than trying to alter it. They had no interest in visiting Europe, in learning to manufacture the items they purchased or received as gifts from the French and English, or in changing their ways in emulation of them. The French, whom they encountered in smaller numbers than the English, became the Micmacs' natural allies; they agreed to pay "rent" on the land and were more generous gift givers than the impecunious New Englanders.

A French ship brought women and children to Port Royal for the first time in 1636, making it a true colony rather than just a trading outpost. These immigrants became the first genuine Acadians. By

1650, the fifty French families who lived, hunted, trapped, farmed, and fished there were developing a distinctive culture bound not only by their shared experiences in the New World but also by kinship. They remained as vulnerable as ever, though, and in 1654, when Oliver Cromwell's government in London commissioned Major Robert Sedgwick, in Boston, to attack New Amsterdam (soon to become New York) as part of its war against the Dutch Republic, Sedgwick seized the opportunity to attack Port Royal instead, even though it had nothing at all to do with the Dutch. Perhaps the best explanation for this unexpected action is that Sedgwick's son-in-law, the future Massachusetts governor Captain John Leverett, had invested in the Maine-Acadia trade, and, as Leverett explained to London officials, the expedition's goal was to enlarge Great Britain's "dominions in these western American parts." True enough; any old excuse to invade French settlements furthered the interests of New England traders and their London counterparts.

A three-day siege of Port Royal ended in French surrender. The victorious New Englanders seized booty estimated to value £10,000 and captured 220 French soldiers. Boston declared "a public and solemn thanksgiving to the Lord for his gracious working." Sedgwick offered Acadians a choice between being shipped back to France with their troops or continuing on their farms "unmolested," with "liberty of conscience allowed to religion," a concession that reflected the invaders' greater interest in commerce than in souls. The Acadians chose to keep their farms in 1654. Under English rule, in comparative isolation and thus independent of France and the Catholic Church, a distinctive Acadian creole culture was beginning to form, an amalgam of Catholic and Huguenot French, Micmac, English, Irish, and even some Spanish influences.

Sixteen years later, in 1670, France regained Port Royal in a diplomatic exchange for some British territorial concessions in the West Indies, a bargain that angered New Englanders, who believed they had captured the prize on their own initiative and were safer without a French military presence in Nova Scotia. A high birthrate among Acadians (six to seven children per woman), peaceful relations with the Indians, a generally healthful climate, and an absence of epidemic disease contributed to the colony's growth from about five hundred in 1670 to fifteen hundred by the end of the century.

The fortunes of the Micmacs rose and fell with those of the French

Acadians, no matter how delicately the Indians approached their diplomacy with the Europeans. The Micmacs were seldom united and could not muster more than eight hundred warriors even if they had acted in concert. Yet they were perceived as a threat by the colonists, as a potential makeweight between the two perennial European enemies and as a genuine force as long as the French and English had only small and scattered outposts that were weakly defended. The Indians continued to mount successful raids on English settlements for another half century, killing eight and capturing fourteen at Dartmouth in 1750, taking scalps outside Halifax in 1756 and 1757, raiding Lunenburg in 1758—and making peace only in 1761.

Joint-stock companies, precursors of modern corporations, played a significant role in the founding of English colonies in North America. Although joint-stock ventures were not new to England in the seventeenth century, the frequency of their creation then and the large size of their financial undertakings in a comparatively poor island nation suggested the grand ambitions England had for empire and trade. The British East India Company, granted a royal charter in 1600 and founded in 1610, was created by London businessmen pooling their resources to enter the Asian spice trade. King James I founded the Plymouth Company in 1606, to minimize the government's risk in establishing colonies in North America. The Virginia Company, which founded Jamestown, was another from the same era. In 1620, the original Plymouth Company was resurrected as the Plymouth Council for New England with forty investors or "patentees."

The settlers of Plymouth Colony in New England were, technically, employees of the Virginia Company to begin with. About half the original group were Separatists from the Church of England, who had founded their own church, a decision that made them vulnerable to prosecution for treason. They fled first from the village of Scrooby, in Nottinghamshire, then from Boston, in Lincolnshire, and thence to a more tolerant haven in the Netherlands. In Holland they felt culturally alienated and worried about the fate of their children in a foreign land, so they immigrated again, this time to North America. The Pilgrims, as we know them, agreed to pay the Virginia Company for their passage with fish, furs, and lumber that they would harvest when they reached Virginia, but storms blew their ship, the *Mayflower,* off course and they landed, in 1620, on what is today Cape Cod. There they occupied a Pokanoket Indian village with cleared fields that the Indians had abandoned during a recent devastating epidemic of smallpox. Half of the 102 Pilgrims died during their first winter from hunger, exposure, and disease, but by 1630 the colony had grown to fifteen hundred people and was thriving.

A decade after the Plymouth settlement, and at about the same time that women and children first arrived in Port Royal, John Dane, a tailor and one of the early settlers of the Massachusetts Bay Colony, another joint-stock venture, said that he had "bent myself to come to New England, thinking that I should be more free here than there from temptations." Dane, like others who made the Atlantic crossing to Massachusetts during the 1630s, fled what they believed to be a diluted religion and a corrupt government, and they founded independent communities based on strict Calvinist principles. They wanted to establish villages of like-minded "saints," free of strangers and nonbelievers. This was decidedly not a heterogeneous population that could worship or not as it saw fit: Other dissenters from Anglo-Catholicism (especially Baptists and Quakers), Catholics, Anglicans themselves, and the unchurched had "free liberty to keep away from us."

Large Puritan migrations in the 1630s brought about fourteen thousand more immigrants, principally from the east coast of England—East Anglia, eastern Lincolnshire, eastern Cambridge, and northeast Kent.* They left a land of martyrs, not just believers: More than 80 percent of the Protestants burned at the stake during the reign of the Catholic Queen Mary (1553–1558), daughter of Henry VIII, had come from those regions; during the reign of Elizabeth I (1558–1603), 75 percent of Puritan ministers were from the eastern counties.

East Anglians were exposed to marauders who attacked from the sea, and they were not above nailing the skins of Danish pirates to

---

* After the 1630s, immigration to New England fell precipitously, with only seven thousand arriving between 1640 and 1700. This meant that the region would be populated principally by descendants of that first wave. Even during the 1630s, though, 70 percent of British immigrants settled in the Chesapeake Bay region and West Indies, including Puritans, who founded the colony of Providence Island off the coast of Nicaragua, which lasted only a decade.

their church doors as warnings to others who might invade their shores to rape, loot, and kill. In the 1620s, there were at least two such raids (1626 and 1627). The East Anglians were also used to defending themselves from what they saw as arbitrary government. East Anglia was the center of several major rebellions, and its inhabitants began to resist King Charles I in 1625. When the English Civil War broke out in 1642, the region sided ardently with parliamentary forces against the monarch. On either side of the Atlantic, the East Anglians were rebellious, rough, religious, stern, literate, uncompromising, devoted to their villages, and opposed to central authority, whether it emanated from Boston or London, a combination of qualities that would shape New England as much as it had East Anglia.

They crossed the ocean mostly in family groups and in the comparatively equal ratio of three men for every two women. Eighty percent of the seventeenth-century New Englanders paid their own way across the sea, making the number of indentured servants, who had signed contracts to work off the cost of their passage over a number of years, low compared to other regions in Anglo North America. As the servants' terms of service expired, subsequent generations usually could not afford to purchase replacement slaves, so New England developed an independent, ethnically homogeneous, largely self-employed workforce. Although only twenty thousand immigrants came to New England before 1700, its robust population approached one hundred thousand when the eighteenth century began.

The Pilgrims purposefully eliminated the top and bottom of English society from their emigration. There would be no aristocracy, and New Englanders strongly discouraged the poor from joining their communities, "warning out" (ordering away) impoverished strangers and refusing to accept prison ships that brought banished British felons to North America. The distribution of wealth was comparatively wide in New England, more so in the villages of the interior than in the coastal towns such as Falmouth, Salem, Marblehead, and Boston. Outside those commercial centers, the wealthiest 10 percent of the population owned, on average, 20–30 percent of the taxable property, a significantly lower concentration of wealth than found in the colonial South or anywhere in Great Britain. New England's wealth-distribution patterns stayed stable for almost a century before the gap between rich and poor began to grow.

New Englanders were attached to their land and local communities, as the rates of internal migration show during the seventeenth and first half of the eighteenth century. In Andover, for example, about 80 percent of the men stayed put in the 1600s; in Dedham, only 7 percent of the population moved during the 1670s. These were closed, corporate communities of believers, who accepted the covenant that bound them to each other and collectively to God. In theory, there was no room for dissent, and the goal was civic and church governance by divinely "elected" leaders.

The settlers brought a town-meeting form of government with them from East Anglia. Participation was generally low, usually 10–30 percent of the men, but it increased considerably when there was important or controversial business to discuss. The goal was a consensus—that is, unanimity—rather than a majority in a democratic vote, and this process generally worked so long as the villages remained small and the populations culturally homogeneous. Consensus remained the ideal, though, long after that. The stark communalism of their seventeenth-century towns reflected the New Englanders' distrust of outsiders, including those just like them from nearby villages. The rivalries were intense, and ill-defined boundaries frequently resulted in litigation, harsh words, and violence. Miscreants were disciplined physically and/or by humiliation, such as confinement in public stocks, whipping in the town square, or lopping off an ear.

Despite the New Englanders' authoritarian ways, town-meeting governance empowered workingmen in a more democratic structure than could be found anywhere else in the British Empire. To royalists and other critics, New Englanders were "republicans," which was an insult that testified to their independence. They saw themselves as diligent protectors of their autonomy from outsiders, which included imperial officials and those who wanted to compete for jobs in their communities.

Aggressive enforcement of town boundaries enabled voters to control their labor force, which maintained high wages and full employment for the colonists' children. Magistrates enjoyed wide authority over families to intervene and rearrange households, assigning single young people where needed as servants and laborers. The annual meeting in Dedham, for example, directed the placement of "young persons in such families in the town as is the most suitable for their good"—and, it might have added, for the good of the community as determined by its elders. The town enforced work discipline, which assured comparatively fair treatment of servants, and this supervision fostered reasonably content workers, who had no incentive to migrate south or to the Caribbean. Stability grew from and enhanced attachment to the villages. Ninety percent of births in Massachusetts towns were to couples who had at least one member born there. Marriages in which both spouses were from the same village produced half the children born in the towns. When native New Englanders did move, it was generally a great distance, to Maine or the western frontier, but rarely to the next village, where they would have remained outsiders for the rest of their lives.

New Englanders did not welcome "interference," nor were they cowed by saber rattling in London. And their republicanism translated into active participation in church affairs, often to the chagrin of their ministers, who balked at their pettiness and ungenerous interpretations of contractual obligations. They sued each other often and squabbled over such matters as how much firewood or food they owed the manse.

The Puritans, with their ascetic work ethic, had expected a mild climate, as Boston was on the same latitude as Rome, but they made the best of rocky soil, rough seas, and weather that was fierce compared to what they had known in England. Hard work and God's blessing could keep them from starving and yield enough to support a large family, but there was no dominant export commodity during the seventeenth century, and thus no risk that their work would lead to wealth and leisure, which they abhorred as signs of moral dissipation. Their labor yielded small surpluses of many products, which led them to trade everything—eggs, milk, grain, fish, tobacco, candles, barrels, shoes, cider, clothing, and cattle—rather than a limited number of staple crops as in the South (tobacco and rice) and the Caribbean (sugar, and its processed derivatives rum and molasses).

By reputation, New Englanders were sharp traders. In 1700, Boston had the third-highest volume of shipping of any port in the British Empire, behind only London and Bristol, most of the profits being from the carrying trade, the freighting of goods between ports, rather than from the sale of locally produced commodities. More than a quarter of the men in Boston owned shares in one or more ships—a much wider investor base than was found elsewhere in the empire.

New England families were large. About 90 percent of Andover's children survived to adulthood, for example, which meant seven to eight children per family, even though the average age at marriage was higher (early twenties for women and late twenties for men) than in England and for men in the American South. And they lived long lives. Male New Englanders in the first generation lived on average to about seventy-two and the women to seventy-one despite the risks of pregnancy and childbirth. This was an amazingly healthy place, with a mortality rate from disease of only 5 percent, which the Puritans counted as a sign of God's grace on their holy experiment.

The Puritans did not believe that work is redemptive, that believers can earn salvation through their own efforts. Indeed, such a "doctrine of works" was abhorrent to them, smacking of Catholic "superstitions." The Puritans believed in grace freely granted by God, which was not theirs to seek or to earn. Only God could grant salvation and did so by his own plan. God required work of everyone, the saved and the damned, both physical labor and the spiritual labor of following the Ten Commandments. They believed in the sanctity of work as a calling, a framing feature of a life purposively led within family and community contexts. They were not pursuing profit as such but worked for the moral satisfaction of working. Financial success was complicated for them. They felt morally obliged to steward their wealth but saw accumulation as a spiritual trap. This inner turmoil led Puritans to reinvest their surpluses, which made them a commercially successful people even before global commerce became their calling. They feared failure yet success troubled them.

These unresolved tensions defined New Englanders during the seventeenth century. When commercial opportunities opened up in the new century, they began to get past their self-flagellation, becoming less troubled and more genteel but still driven by the work ethic that continued to inspire their culture even as they lost the theological rationale for it. As Benjamin Franklin, an eighteenth-century product of this culture, explained, "America is the land of labor." And as Ralph Waldo Emerson, a nineteenth-century New Englander, wrote, "A man is fed, not that he may be fed, but that he may work."

Other principles of New England culture also spread across space and over time. There were Massachusetts Puritans who found the colony too lax in religion, and they left to establish another colony in New

Haven, an outpost of even more conservative Calvinists, which be-came part of Connecticut in 1664. The Puritans banished to Rhode Island radicals such as Roger Williams, who advocated paying Indians for the land taken from them, and Anne Hutchinson, who believed that the faithful, including women, could interpret the Bible for them-selves without the intercession of ordained ministers. Although Wil-liams would have liked to ban slavery from his colony, it became a center of the international slave trade. Rhode Island also received the entering wedge of dissenting groups such as Baptists and Quakers, whom the Puritans persecuted elsewhere in New England.

Jehovah was the Puritans' model for fathers, husbands, ministers, civic officials, and the monarch, rulers of unquestioned authority who governed, when necessary, with iron fists. Out of love, New England Puritans believed they should discipline children from an early age and often "bound them out" as servants to other families, effectively swap-ping children as a way to ensure that they would not themselves be too soft on their offspring. They tried to maintain a godly order, with every-thing and everyone in its place, and did this by force when necessary. Massachusetts villages prosecuted most of their adults at one time or another for breaches of order—violating the Sabbath, disturbing the peace, idleness, drunkenness, or sexual offenses—but the homicide rate in colonial New England was less than half what it was in the Chesa-peake Bay colonies. It was easy to run afoul of local authority in small ways, but the communities successfully enforced a high degree of conformity.

New England enjoyed comparatively low rates of all violent crimes. The seaports were more violent and less homogeneous than towns in the interior, with sailors responsible for more than their share of property crime and drunken brawls. Local law exacted terrible punishments, including burning at the stake, which happened at least twice in the seventeenth century, both times to female slaves—Maria for arson and Phyllis for poisoning her master with arsenic. There were also hangings for capital crimes, including witchcraft, idolatry, blasphemy, homicide, rape, adultery, bestiality, sodomy, bearing false witness, and striking or cursing a parent by an offspring of sixteen years or older.

Witchcraft, defined as "giving entertainment to Satan," was a capi-tal crime in all the New England colonies, and execution of a con-demned witch was generally by hanging. Between 1630 and 1700,

232 cases resulted in 36 executions.* There were certainly more accused, convicted, and executed witches in New England than in other
regions of English North America. Virginia tried only nine, convicted
one man, and whipped rather than executed him. Pennsylvania never
tried anyone for witchcraft, but New England's per capita rates were
roughly the same as England's. The main difference was that witchcraft prosecutions ceased in England by about 1650 but continued
among the Puritans in New England for another half century.

People accused of witchcraft in New England were most often alienated from the community in one sense or another by virtue of their
gender, age, poverty, race, or outlier status—generally powerless, disre-
spected, odd in appearance or demeanor. Often they cultivated their
reputations for having occult powers in order to supplement their
income by telling fortunes or casting spells, and to scare neighbors into
giving them alms or simply leaving them alone. Many were postmeno-
pausal women no longer actively bearing and raising children.

Physical punishments for lesser crimes included slitting nostrils,
amputating ears, boring tongues with hot irons, and branding the face
or hands, sometimes with an *H* for "heresy." Whippings were more
common; a court once ordered the sheriff to strip four Quaker women
blasphemers to the waist, tie them to the back of a wagon, and lead the
convicts through twelve jurisdictions to be whipped by each constable.
Humiliation was the punishment of choice when the villagers passed
judgment on their own people, who suffered even more if they did not
mend their ways: confinement in stocks or pillories, and orders to wear
cloth letters proclaiming the crime—*D* for "drunkenness," *T* for "theft,"
and the *A* for "adultery" immortalized by Nathaniel Hawthorne two
centuries later. New Englanders also imprisoned those awaiting trial,
those who could not pay fines, and sometimes those convicted of a
crime. The "gaols," or jails, were sometimes just holes in the ground,
which provided little protection against the weather. All this would
change over time, as subsequent generations of Puritans lost the edge
of the founders, became more secular, loved unabashedly, and even
rebelled against authority in and outside the home.

---

* This equates to an annual rate of 6.69 per 100,000 for the seventy years 1630–1700.
For comparison's sake, the rate for Essex County, England, was 5.42 between 1560
and 1680.

Militiamen were deputized as posses to supplement law enforcers when this was thought necessary to maintain the public peace. Violent mobs bent on revenge or punishment and lacking any such authorization occasionally disturbed the peace in the coastal towns, but they were rare in the interior. In 1677, after Indians took several fishing crews captive in Marblehead during the Indian-settler hostilities known as King Philip's War, a mob of women seized two Indians as prisoners and literally tore them limb from limb. A witness reported that the women surrounding the Indians kept people "at such a distance that we could not see them till they were dead, and then we found them with their heads off and gone, and their flesh in a manner pulled from their bones. And such was the tumultation that these women made, that . . . they suffered neither constable . . . nor any other person to come near them, until they had finished their bloody purpose."

In these alien surroundings of North America, huddled together against their fears of strangers, dark forests, ferocious winters, devils, and wolves, New Englanders cleared their fields and triangulated their identities vis-à-vis Indian "savages" and all European Catholics, the French in particular, whom they saw as pawns of a corrupt papacy. The Algonquian peoples of the Northeast likewise defined themselves negatively, as being neither Iroquois, English, nor French.

From the very founding of their colonies, New Englanders feared that the wilderness might turn them into savages, and they lived in horror that they would become one with nature. Indians might be "like the very trees of the wilderness," but the English settlers aimed to civilize the forest by clearing it of Indians *and* trees, planting crops and grazing domestic animals, building roads, and using the felled lumber to build towns, shipyards, docks, and ships. Forests harbored dangers but at least had utility in providing fuel and building material. Indians were just plain scary and had to go. Early on, the English had hoped to convert and acculturate them, but they had underestimated the allure of forest over field, hard pew, and stiff leather shoes.

The colonists were not adept at discerning differences among Indian bands, tribes, or language groups, nor were they much interested in the variations. To the Puritans, all Indians were savages. The Abenakis—the largest group inhabiting northern New England, what is today Maine, Vermont, and New Hampshire, who had been there for ten thousand years before the Europeans arrived—introduced the Pilgrims to Squanto, who was to become their celebrated savior; he was a Patuxet, a member of a tributary group of the Wampanoag people. But to the English, they were all the same. A number of distinct tribes were contained under the Abenaki rubric, and the New Englanders expanded it to include both eastern and western Abenakis, Passamaquoddies, Micmacs, Wampanoags, and Maliseets, calling them all "Eastern Indians," principally to distinguish them from the more feared and despised Iroquois. All these peoples followed the game, the tides, the sun, and the seasons, adapting in cycles that varied little if at all across the years; their circular sense of time was very different from the New Englanders' own linear measurements of years, decades, and centuries, and they neither feared nor longed for the future, while the Puritans dwelled at the world's end.

Such incompatible worldviews framed all the conflicts between natives and new settlers over land. From their arrival in the 1620s and 1630s, the newcomers always insisted that they were in authority. This was one reason the Wampanoags initially tried to minimize their contact with the Plymouth colonists; their previous experiences with the English had made them wary. In 1614, for example, six years before the Pilgrims landed, English sailors had kidnapped some of their tribesmen and taken them to England. Squanto was one of the few who survived the ordeal; he returned home to a people that had been all but wiped out by smallpox. But in 1636, the Wampanoags agreed to an alliance with the Plymouth colonists, whereupon their enemies the Narragansetts agreed to a treaty with Massachusetts Bay settlers. One year later, Massachusetts men together with Narragansetts attacked an Indian settlement on the Mystic River in what is now Connecticut, killing hundreds of women and children—they were Pequots, a tribe that had inhabited that region for centuries. The massacre ended the Pequots' dominance, and fear of the colonists led five of their sachems to submit to Massachusetts Bay in 1644, agreeing to "put ourselves, our subjects, lands, and estates under the government and jurisdiction" of the colony, and to "be true and faithfull to the said government." In 1668, ten sachems from western Massachusetts also submitted to the colony and agreed to be "ruled" by its colonists.

Revealingly, none of the Massachusetts treaties after 1643 made any mention of English rule over the colony but simply asserted the colony's direct authority over the Indians. In 1644, the Narragansetts declined the colony's demands for concessions on the grounds that they too were "subjects now . . . unto the same king, & state yourselves are." In fact, Indians throughout the colonies continued for another century to try to enlist the Crown's support in their conflicts with the land-hungry colonists.

By 1665, there were nearly fifty towns in Massachusetts and Plymouth, and more than thirty more in Connecticut, Rhode Island, New Hampshire, and Maine. There were more than fifty thousand settlers in these New England colonies, while only ten to fifteen thousand Indians remained. In 1671, the Wampanoag sachem Metacom, known to the English as King Philip, declined a summons to appear before a Plymouth magistrate. When he met with representatives of Massachusetts, he learned that his efforts to play the colonists against each other had failed, and that the English had agreed that his people were under the authority of Plymouth.* At that point, Metacom agreed that he and his people were subject to the British king, to "the government of New Plymouth, and to their laws." The Wampanoags and other Indians in Plymouth turned over their arms, which diminished the immediate threat of war but created a resentment that would lead to war four years later.

The continuing dispute over authority and subjection was the underlying reason for King Philip's War, a brutal conflict that broke out in 1675, the proximate cause of which concerned land the colonists coveted. The viciousness on both sides aimed at annihilation with the same weapons—knives, tomahawks, and flintlock muskets. The Narragansetts refused to deliver Wampanoag prisoners—loyalty to family trumped diplomatic ties—so the English launched a retributive war with them, too. There was shocking savagery on both sides; the best defense New Englanders could make of their "civilization" was that the Indians had "delighted" in causing pain, while they were disgusted by the violence they had perpetrated. It was a subtle point—and untrue. They reveled in killing Indians, and within just a few years 60–80 percent of the Indian belligerents were dead. After the war, what was left of the tribes in Massachusetts and Connecticut moved north and together, which created both new conflicts and new alliances among them. The Puritans' ferociousness, cultural arrogance, intensive hunting, and

* Plymouth did not officially become part of Massachusetts until 1691.

extensive land use also drove the Indians into alliance with the more tolerable French.

When the Catholic James II abdicated the English throne in 1688 and was succeeded by the Protestant William III the next year, France declared war on England, and soon the two imperial powers were engaged in hostilities in North America, where the Acadians supported James and the Anglo-Americans eagerly embraced William.* This turn of events gave Acadians, who had been trying unsuccessfully to tax the New Englanders who fished off their coast, a pretext for attacking boats sailing from Salem and Boston. In response, seven hundred New Englanders under Sir William Phips, a shipbuilder and merchant (and later royal governor of Massachusetts), besieged the bastion at Port Royal, Acadia's capital, in May 1690. Oral terms of capitulation allowed the defenders to leave the fort fully armed (they were then deported to Quebec) and the local Acadians to keep their homes and continue to practice their Catholic faith without interference. But shortly after the negotiations concluded, fights broke out among the troops, which led to the New Englanders' disarming Acadian soldiers, pillaging the countryside, desecrating Port Royal's Catholic church, and shipping some prisoners to Boston, where they remained incarcerated for years. They also required residents of Port Royal to swear allegiance to the new British monarchs William and Mary. This episode was the beginning of heated enmity between Acadians and New Englanders that persisted for more than a half century.

The New Englanders did not stay to defend their conquest of Port Royal in 1690, but they returned on raids in 1696, 1704, and 1707, and then made a more ambitious assault in 1710, when, during the War of the Spanish Succession (1702–1714), a combined English and New

---

* King James's abdication and eventual flight to France was a response to the invasion of England by Dutch troops under the Protestant Dutch Prince William of Orange, who based his claim to the English throne on his marriage to Mary, James's elder daughter; most Protestants in England supported him. The birth of a son to James and his wife Maria in 1688 had undermined Mary's claim to the throne, however, and William also feared an alliance between the Catholic James and France, which would have been disastrous for the Protestant Netherlands. William and Mary were crowned in England in early 1689.

England force again took Port Royal and renamed it Annapolis Royal. The invaders garrisoned the newly named Fort Anne with 450 men over the winter, 250 of them New Englanders and the other 200 mostly Irish Royal Marines. Some of the Acadians aimed for neutrality and traded with the invaders, while others resisted as best they could. By spring 1711, locals had ceased to supply the fort. When the New Englanders responded aggressively to this treatment, the Acadians' Indian allies ambushed them, killing sixteen, wounding nine, and taking the rest prisoner; they suffered no casualties themselves. Over the summer, Acadians and several hundred Indians from three different tribes besieged the fort. The Acadians also attacked settlements in Maine with the help of Micmac and Abenaki allies, leveled the English fishery station in Newfoundland, and captured the Newfoundland town of St. John's. The rest of the war went badly for France, though, and in the Treaty of Utrecht, which ended it, France conceded Acadia and Newfoundland to Great Britain, keeping only Cape Breton Island and Île Saint-Jean (now Prince Edward Island). The Acadians were, under the treaty's terms, expected to move to Cape Breton, which some of them did despite ongoing tensions with the English who now occupied Nova Scotia.

By 1719, the English in North America had settled on a policy of incorporation of the Micmac into Nova Scotia society, but also, somewhat contradictorily, of respecting their autonomy. Governor Richard Phillips offered cash and land incentives for English-Micmac marriages; not one English settler ever claimed the prize, but Micmac and Acadians intermarried frequently. And they both were provoked to anger by the many New England fishermen who tried to establish settlements on the Atlantic coast. The New Englanders also defied the Micmac by fortifying Canso, on the northeastern tip of Nova Scotia. Micmacs attacked there in 1720, killing three men and destroying the fort under construction. War formally broke out between the New Englanders and Micmacs in 1722 and lasted for three brutal years, with the mutilation of corpses, killing of prisoners, and collecting of scalps for which bounties were paid by Massachusetts. Treaties in 1725 and 1726 acknowledged the Micmacs' right to self-governance but did not settle the question of competing land claims; the two groups tried to stay away from each other on the Atlantic coast, but they got along less well on the Bay of Fundy—which the New Englanders blamed on the Acadians.

At least as early as 1720, James Craggs, the secretary of state for the Southern Department, which was responsible for the North American colonies, had seriously considered expelling the Acadians from Nova Scotia. A financial crisis precipitated by a plunge in the value of South Sea Company stock in 1722 (the so-called South Sea Bubble) stalled such plans, though, and the project was not seriously revived for two decades. That same year, Nova Scotia's own colonial council declared it a crime for Acadians to provide food, shelter, or any kind of assistance to the Micmac. The next few decades were relatively peaceful and prosperous, as a bilingual community developed at Annapolis Royal. By 1730, virtually all male Acadians had taken oaths of fealty to the British monarch, but with the reservation that they were exempt from bearing arms against French or Indian enemies of the English colonies. By the mid-1740s, there were about 10,000 Acadians, 3,000 Micmac, and 500 English settlers in Nova Scotia.

In its January 1, 1745, issue, the *Pennsylvania Gazette* reported that Acadians had taken 135 New Englanders captive in Nova Scotia during the previous five years, and that ten of these captives, now returned to Boston, said they had been "very cruelly treated" while held by the French. According to the *Gazette*, "It is the opinion of many of the returned prisoners that Cape Breton might be easily reduced by a small force from Great Britain, under honest and skillful officers." In February, the *Boston Evening Post* reprinted an article from the *London Magazine* lamenting "the present state of our possessions in North America, which now seem, to the eternal disgrace of their Mother Country, to be left naked and open on all sides to the incursions and ravages of two powerful and irritated enemies." Spain lurked to the south and in the Caribbean, while "on the northern frontier, the effect of our supineness and neglect has been too visible." Colonists estimated that the eight to ten thousand French troops in Canada, plus their Indian allies, were always poised for an invasion. The writer went on to say, "That our colonies in North America are of great importance to the wealth and strength of their Mother Country, is too notorious, and has been too often prov'd, to afford the least pretence for a denial."

Beginning in the 1720s and accelerating in the 1730s, divisions grew within New England's churches and across sectarian lines between those who favored the Puritans' traditional forms of sermonizing and those affected by a new emotional style of evangelical preaching. Declining church membership and a sense that their religion was emotionally dry contributed to the New Englanders' receptivity to the international revivalism of the time, often called the Great Awakening. The amorphous transdenominational assault on the old ways by so-called New Light revivalists split its churches and communities along existing social and theological fault lines, and left a legacy of conflict that was to affect political styles for decades to come. Internal psychological tensions and external social ones, focused on an ever more intense pursuit of economic success, along with guilt about the growing frequency of conflicts with authority, prepared the ground for people to welcome the exorcising effects of a new kind of religious and civic conversion.

Revivalists preached that salvation was a personal responsibility, unmediated by anyone between the sinner and God—the same view that had gotten the celebrated Dissenter Anne Hutchinson and her followers expelled from Massachusetts a century earlier. The faithful heard that they were responsible for their own souls and their own communities; they should not and could not depend on others to discern right from wrong for them. This put moral and political authority in their hands. The New Light ministers also endorsed toleration of other religions, which many accepted but many more heard as an assault on existing institutions and power structures.

Congregants applied this message to their secular lives in ways that the New Light ministry never intended. Once congregants expiated their guilt in emotional revivals, they returned to producing, selling, and consuming without, or at least with less, guilt about their new involvement in the burgeoning international market economy. The Congregationalists, as the descendants of Puritans now called themselves, were less concerned with theological nuance or ministerial sanction than their ancestors had been. They understood that it was now civil authority that bound society together. The New Englanders had shared political values and a devotion to liberty and property—a shared ideology rather than theology. They retained their millennialist habits of mind; apocalyptic temperaments were embedded in their culture, but now these were focused on the battlefield and ballot rather than on the pulpit and pew.

Officers who led New England militias, ministers who pastored their flocks, politicians both appointed by the Crown and elected by the people, and merchants who delivered their goods all had to accommodate themselves to the voices of the majority. New Englanders asserted their independence within the family, town, colony, marketplace, and empire. They had not become rebels, but by comparison to New Englanders of 1690 they were more unruly and sometimes even downright rebellious. And in the communities with the greatest economic expansion, population growth, and geographical spread—like those east of the Connecticut River in the colony of the same name—alienation from authority manifested itself most dramatically.

The New England of 1750 was not that of the founders or even of the recent past. More and more the colonists felt themselves adrift; the ethnically homogeneous, ideologically unified, and socially and economically predictable world they idealized was gone. Change, rather than the stasis their traditions celebrated, unsettled them, alienated them, and destabilized their society.

It is often change rather than any actual experience of deprivation that produces potentially revolutionary environments. Fear of the future can be more unsettling than desperation about the present. Hope that an idealized past can be recovered, or despair because an imagined future is becoming more remote, can turn people's worlds upside down. New Englanders experienced this trepidation in the mid-eighteenth century. Like others before and since, the impulse to blame "outside" forces conspiring against them had tremendous allure, and they had a history of externalizing threats and making them real: the French, Indians, kings, popes, witches, Satan, parliaments, weak-kneed Protestants, some ministers, Catholics, Quakers, Baptists, strangers, and—depending on the locale—the city or the country. New Englanders would look outside to blame and to fight for the moral high ground.

2

✦

COMMERCE

AT FIRST IT WAS JUST A BURGLARY, but a disturbing one. The case had blacks and whites mixing socially, an interracial couple, slaves and servants plotting, prostitutes, and tavern keepers fencing stolen goods. Theft was a problem in Manhattan in 1741, and arson was always a concern. There were gangs of thieves, and prosecutors hoped to get to the bottom, and the top, of organized crime. Each arrest presented an opportunity to probe more deeply into the underworld, to coerce a servant or slave caught red-handed into a plea bargain in which the accused traded the names of coconspirators for her or his life.

It was a cold night in February when three slaves named Prince, Cuffee, and Caesar, alias John Gwin, burgled Rebecca Hogg's shop near the East River docks. The slaves had gotten a tip from a young white seaman that Hogg stashed Spanish coins in a cash box, in addition to the cloth, jewelry, and other luxury items that she sold in her store. Caesar (Gwin) took his share of the loot to the white tavern keepers John and Sarah Hughson, who filled a number of roles in the local underworld. They served liquor to slaves and mixed groups of black and white, male and female customers; received stolen goods; and harbored prostitutes on their premises. The penalty for two counts of burglary was death by hanging, and all those linked in a chain from conspiracy to burglary to fencing stolen goods were complicit.

Allegations made by Mary Burton, a sixteen-year-old indentured servant of the Hughsons, and a young Irish immigrant named Peggy

Kerry, who was rumored to be Gwin's mistress and kept by him at the Hughsons' inn, broke the case. Burton clearly relished an audience, and she played to the crowd. Without her there would have been no case, never mind the raft of convictions and executions that resulted from the stories she told and the predicaments in which she left others, who confessed to whatever it took to survive. By the time authorities questioned the three slaves, prosecutors were more interested in arson plots than in burglaries, and the slaves knew they had to embellish their stories if they hoped to avoid burning at the stake. Eventually, the alleged arson plot morphed into a suspected slave conspiracy connected to the Anglo-Spanish War of Jenkins' Ear, which had begun in 1739 and became part of the larger War of the Austrian Succession in 1742.*

Settlers in many of the colonies, not just in New England, feasted on conspiracies. Central to folk beliefs was the knowledge that there are few accidents but many patterns. Where there is smoke, there is fire, as the saying goes. In 1692, it had taken only a handful of teenage girls who fancied the attention and had malice in their hearts, and a West Indian slave for a scapegoat, to wreak havoc in Salem, Massachusetts, with their accusations of witchcraft. In the beginning it was all a game for them, but by the end, 156 people had been charged and 20 executed as witches; families and congregations were ruined; ministers and judicial officials lost credibility that their institutions would not regain; and guilt spread far and wide. The convictions had been woven of "spectral" evidence, visions of talking birds and dancing dogs that no one but the accusers could see. New York was not Salem and 1741 was not 1692, but they were not so far apart, and the cultures were more similar than New Yorkers and New Englanders would have admitted. About the same number of people were accused in New York's slave conspiracy and even more were convicted and executed on evidence no more reliable than the phantoms offered at Salem fifty years earlier.

---

* The War of Jenkins' Ear between Great Britain and Spain was so named because Captain Robert Jenkins lost an ear in 1731 when he and his crew defended their ship against Spanish coast guards who had boarded it; the ear was displayed in Parliament and became a cause célèbre. The War of the Austrian Succession lasted from 1740 to 1748.

New Netherland was a Dutch West India Company (another joint-stock venture) backwater from 1621 to 1664, never as profitable as the company's holdings in the Caribbean and Brazil, and its managers cared little about the social, cultural, or spiritual lives of the colonists who lived there. The first settlers in 1624 were thirty Walloon families, French-speaking Protestants from the southern Netherlands. Religious diversity, which the company sponsored but the local administration did not, contributed to conflict in the colony. Then groups of New Englanders, principally from New Haven, started moving to Long Island in 1640, building towns each with an autonomous church, town meeting, and communal division of land—a very different settlement pattern from the Dutch one.

In the 1650s and 1660s, Mohawks tried to exploit boundary disputes among the Dutch, the New Englanders, and the tiny colony of New Sweden farther down the coast, on what is called today the Delaware River. According to Peter Stuyvesant, the governor of New Netherland,

> if the boundaries are once settled between us and our neighbors, then the daily quarrels, bickerings, jealousies [suspicions], and claims shall be avoided from either side and a good understanding and correspondence established; these pernicious wars between the Maquaes [Mohawks] and the northern savages would then soon be settled and brought to an end and all the savages could be made to submit or at least to deliberate, when they see the Christians united and drawing a line to keep the barbarians in submission or at least quiet.

Stuyvesant resolved part of the territorial dispute in 1655 by force: annexing New Sweden, which he renamed New Amstel, with six hundred men on seven ships. While he was off on his military conquest, though, Manhattan Island came under siege by a combined force of Mahicans and several smaller native groups seeking revenge for the murder of a woman. The battle spread, and massacres and kidnappings occurred at Dutch outposts in New Jersey as well. Fifty colonists and perhaps sixty Indians died; the Indians destroyed twenty-eight farms, killed five-hundred head of cattle, and burned a large quantity of corn.

In 1664, without any reference to Dutch claims or settlements, King Charles II granted his brother James, Duke of York, lands that we would recognize as parts of Maine, all of Long Island, Martha's Vineyard, and Nantucket, as well as territory up the Hudson River and west of the Connecticut River down to the east side of Delaware Bay. It took only four English ships to secure a bloodless surrender of New Amsterdam on August 26. It would take a generation, though, for the settlement there to make the transition from Dutch to English culture on anything like a large and permanent scale. Even then, the people of New York were less English and more diverse than in any other English colony on the North American mainland. There was even a brief interlude in which the Dutch took back New York in 1673, during the third Anglo-Dutch War (1672–1674), but in the peace treaty that ended the hostilities, the Dutch agreed to relinquish all claims to New York in perpetuity. By this time, the city of New York had about two thousand inhabitants; by 1680, the colony had about ten thousand, and fifteen thousand five years later.

In 1680, the various groups and tribes of Iroquois had completed their "Covenant Chain," a diplomatic union among their league of Five Nations and with the English, which helped them to become a makeweight for either the French or English as they advanced in North America. Soon the English were penetrating farther into the interior than the Dutch ever had—western New York, the Great Lakes region, and the Ohio Valley—bringing English settlers into closer contact and greater conflict with both Indians and the French. This English expansion corresponded with Iroquois invasions of the territories of Illinois, Ottawa, and Miami Indians, which put the Five Nations of the Covenant Chain on a parallel course that initially facilitated English settlement but ultimately complicated it greatly.

The English colonists felt beleaguered both by New York's diversity and by its external enemies. When Catholics began to move into New York, the colonists saw the dangers posed by French Canada increasing; and when rumors spread that the Duke of York had converted to Catholicism (true, as it turned out), their vivid fears of conspiracy against them were sharpened. Iroquois diplomacy was always complex, and the colony's pluralism contributed to its social and political instability, which the increasing number of slaves exacerbated. Then in 1688, that same duke, now King James II, annexed the provinces of New York,

East Jersey, and West Jersey to the Crown's New England colonies, creating a new and larger Dominion of New England. To administer this supercolony, the king appointed Governor Edmund Andros, an imperial official whose authoritarian ways New Yorkers had come to despise during his earlier term (1674–1681) as their governor. Moving New York's official records to Boston, where Andros intended to continue the dominion's administration, created commercial havoc and triggered opposition to the new governance in New York, fires also stoked by false rumors of an imminent attack on Albany by a thousand French and Indians. Lieutenant Governor Francis Nicholson was in charge of this volatile colony, along with the three councilors available to him of the five who made up the council.

But this was no easy task in late 1688 and early 1689, when Dutch troops had invaded the British Isles themselves, deposing King James and installing William of Orange in his place. Nicholson tried to keep the Dutch invasion of England secret "for the prevention of any tumult," but this only fed conspiracy theories when his subterfuge became known. In mid-April, when the news reached Boston, the populace had risen up against Andros and put him under house arrest, replacing his Anglican officials with their own Puritan ones, and as soon as news of this rebellion reached New York, another revolt ensued. In early May, Suffolk County, Long Island, freeholders declared that in light of the invasion of England and rebellion in Massachusetts, they were forced to act for "our own self preservation, being without any to depend on at present, till it pleases God to order better."

On May 31, New York City's militia seized Fort James, disarmed the guards, and demanded the keys, which Nicholson surrendered under duress and on the advice of his councilors. Shortly thereafter, officers drafted an address from the militia to King William, expressing "our exceeding joy" that the Dutch invaders had delivered England from "Tyranny, popery and slavery" and reestablished the "true protestant Religion, liberty and property." They told Britain's new monarch that "we having also long groaned under the same oppression, having been governed of late, most part, by papists who had in a most arbitrary way subverted our ancient priviledges, making us in effect slaves to theire will contrary to the laws of England; and this was chiefly effected by these who are known ennemies to our Religion and liberty." They were now "your Majesties most loyall subjects, having thrown off the papists and pretended Protestants" that James II had imposed on them. Their "only design and intentions was to secure ourselves and country to be wholly devoted to your Majestyes will and pleasure in the disposeing of our Government."

On June 6, Nicholson resigned his office and returned to England "by the first ship, for to give an account of the desperate and deplorable state of the government." The rebels asked Jacob Leisler, a German-born colonist, to assume leadership of their forces; he was one of a number of militia officers—another was Jacob Milborne—who had led the capture of New York's fort and garrison. Not surprisingly, New Yorkers were divided along ethnic, regional, religious, and political lines about whether this rebel government was more or less legitimate than the one it replaced, and also about Leisler himself, who was every bit as arbitrary and rigid as Andros and Nicholson. From the perspective of his supporters, though, they had seized the government from traitors and put it in the "hands of such persons, of whose fidelity and good Inclination to their present Majesties the aforesaid Province is well assured." The royally appointed councilors, on the other hand, believed they had been replaced by "men of meane birth sordid Education and desperate fortunes," who had inflamed "the people with idle and improbable stories and false suggestions."

In January 1690, King William appointed Henry Sloughter New York's new governor, a position that Sloughter did not assume for more than a year. When Sloughter's military vanguard arrived a few months ahead of him, Leisler refused to surrender the fort, fearing the soldiers' real intentions: Rumors persisted of a Catholic plot to seize the colony for France; the two monarchies had been at war since the summer before. There was a standoff and a minor skirmish. When Sloughter arrived on March 19, 1691, he twice sent a military messenger to demand surrender of the fort. Each time, Leisler dispatched an emissary in return to ensure to his satisfaction that it actually was Sloughter and that his commission was truly from William and Mary, not James II. On the third try, Leisler accepted the authority of the new governor, but this concession was his undoing: Sloughter threw him, his emissaries, and his confederates into jail, and took as his advisers men who had been associated with the Andros-Nicholson administration, the very men whom the rebels had ousted, jailed, and otherwise abused a year earlier. After a trial, the court found Leisler and Jacob Milborne guilty of murder and treason, and sentenced them to the usual punishment for traitors: to be hanged "by the Neck and being Alive their bodys be Cutt downe to the Earth and Their Bowells be taken out and they being Alive, burnt before their faces; that their heads shall be struck off and their Bodys Cutt in four parts."

With these executions, Sloughter and his council created two martyrs and ensured the persistence of bitterly waged partisan politics over the following decades. It did not help that Sloughter and his immediate successors were corrupt and retributive. When the political winds eventually changed direction, the bodies of Leisler and Milborne were exhumed and reinterred with all the pomp and ceremony the partisans could muster for their heroes.

Despite the infighting and corruption for which New York became famous, the first assembly to meet after the revolt adopted a bill of rights and privileges that endured, unlike the one of 1685 on which they modeled it and which had been largely ignored. In it, the legislators guaranteed government by governor, council, and an assembly elected annually by the colony's freeholders. They included specific rights guaranteed to Englishmen back in England, such as habeas corpus and trial by jury, freedom of religion and conscience, no martial law except under dire circumstances, and a balance between appointed executive and elected legislative authority. The one qualification put on freedom of worship was as essential to Protestant New Yorkers as it was to New Englanders, both vividly aware of the French power north of them: "Noething herein mentioned or Contained shall extend to give Liberty for any persons of the Romish [Catholic] Religion to exercise their manor of worship contrary to the Laws and Statutes of their Majesties Kingdom of England."

In the new century, the colony became more English without losing its cultural pluralism. The number of lawyers trained in English law doubled by 1710, court decisions began to reflect common-law precedent, and legislation that drew on the English heritage replaced Dutch practices and local innovations. England and France, at war from 1689 to 1697 and 1702 to 1713, did not initiate hostilities in North America, but defense continued to be a preoccupation in the British colonies, which was only exacerbated by the failures in 1709 and 1711 of united colonial expeditions against French Canada; the specter of French and Indian invasions continued to loom. As always, New Yorkers vividly displayed their anti-Catholic bigotry as a patriotic defense against both France and Spain.

By 1740, some New Yorkers were claiming that their assembly had constitutional standing equal to that of Parliament and the authority to administer their government, supersede the directives of the governor, interpret laws, serve as a high court, and control finances. A year earlier, the assembly, in a power struggle with the acting governor, George Clarke, had won the right to levy annual taxes rather than accept Britain's traditional long-term revenue appropriations. This provoked the lieutenant governor, James Blair, to complain that the assembly was using its asserted fiscal powers unconstitutionally, deciding which executive officers to pay, and when and how much to pay them, "thus fixing on themselves the Dependance of the Officers for whom they provided (for Men are naturally Servants to those who pay them), they in effect subverted the Constitution, assuming to themselves one undoubted and essential branch of His Majesty's Royal Prerogative." According to Blair, the New York assembly's overreaching had led Parliament and the king's advisers to question their loyalty, a suspicion that could be disproved only by immediate return to traditional constitutional relationships, including respect for the monarch's fiscal prerogatives. "This, and only this," he warned, in an address to the assembly, "will remove, as to this Province, a Jealousy which for some years has obtain'd in England that the Plantations are not without Thoughts of throwing off their Dependance on the Crown of England."

Commerce in Manhattan waxed and waned, its health depending on Boston's economy and the rhythms of English wars. But the general trends were upward: 40 ships cleared New York harbor annually in the 1690s, an average of 64 per year in 1714–1717; by 1721, the annual average leaped to 215. Between 1708 and 1715 alone, the number of locally owned vessels increased 150 percent; the tonnage of imports from England grew annually, on average, about 7 percent in the 1740s and 1750s.

Even as commerce grew so hugely, so did poverty. As the gap between rich and poor, and the number of landless poor both increased, the social challenges presented by a permanently dispossessed class and more crime became enduring features of urban life. Between 1723 and 1735, the city's annual budget for poor relief averaged £523; by

1734 it was £649. Taxpayers complained, and in 1734 New York's first poorhouse was ordered built: The "House of Correction" laid the blame where taxpayers thought it belonged, on the "idle poor" themselves.

As the polyglot city became more socially stratified, it remained culturally divided from the primarily Dutch Hudson Valley and English Long Island. Highland Scots and Scots-Irish settlers began moving into the Hudson Valley, as did Palatine Germans and Huguenots. At midcentury, New York lagged behind other English colonies in population growth, which some attributed to the fact that huge estates along the Hudson River closed off the land market in that region and made only rentals available.

Slavery also had a major effect on New York society. Already in 1700, about 11 percent of the colony's population was black, and by 1723, blacks represented 15 percent of the city (as they did through the rest of the colonial period). In 1731, there were sixteen hundred slaves in New York City and Long Island, and almost five thousand in the New York–New Jersey region; 18 percent of the city's population was enslaved. In 1738, the more than seventeen hundred blacks in New York City were all but a few of them slaves. The city accounted for more than half of all crimes reported in the colony, and 10 percent of the convictions were of slaves. (The conviction rates for slaves were 65 percent compared to 45 percent for free whites.) More than 95 percent of prosecutions were for violence and disturbance of the public peace, often for street fights involving only whites; slaves were more often convicted of property crimes, which the sheriffs believed, in 1740–1741, were becoming more frequent.

Prevention was of course the best protection against crime, and the laws that restricted slaves give us clues as to how the authorities viewed the situation: It would help to keep the slave and servant populations apart, segregate the city's nine thousand white servants from its two thousand slaves, and cow the slaves with harsh physical discipline. A 1702 law already gave masters total discretion in punishing their slaves' misconduct, forbade gatherings of more than three slaves without their masters' explicit permission, and barred slaves from commerce on the public streets. A 1708 law made it a capital crime for slaves to conspire to commit the murder of whites. A 1712 act required masters who manumitted a slave to post a bond of £200 to guarantee the slave's good behavior. In 1730, the assembly adopted a statute that made it a criminal offense for anyone to "entertain" slaves, a law aimed at innkeepers who served slaves liquor and permitted slaves and servants to gamble on their premises. Finally, in this series of increasingly strict regulations of slaves' mobility, a 1731 law required any slave out after dark to carry a lantern, which was intended to serve as a beacon of possible trouble and cut down on muggings and burglaries, and it also banned gatherings of more than three slaves after dark, no matter what their masters had authorized. If the town could control concealment and conspiracy, perhaps it could reduce crime, but without a significant enforcement arm, the legislation had only spotty success.

White New Yorkers believed that the prevalence of black seamen on the docks was a threat to the public peace at all times of the day. They were just as rowdy as the white sailors, yet from the whites' point of view, they embodied an alternative life for the city's black slaves and suggested an escape from servitude. If slaves could blend in with them and sail off, they would be free. If the black seamen conspired with white servants, seamen, and roustabouts, the safety of the middling and upper classes would be at risk and their slaves would imperil New York's entire social structure. The presumption that resentment, revenge, and a desire to overturn the city's social hierarchy drove crime was accurate. Although economic motives propelled property crime, it was never just about money.

New York had had a slave rebellion back in 1712, so Manhattanites knew what they feared. Twenty-four slaves had set fire to barns and outhouses, and then, when the fire brigade responded to the alarm, they attacked them with guns, axes, and swords. Slaves killed or wounded about twenty whites, then fled to the largely uninhabited northern end of Manhattan Island, where two of them committed suicide to avoid capture. Eventually, prosecutors indicted twenty-one slaves and juries sentenced eighteen to death. Some of those convicted burned at the stake, one hung in chains until he starved to death, and others were dismembered alive (drawn and quartered). Authorities publicly displayed the severed heads on pikes as a warning to other slaves.

Fear of arson increased as the city's population grew because the proliferating wooden buildings made New York a tinderbox. In 1721 and 1730 there were scares, but nothing came of them. Still, societies with slaves were always on edge, and New York was no different in this regard. There was a slave rebellion in South Carolina in 1739, in which twenty-five whites died. All this was in the background when slaves were prosecuted for property crime.

New York authorities were still investigating the web of connections that led the three slaves to rob Mrs. Hogg's store in February when a major fire broke out on the night of March 18, 1741. It seemed to begin in several places at once, all frighteningly close to the weapons and ammunition stored at Fort George. Flames from the roof of the fort spread to the governor's mansion, chapel, and armory. High winds hindered the firefighters, but a pouring rain stopped the fire from spreading to the ammunition or beyond the fort. Providence saved the city from a disaster.

A slave named Quaco Roosevelt eventually confessed to starting the fire because his master had denied him permission to visit his new wife. Thirteen other fires over the next three weeks were apparently inspired by Quaco's arson, and other slaves intended to use fire as a cover for thefts: While whites were fighting the fires, slaves could rob their homes. A black man leaped from a warehouse window during one fire; rumor had it that several African-Spanish sailors who had been sold into slavery were involved. From that suspicion, it was a short step to imagining slaves, Spain and France, Catholicism, the pope and priests, and the ongoing War of the Austrian Succession as inspiration for a plan to burn New York and kill its white inhabitants.

New Yorkers had their own 1712 rebellion as well as the Stono slave uprising in South Carolina and the war very much in mind as prosecutors interrogated informants during March and April about the robbery of Mrs. Hogg's store. As the questioning continued, though, it was not only a burglary and fencing ring that emerged; other suspected felons broke under the threat of the gallows or worse, and the prosecutors cast a wider net. There had been more fires than usual over these months. Was arson the cause? Was the burglary ring also an arson squad? Was this the beginning of a full-blown rebellion? Was the burglary connected to the war, and inspired by French and Spanish spies?

In the end, with the help of imaginative "witnesses," the authorities answered all those questions affirmatively, and now they wanted to find the lead conspirator. A letter from James Oglethorpe, the British officer who had recently arrived in Georgia to form a new English colony there (one that did not permit slavery and that served British interests as a bulwark against Spain's colonies farther south), alleged that "the Spaniards had employed emissaries to burn all the magazines and considerable towns in the English North-America . . . and that for this purpose many priests were employed, who pretended to be physicians, dancing-masters, and other such kinds of occupations; and under that pretence to get admittance and confidence in families." So resourceful informants delivered up a priest as the alleged leader of the plot. At least, he was rumored to be either a Catholic priest or a nonjuring minister—that is, a member of a Protestant sect like the Moravians or Quakers who declined to take oaths on religious grounds.*

"Ury the priest," as prosecutors called him, was an itinerant schoolmaster and tutor who read Latin and Greek. Priests were known to read and speak Latin. Although Ury denied ever having met the Hughsons or patronized their tavern, witness after witness testified to seeing him at the tavern in hushed conversations with known conspirators. The court indicted him for "counseling, abetting, and procuring, etc. a negro man slave called Quack, to set fire to the king's house in the fort." A second charge alleged that Ury, "being an ecclesiastical person, made by authority pretended from the See of Rome, did . . . come into the province and city of New-York, and there remained for the space of seven months, and did profess himself to be an ecclesiastical person, made and ordained by authority from the See of Rome, and did appear so to be, by celebrating masses, and granting absolution &c."

The daughter of the innkeepers testified that she had "often seen Ury the priest at her father's house, who used to come there in the evenings and at nights, and has seen him in company with the negroes, and talking with them about the plot of burning the town and destroying the white people." She heard slaves say that they "used to go to Ury's lodging, where they used to pray in private after the popish fashion, and that he used to forgive them their sins for burning the town and destroying and cutting of the people's throats." Elias Debrosse, a confectioner, testified that Ury tried to buy wafers from him—evidence that Ury provided communion in the "popish fashion" at an altar

---

* Nonjurors rejected all forms of swearing. Ury, however, may have been a nonjuring Anglican, one who did not recognize the Hanoverian succession and refused to swear allegiance to George II.

constructed in his room. Joseph Web, the carpenter who built the "altar," gave evidence that "Ury in some of his conversations with him upon religious topics, expressed himself in such a dark, obscure, and mysterious manner, that the deponent could not understand him; he would give hints that he could neither make head nor tail of." Priests were known to obfuscate, to speak in dead languages and on arcane subjects, so the mere fact that Ury was obscure was further circumstantial evidence that he was a spy and a priest.

Prosecutors applied a circular logic born of bigotry against slaves and Catholics and fears of arson, slave conspiracies, and the war against France to which New Yorkers had troops committed. They had little trouble convincing the Anglo-Protestant jury that Ury the priest was the architect of a slave conspiracy inspired by "other popish priests and emissaries, and his zeal for that murderous religion." The method of Catholic spies was trickery to "pick the pockets of credulous people." And who, prosecutors asked rhetorically, were more credulous than slaves?

According to one witness, Ury had slipped several times and referred to endeavors of "we priests." Another letter like Oglethorpe's had appeared in English newspapers warning that France also intended to "turn the tables upon the English in America, by exciting revolts and disturbances in their possessions, and by doing every thing in its power to traverse the designs and even to distress the English." And there was a pattern into which this particular conspiracy fit, one that united Irish immigrants, English priests, and the war aims of Spain and France, "so that this is a fourth instance of suspicious schoolmasters infesting these parts, correspondent to general Oglethorpe's letter of advice." According to Daniel Horsmanden, chronicler of the trials and one of the judges, "If such priests had not been here . . . there would have been no such plot; for upon this and no other footing can it be accounted for."

All told, prosecutors accused more than 150 slaves and 25 whites of conspiring to burn down New York City and kill its white inhabitants, and sentenced eighteen convicted slaves and four whites to be hanged. Thirteen slaves burned at the stake; seventy more, who confessed and pleaded guilty, were banished to the West Indies. Given the alternatives, confession was the right move no matter what was the truth.

In a culture prone to conspiracy theories, it was a short step from blaming Catholicism and priests for this audacious crime to indicting Protestant ministers for their naïve efforts to convert slaves to Christianity. As one witness explained, "It was through the great encouragement the negroes had received from Mr. Whitefield, we had all the disturbance, and that he believed Mr. Whitefield was more of a Roman than any thing else, and he believed he came abroad with no good design."

George Whitefield was an Anglican priest who had come to America for the first time in 1739. Eventually he preached sermons to a total audience of hundreds of thousands, sometimes in open-air venues with six to eight thousand or more at a time (this when the population of Philadelphia, the Anglo-American colonies' largest city, was ten thousand). Whitefield was the best known of the evangelical ministers of the Great Awakening whose preaching style was sweeping through the colonies at this time. Whitefield was a Calvinist, and he believed in predestination, while his mentor John Wesley, a contemporary and the founder of Methodism, was not. Wesley believed in "universal redemption" and claimed that salvation will come to all those who accept it. Whitefield did not think humans had any agency in their salvation and therefore merit was inconsequential.

The Great Awakening included both people and belief systems in its transatlantic, transsectarian sweep; it even reached beyond Protestantism. The revival was not about church affiliation but about the "new birth" in which both Wesley and Whitefield believed, a conversion experience that often came in an ecstatic flash. Although Whitefield denounced ministers who played on the emotions of their congregations, his listeners, too, included people fainting and engaging in histrionics, which critics ridiculed. Like other New Light ministers, he offered certainty, a clear message that they were damned and worthless unless gifted with a salvation they did not deserve. If they were saved, there would be no doubt; if they were not, their fate was ordained. As Benjamin Franklin commented, "The Multitudes of all Sects and Denominations that attended his Sermons were enormous, and it was [a] matter of Speculation to me who was one of the Number, to observe the extraordinary Influence of his Oratory on his Hearers, and how much they admir'd and respected him, notwithstanding his common Abuse of them, by assuring them they were naturally *half Beasts and half Devils*."

Secular and ecclesiastical authorities perceived the revivalists as antiauthority, so it is hardly a surprise that church officials denied Whitefield permission to preach at an Anglican service in New York City in late 1739, and constables were posted "at the door of the English Church, lest [his] adherents . . . should break it open and take it by force." This was why Whitefield instead preached in open fields. "The people seemed exceedingly attentive," he wrote in his journal, "and I have not felt greater freedom in preaching, and more power in prayer, since I came to America, than I have had here in New York. I find that little of the work of God has been seen in it for many years." Nonetheless, the Awakening probably had less effect in New York than in any of the other mainland colonies north of the Carolinas—perhaps because there was no deep or unified religious tradition in the colony, and because no ministry followed up on the revival afterward. With no ministry to rebel against, it was harder to drum up religious fervor. "As to religion," a visitor wrote about New Yorkers a few years later, "they have little of it among them, and of enthusiasm not a grain."

Not all of the itinerant preachers were ordained, and they explicitly challenged established church structures and traditions. Their evangelical style was emotional, in contrast to the more reasoned approach of Puritans and Anglicans, and their work often divided communities and congregations along existing lines of stress, separating out "New Light" adherents from the entrenched "Old Light" figures in the pulpit and vestry. The revival brought more people to church, more to church membership, and more outward displays of religiosity. As Franklin reported, "It was wonderful to see the Change soon made in the Manners of our Inhabitants; from being thoughtless or indifferent about Religion, it seem'd as if all the World were growing Religious; so that one could not walk thro' the Town in an Evening without Hearing Psalms sung in different Families of every Street."

Wealthy and powerful men throughout the colonies feared that the outdoor revival meetings shattered the symbolic ordering of society as expressed in the churches' pews. The spontaneity of revival meetings, of preachers haranguing their audiences for hours, often without prepared, written texts, was also in strong contrast to the familiar, repeated forms of worship in Anglican churches. In Virginia, for example, readings from the Book of Common Prayer and a sermon of never more than twenty minutes was the Anglican norm. The revival meetings were democratizing religion, with their huge gatherings of the under-classes that those of wealth and influence were powerless to control. The emotional freedom celebrated by the itinerant preachers directly challenged those who had enjoyed a monopoly of power across social, political, judicial, and church lines.

Another sort of social democratization was at work as well. White-field's ministry during the Great Awakening coincided with an explosion in the transatlantic market economy, with the colonies welcoming new products, new commercial practices, and increased credit and debt. Merchandising reached a whole new category of consumers, including the working classes, who now aspired to own possessions that in some cases they had not even known existed a short time before, and to behavior it would previously never have occurred to them to affect. One credulous historian later reported as fact that when tea first arrived on Long Island, people knew they wanted it before they knew what it was. "One family boiled it in a pot and ate it like . . . porridge," he explained; "another spread tea leaves on his bread and butter, and bragged of his having ate half a pound at a meal." When the first teapot followed, "some said it was for one thing, and some said it was for another. At length one, the more knowing than his neighbors, affirmed it to be the ship's lamp, to which they all assented."

Population growth, falling agricultural prices, and increased productivity per worker in England had spurred demand for manufactured goods, and demand drove production. Demand from the colonies grew significantly, too. In turn, improved transportation, both overland and overseas, was an essential consequence and a facilitator of market growth. In the first half of the eighteenth century, the time required for overland travel from London to Edinburgh declined by 40 percent; over the same period, clearances of ships in colonial ports doubled, and schedules became more regular and thus predictable. The transatlantic voyage was also becoming shorter. In the second decade of the eighteenth century, news datelined London appeared in colonial newspapers on average 162 days later; by 1739, the year of Whitefield's arrival, the lag was about half that, 83 days.

In 1700, colonial America had no newspapers, but there were eleven by the time Whitefield arrived. Over that same forty years, the number of printing shops in Boston doubled. In New York, twenty-two different newspapers were published between 1725 and 1776. There were four printing shops in the city by 1742, five in 1750, six in 1762, and twelve by the 1770s. The average number of books published annually in New York rose from twenty in the 1730s to twenty-five in the 1740s, thirty-two in the 1750s, fifty-five in the 1760s, and by 1774 there were 155, as the market for everything from political pamphlets to abridged novels to narratives of Indian captivity rose exponentially.

Before the end of the colonial period, Americans were spending 20 percent of their income on goods produced outside the colony where they lived. They were deeply in debt to creditors they never met, at the mercy of international finance they did not understand, and addicted not just to tea but also to products grown (spices), processed (rum, sugar, molasses), and manufactured (cloth, carpets, porcelain) in Europe, the Caribbean, and Asia. This proliferation of commodities perplexed some colonists and sometimes contributed to conflict, especially when the goods were politicized: Sometimes they became the material embodiments of rights, since the colonists paid taxes on them; sometimes they were evidence of corruption, since the debts incurred to buy them and the interest on those debts were devouring the colonists' income. The complexities of trade made some commodities emblems of self-fashioning and self-flagellation at the same time.

Expansion of commerce led to more dealings with strangers and new credit relationships, which in turn seemed to threaten traditional community values and to undermine the consensus about just prices for goods. In 1710, a Boston crowd hacked the rudder of a ship bearing grain to keep it from leaving the harbor during a bread shortage. In 1736, also in Boston, a crowd of five or six hundred men destroyed buildings that had housed two public markets that, they believed, rich merchants had designed to control commerce and the lower classes. One advocate for the merchants had argued that the public markets would keep children and servants sent to the city to sell produce from "idling and playing about the town." Boston abandoned the public markets to quell the unrest they fostered.

George Whitefield knew how to use up-to-date marketing methods without upsetting his followers, and he sold his message in newspaper advertisements for his meetings that appeared before his arrival in town. He also published and sold books and other revival materials both in shops and to the crowds attending his sermons. He offered quantity discounts, incentives to prepay for serialized publications, and home delivery. His representatives even touted the packaging. The irony here is that Whitefield was using the market to attack it, thereby contributing to the ambivalence with which people welcomed their new possessions and new market relationships. He denounced the corrupting influence of style, fashion, and consumer goods, but he did so in print materials that he marketed and sold, in sermons that he advertised in the same ways, in the same newspapers, and sometimes on the same pages that advertised varieties of cloth, carpets, gloves, tea, dinnerware, and eating utensils that the previous generation had not even aspired to own.

The many relationships among production, supply, advertising, credit, and the spread of print culture were reciprocal. Advertisements fueled the spread of newspapers, which circulated news more widely and quickly than ever before to more people than had previously had access to either the goods or the news. High literacy created an environment in which print culture could expand. The books, pamphlets, and newspapers available in greater quantities, varieties, and locales promoted literacy as well as political awareness; news of the goods and events they advertised spread across colonies and regions to the most widely literate population in the world. In the fifty years prior to 1740, male literacy had increased by 35 percent among whites in Virginia and by about 50 percent in New York. In New England at midcentury, 75 percent of men and 60 percent of women could read.

The circulation of news also changed when it became common for a customer in a tavern to stand on a box to read the latest newspaper aloud. This democratization of information was an essential dimension in the growth of a revolutionary environment in which Americans reacted quickly, in eighteenth-century terms, to news from abroad and from other colonies. News about wars, revivals, and New York's slave conspiracy spread quickly throughout the colonies. Misinformation, rumors, and other conspiracy theories spread just as rapidly, and colonists often accepted them as fact.

Whitefield could not even have imagined, never mind realized, a transatlantic or even an intercolonial revival before this print and commercial infrastructure existed to promote it. He could not have drawn his unprecedented crowds without his itinerary being advertised. And the revivalists would not have connected with their audiences were it not for the unsettling nature of all these changes. The goods were pleasing and alienating at the same time. They unsettled traditional relationships based on barter, cooperation, and an ideology of local sufficiency. Traditional communities were under siege in some places and transformed in others, questioned by some and heartily adopted by others. Ethnic and ecclesiastical homogeneity were shattering, generational conflict reared its head, and social problems multiplied and seemed increasingly complex. The marketplace heightened personal ambition and the desire to stand out from the crowd that had once defined one's identity more than individuality did. Indeed, the very sense of the self as distinct from family and community was changing. Expanding networks of commercialization offered new models and new ambitions for those at the bottom of society as well as at the top. Elites could aspire to higher standing in the British Empire as it grew, and those at the bottom could aspire to own things and to have experiences previously unimaginable to them.

Evangelists provided a model for a new world that would be simpler and more traditional; hence their appeal and the controversy. They preached a gospel that had social implications that the ministers often did not, but sometimes did, intend. The democratizing, class-upending implications of their sermons were by-products of their spiritual message about the autonomous soul and the leveling of personal spiritual standing so that lower-class people could be equal to or above their social betters. The ministers also challenged the forces of secularization and commercialization, asking society to recall the higher value of the soul versus the purse, to consider the relationship between virtue and profit, corruption and mortality, community versus individual ambition. They appealed to values, to principles, to higher truths, and to unnegotiable right against unconscionable wrong. And they spoke in a language that people steeped in the Bible understood. Their parishioners were not rudderless, but quite possibly they were unsettled, unsure, adrift in the beckoning new world.

Not all Americans were changing; not everyone had the same access to commerce, credit, and the high road to the next market, or welcomed the complexities of community transformation. But a process was in motion that brought change to many, and for more and more Americans flux was the norm. The population had grown exponentially since 1700, when about 250,000 people lived in the British colonies on mainland North America, up from about 50,000 in 1650; there were well over a million by 1750 and 2.5 million by 1775. (The rate of increase between 1700 and 1750 was about 35 percent per decade.) And the racial makeup of the colonies was changing almost as quickly. In 1750, 97 percent of New Englanders were white and 3 percent black; in the Middle Colonies (New York, New Jersey, Pennsylvania, and Delaware), 93 percent white and 7 percent black; in the South, 60 percent and 40 percent. But by the time of the Revolution, about one out of every five colonists was a black slave, and half of all Americans lived in the South. More than half the population of South Carolina was black, and the percentage in Virginia was not hugely different; the populations of North Carolina and Maryland were more than 70 percent white. In all the colonies, Indians represented a very small percentage of the population and were mostly found in the backcountry.

Immigrants shattered the ethnic homogeneity of the colonies, however. In the 1760s, about one-third of the white population was not English, though in New England that fell to one-quarter. Pennsylvania was the most mixed, with only 20 percent English, about one-third German, and more than 40 percent Celtic (Irish, Scottish, and Welsh).

Boston, the largest city, grew rapidly until 1740, and ten years later Philadelphia surpassed it. The only Southern city was Charleston, if you do not count New Orleans, still under the control of Spain or France. The percentage of the population that lived in cities never rose much above 6 percent and actually shrank after the Revolution. All told, about a million people, counting all races and ethnicities, immigrated to Anglo-America during the colonial period; natural increase accounted for the other 1.5 million Americans by midcentury.

In some of the older colonies, population density was also rising quickly, to a point where some counties became as crowded as an English shire. This created the need for more institutions and made for new specializations—two churches and two schools in a county that had had only one of each in 1720, for example, a process accelerated by the growth of the Anglican church in North America and by the church conflicts brought on by the Great Awakening. The larger population also led to concentrations of like-minded or similarly employed residents who would then form groups—Baptists, for example, or innkeepers—that could petition the government about their shared interests and perceived abuses. Towns or villages that had previously had a single farmer-merchant were able by midcentury to support at least one full-time storekeeper. And some farmer-artisans had enough business to become full-time artisans.

In older, more established counties, the number of acres under cultivation was in decline, as communities reached their limits of growth and butted up against others. Fathers could no longer bequeath enough land to all their sons to allow them to become self-sufficient farmers at home, and this constriction increased both the rate of out-migration and the number of subsistence or near-subsistence farmers. More and more wealth in the hands of fewer and fewer individuals made for social polarization and a geographic concentration of wealth, usually in cities. And widespread commercialization, growing even more quickly than population density, meant that a higher percentage of the colonists' income fluctuated in response to external market forces. They were prisoners as well as beneficiaries of the market.

All this change, some of it selectively painful for some sectors of the population and all of it polarizing, was experienced by social groups that valued stability, tradition, community, consensus, and local control. As population and density increased, so did the problems that could be resolved only with the assistance of political agencies outside the people's own communities. In return for help solving larger problems, they were sacrificing autonomy. As parents became unable to establish their children in life as their ancestors had, with bequests of land and personal property, they lost influence over the next generation. In rural New England, premarital pregnancy rates rose, to the horror of parents, who interpreted their children's behavior as a challenge to their authority. Some young people chose partners without making traditional dowry arrangements. In the home, at church, and in politics, Americans were facing problems that seemed to them new.

The stresses of change contributed to nostalgia, and to calls for simplicity, virtue, and a return to the old ways. Some advocates for the new developments themselves looked back to the old virtues, while a new, cosmopolitan, commercial populace, notably in the cities, looked forward with eager anticipation to ever more change. The cosmopolites advocated an America modeled in many ways on Europe, which is precisely what British imperial interests and fellow colonists living on the land dreaded. Were the colonies sinking into feudalism, into a society marked by the very wealthy and very poor, or would there be a new world led by American entrepreneurs?

From the perspective of the British colonial officers in London, the growth of Britain's empire, both in numbers and across space, clearly dictated institutional changes. But that same growth enabled the colonists to resist any revisions of imperial relationships made by a bureaucracy spread thin in managing its global responsibilities. American colonists in the 1740s and 1750s did not imagine separating from the empire, but they grew more independent and more aggressive in asserting their right to local control. The colonial communities became more distinctively marked by mixed ethnicities, multiple classes, and interregional conflict as the backcountry settlements grew and the cities became socially stratified.

In the 1740s, New Yorkers were not the only colonists to imagine that property crime, social rebellion, and the play to emotions made by evangelical preachers such as Whitefield were somehow linked. Their conspiratorial mind-set encouraged the notion that external threats and internal challenges were inevitably connected. In the early stages of a market revolution, the colonists worried that their increased consumption—made possible by the proliferation of small shops like Mrs. Hogg's, which offered an array of consumer goods such as the ones stolen by the three slaves—made them vulnerable to thieves. After all, the more one had, the more there was to lose, and the more one had, the more jealous dispossessed people became, especially in the city. The colonists recognized that the evangelical style affected politics and social relations as much as it did religion, and they sensed that the European wars and the social upheavals of their times were connected rather than simply contemporaneous.

Thus to many New Yorkers, it was clear that Catholics, spies, Spain, France, war, and itinerant preaching to impressionable slaves were the driving forces behind a slave conspiracy. Without outside instigators, they believed, there would have been no rebellion. And war framed events in that spring and summer of 1741. New Yorkers had raised troops the previous two years in support of British naval expeditions against the Spanish in the Caribbean and along the coast of South America. And while the conspiracy cases were unfolding in the courts, they learned that fever had broken out among their troops, that men had died in the assault on Cartagena, New Granada (now Colombia), in early April, and that battles were being fought for and off the coasts of Hispaniola (now Haiti and the Dominican Republic) and

Cuba. Newspaper reports of the naval actions crowded out details about the court cases, but that the two were connected did not seem in the least surprising. According to a report in the *New-York Weekly Journal* in mid-June, "The Spanish Negroes (of which there are many in this place) were deeply concerned and active in the Business; and whatever Encouragement or Assurances they might receive from abroad, or hellish Incendiaries at home, they were persuaded that an attempt on this Province would be made by the *Spaniards* and *French*, for whom they agreed to wait some Time."

What, then, had happened? New Yorkers thought that "Wicked White People" had conspired with a "great number of Negro Slaves" in "barbarous designs" to burn down New York and murder its white inhabitants. There were rumors in late June, as the trials and executions continued, that Spanish forces had landed on Long Island. This was not true, but the reports further unsettled the edgy populace, just as such a rumor about a French invasion in 1689 had triggered Leisler's Rebellion. Surely, then, the "fomenters" of the "Negro Plot" included not only the two innkeepers, Spanish and French spies, "divers Spanish Negroes," and Ury the priest, but also other, unwitting figures, who prepared the ground for the slaves' villainy.

New Yorkers theorized that the larger numbers of servants and slaves, and more white people leaving their homes to attend church, created the opportunity for conspiracies: "Fetching Tea-Water on Sundays has been found to tend to the forming of the said Conspiracy, by giving Occasion to great numbers of them to meet in the same place." A few decades earlier, before the fashion for Sunday afternoon tea had developed, there was no call for fearing such a thing, and moreover, during the Great Awakening both white masters and black slaves went more often to church.

In the aftermath of the "Negro Plot," the grand-jury members petitioned the assembly for several new laws to restrict the movement and gathering of slaves, including one specifically "to restrain Negroes from fetching Tea-Water on Sundays." Later in the century, similar efforts were made to curb tea drinking—for political reasons of even greater moment than a merely local conspiracy of slaves. And colonists came to believe that other outsiders, this time British officials, were fomenting slave revolts in Virginia and North Carolina that threatened the independence of all white Americans.

3

✦

WARS

A S THE BRITISH EMPIRE became a global one during the seventeenth and eighteenth centuries, its rulers had the ambition to tighten their authority and rationalize the administration of their colonies, to make policies consistent across the globe, to create a structure in which one size, one policy, would fit all the colonies from India to the Ohio Valley, from Nova Scotia to Georgia and the Caribbean. There were many distractions, though, and the resources available for colonial administration over an ever greater expanse of ocean and land were limited. Parliament and the king adopted laws, issued edicts, and asserted authority that would not and could not be enforced. Frequent wars would draw attention to the problems, but they made it all but impossible to enforce the imperial regulations consistently. From the colonists' perspective, lax enforcement allowed them to ignore policies emanating from London that did not suit them; from the British perspective, disloyal and lawless colonists needed a stronger governing hand to bring them into line. Neither the perspectives nor their implications changed over 150 years; what changed were the global contexts, the perceived significance of the mainland North American colonies in the empire, the colonies' ability and desire to resist, and the resources the empire could and did devote to administration of its colonies.

After the execution of King Charles I in 1649, Massachusetts colonists continued to rule themselves in a representative government that had evolved from the founding charter of the joint-stock company that had brought them to America. They interpreted the charter expansively as a sacred and binding document, a written constitution that assured them the same civil liberties that they believed Magna Carta guaranteed all Englishmen. They took the assertion of rights even further, though, believing their elected officials held coequal status with members of the Parliament in London. In 1661, representatives in the Massachusetts assembly declared that "wee conceive any imposition prejudiciall to the country contrary to any just lawe of ours, not repugnant to the lawes of England, to be an infringement of our right." They were toeing a delicate line, as shown in the colony's passage of Navigation Acts in 1682 that were identical to those of Parliament, but on its own legislative authority, "haveing Considered the Statu[t]es of England, his Majestie's Commands and our owne Laws Refering to trade and navigation."

The colonists were obviously not challenging the purpose of the Navigation Acts—although decades later they sometimes did, after circumstances and perceived interests had evolved. The goal of the Navigation Acts was to require that goods on an enumerated list of raw materials from the colonies (including sugar, tobacco, and wool) be shipped only to British ports and only in British-built ships. At the start the idea was to deny the Dutch profits from any colonial trade, but the broader ambition was to protect British merchants and manufacturers from all of England's European competitors, including Spain and France. The Massachusetts colonists believed that in passing laws of their own they were challenging Parliament's authority to legislate for them without their consent. For them, it was a question of rights, interests, and independence within the imperial structure.

In 1683, King Charles II requested that Massachusetts voluntarily submit its charter for revision, and the colony declined. The Lords of Trade and Plantations, a committee the king had set up in 1675 to provide stronger administration of the colonies, filed legal action to dissolve the charter on grounds that the colony had run amok—minting its own currency, denying freedom of worship to Catholics and Dissenters ("repugnant to the Lawes of England"), imposing duties of its own creation on imported goods, levying taxes as it saw fit, establishing its own admiralty office, setting forth its own rules about extension of the franchise based on religious affiliation, and exceeding the authority of the charter in sundry other ways. All these charges were more or less true. Within a year, on the advice of the same Lords of Trade and Plantations, King Charles revoked the charter; he wanted to rein in the unruly Puritans and bring some uniformity and centralized administration to the empire. And one year later, the new king, James II, backed an even more ambitious centralization project.

New Englanders had feared the Catholic leanings of King Charles, and they abhorred James's open avowal of his Catholic faith, his outright claim to rule by Divine Right, his issuance of a Declaration of Indulgence, which freed many of the Protestant Dissenters (such as Quakers and Anabaptists) who were thorns in the Puritans' sides, and his exempting Catholics from the existing restrictions on the practice of their religion and service in government. Then he went even further, putting avowed Catholics in leading military and political positions. New Englanders feared he would do the same in the colonies.

When King James brought all the New England colonies together with New York, East and West Jersey, and Pennsylvania in a new, enlarged Dominion of New England under the rule of Governor Edmund Andros in 1688, the Massachusetts assembly was abolished. Andros had "full power and authority, by and with the advise and consent of our said [appointed] Councill or the major part of them, to make constitute and ordain lawes statutes and ordinances for the public peace welfare and good government of our said territory & dominion and of the people and inhabitants thereof." With no charter, no elected legislature, an arbitrary governor, and an authoritarian Catholic monarch, Massachusetts was poised for revolt.

During the winter months of 1688–1689, French colonists and traders in Canada gave support to various Indian groups that were attacking remote English settlements in what is now northern Maine. Governor Andros sent British regular soldiers and drafted colonists to eradicate this danger on the frontier. The draft and the timing of this march, in the middle of a brutal winter, were extremely unpopular. Massachusetts critics castigated the governor for the losses in the harsh weather, for what they thought was his lenient treatment of captured Indians, and for his attempts to distinguish hostile from friendly Indians. False rumors spread that Andros was plotting to turn the colony over to the French.

In the second week of April 1689, word reached Boston that the Protestant Dutch Prince William of Orange with a considerable body of troops had invaded England "for the Rescue of the Nation from Slavery and Popery"—a major development that had occurred in November 1688. The news encouraged the colonists to declare that the "Body of our People" would "assert our *Liberties* against the Arbetrary Rulers that were fleecing them." On the morning of April 18, in the north end of Boston, one witness "saw boys run along the street with clubs in their hands, encouraging one another to fight . . . And then immediately the drums began to beat, and the people hast[en]ing and running, some with and some for arms." Some of Boston's leaders feared that a detachment of deserters from the Indian war might join the mob, "make a great stir, and produce a *bloody Revolution* . . . The People were so driving and furious, that unheaded [without leaders] they began to seize our public Oppressors, upon which the Gentlemen aforesaid found it necessary to appear, that by their Authority among the People the unhappy Tumults might be a little regulated."

At about noon, these leaders met in the council room as a Committee of Safety and drafted a "Declaration" in an attempt to control the rebellion. The document began with predictable expressions of anti-Catholic bigotry and paranoia, always popular themes in Anglo-America. Massachusetts was rebelling against an "infamous Plot . . . to crush and break a Country so entirely and signally made up of Reformed Churches, and at length to involve it in the miseries of an utter Extirpation." The ousted Catholic monarch James II had sent to rule over them "such as were intoxicated with a Bigotry inspired unto them by the great Scarlet Whore," the pope. The first step in the conspiracy had been to vacate their charter; the next was to impose the Dominion of New England under a commission "absolute and Arbitrary, with which Sir Edmond Andross arrived as our Governor: who besides his Power, with the Advice and Consent of his Council, to make Laws and raise Taxes as he pleased, had also Authority by himself to Muster and Imploy all Persons residing in the Territory as occasion shall serve; and to transfer such Forces to any English Plantation in America." In furtherance of this plan, "several Companies of Souldiers were now brought from Europe, to support what was to be imposed upon us, not without repeated Menaces that some hundreds more were intended for us." Then, the empire gave patronage appointments to "such Men as were Strangers to and Haters of the People," men who extorted extraordinary and intolerable "Fees . . . from every one upon all Occasions, without any Rules but those of their own insatiable Avarice and Beggary."

As a consequence of such perfidy, "the People in New-England were all Slaves, and the only difference between them and Slaves is their not being bought and sold." To add insult to injury, "it was a Maxim delivered in open Court unto us by one of the Council, that we must not think the Priviledges of English men would follow us to the End of the World."

New Englanders did indeed believe that they had lost their rights, being tried without juries, taxed without elected representation, overseen by foreign mercenaries in red coats and a "gang" of strangers from New York, and having had their land titles questioned and revoked to feather the nests of their corrupt masters: "We were every day told, That no Man was owner of a Foot of Land in all the Colony." The governor "Briar'd" them, got them stuck in another Indian war even though the Indian enemies numbered not more than one hundred, drafted a thousand farmers to fight this handful of Indians, and put them under "Popish commanders (for in the Army as well as in the Council, Papists are in Commission)." Nothing good had come of this activity: "Not one Indian hath been kill'd, but more English are supposed to have died through sickness and hardship, than we have Adversaries there alive; and the whole War hath been so managed, that we cannot but suspect in it a Branch of the Plot to bring us low."

The New Englanders, like other British colonists, were "alarmed with just and great Fears, that they may be attaqu'd by the French, who have lately ('tis said) already treated many of the English with worse then Turkish Cruelties." Finally, the attempts Governor Andros had made to keep them from hearing the news of the arrival of William of Orange in England could be understood only as part of a conspiracy to attack the rights bestowed by Magna Carta.

The Massachusetts Declaration calmed inflamed passions, established the credentials of the more moderate men who had drafted it, and brought order to the unruly crowd. But the rebellion continued. At about 4:00 p.m. on that same day, the rebels demanded that Andros's men surrender Fort Mary, where those among them who had not been captured had retreated for protection. The armed crowd seized the battery and turned its cannons on the fort. By this time, "the country people came armed into the town . . . in such rage and heat, that it made us all tremble to think what would follow." Calm prevailed none-theless, and not a life was lost in this bloodless seizure of the colony from imperial officials and their mercenaries.

Two months later, the leaders of New England's Glorious Revolu-tion proudly argued that "no [other] part of the *English America*, so powerful and united as *New-England* was, could have endured half so many Abuses as we have bin harassed withal, with a tenth part of our *Patience*." It was only because they were such a religious people, they claimed, that they had endured so much for so long. They had been burdened with a government that was "as Vexatious as the *Constitu-tion* of it was Illegal" and yet "*scarce one half is told you. The Declara-tion* was composed so much in the Hurry of Action that it comprehends not all our *Grievances*; However, you may guess from the *Clawes* there pourtray'd, what sort of Creatures were devouring of us."

There had been a "*Plot to bring the Indians upon us*" and a conspir-acy to keep news of William's conquest from them. They had heard that the governor conspired to abdicate his office as James had and to join him in France in preparation for an invasion of New England by the French fleet stationed in the West Indies. Nonetheless, the Declara-tion boasted, the people of Massachusetts had responded with moder-ation and "no man underwent any Confinement, but such as the people counted the Enemies of the *Prince of Orange*, and of our *English Liber-ties*." In sum, they had acted as loyal subjects rather than rebellious ones, in behalf of constitutional order rather than against it, and to crush "*the worst of Treasons*, even a Treasonable Invasion of the Rights which the whole *English* Nation lays claim unto; every true *English-man* must justifie our Dissatisfaction at it, and believe that we have not so much *Resisted the Ordinance of God*, as we have Resisted an intolle-rable Violation of His *Ordinance*."

In May, the people of Massachusetts, still leading and with their leaders trying to keep up, reinstated their old government under the revoked charter. The governor and legislators from 1685 were recalled to their offices. Many of the drafted soldiers deserted the Maine fron-tier and came home, while some of them enlisted for an attack on the French community at Port Royal on the Bay of Fundy.

It would take two years for the English ministers to sort out these colonial affairs, which were, as usual, of less concern to them than domestic matters and imperial ambitions. Not surprisingly, during those two years the London officials heard about the overthrow of the government in Massachusetts from others. One man whom the rebels had imprisoned said the colonists were possessed by a "violent and bloudy zeal stird up in the Rabble acted and managed by the preachers." Eventually, London concluded that the New Englanders were challenging their subservient place in the empire and would go still further if they were not subdued. According to Sir Robert Southwell, a civil servant advising the Earl of Nottingham, "If New England be restored to the usurped Priviledges they had in 1660 . . . it will soe Confound the Present settlement in those Parts, and their Dependance on England, that 'tis hard to say where the Mischeif will stopp, or how farr the Act of Navigation will be over throwne thereby."

English officials did not view the Glorious Revolution in America as a reflection of the event in England, performed in the same way for much the same reasons, and acted out with the same restraint and high-minded ideals. The Lords of Trade and Plantations questioned Increase Mather, the influential clergyman and the Massachusetts agent in London, "Who are they that made these objections" to the governance of Sir Edmund Andros? Mather answered, "The Country, my Lord, the people of the place, who being under the oppression of an arbitrary Government did there as we did here, arose as one man and tooke the opportunity from the News they had of the Revolution here to free themselves from such a yoake." Sir John Somers, who was perhaps King William's closest adviser, could not or would not comprehend: "You say it was done by the people, but it was by the Rabble spirited by the faction to overthrow the Government." Mather was adamant: "It was done just as it was here by a general concurrence of the people of all degrees, and if you will say the Revolution here was done by the Rabble, you may. They acted like Englishmen and good subjects." Significantly, given the later conflict between the empire and the colonists that led directly to the Revolution, Sir John could not or would not comprehend this. "You say it was done by the country and by the people, [but] that is nobody," he protested. The colonists' concept of "the people" was not one that British aristocrats would ever grasp.

The controversy took all of Mather's considerable diplomatic talents to resolve. In 1691, after years of twists, turns, inaction, and preoccupation with more pressing matters, the king authorized, and the bureaucracy issued, a new charter for Massachusetts. The colony lost some important privileges, but it was back on firmer ground with a new "constitution" to which colonists could look with pride and a feeling of greater security.

The colonists were disappointed that their governors would be appointed ones, but they did get back their elected legislature. The original stipulation that church membership be required of voters was replaced by a property-based franchise, a 40-shilling freehold. This was more inclusive and became even more so over the next century. The British Empire was dragging Massachusetts toward wider religious tolerance and imposing a more republican form of government on them. The nature of the guarantees, though, continued to be a matter of debate, with New Englanders believing they had all the rights of Englishmen and a legislature with sovereign powers, while the British ignored these claims and believed nothing of the sort.

The Glorious Revolution of 1689 no more resolved New England's disputes with English authorities than the savage King Philip's War had ended violence on the French and Indian borderlands in 1676. The French were still in Canada, attacking the frontier town of Deerfield, in western Massachusetts, for example, six times in the 1690s; again, in February 1704, a combined force of French, Abenakis, Hurons, and Mohawks surprised the town. There were deaths by torture, prisoners taken, and captives marched through snow, ice, and mud, across frigid rivers and streams, reaching Montreal on April 25, almost three months later. Negotiations eventually achieved the repatriation of two or three hundred French and English prisoners over several years. Between King Philip's War and the Treaty of Utrecht in 1713, raids and reprisals were common, settlers withdrew to garrison towns, and the Indians moved deeper into the wilderness, which created hardships for both sides. The Abenaki and Micmacs aspired to be middlemen between the Europeans and other Indian tribes, but more often they were stuck in violent, insecure borderland relationships.

On Cape Breton, the French renamed Havre à L'Anglois as Port Saint-Louis, and then in 1719 built a substantial fortress and naval base there and renamed it again, as Louisbourg. By 1740, when the British were again at war with France and Spain, Louisbourg had about four thousand residents and was the fifth-busiest harbor in North America (behind Quebec, Boston, Philadelphia, and Charleston). This French thorn pained Britons on both sides of the Atlantic.

The strategic importance of Cape Breton was immense, as the English well knew. It was, according to an anonymous letter written by a Frenchman there in 1745, "a prodigious Addition to the riches and strength of France," and, if lost, the French would have "no other Shelter for their Fishery nearer than Old France." The island dominated navigation going up the St. Lawrence River, so its possession by Great Britain would cut off "all Communication with Quebeck, by which Means the whole Country of Canada must in a little Time fall into the Hands of the English." The fall of Canada, in turn, would result in France's loss of the principal market for the rum and molasses made in its island possessions in the Caribbean and the return market for Canadian lumber. If Britain controlled Canada, then it "must have a boundless Vent for all Kinds of coarse Woollens, and many other Kinds of their Manufactures, and command the valuable Trade in Fur, with all the Indian Nations. And those of them who live near the English Settlements, will have no French Missionaries to stir them up to a mischievous and expensive War." But as long as the French held Cape Breton Island, "all the British Plantations in North America will be liable to perpetual Annoyance from their Parties and Indians by Land, and all the British Navigation to and in America."

For roughly twenty-five years after it was built, the fortress at Louisbourg harbored the French vessels guarding the water approaches to Quebec, embodying a warning, if not a threat, to any expansion-minded English colonists. As Thomas Pichon—who worked for the French governor at Louisbourg but later was discovered to be a British spy—explained in his *Lettres et Mémoires* (published in 1760),

> Isle Royale [Cape Breton] protects all the French trade in North America, and is of no small consequence to the trade they conduct further south. If they [the French] had nothing in this part of the world, their ships which come back from Saint-Domingue or Martinique, would not be safe on the Grand Banks of Newfoundland, especially in times of war. Finally, being at the entrance of the gulf [of St. Lawrence], she controls totally that river.

There was, therefore, always cause for an Anglo-American attack on the place; the questions were only about timing, strategy, and logistics.

The British campaign against Cape Breton Island in 1745 was but another episode in the long history of cross-border aggression, to be sure, but French assaults on Canso and Annapolis Royal in 1744 had aroused legitimate defensive concerns for the English.* "It can't be reasonably doubted but that the French were meditating another attack against Annapolis Royal," the *Boston Post-Boy* reported after New England's troops debarked from Boston, "in which they expected to be joined by a naval force from France." Anglo-American raiders would also be striking a British blow in the War of the Austrian Succession, a European conflict in which Britain and France had declared themselves adversaries, and in which French defensive resources had been stretched thin. Louisbourg was undermanned and short of supplies. Reinforcements from Quebec, France, or the West Indies would be unable to arrive on short notice, and this was a good reason to attack with dispatch.

The initiative came from Massachusetts governor William Shirley and William Pepperrell, a merchant and militia commander. Initially the Duke of Newcastle, secretary of state for the Southern Department, had rejected the proposal, which had asked the admiralty to bear the full cost of six or seven warships that would shell Louisbourg's walls from offshore, before landing a thousand marines to overrun what was left of the ramparts. But he supported the plan when it was reconceived as a collaborative Anglo-American enterprise with the colonists as cannon fodder.

In January 1745, while Pepperrell was away, Shirley swore the Massachusetts assembly to secrecy and then presented his plan. He wanted to land *two* thousand colonial militiamen, apparently figuring—not unreasonably—that it would take twice as many provincials as British marines to pull off the invasion, to destroy the out-settlements and fisheries before reducing the town to ashes and occupying the fort. The assembly liked the idea, but not if Massachusetts had to bear the full financial burden. When Pepperrell returned, he and Shirley lobbied merchants in Boston and Marblehead, who petitioned the assembly to

* This invasion of Canso led Massachusetts to declare war on the Micmac and renew its bounty on Micmac scalps.

reconsider and recommended that the colony raise *three* thousand volunteers and pay them with plunder from the French; they added that provisions for four months would be needed. In a close vote, the assembly endorsed a bounty of one pound of ginger and a pound and a half of sugar to each volunteer, and forbade a draft. The colony would pay enlisted men 25 shillings a month and give each a blanket. This was not much, but there were colonists eager for income supplements in their cash-poor economy. A year's hard labor on a farm or a season of fishing on dangerous seas might not bring them as much in cash as the hoped-for bartered trade goods, liquor, and food.

Pepperrell, who came from Kittery (in what is now Maine) and was the wealthiest man in Massachusetts and one of the richest in mainland North America, was to command the troops on land. Captain Edward Tyng, a seafaring man from Falmouth, another coastal town in what is now Maine, was to sail on the *Massachusetts*, a new ship of four hundred tons armed as a frigate, and command the New England flotilla of ninety transports and thirteen armed vessels. The drums of war and an opportunity to eliminate the French menace on the frontier spurred patriotic volunteers for the expedition. An anonymous militiaman noted in his journal "the news of our Government's Raising an army" to attack Cape Breton, "which was like to prove Detrimental if not Destroying to our Country." The news "so affected the minds of many (together with the Expectation of seeing great things, etc.).—As to Inclind many, yea, Very Many to venture themselves and to Enlist into the Service Among whom I was one."

New Hampshire and Connecticut each committed 500 men. Rhode Island, always a recalcitrant neighbor, offered a sloop and 150 men, which arrived too late to take part in the siege. New York, which was farther from the fray, lent some rifles and donated £5,000. New Jersey sent £2,000 worth of provisions, and Pennsylvania contributed £4,000 for provisions and clothing, thereby assuaging Quaker consciences by supplying no weapons for the military operation. Not bad, as intercolonial cooperation went, not bad at all; the colonists repeatedly berated each other, and the British repeatedly berated all of them for their inability to cooperate on their collective defense against Indians and the French, but not this time. As Britons they could unite around their Protestant (and anti-Catholic) identity and their shared discomfort with the French presence to the north and west. "I doubt not the cause is God's," a Puritan minister assured the troops on the eve of their departure. A correspondent for the *Boston Evening Post* was more measured: "Every Man who loves his Country, ought to pray for the Success of the present Expedition."

Commodore Peter Warren, an Irishman who had enlisted as a common seaman in the Royal Navy at the age of thirteen, was cruising in the West Indies with his fleet when he received orders from the admiralty to support the invasion. Warren set sail for Boston from Antigua on March 13 with three warships, two smaller armed vessels, and ten sail of merchantmen, and reached Nova Scotia in early May to reinforce the blockade of the harbor and the assault on the fortress. The invading force from New England—five thousand men and sixty-three sail—set off on March 24. It was a "rough and tedious" journey, an anonymous militiaman reported in his journal. "Our Vessel was A Very Hospital, wee were all Sick, in a Greater or lesser degree." Then things got worse. "Our distress increased," he went on, "inasmuch as our Sickness, not only continued, but the weather Grew thicker and more stormy. And our captain, upon whom (under God) was our dependence, began to drink too hard." With both the captain and first mate drunk, it fell to an old fisherman to see the ship through the storm. Under his command, they made it to Nova Scotia, but only after a close escape from a French privateer.

Ice slowed the advance on Louisbourg by land and sea, but on April 29 a thaw made movement on the fort possible. Until this time, the French had underestimated the size of the force that was attacking them and found the New Englanders' blockade of the harbor permeable. But now, with the arrival of Warren's flotilla, they sent word to France, on a ship that slipped through the blockade, that they were in desperate straits and required immediate reinforcements. The acting governor and commander, Louis du Port Chambon, lacked courage, experience, fortitude, imagination, and good judgment. As badly equipped and dilatory as the Anglo-American militiamen were, they had at least made plans for engagement with the enemy. But it was not until the fort's lookouts could see raiders landing on the beach that the French even began to discuss the question of defense. Eventually fifty civilian volunteers and a contingent of twenty-four soldiers left the fort to repulse the attack. On the beach, they engaged the fifteen hundred New Englanders who had already landed. In the ensuing skirmish and

French retreat, the English had only two or three wounded; the French, seven killed and nine or ten wounded.

By nightfall, two thousand New Englanders were on the ground, and they completed their landing on May 1. In their first few weeks on Cape Breton, the New Englanders plundered civilian properties and scavenged for food and supplies. A member of one roving band reported capturing five cows; the hungry invaders ate three of them and kept the other two for milk. Within three weeks, the colonists had left not a single house or barn intact and had consumed, burned, carried off, or scattered their contents to the wind. Plunderers killed two French noncombatants for their gold and other possessions. Such engagements as occurred came in the course of thefts, when owners returned to defend their properties. One New Englander reported that 140 French and Indians (a gross exaggeration) attacked him and four others who were "in a house upon plunder"; three of the five escaped, and the other two died in combat. One officer informed Colonel Pepperrell that "three fourths of the men . . . are partly employed in speculation on the neighbouring hills and partly employed in ravaging the country." Pepperrell fully comprehended the problem, calling marauders the "greatest fatigue I meet with; hope to reduce them to a better discipline soon." He failed.

On May 23, "about eight hundred of us went to take the Island," wrote an anonymous diarist, "but our head officer being a coward, we rowed about all night and never landed." Three days later, New Englanders attacked the Island Battery, which between sixty and eighty French soldiers defended. French cannon fire held Commodore Warren's fleet at bay, keeping most of his vessels from entering the harbor, and rough surf made it almost impossible for the militiamen to land, but those who made it outnumbered the French garrison by about two to one. Yet in a muddled assault, the aggressors suffered heavy casualties and failed to take the island. They tried again and again, cajoled and bribed by commanders who agreed that "if a number of men to the amount of three or four hundred appear as volunteers for the attack of the Island Battery, they be allowed to choose their own officer and be entitled to the plunder found there." After five unsuccessful charges, they still had not captured Louisbourg and had lost upward of 189 men killed and wounded, by Colonel Pepperrell's estimate.

Eventually, it occurred to the British commanders that they could bombard the Island Battery from the shore, where they constructed their own battery on a spit of land with a lighthouse about a thousand yards across the harbor. They began shelling the French in mid-June, and this was a much more successful strategy. Seventeen of the first nineteen shells hit the Island Battery's fort, one of them setting fire to the magazine and driving the terrified French soldiers into the surf to escape the flames and relentless bombardment.

With their main defensive batteries silenced and the walls of their fort and town reduced to rubble, with only one house undamaged by the British cannonade, and ammunition almost expended, the French surrendered. On June 17, after some squabbling over terms, New Englanders occupied the fort and town, struck the French flag, and took two thousand prisoners; the English planned to ship them, along with their personal effects, back to France on captured French vessels—a fate that was spelled out in the terms of surrender. The casualty estimates reported in Boston newspapers were lower for the whole siege than Pepperrell's for that one engagement at the Island Battery (101 of the attackers dead by gunfire and 30 by disease), and the New Englanders put French losses in the siege at about three hundred dead. Commodore Warren also had his prizes, including the sixty-gun French warship *Vigilant*. "And as the French were allowed to carry off their effects," reported one diarist, "so our guards took all the care they possibly could to prevent the common soldiers from pilfering and stealing."

There was the rub, as far as the victorious volunteers were concerned. They had expected payment in plunder, as the recruiters had promised them and as was traditional for armies long before and after 1745. Granting the French their possessions in the official terms of surrender was, the New Englanders thought, stealing from *their* pockets. Even though they had not done much fighting, and many of them had fought only civilians in armed robberies, and even though they had been plundering for two months, they had weathered harsh conditions and short rations, and they felt entitled to the booty. According to Pepperrell's diary entry for June 19, there were "many complaints of abuses done by the English soldiers to the French inhabitants." Since the "abuses" are unspecified, it is not clear whether the men did any more than admire the "hansom ladeys," but we do know that they ravaged the countryside and attempted to relieve prisoners of whatever was left for them to carry on board the ships that would take them back to a homeland some of them had never known.

The prisoners obviously could not take their fishing boats with them on the transports, so those at least were up for grabs and were valuable acquisitions. It was the gold, coin, and jewelry, though, that the New Englanders begrudged the French, whom they insulted and assaulted repeatedly. Finally the process of shipping off the four thousand prisoners commenced on July 4 in eleven overcrowded ships. This was the beginning of the Acadian expulsion, an enterprise that took more than a decade to complete but was always high on the list of the New Englanders' ambitions.

The heroes returned home triumphant but irked, but the civilians who welcomed them back were unabashedly thrilled, and even the English were uncharacteristically complimentary about the New England colonists. News of the great victory appeared in Boston newspapers on July 15. The *Evening Post* gushed that the taking of Louisbourg "can scarce be parallel'd in History" and challenged "any Army in Europe to produce Three Thousand stouter, braver Men, fired with more Resolution and Stronger Resentments." A French prisoner was reported to have said that "he doubted whether Ten Thousand Regular Forces" from any of Europe's armies could have accomplished the same. New Englanders proclaimed their traditional providentialism in the pulpit and press: "Never any Affair seem'd to be more under the immediate Influence of Heaven, than this has been." Not once in twenty years would the fleet have experienced such good weather in February and March; "not one storm in that ordinar[ily] tempestuous season . . . ruffle[d] our Fleet in their Passage." God had "triumphed gloriously over his and our antichristian enemies," and there was good cause to foresee "from the Eastern to the Western sea, and from the river of Canada to the Ends of America," a Protestant English empire.

Newspapers reported lower losses than the field estimates did: about one hundred New Englanders on land and one ship of fifty men, the *Prince of Orange*, a Massachusetts scow lost at sea in a storm that had not been counted against the providential good weather. Newspapers reported that the French had lost eighty-seven men within the walls of the fortress at Louisbourg, but there was no body count for those outside the fort—Indians, civilians, seamen, and Acadian militiamen. For the spent blood, Britain's colonists counted themselves safer on the seas and in port, and believed they were poised to profit from unfettered exploitation of the cod fishery in the North Atlantic.

On July 24, 1745, a French vessel named *Charmont*, "richly laden from Bengal," waited for a pilot to guide it into the port at Louisbourg. Instead, the *Princess Mary* and the *Canterbury* attacked the ship, whose officers and crew knew nothing of the Anglo-American invasion, and towed it into what was now an English harbor. This was New England's first windfall from the capture of Cape Breton. When the news reached Boston in early August, several merchants set sail for the port in anticipation of purchasing the booty for a pittance of its worth: "Muslings of various Sorts, plain and embroidered, and all other Sorts of Cottons, a large Quantity of Handkerchiefs, of various Sorts for Men and Women, plain and embroidered, Seersuccers, a large Quantity of raw Silk and Kirman Wool, Table Linnen, a large Quantity of pepper and a variety of other valuable Merchanndize yet unknown." Never had such a cargo reached Boston's consumers, and for a "Pennyworths" of its true market value.

Massachusetts governor Shirley warned against unbridled elation. Vigilance was essential, as the French could be expected to try to retake Louisbourg at their earliest opportunity. He thought the time seemed ripe to drive out the Acadians from Nova Scotia completely, thereby securing Cape Breton, Nova Scotia, and New England with one blow. "It grieves me much," wrote Shirley, "that I have it not in my power to send a party of 500 men forthwith to Menis [Minas, a Nova Scotia settlement on the Bay of Fundy], and burn Grand Pré, their chief town, and open all their sluices, and lay their country waste." But Shirley did not have the men.

The need to defend the fort against an anticipated French assault dictated that two thousand of the New England volunteers must stay behind. There were fewer volunteers and much less enthusiasm for this extended duty over the harsh winter. As Captain Joseph Sherburne confided in his diary, Governor Shirley averted a mutiny in mid-September only by promising high wages and ample supplies, which he allowed the men to delegate fifty of their number to return to Boston to procure. Shirley appealed to their honor and patriotism, and he warned them of "the ignominy and Disgrace they would bring on themselves" if they mutinied, and "the Damage to their Country, [and] the Advantage they would give the Enemy should they leave the place exposed."

Ultimately, more than a thousand of the soldiers died from un-named diseases—about ten times more than had died in battle—after the French surrender, and once they were living in the closer quarters of the damaged fort; the death rate continued to climb over the fall and winter of 1745–1746. The journal of Chaplain Stephen Williams, who arrived after the battle, records little else but illness, death, and his fears for his own life during a protracted illness. Williams had been a captive of the French and Indians when he was a boy, and the circum-stances under which he was living in Louisbourg brought back painful memories of that traumatic time of his life. "This day fourty years ago," he wrote on November 20, 1745, "I arrivd in Boston, from Canada, where I had been a prisoner." He prayed that, though he was unworthy, God would redeem him again. He ministered to soldiers through their fevers, fears, fits, and deaths, until he could no longer rise from his own bed, and was carried, near death himself, to the ship that returned him to Boston, a shell of the man who had left the city six months before.

New Englanders had lost many men and spent much of their wealth for their victory on Cape Breton Island, so they remained vengeful, which many Acadians did not understand. Some of them had supplied Louisbourg before the New England invasion, but most had tried to remain scrupulously neutral. "But would you damn the innocent many for the guilty few?" one asked after the siege, when he learned that New Englanders' bellicosity had not been sated. The answer was yes, New Englanders damned all twenty thousand of the "heathen," "papist" settlers of French ancestry on their northern border, as well as their "savage" allies. The Nova Scotia Governor's Council agreed that Acadi-ans were traitors with a "Natural disposition" to support the French, regardless of their declarations of loyalty to the British Crown. "Upon the whole," it concluded, "it is most humbly submitted whether the said French Inhabitants may not be transported out of the Province of Nova Scotia and be replac'd by good Protestant Subjects."

Back in London, the government decided against supporting a sec-ond invasion in 1746. The Duke of Bedford, for one, advised Newcastle against it on the grounds that an American conquest would create an "independence . . . in those provinces towards their mother country, when they shall see within themselves so great an army possessed in their own right by conquest, of so great an extent of country." Governor

Shirley was willing to go it alone, but he could not convince the Massachusetts assembly to fund an expulsion of the Acadians in 1746, given the high cost and the toll that would be taken by another Cape Breton winter for militiamen left behind to guard Louisbourg.

When the Acadians caught wind of Shirley's ambition, they were understandably frightened, as they made clear to the Nova Scotia Governor's Council:

> You know the condition in which we are placed both by the French and the Indians in all their operations. The latter ravage, plunder, and kill us; the former overwhelm us with work and trouble, not giving us a moment to breathe. And now from another side we are made to understand that out of Boston will come those intent on destroying us entirely, which would not be difficult, since we are already crushed in all ways.

Britons on both sides of the Atlantic recognized that the Louisbourg victory belonged principally to Massachusetts. An article that first appeared in the *Westminster Journal* and was widely reprinted in America graciously acknowledged that New England had "so much Right to the Glory of this Plan, that I am afraid scarce a Glimpse of it can ever reach the Old." Nonetheless, all Britons would be beneficiaries of a complete French expulsion from Cape Breton Island: "When this Island was given to the French for the Sake of a Peace [in the 1715 Treaty of Utrecht], we parted with a Mine of gold, or indeed with a better Thing, since if we keep and fortify Cape-Breton, and improve the Fishery there to the Degree of which it is capable, it will very soon produce to this Nation between two and three Millions Sterling per Annum." Another wrote that "Cape Breton . . . is alone worth a little Kingdom." Had the English authorities the foresight to invade earlier, without abdicating the responsibility to its colonists, "Quebec might by this Time have fallen into our Hands."

Perhaps, some in England speculated, the greatest threat in North America was no longer France but Massachusetts. "I know what may be said on this Occasion," wrote a contributor to the *London Magazine*, "as it has often been said on others. There is Danger in making this Colony too powerful, lest the People should, at some Time or other, throw off all Dependency on the Crown of England, and erect themselves into a Republick, according to the Principles of the Majority among them." Through the 1730s, the ruling assumption had been that "while Canada is so near, they cannot rebel." But beginning in the 1740s there was increasing doubt that the French could hold Canada indefinitely.

So long as the French remained in North America, there was no reason to fear an imminent revolt in Massachusetts but every reason to think that New Englanders' longer-term loyalty was contingent on British policy. According to an article in the *Westminster Journal*, "There will be no Room to fear it hereafter, while we give our Brethren, together with Protection, all the Advantages natural to their Situation, I will venture to predict. When a Colony thus deserts her Mother, it is usually the Effect of some ill Treatment, which, I hope, therefore, it is not thought necessary to give, in order to secure Obedience."

The French immediately began to plan a reconquest of Louisbourg's fortress and valuable harbor. In the opinion of one informant from French Canada, "If Louisbourg had been attacked during the winter [of 1745–1746] by three hundred Indians, it might have been taken" from the New England militiamen who were guarding the prize. A major expedition left France later in 1746 only to founder on the bad fortune of storms at sea and rampant disease. In early September, Bostonians learned that the Royal Navy had captured two French ships from a fleet of more than fifty armed vessels that carried three thousand troops ordered to retake Louisbourg, invade Annapolis Royal, and then attack Boston. After a brutal Atlantic crossing, the French flotilla anchored in the harbor that three years later would become English Halifax, unfit to fight anyone, and then sailed home again, having lost twelve hundred men at sea, including its commander, its second-in-command by suicide, and hundreds more to disease without ever engaging the Anglo-Americans. Jubilant Britons hoped, but did not expect, that they had seen the last of French invasion forces. American newspapers reported that the British fully appreciated the significance of the victory at Louisbourg in 1745. According to the *Philadelphia Gazette*, "We hear it is determined that no Treaty of Peace shall ever be set on Foot with France, to whom we have shewn ourselves so much superior by Sea, unless it be previously agreed, that the Restoration of CAPE BRETON shall not be so much as mentioned in the Negotiations."

Be that as it may, during a snowstorm in late January 1747, a combined force of about 240 Canadian militiamen, a few militant Acadians, and 60 Indians (Micmac and Maliseets) attacked a New England militia unit that was occupying Minas. Six members of the assault party died and about fourteen were wounded, but the New Englanders suffered heavy casualties; again the sources vary in their estimates but agree that at least one hundred died, twenty-five were injured, and more than fifty were taken prisoner. The remaining 250 New Englanders surrendered on terms that required them to go home and not return for at least six months. Nonetheless, in April, three hundred replacements from Boston occupied Minas, and over the summer the Royal Navy thwarted yet another French invasion of Louisbourg, capturing between four and five thousand troops on the high seas. In October, Governor Shirley tried to calm the waters by offering royal protection to those Acadians who remained loyal to their oath of allegiance to the British Crown. At the same time, he offered a bounty on the heads of twelve traitors, who then fled with their families to Île Saint-Jean (Prince Edward Island). New England militia burned their houses to the ground as an example to other Acadians.

The invasion in 1745 had been a costly adventure for the colonies, upward of £225,000, and the costs the colonists bore for defending their conquest were adding up, too. It took years for the British accountants to pore over invoices and for the higher-ups to determine the terms of compensation. Meanwhile, New England militiamen grew weary of guard duty on dank Cape Breton Island, bitter about the tardy delivery of pay and short supplies, and fearful that their enlistments might extend indefinitely.

Governor Shirley had plenty of problems back in Massachusetts, where elation over the victory was mixed with mourning the dead militiamen and suffering the economic hardships that resulted from the unreimbursed expenditures. Things came to a head during the night of November 16, 1747, when Commodore Charles Knowles, who commanded a British fleet that had been anchored in Boston Harbor for two months, was short of hands to man his ships and instituted a "press," an armed effort to capture deserters who had either signed on to commercial vessels or were hiding out on land and seeking other work. Knowles's press took forty men, which would enable his fleet to set sail for the West Indies.

One problem with a press was always its violence; another was the marines' indiscriminate approach to the men they were taking, being none too careful about whether they were truly deserters; and they were brutal. Seaboard towns feared and resisted the press. But Knowles's press differed from others mainly in the Bostonians' response to it, and it is possible that the violent rioting, which brought several thousand into the streets, stemmed from anger at the losses in the Louisbourg attack and frustration with London's lethargy in reimbursing the colony for its expenses, both of which contributed to hard times; there was also a vitalized sense of the colony's independence, now that it had ousted the French from the Cape Breton fort.

In any event, the next day a mob of Bostonians kidnapped English naval officers onshore in retribution and held them hostage pending the release of the local men who had been impressed. The crowd also lashed out at local authorities, assuming their complicity, beating the deputy sheriff and locking him in the stocks before burning a barge they mistakenly believed was the property of the naval detachment. Governor Shirley tried to calm them down, but when he "went out to 'em and demanded the cause of the Tumult . . . one of 'em arm'd with a Cutlass answer'd me in an Insolent manner it was caused by my unjustifiable Impress Warrant, whereupon I told 'em that the Impress was not made by my Warrant, nor with my knowledge." It is unlikely that many Bostonians believed this.

The insolence, the violence, the size of the mob, and the refusal of militiamen to turn out in response to the governor's call were unnerving. Shirley and other officials fled to Castle William, a fortified island in Boston Harbor. Commodore Knowles was not helping, for he refused to negotiate, with Shirley as middleman, an exchange of kidnapped officers for the impressed Bostonians, and threatened to reduce the town to rubble. This breakdown of civil authority and resistance to British military force was the beginning of a new phase in imperial-colonial relations.

The resurgence of conflict over impressment had come after a half century of more or less amicable relationships between British naval officers and New Englanders. There had been conflict over impressments in the early 1690s, but an accommodation had been reached in 1696 that only warrants issued by the colonial governors could authorize a press, which explains the exchange between Shirley and the man who blamed him for the November 16 press. The requirement for warrants had been supplemented in 1707 by "An Act for the encouragement of Trade to America," which contained a clause popularly referred to as the "Sixth of Anne" (the year of the queen's reign in which it became law) stipulating that no "mariner or other person, being on shore in any part [of America] shall be liable to be impressed or taken away by an officer or officers of or belonging to any of her Majesty's ships of war empowered by the Lord High Admiral, or any other person whatsoever, unless such mariner shall have before deserted from such ship of war."

The accommodations, which Americans saw as rights protected in law, lasted until 1740 and the hostilities in North America connected to the War of the Austrian Succession. One incident in Boston had occurred in 1742, pitting Governor Shirley against an impatient Captain James Scott, who wrongly anticipated that the governor would not issue a warrant to impress fifty deserters known to be living in Boston. Scott preemptively ordered a press, and when Shirley ordered the release of the illegally impressed sailors, Scott defied his order. This unprecedented breach of the law was followed in 1745 by a legally sanctioned seizure of two hundred Bostonians to man British warships for the invasion of Louisbourg. The Massachusetts assembly sanctioned the press, considering it the equivalent of a militia draft during time of war.

So local officials thus helped to politicize the press and reignite popular resistance to it. It was one thing to be drafted into the local militia and another to be forcibly enlisted in the Royal Navy. This point seemed overly subtle to the Massachusetts assembly and irrelevant to the British naval officers, but in 1746 the petitioners made the argument that impressment was a breach of Magna Carta as well as the province's charter and an act of Parliament. In other words, it was unconstitutional, an American construction that was to be resurrected time and again in the next decades, one that Americans took for granted and the British never accepted.

Governor Shirley shared the imperial view that the 1707 law regulating impressment had "expir'd." He was frustrated with the "perswasion they have all over the Continent, that the Impressing of Seamen within any of his Majesty's Plantations, is illegal, by virtue of a Clause in a Statute of the [Sixth] of Queen Anne, which they conceive to be perpetual." And he was exasperated by the anarchic "constitution" of the mob and the city. Kidnapping, bludgeoning, and imprisoning rightful authorities, destroying private property, and rescuing prisoners were commonplace. The democratic traditions of the town meeting were most threatening, "one of which may be called together at any time upon the Petition of ten of the meanest Inhabitants, who by their Constant attendance there generally are the majority and outvote the Gentlemen, Merchants, Substantial Traders and all the better part of the Inhabitants."

That same year, Parliament compounded the constitutional problem by adopting a law much like the Sixth of Anne but specifically referring only to impressment in the West Indies, which it forbade. Since the law did not mention Britain's mainland colonies, it could be understood to exclude them from its protection, therefore effectively repealing the act of 1707. This, at least, was the way the governor and Commodore Knowles understood it, and they recognized that it would arouse fierce opposition: "The [1746] Act against pressing in the Sugar Islands, filled the Minds of the Common People ashore as well as Sailors in all the Northern Colonies (but more especially in New England) with not only a Hatred for the King's Service but [also] a Spirit of Rebellion, each Claiming a Right to the same Indulgence as the Sugar Colonies and declaring they will maintain themselves in it."

A pamphleteer who signed himself *Amicus Patria* (a Lover of His Country)—generally believed to be Samuel Adams, cousin of John Adams and a rabble-rouser extraordinaire—wrote shortly after the Knowles Riot "to inspire the minds of the people in this Province, especially in this Town, with a proper Sense of the imminent Danger their Lives, and Liberties, are in." They had already been subjected to the "Inhuman and barbarous Murder" of illegal presses during the 1740s. It was no wonder that citizens ran together in a mob for their mutual defense against such a surprising and unwarranted attack in Boston. It seemed to him outrageous that anyone believed "*Pressing has been so long a Custom as to become a Part of the Constitution.*" The town of Boston was under attack by the Royal Navy,

> despite the great Losses the trading Part of this Province has met with
> by Sea; The Captivity of many Hundreds of Her Inhabitants by the
> *French*, and *Indians*, upon the Frontiers: The Lives lost, and immense

Sums spent, in Defence of His Majesty's Province of *Nova-Scotia*; And above all, the Blood, and Treasure, spent in the Reduction of *Louis-burgh* to the Crown of *Great-Britain.*—An Action, which I am sure, must ever be remembred to the Glory of *New-England.*

In January 1748, London still had not compensated the colonies for the invasion and defense of Louisbourg. New Englanders were still mourning their losses, more militiamen were dying of exposure and disease in another brutal winter of guarding it, and Bostonians had not yet recovered the men taken in the Knowles press. Colonists heard rumors that, contrary to their assumptions and former understandings, there "was talk of restoring Cape Breton in exchange for Madrass" in the peace negotiations between England and France then being conducted in Europe. And by February the colonists knew that the rumors were true. According to a story in the *Boston Gazette,*

> Cape Breton and Madrass shall be reciprocally restored. Our ministers had accepted the most disadvantageous terms of the enemy. They had been . . . bullied into the acceptance of these terms by the address and threats of France, at a time when we were more capable than ever of continuing the war, and France less so. And . . . we had basely and wickedly surrender'd Cape Breton, a fortress of the utmost consequence to the trade & navigation of Great Britain, without receiving any equivalent in return.

In March, colonists heard that Parliament had finally authorized reimbursement for the Louisbourg invasion. By the time Massachusetts received its £183,649 and the other New England colonies got their lesser amounts in 1749, another whole year later, the French had doubled the size of the garrison guarding Louisbourg and rebuilt the fortress. French Louisbourg was now larger, reaching a population of about forty-five hundred souls within a couple of years, was better armed, and harbored more warships than ever.

Anglo-Americans, and especially New Englanders, were bewildered. Clearly, British officials, Parliament, and perhaps King George himself had not appreciated their great victory. They were sensitive on this score anyway and felt devalued in relationship to other parts of the empire, first the West Indies and now India. The Treaty of Aix-la-

Chapelle bringing the War of the Austrian Succession to a close rubbed Anglo-Americans' low status in their faces. By returning Louisbourg to the French, it showed how little their sacrifice and safety mattered to England. Men had died, others had suffered, all had paid. Rather than sharing in the British Empire's victory over France, they felt defeated, humiliated, inconsequential, and impotent to affect policies that bore on their lives.

The Knowles Riot was the first time that mob violence had challenged imperial authority in Massachusetts. After it, the ministry ignored the colonists' petitions against impressment, which was frustrating. "It is a sad symptom of a declining State," wrote one disgruntled Bostonian in 1748. Not only had the costs in lives and supplies been in vain, but "we have not appear'd respectable enough to obtain any Relaxation from Impresses." New Englanders were, as they always had been, stubbornly devoted to local governance, and they were angrier at the empire than they had been at any other time in memory.

British officials also abandoned their tolerant approach to imperial administration, aiming instead for closer supervision; they worried that the colonists had grown so used to bureaucratic lethargy that they perceived benign neglect as a constitutional right. The colonies' growth in size and economic power made the bureaucrats anxious that their continued relative independence might lead to rebellion. They convinced themselves that it was therefore necessary to tighten the administrative screws, thereby hastening the very process they feared.

The peace of 1748 created an opening for new approaches to colonial administration. The growing importance of India and North America to the economic health of the entire British Empire gave impetus to plans for a global rationalization of the bureaucracy, and relative calm in the British Isles themselves for the next several years freed the imperial gaze for closer scrutiny of the colonies. Officials paid more attention to their colonial governors' chronic complaints of being powerless in the face of recalcitrant local legislatures. The ministry also decided it must do something about merchants for whom smuggling had become a standard business practice and colonists who routinely ignored its edicts.

Given the recent past, interested parties in North America, Paris, and London might have anticipated that the next conflict would come again in Louisbourg or this time in Boston, or on the European mainland, in the Caribbean, or even in India. Shrewd analysts on both sides of the Atlantic would not have been surprised if armed conflict broke out on more than one of these fronts, as the competing empires were now stretched thinly across the globe and constantly reassessing their own priorities and their opponents' vulnerabilities. All were shocked, then, when hostilities ignited in the Ohio Valley, a place that very few members of Parliament could have located on a map.

4

✦

BATTLEFIELDS

IN MAY 1754, forty Virginia militiamen, minus seven lost in the woods, under the command of twenty-two-year-old Lieutenant Colonel George Washington, fired an opening volley in the American Revolution. It was a preemptive strike against thirty-five French soldiers, less one Canadian who had deserted, in Pennsylvania's backwoods. Seneca Indians had betrayed the French position to Washington, who marched the contingent of his 159-man company into the forest, a perilous journey in the rainy, dark night—"black as pitch," he said—where they stumbled over roots and into trees and each other, and then attacked the startled Frenchmen. Or the French fired first. The accounts conflict.

In the ensuing battle, between nine and twelve of the French soldiers died and one was wounded. After the combat ended, the commanding French ensign was either shot by a Virginian as he tried to read out his orders or clubbed with a hatchet by an Indian, who then scalped his victim and washed his hands with the Frenchman's brains. The Americans lost one man or none, depending on which account is accurate, and took twenty-one or twenty-two captives.

The French survivors showed Washington a declaration from their commander at Fort Duquesne, which ordered the withdrawal of English colonists from the Ohio Valley. They insisted that their mission had been peaceful, that they were combing the wilderness for Englishmen to warn. Washington did not believe it; he knew the French had been spying on his encampment for at least two days. Under torture, the captives confessed they were spies and the declaration merely a cover for their intrigue.

The skirmish was about land and empire, and in this case there was no difference between the two. Anglo-American shareholders in the Ohio Company, not coincidentally including Washington, intended to profit from a five-hundred-thousand-acre grant bestowed on the company by King George II in 1749. Conditions placed on these speculators included the obligation to build a fort and lure one hundred settlers to live on the land within seven years. Eventually the investors failed, but in the short term they stirred up a hornets' nest of trouble, expedited settlement of what historians call the Old Northwest, exacerbated tensions among the colonies of Virginia, Maryland, and Pennsylvania, all of which had ambitions in the region, and significantly assisted in provoking war with the French and Iroquois.

The confluence of the Mississippi, Ohio, and Monongahela Rivers was one place where British and French ambitions clashed, and where Virginia land speculators staked their claim in blood.* France based its claim to the region on the explorations of René-Robert Cavelier, Sieur de La Salle, in 1669–1670, while the English insisted it was part of their original Virginia grant of 1609 and among the concessions they had extracted from the Iroquois in the Treaty of Lancaster (1744). The Indians had quickly repudiated the latter claim, saying that it was a misunderstanding or willful misrepresentation of their agreements. At Quebec in 1748, the Iroquois repeated the assertion that in the treaty they had not ceded any lands to the English. This was true, up to a point. They had agreed at Lancaster to disclaim "all lands within the said colony" of Virginia, but they had not known that Virginians claimed their charter extended from sea to sea, entitling the colony to nearly half of the continent.

Even as the Virginians thus precipitated conflict with the French in the contested backcountry, immigrants without documented land claims were beginning to populate it. About fifty thousand people left Irish ports on ships bound for Philadelphia during the colonial period, and many of them ended up in this region. Among them was a high proportion of Scots-Irish who spoke English, not Gaelic; most either had come from Scotland to Ulster before crossing the Atlantic or were

---

* First, the French built Fort Duquesne; then the English constructed Fort Pitt, which was followed later by the frontier town of Pittsburgh.

members of families that had left Scotland not long before. Every year between 1718 and 1775, about five thousand of these "borderers," so-called because of their borderland origins, arrived in Philadelphia and Newcastle from Ireland, Scotland, and the north of England.

The Scots-Irish paid their own way, and very few of them in the early waves were indentured servants. They may have been economically humble, but they were not impoverished; they were free of debt and attachments, and fiercely independent. Many of them were Presbyterians, which contributed an evangelical spirit to their assertive lay culture and commitment to secular education. They were not as well-off as the typical New England Puritan or Quaker immigrant in eastern Pennsylvania or West Jersey, but they were proud even in rags. Indeed, they demanded respect and were known for their stubbornness. Since most of them came to America in family groups, the ratio of men to women was more or less equal, closer to that of the Quaker and Puritan migrations than to that of seventeenth-century Virginia, which was heavily male for the first fifteen years. They had been, by and large, farmers and farm laborers but had not owned the soil they tilled. These borderlands peoples made the Atlantic crossing for land, to escape from the iron clutches of landlords, and to confound the expectation that they and their descendants would always be poor. And they shared a legacy of violence.

The immigrants moved west and south through regions that had no roads, through dense deciduous forests—principally oak, hickory, and chestnut, changing to birch, evergreens, and maple in the mountains. The settlers walked on lands the Indians believed were already too crowded: In the North, the Shawnee and the Iroquois Confederacy fought over territory; farther south, Cherokee, Creek, Choctaw, and Chickasaw Indians disputed overlapping claims. The Scots-Irish intended to fight for land against all comers—the climate, Indians, Ohio Company agents and land claimants, absentee landlords, and whoever and whatever else got in their way. They would fight the French *and* the English if they had to. They became the dominant culture of the Appalachian region, accounting for about 75 percent of Kentuckians and Tennesseans by the time those states broke off from Virginia and North Carolina in the 1790s, and almost 100 percent of the settlers in the Hillsborough region of North Carolina. But they did not get along any better with each other than they did with their neighbors.

These north Britons were exceptionally independent, and they defined independence more extremely than other Anglo-Americans did. They favored a "natural" freedom from restraint that ran the range from libertarian to anarchic. They had little use for institutions or the rule of law. In some ways their notions of independence were like those of the Indians, but their individualism was the opposite of the communalism practiced in the Iroquois longhouses. Writing in 1783, a German traveler named Johann Schoepf found that "they shun everything which appears to demand of them law and order, and anything that preaches constraint. They hate the name of a justice, and yet they are not transgressors. Their object is merely wild. Altogether, natural freedom . . . is what pleases them." They relished the remoteness of the frontier and their distance from centers of power and authority. They abhorred taxes and favored no government services over any demand to pay for them. The Patrick Henrys, Davy Crocketts, and Daniel Boones of the American frontier would be products of this culture.

It is difficult to imagine two less compatible groups of Britons than the Ulster Scots and the Quakers who founded Pennsylvania in the 1680s, unless it was Quakers and New England Puritans. The persecutory environment of seventeenth-century England had propelled the Quakers to emigrate, just as it had the Puritans, and those who crossed the Atlantic tended to be the most radical and least inclined to compromise in their faith group; more flexible ones stayed behind. Unlike the Puritans, Quakers came from counties all over the British Isles, but the preponderance of the Pennsylvania and New Jersey Quakers hailed from the north Midlands counties of Cheshire, Lancashire, Yorkshire, Derbyshire, and Nottinghamshire. The Quakers adopted their "plain" style of dress from the traditional clothing of the north Midlands. None of the Quakers came from East Anglia, the font of Puritan immigration to the New World.

Between twenty and twenty-five thousand Quakers arrived on American shores between 1675 and 1715, and they then represented about half the European population of Pennsylvania, the colony that had been founded by the Quaker William Penn, recipient of a vast land grant from King Charles in 1681–1682.* By the mid-eighteenth century, the colony had about 70,000 Quakers—a significant minority—

* Penn's "Frame of Government" for Pennsylvania carefully safeguarded the tradi-

and they composed the third-largest religious denomination in Anglo North America, behind only Congregationalists and Anglicans. Their influence in Pennsylvania was dropping, though; within a few decades they were only the fifth-largest faith group and no longer a political force.

The Quakers were, again like the Puritans, "middling" class, and on average poorer than Anglican immigrants when they arrived. They looked aggressively for land to buy, not just for economic security but also because real property was a glue that would keep families together, and families were the moral center of their faith. But Quakers were less authoritarian than Congregationalists and less inclined to inflict corporal punishment on their children or on criminals. They did not believe in original sin or magic and witchcraft, nor did they share the Calvinist view of predestination. (Although the courts never prosecuted anyone for witchcraft in Pennsylvania, folk beliefs did lead to the murder of an accused witch on the streets of Philadelphia as late as 1787.) Theirs was a God of love and light, while the Puritans worshipped an inscrutable deity.

And they were more egalitarian than the colonists who ruled New England and Virginia—a quality that reached across gender as well as class and racial lines. Some of the Quakers were pacifists, and the collectivity was moving in that direction, as well as toward becoming the first corporate group to abolish slavery among its members. They believed, like the Puritan Roger Williams before them, that they should pay Indians for the land they took, and in a paternalistic way they believed they were responsible for the Indians. The Quakers also believed that they should not sell arms or liquor to members of the tribes they lived among, but other colonists fairly criticized them for sharp dealing and for casting a blind eye on the sale of liquor to Indians by non-Quakers. They also took a long time, about a century, to rid themselves of slaves, and profited heavily in the interim from the carrying trade in which they bought slaves and sold them to others.

Nonetheless, for all the ways the Quakers fell short of the utopian vision of William Penn, they did enjoy better, more peaceful relations with Indians than did settlers in other English colonies. Few Indians

tional rights of Englishmen and guaranteed free and fair trial by jury, freedom of religion, freedom from unjust imprisonment, and free elections.

had been living in the territory that is now southeastern Pennsylvania when Quakers began arriving there in the 1680s, and there were even fewer a half century later, principally Iroquoian speakers. By then, the region had German, Scots-Irish, Welsh, and English settlers, most of them farmers or artisans, with the German population growing the most quickly. The middling class predominated, but even here, in the colony with the most equitable division of property, there were more and more landless laborers. Farms in southeastern Pennsylvania ranged between 100 and 500 acres, with 125 as an average, which fell as land prices climbed, as the population grew, and as partible inheritance— heirs dividing the estate rather than the land going to the eldest male— reduced each generation's individual shares of family estates.

Two political parties emerged early in Pennsylvania's history as the colony became culturally more heterogeneous. Beginning in the 1720s, a split pitted the Quaker party on one side, which also included German Pietists who shared many of the Quakers' social values, and the Gentleman's party on the other, composed principally of Anglican merchants, seamen, and Scots-Irish immigrants. For the next decades, Quakers continued to dominate Pennsylvania politics as they did its culture: 60 percent of assembly members were Quakers in the 1730s, and Quakers reached a peak of 83 percent there in 1745; it was as high as 75 percent as late as 1755, when Quakers began their collective withdrawal from politics, focusing instead on internal reforms that aimed to purify the faith and its members. Quaker enthusiasm for the inward-looking spirituality of Pietism encouraged many of them to disengage from the world. Increased violence with Indians at the beginning of the French and Indian War in the 1750s challenged their pacific traditions at precisely the moment they were experiencing this reinvigorated faith, and Quaker assemblymen who supported the war came under withering criticism for compromising the principles of their religion, which they always had. Still, half the assembly members were at least putatively Quakers as late as 1773.

Three-quarters of the 111,000 Germans who immigrated to North America in the eighteenth century settled in Pennsylvania, a high proportion of them between 1747 and 1753. The prospect of land ownership and rich soil had drawn them to the New World. They were not fleeing persecution, they were not utopians or religious refugees, and they were not impoverished, being mostly low- to middling-class farmers from southwestern Germany. They had secular ambitions for themselves and their families, and they readily settled in the backcountry, where reasonably priced land was still available. Germans who came later were poorer, usually single males paying for their passage with future labor (indentures). Many of these late arrivals never did own land; they became foot soldiers in George Washington's army during the Revolution, lured to enlist by the bonuses, supplies, and salaries, such as they were. The earlier German arrivals fought, too, but for their land.

Although their actions along the Ohio River in 1754 were provocative, the French really did not want another war in North America, at least not so closely on the heels of the last one. The War of the Austrian Succession had been expensive, and Canada was costing far more than it returned in tax revenue and trade. The colony's commandant acknowledged that Canada had "always been a burthen to France" but believed it made the "strongest barrier that can be opposed to the ambition of the English." French colonists were widely but thinly dispersed throughout Canada and the Louisiana territory, which made central administration costly and ineffective: In the 1660s, the European population of Canada was smaller than that of tiny Rhode Island; a century later Canada had about fifty-five thousand French to Rhode Island's forty thousand English souls. In the mid-eighteenth century, Quebec's population was one-third that of Philadelphia's; Montreal's, half the size of Quebec's and smaller than New Haven, Connecticut's. In the mid-eighteenth century, the European population of New France was perhaps 5 percent of that of the English mainland colonies. Poor harvests and Canada's brief growing seasons meant frequent shortages of grain and, hence, bread. Even in peacetime, Canada ran an annual deficit of almost two million livres in the mid-eighteenth century.*

In 1749, the French sent a two-hundred-man military expedition on a three-thousand-mile round-trip journey from Montreal down the Allegheny and Ohio Rivers to the Miami River and back. The assignment was to secure lead-and-copper plates engraved with French

---

* This equates to about £87,500 sterling in the mid-eighteenth century or almost $12 million in 2007.

claims to the land at various key points along the rivers, to warn off the English and to threaten Indians who did not deal exclusively with French traders. But in the competition for commerce with the Indians, the English had a number of advantages: The Indians favored English cloth and English iron kettles over those of the French not only for their quality but also for their low prices, usually one-fourth the French ones, thanks to England's more developed manufacturing industry, larger trade network, and lower expenses on the frontier (the English were not supporting, as the French were, a heavy military presence in the region). The lead plates were a kind of bluff, an assertion of dominance the French had no real desire to enforce, but their attempt at intimidation failed. The Indians later "gave the French to understand that the land was theirs and that while there were any Indians in those Parts they would trade with their Brothers the English."

In that same year of 1749, the Ohio Company established frontier headquarters at Wills Creek, today's Cumberland, Maryland, and by 1750 it began surveying its grant from the king. The agent doing this work felt no more welcome in the backcountry than had the French. The Indians "began to suspect me," he reported, "and said, I was come to settle the Indians' Land, and they knew I would never go Home again safe. I found this Discourse was [likely] to be of ill consequence to me." In 1752, the company set up a second store on Redstone Creek, in southwestern Pennsylvania, and in June and July sent men to attend a conference with Indians who had been convened by Virginia at a settlement on the banks of the Ohio River called Logstown. The Indians agreed to allow the English to build a fort at the forks of the Ohio and Monongahela Rivers in return for gifts the Virginians offered. But they also "desired to know where the Indians' Land Lay, for that the French claimed all the Land on one Side [of] the River Ohio and the English on the Other Side."*

There were almost as many conspiracies as there were people at the Logstown conference. Two of Virginia's three delegates represented

---

* It is difficult now, as it was then, to sort out the different bands and tribes, and the number of Indians in the region. Estimates put somewhere between twenty-five hundred and four thousand Indians in the Ohio Valley, some of whom spoke Iroquoian, others Algonquian languages. Also, previously distinct tribes were now combining and re-forming in the changed circumstances. Estimates of Iroquois in New York and around the Great Lakes range up to fifty-five hundred.

interests that competed with those of the Ohio Company investors (one of whom was Virginia's lieutenant governor Robert Dinwiddie). The company sent its own man with a different set of instructions. One agent, something of a double agent, also informally represented Pennsylvania's interests, while the interpreters, who had their own agendas, intrigued on behalf of whoever paid them. As for the interests of the Indians in attendance, Iroquois claims conflicted with those of the Delaware and Shawnee.

No Frenchmen were present to stake their claims against those of the two colonies, the various tribes and companies, and the freelance speculators who conspired against each other and paid no attention to policies formed in London. The imperial interests of Great Britain conflicted with those of all the other parties in any case, but the British Empire, like the French one, had no representation at the conference. What is more, neither of the colonies and none of the Indian delegates had the power to enforce whatever agreements were reached. When the Iroquois secretly sold out the claims of the Delaware Indians to Virginia, they also undermined New York's and Maryland's interests.

When enemies of the Miami Indians learned that they had sent delegates to this Logstown conference, a combined party of Ottawas, Chippewas, and Potawatomis attacked the principal Miami village, killed the chief, and ritually feasted on his body. The same warriors also killed an English trader and took prisoners to Detroit. All this had the desired effect of intimidating the Miami and bringing them back into the French fold. The French also led or supported other raids on English traders in the Ohio country, and they began building forts, against which the British were powerless to respond, since they had no troops in the region.

In February 1753, the French sent a force of about two thousand men to occupy the Ohio frontier. During this move south, the French encountered Tanacharison, the half king, a Seneca chief who represented the Onondaga Council of the Six Nations, or Iroquois Confederacy— and who favored the English. He warned them off, but the French retorted accurately that the chief did not represent all Iroquois, only his band.

The English rightly feared a pan-Indian alliance with France. William Trent, an English trader, wrote to Lieutenant Governor Dinwiddie in August 1753, "Now is our time; if we manage well all the Indians may be brought to join against the French, otherwise they will join the French against the English." Dinwiddie had already communicated an alarm to Pennsylvania governor James Hamilton about the French ambition to dominate the Ohio region: "I have sometime ago heard of their robberies and murders, and if they are allowed a peaceable settlement on the Ohio, I think the consequence will be attended with the ruin of our trade with the Indians and also in time will be destruction to all our settlements on the continent." He also had written to the Board of Trade in London for permission to deal with the French intrusion and for support.

On August 18, the board forwarded the letter to King George. Ten days later, it asked Dinwiddie to verify rumors of a French invasion of Virginia and instructed him further: "If you shall find that any number of persons, whether Indians or Europeans, shall presume to erect any fort or forts within the limits of our Province of Virginia . . . you are to require of them peaceably to depart and not to persist in such unlawful proceedings." If the French were to ignore such warnings, "we do hereby strictly charge and command you to drive them off by force of arms."

It was with this authorization that Dinwiddie and his council had accepted George Washington's offer of service and had ordered him to the Ohio Valley. He was to inform the half king of his mission and request warriors as bodyguards; then he was to scout the enemy's constructions and troop strength, determine its intentions, and deliver to the French commanding officer the order to abandon the region: "After waiting not exceeding one week for an answer, you are to take your leave and return immediately back." The French answer was no, and Washington returned to Williamsburg by January 1754. Then Dinwiddie secured funding from the Virginia assembly, raised troops, promoted Washington from captain to lieutenant colonel, and sent him and the militiamen back to the Ohio River.

When Washington and his troops left Alexandria on April 2, tribes in the Ohio Valley and the land of the six Iroquois nations were already agitated and the French had panicked. Three weeks later, at the fork of the Monongahela and Ohio Rivers, Washington learned that General Pierre Paul de la Malgue, commander of French forces in the Ohio Valley, had died over the winter. He also heard, probably from the Seneca, that eight hundred of the French troops had retired to winter quarters in Montreal, leaving a garrison force of only about six hundred, divided up to defend the four existing forts: Machault at Venango on French Creek, LeBoeuf farther north, Presque Isle on Lake Erie, and Niagara.

With the eye of a speculator and the skill of a surveyor, Washington scouted the area for quality land and for suitable spots to build a fort. At Logstown he interrogated four French deserters who gave him more details about troop deployments. The half king also told Washington what he had said to the French: "Fathers, both you and the English are white. We live in a country between, therefore the land does not belong either to one or the other; but the GREAT BEING above allowed it to be a place of residence for us; so fathers, I desire you to withdraw, as I have done our brothers the English, for I will keep you at arm's length."

Both the French and the English saw Indians alternatively as pawns, allies, or obstacles that had to be cleared, just like trees, if commerce (for the French) or settlement (for the Anglo-Virginians) was to stretch farther inland. Soon, very soon, it would come to war. The outcome of that war—called the French and Indian War by Americans and the Seven Years War by Europeans—brutally cleansed Nova Scotia of Acadians, bloodied the frontier, and increased the likelihood that Anglo-American colonists would clash with the British Empire. Land hunger bordering on gluttony, profit seeking propelled by greed, atrocities driven by both, and a deeply ingrained bigotry against Indians were marks of the ugly, unacknowledged motives of the contending empires.

Over the previous century, representatives from the various English colonies had met at a dozen treaty conferences, as they were called, to discuss how they might cooperate in dealing with hostile Indians, or French, or Spanish. Some were more successful than others, but all of them showed the limits of cooperative defense. Benjamin Franklin had earlier proposed the idea of a compulsory confederation, and then raised it again at the Albany Conference in June 1754 called by the Lords of Trade, but it was more ambitious than anything the Lords of Trade had proposed or announced.

The Board wanted a "concert" of the colonies rather than a "union," and meant the colonies to be consulted only on the limited issue of raising funds after the governors-general had fixed the amounts. Seven of the nine invited colonies agreed with this arrangement. But Virginia, which had another Indian conference going on at its southern border at the same time and its attention focused there, and New Jersey, whose assembly decided that Indians were not its problem, ignored the summons to Albany. New York's lieutenant governor James De Lancey also ignored the New York assembly, but he agreed to have the conference in Albany and presided over it as acting governor of New York. About two hundred Indians attended, along with twenty-four representatives of the seven colonies, including Thomas Hutchinson of Massachusetts, Stephen Hopkins from Rhode Island, De Lancey and William Johnson of New York, and Franklin representing Pennsylvania.

The conference focused on common defense against France and the restoration of close relations with the Iroquois and other Indians. The main outcome was the Albany Plan of Union, which recommended that the Crown appoint a president general to preside over a Grand Council in which all the mainland colonies except Delaware and Georgia, which had much smaller populations and far fewer resources, would be represented proportionally by between two and seven delegates, according to a formula that roughly linked population and the funds each colony could be expected to contribute to the council's work. After three years, the number of delegates representing each colony would be reallocated based on the actual support provided. Council members would be elected by their respective colonial assemblies to serve three-year terms.

The business of the general government would be "to make peace or declare War with Indian Nations." It would regulate trade with the Indians, settlements on the frontier, and all land purchases from Indians; it would raise armies and pay soldiers, build forts, and legislate taxes to cover the costs of diplomacy with the Indians and frontier defense. The council's decisions would not be "repugnant but as near as may be agreeable to the Laws of England and shall be transmitted to the King in Council for approbation . . . and if not disapproved within three years after presentation to remain in force."

The assemblies of not a single colony approved this plan. Some rejected it. Others ignored it. All of them interpreted it as an entering wedge for British intrusion into their local affairs and thus as a potential challenge to their independence.

In the days following the May 1754 victory of Lieutenant Colonel Washington's militia and its Seneca allies over French "spies" in the Ohio Valley, the Virginians constructed a makeshift circular stockade about fifty feet in diameter with seven-foot-high walls. Around it, they dug trenches intended to give cover to infantrymen outside and inhibit attackers who might try to scale the shaky barricade, which would have been easier to push over. The Seneca wanted nothing to do with "that little thing upon the Meadow"; it was badly situated for a fort but would have been a good place to farm, being in a valley surrounded by hills from which an enemy could rain down arrows and lead shot. The headstrong and inexperienced lieutenant colonel ignored the half king's advice and huddled his sixty or seventy men and their ammunition in the tight space they called Fort Necessity.

Reinforcements arrived in mid-June, and Washington decided to march on the French stronghold at Fort Duquesne, almost a hundred miles away, with his combined force of about three hundred men, small cannons, and supplies. The Indians thought this a foolhardy plan and saw no reason to enrage the French by following an ill-tempered novice who tried to order them around. Seneca, Shawnee, Delaware, and Mingo warriors all decided to withdraw. The hundred British regulars who arrived on the scene that month also declined to support the Virginians, which left them to slog alone through the forest for several weeks, driving their horses to death and then hauling everything themselves under the lash of Washington's command.

On June 28, Washington retreated when he learned that a combined French and Indian force coming from Fort Duquesne was closing swiftly on them. The Virginians' forced withdrawal returned them to the dubious protection of Fort Necessity shortly before the French and Indians arrived. Most of Washington's troops spent the night of July 2 exposed in a drenching rain, huddled in the trenches that had become a moat around the fort. Late on the morning of July 3, the French and their Indian allies fired from the umbrella of trees above the fort. The Virginians' weaponry was soaked and useless.

By nightfall, at least one-third of Washington's force was dead or wounded.

The French mercifully offered the Virginians terms of surrender. Washington had to sign an admission that he had "assassinated" the French ensign at the earlier battle in the woods,* agree to return the prisoners his troops had taken, pledge that he and his troops would vacate the Ohio country and not return for a year, and leave behind two officers as hostages to ensure compliance. In return, the Virginians would be allowed to withdraw unmolested with their weapons, personal possessions, and flag. The alternative was renewal of the battle at dawn. Washington was in a poor bargaining position and understood that his signed admission was a casus belli that could, and did, provide the excuse for another world war between England and France.

On July 4, Washington evacuated Fort Necessity, having lost thirty killed and seventy wounded. The French and Indians together had only three dead. The defeated Virginians could see as they filed out that their Indian enemies included some whom they had considered allies— Delaware, Mingo, and Shawnee. Incidents such as this one helped Washington rationalize his view that all Indians had "nothing human except the shape."

It took the militiamen five days to traverse the fifty miles back to a safe encampment at Wills Creek, where the wounded could rest and be cared for. Many of those who were well enough to walk deserted, which their commanding officer understood perfectly well, if not sympathetically: "The chief part are almost naked, and scarcely a man has either Shoes, Stockings or Hat . . . They will desert whenever they have an opportunity. There is not a man that has a Blanket to secure him from cold or wet."

When the Duke of Newcastle, the secretary of state, learned of the debacle at Fort Necessity, he realized its dire implications. Britain's North American colonies were at risk if the victory emboldened France. The British goal, though, was to dislodge the enemy from the Ohio country without provoking another global war. Shortly after an official dispatch from Dinwiddie informed London of Washington's ignominious defeat, the monarch followed the advice of his younger

---

* The commanding officer of the French expedition was the brother of the ensign killed in the previous engagement with Washington's militia unit.

son William, Duke of Cumberland, and authorized the deployment of two regiments of Irish infantry to the Ohio Valley under the command of General Edward Braddock.

Cumberland had been the hero of the House of Hanover's victory in the Battle of Culloden in 1746, when he had led an English army (along with Austrian and Dutch troops) to victory over Scottish troops (aided by the French) who were fighting for, and led by, Charles Stuart, the "Young Pretender," grandson of the exiled King James. "Bonnie Prince Charlie" had wanted to overthrow King George and retake the British throne, but the defeat at Culloden ended the hopes of a "Jacobite rebellion," and King George put Cumberland, known as "the Butcher," in charge of the infamous Highland Clearances, the forced removal of several thousand Scottish Highlanders as punishment for the Scots' support of the Stuart cause. In 1754, Cumberland, the most bellicose of his father's advisers, recommended which officers should be sent to prosecute the North American conflict in its early stages; Braddock had been with him at Culloden.

Braddock was to command garrisons stationed in Nova Scotia, New York, and South Carolina; he was also to reactivate and recruit to full strength two regiments that had been disbanded after the War of the Austrian Succession. As sole administrator and operational commander, it was understood that Braddock would supply his forces from a common defense fund provided by the colonies and requisition what he needed from locals along the path of his march. An Irish contingent would proceed from coastal Virginia into the backcountry, take Fort Duquesne and the lesser French bastions there, then march north and east to the frontier with New York, which would have troops already stationed there to reinforce it. The combined force would then overwhelm the French fortifications on Lake Champlain. In a third stage, Nova Scotia regiments would join the expedition and dislodge the French from the isthmus connecting Nova Scotia to the mainland.

This bold imperial plan showed considerable ignorance of the terrain, the plenitude of forests and dearth of roads, and the distances over which Braddock's regiments would have to clear trees, haul equipment, provision themselves, and engage Indians and French militia who did not fight the kind of battles for which British infantry were trained. The distances alone, even if they had every good break in the weather and every cooperative gesture from the Anglo-American colonists, could not be traversed in one season of campaigning. And provisions for gifts to Indian allies were totally inadequate, given the realities of diplomatic competition with the French. In any event, Braddock would not have good fortune, fair weather, Indian allies, or submissive colonists to support a sweep across the northeastern tier of the continent.

Meanwhile, the French were not idle. They planned to send the equivalent of seven British regiments* across the Atlantic when weather permitted in the spring of 1755. And on the diplomatic front they attempted to dislodge Austria as a British ally. Back in the Ohio country, the Iroquois League's neutrality was breaking down, to the advantage of France, while farther north the Mohawks complained that English colonists were encroaching on their ancestral lands.

Braddock took command of North America even before the two Irish regiments arrived on March 10, 1755. He called the governors of Massachusetts, New York, Pennsylvania, Maryland, and Virginia to an April meeting, where he did not ask anyone's advice but simply ordered them to raise, supply, and pay the troops that he needed for his four-pronged assault on the French. Within days of Braddock's arrival at the newly built Fort Cumberland, in Maryland, where his troops prepared for their march into the wilderness, he drove away Indian allies by forbidding their women to accompany the expedition. He also told them that when he threw the French off the continent, none of it would belong to them: "No Savage Should Inherit the Land." He declined their advice on strategy and the terrain, ignored the gift of a detailed map of Fort Duquesne, and insulted every Indian he met. When his twenty-two hundred troops left the staging area, there were only eight Indians in the party.

Mountains, forest, and mud lay between the two English regiments and the French. Braddock's men had to clear trees and make a road over which they could drag their heavy ordnance and supplies. It was slow going at best, and the expedition fell behind schedule almost immediately. Braddock divided the troops into two divisions, the first told to move faster, about five miles a day on average. The second, bringing equipment and supplies, eventually fell sixty miles behind. By July 9,

* In theory, an eighteenth-century British regiment was composed of one thousand men.

the forward division of 300 infantrymen under Lieutenant Colonel Thomas Gage was about ten miles from Fort Duquesne. Behind them, another 250 soldiers guarded the laborers who cleared trees. The main body of 500, including Braddock and his aide-de-camp George Washington, who was incapacitated by dysentery and hemorrhoids, came next with long lines of wagons, animals, and camp followers of the very sort that Braddock had forbidden to the Indians. Last was a rear guard of about a hundred men. Scouts flanked the whole contingent.

About sixty-six hundred French regular troops, Canadian militia, and Indians were waiting at Fort Duquesne for Braddock's forces. On the morning of July 9, the French commander, Captain Claude-Pierre Pécaudy de Contrecoeur, ordered eight or nine hundred regulars, militia, and Indians to launch an assault on the English before they reached the fort. Although the English spotted the French and Indians first, and killed the French captain in the first volley, the terrain favored a French retreat into the woods from which they and the Indians could fire withering volleys that reduced the exhausted British forces to bloody disarray. The Americans, too, took cover and fired from behind trees, while the British regulars fought in the open as they had been trained to do.

Braddock, who commanded from horseback and waited in vain for the irregular forces arrayed against him to give way before his disciplined troops, died on the field of battle. Washington had two horses shot from under him but survived unscathed. Three-quarters of his fellow officers, sixty-three of eighty-six, and nearly one thousand of Braddock's fourteen hundred men either died or were wounded, while the French and Indians lost only twenty-three dead and sixteen wounded. Once regrouped far from the scene of battle, about thirteen hundred of Braddock's total troops remained, more than enough to launch another attack on Fort Duquesne, which the Indians had now left for a journey home with their prisoners and booty. But an offensive was the last thing on the minds of the British soldiers and Virginia militiamen. They were still in shock from the horror of their total battlefield defeat.

The Indians would have dissuaded Braddock from his ill-fated plan if he had been willing to listen. The colonists would have warned him if he had asked. Everyone questioned Braddock's competence, the wisdom of those who sent him to North America, and the battlefield prowess of the troops that could only stand their ground as enemies mowed them down. Braddock's was another bungled beginning, this time of a major war, which emboldened enemies, thwarted imperial plans, and weakened the links that bound the New World to the Old.

The restoration of Cape Breton Island to France in the 1748 Treaty of Aix-la-Chapelle had stoked New Englanders' eagerness to expel the Acadians from Nova Scotia. Otis Little, a Massachusetts attorney and correspondent of Governor Shirley, voiced sentiments widely shared in New England: "It must surely be deemed impolitic to suffer such a Colony of French Bigots to be reared up under the kindly influences of a British Administration, to cut our own People's Throats whenever the Priest shall consecrate the Knife." But New Englanders knew that the cost of violent expulsion would be high in blood and money, and forcing the Acadians to Cape Breton or Quebec would strengthen the French footholds there, thus solving one problem only by creating another.

One alternative was to recruit immigrants from Europe and to subsidize the settlement of Irish, German, and English Protestants in Nova Scotia. That would dilute the Acadian presence and make it possible to supplement the militia units defending the colony from French and Indian attacks. The Earl of Halifax, in his position as First Lord of Trade and Plantations, presented such a plan to the Board of Trade in March 1749. It would fund free passage to the colony for up to three thousand settlers and provide them with food, arms, tools, and grants of land immune from taxes for a decade. The endeavor ended up costing the British about £100,000 per annum, twice the original estimate. In May, about twenty-five hundred colonists sailed from London along with their thirty-six-year-old governor, Colonel Edward Cornwallis, another veteran of the Battle of Culloden and protégé of the Duke of Cumberland. His qualifications for the post included his bloody "pacification" of the Scottish Highlands, where he supervised the burning of Catholic churches and the torturing of priests.

Within a month of their arrival, more than a thousand of the new colonists had absconded to New England and elsewhere. By September, no more than three hundred able-bodied Protestant men were left to finish building houses in Nova Scotia before winter. Without Acadian help, these new settlers would have died before the end of their first winter. And, since the Acadians recognized that the enhanced

English presence "can be nothing but very dangerous for us," many of them evacuated the colony that same fall and in increasing numbers over the next few years. In December, Indians supplied by the French along with a few Acadians (who claimed to be participating only after being threatened by Abenaki and Micmac warriors) attacked the English contingent at Minas and took nineteen prisoners, who spent several years in captivity before being ransomed.

The same directive from the Board of Trade that Virginia lieutenant governor Dinwiddie had interpreted in 1753 as authorization for sending Washington and his militia unit into the Ohio country also served the purposes of Massachusetts governor Shirley. In March 1754, Shirley reported that "rebel inhabitants" (i.e., Acadians) were settling on the Kennebec River in central Maine and that Jesuit priests were fomenting Indian violence against New Englanders. It was the "rebels'" intention "to break up all the Eastern settlements of this province," which constituted a threat to New England. This inflammatory rhetoric convinced the Massachusetts General Court to authorize raising five hundred militiamen to expel the rebels and establish fortified outposts against their return. The absence of any French, Acadians, or Abenaki on the upper Kennebec did not dissuade New Englanders from moving immediately on the Minas Basin in Nova Scotia, which, they imagined, might be a French stepping-stone for the invasion they predicted: "Should the French make themselves Masters of Nova Scotia, which is a Country fruitful of all kinds of Grain and Provisions, they would be in a Condition to introduce and subsist a Body of Troops strong enough with the French *Acadians*, and inhabitants of *Cape-Breton* and *Canada*, together with the *Indians*, to reduce all the English Colonies."

New England's only chance, the argument went, was a preemptive strike. For starters, the English governor of Nova Scotia, Charles Lawrence, extracted supplies and labor from the Acadians by force in the summer of 1754. In November, Lawrence received the ministry's reply to Shirley's erroneous report of a French infiltration of Maine. It instructed both governors to proceed "as will frustrate the designs of the French." Shirley explained the directive more expansively to Lawrence: "I construe the contents to be orders to us to act in concert for taking any advantages to drive the French of Canada out of Nova Scotia."

In the spring of 1755, the combined Massachusetts and Nova

Scotian forces mounted an assault on Fort Beauséjour, on Chignecto Bay. Only two hundred Canadian and Acadian troops occupied the fortress there, which was intended to hold four times that many defenders. The first assault, on June 4, took less than an hour; the Canadians and Acadians killed three Britons and wounded about twenty. Four days later, the English seized the high ground overlooking the fort. By June 13, the invaders had their cannons in place and began a brutal bombardment early in the evening. The next day, the defenders learned that no troops from Louisbourg would reinforce them, nor was relief coming from elsewhere in Canada either. The Canadians and Acadians formally capitulated on June 17, ten years to the day after the 1745 surrender of Louisbourg. The terms were transportation to Louisbourg on their pledge not to bear arms for six months.

Several hundred Acadians, who surrendered their weapons over the days and weeks after the battle, were set to work cleaning up the rubble. Then, at the end of June, word came that three thousand reinforcements had reached Louisbourg from France, slipping past the British warships meant to intercept them. Now the Nova Scotians and New Englanders had greater cause for concern. They had better reason to believe, as they had imagined all along, that the only way to secure their military gains was by "totally extirpating the French." As Governor Lawrence explained, "by the French I mean both Acadians and Canadians." The French and Indian War was now presenting New Englanders with an opportunity to fulfill their long-standing ambition to clear their northern border of French speakers of whatever national attachments. Neutrality was not, as it never had been, an option on this imperial borderland.

Disarming the Acadians was the next step toward their expulsion: "It was thought advisable *to Draw the Teeth* of all the Neutrals in the Province by a seizure of their arms and ammunition, which in these parts was effected with great secrecy and expedition." Governor Lawrence issued a proclamation declaring that any Acadians caught with weapons "should be treated as rebels to His Majesty's Government," and the English confiscated several thousand guns. The governor also forbade Acadians to ship goods from Nova Scotia and posted armed guards to limit communication among them. Lawrence believed they were "of no use to the province" and an "obstruction to the King's intentions in the settlement."

The Acadians remained willing to swear oaths of "fidelity," but not the full and unconditional allegiance that English authorities required in the summer of 1755. The Acadians' appointed deputies agreed only to the renewal of previous oaths that allowed them a position of neutrality in wars between France and Great Britain: "Since we are asked only for a yes or a no, we will all answer unanimously, no." They were then arrested.

The question was where to send the Acadians after confiscating their property and expelling them from Nova Scotia. John Winslow, a Massachusetts militia commander, summarized the proceedings as follows: "They were declared rebels. Their Lands, Goods and Chattels forfitt to the Crown and their Bodys to be Imprisoned." Contrary to the Acadians' expectation that they would be sent to Louisbourg or to France, as in previous wars, the English were determined that they must not return as enemy combatants bent on revenge and recovery of their land. So the victors shipped the Acadians off to English colonies where their alien status would make them easier to watch and make it more difficult for them to return. The "most Rebellious," those from the Chignecto region, were sent the farthest, to South Carolina and Georgia. The New Englanders scattered the rest of them, in groups of fewer than a thousand each, among Virginia, Maryland, Pennsylvania, New York, Massachusetts, and Connecticut.

The militia rounded up parish priests and exposed them to public humiliation in Halifax. New England and Nova Scotia militia units also destroyed deeds, parish records, and other legal documents, erasing all evidence of the lives and rights of those whom they expelled. Then the militiamen torched the villages. About two dozen ships, most from New England, assembled for deportation of the Acadians, who were permitted to take only "ready money and household furniture." They had to forfeit domestic cattle and horses to underwrite the cost of their own deportation, and were strictly forbidden to sell anything.

After the New Englanders forcibly evicted the Acadians from their homes and burned down their towns, provided and manned the ships that transported the unlucky people to distant ports, and took possession of confiscated farms, they enjoyed the complete victory they had sought for more than half a century, a resolution of Nova Scotia's borderland status, and a windfall. Acadians would no longer compete with New England's fishermen or smugglers from Boston, Newport, and

Halifax. The children of New England farmers, who had reached the limits of heritable land, could acquire affordable farms on "as good Land as any in the World." There would be no Catholics on the border, no alternative European allies to whom the Micmac and Abenaki could turn, and only a weakened Louisbourg, given its loss of a source of supplies. There simply was no downside that Anglo–Nova Scotians and New Englanders could see: "We are now upon a great and noble Scheme of sending the neutral French out of this Province, who have always been secret Enemies, and have encouraged our Savages to cut our Throats. If we effect their Expulsion, it will be one of the greatest Things that ever the English did in America."

Braddock's defeat, naturally enough, encouraged Ohio Valley Indians and the Iroquois to make alliances with the French. The Iroquois League was in shambles yet still able to launch successful raids from the Ohio Valley. Pennsylvania, Maryland, and Virginia were exposed. Indians routed the troops of Colonel Thomas Dunbar, who had taken over command of British forces in the region after Braddock's death and then, contrary to orders, marched his sixteen hundred men into winter quarters at Albany. Dunbar's abandonment contributed to a "general desertion" of Virginia's militia. According to newspaper reports, within a month of his exit "the Frontiers of Virginia had been reduced to one universal Waste by the Burning, Murdering and Scalping committed by the Indians." Six months later, Colonel Washington reported that the "Bleu-Ridge is now our Frontier . . . There will not be a living creature left in Frederick-County: and how soon Fairfax, and Prince William may share its fate, is easily conceived."

Three British forts in Pennsylvania fell like dominoes. Before the end of 1756, dispatches from Canada to France claimed that the French and Indians had "disposed of more than 700 people in the Provinces of Pennsylvania, Virginia and Carolina, including those killed and those taken prisoner." In Pennsylvania alone, Delaware and Shawnee from the Ohio Valley killed at least 326 settlers and took another 125 captive. Newspaper accounts note that the Scots-Irish frontiersmen were "in great consternation, but being undisciplined and mostly without arms, they can do very little good." In New York, Indians took twenty scalps and five prisoners at Oswego, when the fort fell to French infantry under the command of the Marquis de Montcalm, and at Fort Bull a combined force of French and Indians "put every one to the sword they could lay hands on." Combat losses, combined with cold weather and disease, substantially weakened Virginia's militia the following winter.

Around the world, as in North America, the British were losing out to France. Calcutta fell to French forces, and in Europe the French were poised to attack the British Isles: There were reports that 118 infantry battalions and 28 cavalry squadrons awaited six hundred transports to shuttle them across the English Channel. This would have been an overwhelming force, but the massing of British sea power convinced France to strike at weaker points left unprotected as the British hunkered down at home—and then declared war on May 17.

Great Britain's conflict with France was going equally badly in the Mediterranean. In April the French had invaded the British-held island of Minorca, and on May 20, in a naval battle off its shores, the British lost the service of half a dozen ships and more than five hundred men dead and wounded, which meant they could not reinforce their twenty-eight hundred beleaguered troops on the island. After a seventy-day siege, Minorca fell to about fifteen thousand French infantry. Three weeks later—and two years after the fighting had begun on the Virginia frontier—France declared war, too.

Several months after that, the celebrated orator and parliamentarian William Pitt was named secretary of state for the Southern Department and took over responsibility for directing British forces in the war. Pitt's team, which included George Anson, already First Lord of the Admiralty, and John Ligonier, who became commander in chief of the forces, succeeded brilliantly where the previous administration had failed. Pitt shifted the central theater from continental Europe and the Mediterranean to North America and the Atlantic, and the Royal Navy successfully blockaded French ports and intercepted French ships carrying supplies to Canada.

In 1757, the British command prepared to send eleven thousand infantry to take the fort at Louisbourg, along with ships, weapons, ammunition, and supplies to support them in the confrontation (which ultimately did not occur until the following year). They moved half of the needed infantry from New York, but this gave the French an opening to attack weakened English fortifications there. Most famously, the

French assaulted Fort William Henry, on Lake George, with a force of about eight thousand and overwhelmed its twenty-four hundred defenders—English regular troops and colonial militia. As the disarmed prisoners filed from the fort, Indian allies of the French attacked them, killing about fifty and dragging six hundred captives into the forest. Greatly exaggerated reports of this massacre affected the tenor of the war thereafter, just as did tales about the grisly sufferings of British soldiers in a dungeon in India—the Black Hole of Calcutta—which began to circulate at about the same time.

It was late spring 1758 before Britain had its fleets and forces in place for the decisive battle of Louisbourg. Three French squadrons had sailed early in the year—eighteen ships of the line and five frigates with a total of fourteen hundred cannons on board. But the French lost not only ships captured by the British as they left Mediterranean ports and more that were waylaid on the high seas but also ten ships off the coast of Île Royale during the first five months of 1758. Just one of those carried fifteen hundred mortar shells, four hundred barrels of powder, seven hundred barrels of flour, four hundred barrels of pork, four chests of money, and twelve hundred rifles. This ship alone was a catastrophic loss.

The French had committed more ships and soldiers to Louisbourg since its recovery in 1749 than they had in the previous thirty years since its founding. About 20 percent of the entire Canadian budget went to the fort, double what it had ever been before the War of the Austrian Succession. And still, the fort gave the impression of being weak and run-down, no stronger or better defended than it had been when the New Englanders last overran it in 1745. As one informant believed, "If Louisbourg had been attacked during the winter by three hundred Indians, it might have been taken." Progressively worsening Canadian harvests in 1756, 1757, and 1758, and the Anglo-American expulsion of the Acadians also weakened Louisbourg. Almost all the town's supplies had to be shipped across the Atlantic from France, given the loss of Acadia's farms, farmers, and fishermen. The best hope for a successful defense, then, rested not with the small number of healthy troops, the weak fortifications, or the warships in the harbor, but rather with the weather. Rough seas and thick fog would hinder any assault on the fortress.

French lookouts counted seventy British ships off the coast on

June 1. There were actually two hundred, with thirty thousand people on board, including cooks, laundresses, nurses, and servants. On land, about ten thousand French could be found behind the ramparts that day, including children, the elderly, and the infirm. Major General Jeffery Amherst led the British assault with thirty thousand infantrymen, while Admiral Edward Boscawen commanded the fleet with about two thousand mounted cannons and crews of more than fourteen thousand. A total of twenty-seven thousand soldiers and sailors participated in this military operation, the largest that Great Britain would ever mount in North America, larger than the combined force that invaded Quebec the following year and the ones that fought the American Revolution.

When the fog cleared, albeit briefly, on June 2, the British could see Louisbourg from their ships anchored in Gabarus Bay, southwest of the fort. The next day, Amherst decided that the rough surf made it "impossible to land." On June 6, the infantry prepared, but failed, to debark in fog and rough seas. Brigadier General James Wolfe, at thirty-one the youngest of the senior officers, tried again on June 8 with a small handpicked squadron and initially failed in pounding waves and under withering fire from the French trenches. Those who were not shot or had not drowned drifted to a sheltered landing, from which they flanked the enemy and drove them from their embankments. The French barely escaped the onslaught as they retreated to the fort, leaving behind their munitions and supplies.

At a pace about twice that of a leisurely ramble, the British had routed the enemy and absorbed surprisingly light losses in the effort. Had the French held their fire until the British landed and then blasted them at point-blank range, had they mounted a lookout on the highest point who could observe the covert landing and issue a warning before the surprise assault, or had there been reinforcements nearby to back up the entrenched defenders, the outcome would likely have been different that day. But Wolfe's bold and lucky assault overran the inadequate defense and prepared the ground for subsequent landings of much larger contingents of men and their weaponry.

The French were dispirited, having banked their whole strategy on preventing a landing. The rout on June 8, "this unfortunate occurrence which we had hoped to overcome," wrote Governor Drucour, "casts dismay and dreariness over all our spirits, with every reason, for it decides the loss of the colony." The few Micmacs and Acadians still living in Nova Scotia fought independently of the French soldiers and contributed little other than occasionally picking off a lone British sentry or sailor who wandered out from protected sites.

Wolfe had chosen his men from Highland regiments he had fought against in 1745–1746 so that he would not have to rely on New Englanders or young, less seasoned troops. "The Americans are in general the dirtiest, most contemptible cowardly dogs that you can conceive," Wolfe complained. "There is no depending upon 'em in action. They fall down dead in their own dirt and desert by battalions, officers and all. Such rascals as these are rather an incumbrance than any real strength to an army." The colonists would not be necessary, or even useful, for this assault on Louisbourg, and the experienced Scots had shown the mettle in a losing cause that had impressed Wolfe twelve years earlier.

When a thick fog lifted on June 12, crews of French warships in the harbor noticed that British troops were digging in on Lighthouse Point, a strategic objective that had cost New Englanders hundreds of lives in 1745. This time Brigadier General Wolfe landed his men without a shot being fired. On June 14, again under the cover of fog, the British unloaded supplies, cannons, and mortars. By June 19, their battery was in place and Wolfe ordered the bombardment of French warships during the night. On June 21, the French captains moved their ships to the end of the harbor closest to the fortress, which enabled them to avoid the British guns at least for the moment. By June 25, the bombardment had silenced the Island Battery, which enabled the British to advance on Green Hill, the highest point of land from which they could fire down on the fortress. For the third time, Brigadier General Wolfe led the charge, and on June 26 his troops took the hill by nightfall. In total, only a dozen British lives had been lost since the initial landing on June 8.

On July 1, Wolfe and his men closed within eight hundred yards of the fortress's West, or Dauphin, Gate. The only question was how long it would be before the French surrendered. Their commanders were now fighting for their careers, trying to ensure that the defeat would not be a total embarrassment.

The British were none too careful about civilians. Their constant bombardment of the docks and fortress often "missed" the military targets. French complaints about civilian casualties received derisive responses. "When the French are in a scrape," groused Wolfe, "they are ready to cry out in behalf of the human species; when fortune favours them, none [are] more bloody, more inhuman." In a reference to the massacre at Fort William Henry the year before, Wolfe continued, "Montcalm has changed the very nature of war, and has forced us, in some measure, to a deterring and dreadful vengeance."

At the end of the first week of July, the French command calculated that losses were insufficient to justify surrender, especially since the officers expected harsh terms from the British. At that point, they had nineteen wounded French officers and about one hundred enlisted men incapacitated by injuries (they did not report a death toll). On July 8, two hundred French soldiers sneaked from the fort between midnight and 1:00 a.m. to make a bayonet attack on British laborers building a forward siege works. They surprised and overwhelmed the worksite, destroying the structure and engaging in hand-to-hand combat. They lost one officer and seventeen enlisted men; the British claimed to have five dead, including a captain killed in his sleep, seventeen wounded, and eleven missing.

During the second week of July, the British continued bombarding, building roads for the transport of supplies, and building earthworks ever closer to the fort from which they could more effectively shell the French defenses. Under cover of night on July 16, Wolfe commanded an advance on the hills overlooking the West Gate, about 250 yards from the fortress walls. Now the combatants were within distance of musket fire as well as bombardment, and the toll of injured and dead rose precipitously on both sides. Over a twenty-four-hour period on July 17 and 18, the British lost eighteen officers and men. On July 19, twenty of the French died inside the fort. There was no official estimate of civilian casualties at this point, but on July 21, according to a French engineer, the town had endured "a great many people injured and killed either by the cannon or the bomb." On the same day, a British cannonball aimed at one of the French ships struck gunpowder, and the resulting conflagration spread to two other ships, for a total loss of all three and many of those on board. The number of French defenders had been halved over the previous month, from four thousand on land and sea to two thousand left to fight.

On July 22 and lasting for three days, the British dramatically increased the frequency of their bombardments of the fort and town; both were in flames by nightfall on July 23. The barracks built by New Englanders in 1745 burned to ash. Desertions increased. On July 24, the British spotted breaches in the fortress walls. According to existing protocols of war, once the invaders breached the walls, the French commanders could, without shame, consider surrendering. The siege had now lasted for seven weeks.

After midnight on July 26, British marines boarded and captured the two remaining French warships. By 10:00 a.m. that same morning, the French raised a white flag. There were no negotiations. The British commanders insisted on total capitulation, again in retaliation for the massacre at Fort William Henry. The terms of surrender signed that day were simple and blunt: The British would load the French garrison—roughly 5,600 men—onto British ships and transport them to England as prisoners of war, and they would return the roughly 3,500 civilians to France. The British had lost about 200 dead and 700 wounded. The French estimates were about 100 killed and 250 injured, far fewer than the British but from a much smaller force, and the French casualty list did not include civilians and Indians.*

The British decided it was too late in the year to invade Quebec, but they did take Île Saint-Jean by force. Then about two thousand troops from New England sailed up the Bay of Fundy in September and October, and built Fort Frederick at the mouth of the St. John River, in what is today the Canadian province of New Brunswick. The New Englanders conducted forays into the forest in search of Acadians, whom they captured or killed on sight. Brigadier General Wolfe commanded land forces in an expedition up the Atlantic coast of the Gaspé Peninsula to the same end, killing and burning a path toward Quebec.

Bostonians lit a massive bonfire upon receiving the news of the conquest of Louisbourg. In Newport, Rhode Island, there were fireworks. Church bells rang in Philadelphia. There was an official dinner and artillery salutes in New York. From Boston:

* Île Royale was again Cape Breton Island and part of Nova Scotia, which it remained until the arrival of Loyalist exiles after the American Revolution, when the island became a separate British colony. In 1820, the island again became part of Nova Scotia and remains so today.

Mark with what different Zeal each Nation arms,
Which Slavery *abjects, and which* Freedom *warms;*
France *to oppress, the Sword of rapine [pillage] draws;*
Britain *contends for liberty and LAWS:*
The venal Frenchman, *spoils, insults, enslaves;*
The generous BRITON, rescues, pities, saves:
In freedom's glorious Cause, who nobly dare,
VIRTUE which bids them conquer, bids them spare.

The colonists' self-identification as Britons could not have been more imperially unifying as 1759 began. Their constitutional rights as Britons, their freedoms, had never seemed so secure. Making cultural contrasts with the French was an essential part, and defining characteristic, of their transatlantic identity. Anglo-Americans believed that the nobility of character, the liberty protected by law, the virtue, generosity, and courage of the British had all contributed to the superiority that manifested itself in battle as it would in a restored peace.

Memories of 1748, though, could not be shaken off among New Englanders: "Now that Cape Breton is happily fallen again into our hands, it is to be hoped due care will be taken that it shall ever remain with us." Correspondents wondered, of course, whether the conquest would again "slip out of our hands" by a "pusillanimous administration" that might restore it to France. No, not this time, with Pitt and his ministers displaying "spirit, integrity, and vigilance" at every turn. Such men would never lose sight of the inextricable link between Britain's and America's "immediate interest" or the fact that those interests were one and the same for the future. Pitt and King George both knew that "we must keep Cape Breton, take Canada, [and] drive the French out of America." On the other side, France remained clear that whatever happened, it might be willing to cede Canada to the English, but never Cape Breton.

"Canada must fall next year" was a sentiment widely shared in American newspapers as 1759 began. "A Fleet of Men of War will soon Sail for Louisbourg, for to be ready to go up [the] St. Laurence River as soon as it is clear of Ice," Boston newspapers reported in March. In early April, the newspapers reported that the British would launch an expedition up the St. Lawrence River through Lake Champlain by May 1, with the ultimate destinations of Montreal and Quebec.

5

✦

GLOBAL EMPIRES

ON JUNE 23, 1757, the American Revolution also commenced on the other side of the world, in a place neither William Pepperrell and his New England volunteers nor George Washington and his Virginia militiamen had ever heard of. English East India Company mercenaries in rural Bengal won a skirmish with about fifty French artillerymen and some thirty thousand indigenous troops, most of whom sat out the fight. Like Washington's and Pepperrell's victories, this was not a great battle on a Tolstoyan scale, but it was, in retrospect, a decisive one, with implications that endured. The Battle of Plassey and the subsequent withdrawal from Bengal of the French Compagnie des Indes—a mortally wounded combatant that bled for four more years before giving up the ghost—confirmed Great Britain's new self-image as an invincible power across the globe. Plassey, along with victories in North America in 1759, helped to transform Britain's imperial ambitions and, in short order, to bring further conflicts to the colonists in the New World.

Before Plassey, English imperial and mercantile interests in India sometimes worked in concert and sometimes were at odds, but they were distinct. The East India Company, with its Royal Charter from 1600 and its private army, which fell outside the authority of imperial command, set policy and pursued military and political goals that should have been, according to the eighteenth-century ideology of empire, the government's domain. But it was profit and not empire that the East India Company was after. Before Plassey, even declarations of peace and war by the British government had, at most, ripple effects on the India trade. The East India Company's campaign to overthrow the nabob* of Bengal in 1756–1757, though, drew the British government into the vortex of Indian politics. After Plassey, Great Britain moved aggressively into the power vacuum created by the withdrawal of the French and the disintegration of the Mogul Empire.

Britons dated the birth of their Indian empire to Plassey. Although previously it had been possible to imagine a British Empire that included India, after 1757 it was plausible to claim one, and to perceive a need to institute imperial reforms that would rationalize British governance in its colonies around the globe. The Newcastle ministry believed that to keep the empire, the government would have to defend and rule all of it, and recoup at least some of the costs of this immense task from the colonies themselves. Collecting duties, taxes, loans, and fees from the East India Company was fairly straightforward, while assessing colonists in North America would bedevil the imperial bureaucrats. But ruling the empire in Asia, the Caribbean, and mainland North America were aspects of one problem now, and each colony needed to be considered in the light of the others. That was the rub, but not quite yet; there was still time to bask in the glory of the victory at Plassey and what the English construed as a French defeat.

In the eighteenth century, Bengal was the easternmost province of India and, then as now, one of the most densely populated regions in the world. It is today principally divided into the independent nation of Bangladesh, formerly East Pakistan (1947–1971), and the Indian state of West Bengal. Parts of what was once Bengal have also been incorporated into the neighboring Indian states of Bihar, Tripura, and Orissa. But from the seventh to the eleventh century, Bengal was a single province in an indigenous Buddhist empire, to which a shorter-lived Hindu dynasty succeeded. Sufi missionaries introduced Islam to Bengal in the twelfth century, and then in the sixteenth century the Muslim Moguls conquered it and ruled largely through their nabobs. The seventeenth century was the great age of the Moguls, whose pomp, pageantry,

---

* Also *nawab*, a governor under the Mogul Empire; the word also described Englishmen who had made great fortunes in India.

and alluring wealth fascinated the Europeans, but by the eighteenth century, the Mogul Empire was in precipitate decline, undermined by religious movements such as that of the Sikhs and by the political ambitions of the Marathas, Hindu warriors from what is today the Indian state of Maharashtra. From 1681 until 1707, the Moguls and Marathas were at war, and though the Marathas lost, they never entirely gave up and instead became guerrilla fighters, continuing to harass the Moguls, inflicting losses and costs for defense that contributed to the empire's decline. In 1738, the Marathas reached the outskirts of Delhi and dictated terms to the weakened emperor, but this did not end the fighting. In 1748, Afghan invaders threatened, the Mogul emperor died, and civil war ensued. Now the Moguls wanted an alliance with the Marathas.

The Mogul Empire, under siege from without, was vulnerable to revolt from within, too, and in Bengal's mixed population of Hindus and Muslims, the Hindus, constituting a large majority, came to resent the Moguls' Islamic rule. Europeans could exploit the many political tensions in this situation, and when the Mogul Empire fell, the English were the beneficiaries—thanks to good timing, able East India Company employees, and their own comparatively strong state.

For centuries, the great variety and cheapness of Indian products had lured European traders, who hoped to break into the subcontinent's huge market for woolens, weaponry, tools, and other manufactured metal items. The Portuguese were first, but the Dutch eventually supplanted them as the major European trading power in India. That is where things stood when the English arrived on the Indian scene comparatively late, just as they did in North America. The English traded in the Asian market only sporadically until the formation of the East India Company, which was incorporated on December 31, 1600, not as a public-private endeavor like the state-sponsored Dutch East India Company but as a private business enterprise licensed by the Crown but operating independently of it and Parliament. The company, getting off to a slow start, began trading in Bengal in 1633 and built Fort St. George (the future Madras) in 1639 on the southeastern Indian coast—called the Coromandel Coast, where the Portuguese and Dutch already had trading posts. At first the company's principal export to Great Britain was spices, but then it broadened out to calicoes and other cotton textiles including Madras prints and silk—all of which became popular in England and affected fashion and other consumption trends. But by the end of the seventeenth century, tea dominated the company's Asia trade.

After the disruptions and upheavals of the English Civil War, the East India Company's profits rose on the wave of economic prosperity that European trade enjoyed in the last decades of the seventeenth century. It introduced tea from China and India to the English populace in 1667, which became a fashionable drink in the 1680s when complemented with sugar from the West Indies. Within a few decades, England had become a nation of tea drinkers, and new retail tea companies such as Twinings were prospering. The brew introduced caffeine into the English diet, and people would drink up to fifty cups a day to secure what were advertised as its health benefits; they drank so much tea that the ale breweries suffered. And this was just the beginning. The company was exporting from India about thirty-three thousand pounds of tea a year by 1717; by 1757, it was shipping three million pounds annually.

Tea and textiles from India, fueling the growth of England's consumer economy, also fueled the increase in value of East India Company stock. During the early eighteenth century, shareholders enjoyed regular dividends and the security of rising stock prices; by 1709, the company was a major financial institution, lending vast sums to the government, increasing England's domestic trade, and contributing significantly to what has been called a "financial revolution." In that year, the company lent the government £3,200,000 as a condition of renewing its charter, and its exports to Asia were £552,154. Most of the company's profits would always come from what it shipped from India to Britain, but exports *to* India also increased 100 percent between 1709 and 1748. And the company achieved this economic growth with relatively few employees on the ground in India; by midcentury, it still had fewer than seventy employees in Calcutta and defended its interests with an army of only three hundred in Madras and about five hundred in Bengal, military forces that historians have characterized as ill trained, poorly armed, unmotivated, and incompetently led.

The British government kept its hands off India and the East India Company for the first six decades of the eighteenth century. Laws enacted during that time protected the company against competitors and introduced only minimal regulation. The French Compagnie des Indes, on the other hand, was a creature of the state that had founded it. The French king and his ministers regularly interfered in company business, filled its ranks with patronage appointees, and destabilized it by changing policy and personnel with every ministerial transition. The compagnie's fortunes were so linked to those of the government that its profits rose and fell closer to the rhythms of politics than to those of the marketplace. The state guaranteed its dividends and subsidized its investments, but the price was high and ultimately made the compagnie a less flexible and less competitive entity; it proved unable to compete with the more independent English enterprise.

Eventually, officers of the East India Company used the French presence in India to convince the British government to expand its naval power in South Asia. It has been said that the English owed their Indian empire to the French, since without them the East India Company could not have made its case and the British would have focused their military resources elsewhere. But Britain's designs in India were always commercial and never included the ambitions for settlement that spurred colonization in North America. And, as has been said quite rightly, the British and French "empires" in India until the mid-eighteenth century were imagined rather than realized. Whatever loose policies and bureaucratic interventions the European governments tried halfheartedly to implement, it was the companies that ruled—often in conflict with French or English policy, for they were attuned to the rhythms of world commerce rather than diplomacy plotted in London and Paris.

Although the two companies competed, their employees in India were not always in conflict, and their relationships were usually affected more by company policy and local Indian politics, by the cupidity of nabobs and the capriciousness of native armies, weather, personalities, and contingencies of the international market, than by war declared and peace negotiated by their governments. Indeed, relations between the French and English traders were sometimes better than those between the merchants and their home governments. There were inevitable conflicts over rank and authority between the East India Company's private army and Crown officers, but Britain's assertion of imperial hegemony was fitful and fleeting, mostly expressing fantasies about the locus of power. For the most part, the company was free from bureaucratic restraints in India and enjoyed the same sort of "salutary neglect" as American colonists did during the term of Robert Walpole, Great Britain's first prime minister. It was said at the time that Walpole, who led the Whigs' parliamentary majority from 1715 to 1742, never got in the way of his revenue sources, which in this case meant that he left the East India Company alone as long as it remained a cash cow for the government.

Until the 1740s, the Europeans believed themselves in India at the nabobs' whims, and the English and French seemed to both sides evenly matched there. As late as 1745, according to a nineteenth-century English military historian, the "European trader was simply the permanent occupier, on a fixed rental, of a portion of the lands of the lord of the country. He possessed the right only to claim the protection of that overlord when he might be attacked." When the nabob of the Carnatic—the region of southern India that included the Coromandel Coast, where the English post at Madras and the French one at Pondicherry were located—told the British to refrain from hostile action against the French under his protection, the British generally obeyed.

The nabobs were just as capable of playing the French and English against each other as the Europeans were at manipulating local politics, and they dramatized their power with huge armies that vastly outnumbered European forces in India. The companies, in turn, used their private armies, which as of 1744 included indigenous soldiers, called sepoys, as bargaining chips, since the nabobs found these European-led forces useful when they were rebalancing power relationships with their political enemies, much as the Indian tribes did in North America. The companies often traded pledges of military support to the nabobs in return for taxable territory, but they had to renegotiate terms with each succeeding nabob who conquered or inherited his realm.

Then, in 1746, the balance of power shifted as swiftly as the monsoon winds, surprising everyone when the Europeans began to back up their previously unwarranted arrogance with military victories. In that year, a French fleet captured Madras from the English, and the English laid siege to Pondicherry. But the Treaty of Aix-la-Chapelle in 1748 restored Madras to Great Britain in return for Louisbourg and Cape Breton Island—and thus British imperial priorities were linked around the globe. Although the two nations were putatively at peace between 1748 and 1756, their East India companies continued to wage commercial wars, in which the nabobs were proxies and allies. The second Carnatic War (1751–1753), for control of that coastal strip, for example, was independent of French or English imperial ambitions. Sometimes, depending on the vagaries of the market, it was more profitable to go to war to gain control over taxable territory than it was to trade, so the companies ignored signals from London or Paris.

The apparent balance of power between the French and English in India during the 1740s had been an illusion, however. The profits of the Compagnie des Indes were insufficient to maintain troops in India over the long haul, and France itself lacked the financial resources and the will to build an empire there. Once the English in India had competent field commanders, which they did by the 1750s, the balance shifted decisively to them. Battlefield victories, expanded trade, domination of local politics, and the acquisition of territory, especially in Bengal, cumulatively bestowed on Great Britain the power it needed to rule India for almost two centuries. In 1751, a company contingent of 210 mercenaries under Robert Clive captured the city of Arcot, capital of the Carnatic, from the French, an accomplishment that Clive and his supporters successfully exaggerated, and it became the basis for his reputation as a military genius: Baron Clive, the iconic "Clive of Plassey," and then "Clive of India" in the eighteenth- and nineteenth-century histories of the British Empire.

Their independence notwithstanding, the East India companies greeted news of wars declared in Europe as bad news. The Seven Years War (1756–1763) cost the East India Company £75,000—mostly to hire mercenaries to defend its trading posts against possible enemy attack. In Bengal alone, the company's annual military expenditures increased from £375,000 to £885,000 over the decade after the war began. The first royal squadron of 900 men, under the command of Lieutenant Colonel John Aldercron, arrived in 1754, on "loan" to the company but not fully under its control, thereby blurring the line between commerce and empire. The company paid for maintaining this and another regiment, but Aldercron and other royal officers were not about to take orders from the likes of Clive, who had no military training when he arrived in India as a company employee. The increased defense expenses required the company to reduce its dividends and borrow money; no wonder the value of its stock declined by 20 percent during the war. On the other hand, that same war forged the government's commitment to an empire that included India. The Newcastle ministry accepted the company's argument that ousting France from the subcontinent was in Britain's economic and strategic interests, and it assumed the financial burden of that policy at war's end.

Again, though, it was local politics in India more than policies in London that inspired the company's actions in India. In 1756, nineteen-year-old Mirza Muhammad Siraj ud-Daulah succeeded to the office of nabob upon the death of his grandfather, and for reasons both xenophobic and financial he began a campaign against the English in Bengal; he also held a grudge against the English for conspiring with two rivals to his throne. He hoped to plunder the foreigners and perhaps to expel them from Bengal. He resented the way the English paraded their wealth, abused duty-free trade privileges granted to them by his predecessors, and moated and extended their fort without his permission. "I swear by the Great God and the prophets," he wrote to an ally, "that unless the English consent to fill up their ditch, raze their fortifications, and trade upon the same terms they did in ... [1725], I will expel them totally out of my country."

Siraj ud-Daulah's indigenous enemies and disloyal allies created openings for conspiracies against him fomented by the English. Hindu and Jain merchants and bankers who opposed the Muslim rulers, including the nabob, were natural allies for European mercantile interests. Although the Mogul Empire was crumbling, the English still had legal standing under various existing imperial firmans (edicts licensing trade), which the nabob resented because they undermined his local authority and reduced his revenues.

With this long list of grievances, suspicions, and economic self-interests to motivate him, Siraj ud-Daulah attacked the English at Calcutta in June 1756 with an army estimated at between thirty and fifty thousand men, impressively accompanied by 150 elephants and camels. The English defenses were actually weak, contrary to the nabob's fears: At full strength, five hundred men would have staffed the garrison, but there were only one hundred eighty, forty-five of whom were Europeans, at the time of the attack. Both the commander and the governor of Calcutta were famously incompetent—a common problem in England's far-flung possessions at this time. The nabob's troops took the company's settlement after a siege that lasted four days, captured its inhabitants, and confiscated their trade goods, stores, and cash, which he found far less valuable than he had anticipated. According to Robert Orme, the company historian, "Most of the merchandizes provided in the country had been shipped to different ports before the month of April, after which time vessels cannot go out of the river. None of the company's ships were arrived from England; and none of those belonging to private merchants were returned from their voyages; and the greatest part of the commodities imported in the preceding year were [already] sold."

The infamous Black Hole of Calcutta catastrophe occurred after this conquest, when between 18 and 123 out of between 39 and 146 English prisoners expired from asphyxiation in an eighteen- by fourteen-foot underground cell (black hole) that was too small to hold them.* Orme reported, "It was the hottest season of the year, and the night uncommonly sultry even at this season. The excessive pressure of their bodies against one another, and the intolerable heat which prevailed as soon as the door was shut, convinced the prisoners that it was impossible to live through the night in this horrible confinement; and violent attempts were immediately made to force the door; but without effect, for it opened inward: on which many began to give a loose to rage." When the ranking officer among the prisoners offered their jailor a bribe to separate them into two cells, the attendant told him that the nabob was asleep, no one dared to awaken him, and the guards followed their orders. The event was not an atrocity planned by the nabob, as legend would claim in the nineteenth century, when casting indigenous peoples as barbarians was one way to rationalize conquest as a civilizing force that was good for the natives.

After exacting tribute and testaments of loyalty from French and Dutch officials, Siraj ud-Daulah refocused his plans to oust the English permanently from Bengal. Meanwhile, the English were in disarray. On the Coromandel Coast, where French and English forces were evenly matched, English spies reported that a contingent of about ten thousand French soldiers was on its way, which would leave the English

* "Black hole" was the term used by the British military for any cell or lockup until well into the nineteenth century. The lower numbers of prisoners are more credible; the higher ones appear to reflect ideological agendas that rationalized empire, especially in the nineteenth century.

outnumbered five or six to one. It looked as though the war between the two powers that had started in North America only two years earlier and had recently spread to Europe was about to engulf India.

The English felt ill equipped to hold their ground either in Bengal or on the Coromandel Coast. Opinion among the English diplomats, company officials, and military personnel in India was divided on whether to send reinforcements from Madras to support the overwhelmed contingent in Bengal. In the end, the debate boiled down to whether they should send almost all the troops from Madras to Bengal or move none of them. The company's governing council in Madras reached the unanimous decision to adopt the plan argued by Clive: to station the maximum available troops in Bengal, about eight hundred Europeans and at least fifteen hundred sepoys. His reasoning was that "the squadron, if divided, would be of little service any where." There would be time before the end of the monsoon season in September, Clive believed, for the English to recover Bengal, thus keeping the French from landing there, and the British troops could then return to defend Madras.

The question of military command remained controversial. The council decided on Colonel Clive, a resolution that was not at all satisfactory to, among others, Colonel Aldercron, who was, after all, a Crown officer commanding a regiment of British troops, albeit on loan to the East India Company, while Clive was a mere company officer, appointed by the directors to command its security force. To Aldercron, the choice of Clive was an insult; an officer in His Majesty's armed forces always outranked a company man, as any royal officer would have agreed. The dispute had a parallel in the American colonies, where British officers outranked all colonial militia officers. But Clive it was, and under his command he would have 528 European foot soldiers, 109 artillerymen, 940 sepoys, and 160 lascars—indigenous camp followers who hauled water, pitched tents, dug latrines, and carried ammunition.

Clive was also unpopular with the Bengal Select Committee, the British civilian authorities who returned to Calcutta with him. They, too, resented his appointment as undermining their authority and rightly perceived it as a judgment against their competence. Throughout the campaign, they would snipe at Clive and obstruct his efforts in order to discredit him with the company. The division of authority, the quarrels, the jockeying for power, and the incompetence of both civilians and military personnel were hardly a formula for empire building, but Clive's personality, skill, and luck prevailed in these internecine conflicts and prevailed over his enemies on the field of combat as well. Decisive actors such as Clive pursued policies that were never endorsed by conservative politicians and company directors back in London; they seized an empire and delivered it to the nation as a fait accompli. Clive, the company, and Great Britain's imperial ambitions all benefited greatly from slow communication between Calcutta and London.

The troops under Clive set sail from Madras on October 16, 1756, in bad weather that blew them as far south as Ceylon. It was not until December 5 that they landed in Bengal, weakened from their seven-week journey on rough seas, during which they had been on half rations and scurvy had broken out. Clive had a malaria attack shortly after they debarked.

Nonetheless, in January 1757, Clive's troops fought a series of skirmishes and had a few pitched battles with Siraj ud-Daulah's forces. That same month, naval bombardment allowed the English to retake the fort at Calcutta without resistance from the deserting Indian forces. The next day, the Select Committee went back to work. Orme reported that "the greatest part of the merchandizes belonging to the company, which were in the fort when taken, were found remaining without detriment; for this part of the plunder had been reserved for the Nabob; but every thing of value belonging to the inhabitants had been removed out of the settlement."

It was only now that the English in Calcutta learned that France and Britain had declared war eight months earlier, in May 1756. As they were already fighting their own war with the compagnie and Bengali forces under Siraj ud-Daulah, the news did not affect the company's plans to reclaim the territory taken from it while the two nations had been officially at peace. What Clive feared, however, was an active alliance of the French and the nabob; indeed, Siraj ud-Daulah had suggested to the French that such a partnership was needed to drive the English from Bengal. Nonetheless, according to Orme, the French proposed to the English "that the two nations should engage by treaty not to commit hostilities against each other in Bengal during the continuance of the war in Europe."

The inversion—local war during international peace and local

peace during international war—made some sense because the companies could not count on reinforcements and a steady flow of supplies
while their nations' armed forces were engaged elsewhere in the world.
Yet the European war made the situation in Bengal potentially more
volatile, since both European companies became more vulnerable to
the nabobs. The English interpreted the French peace proposal as a
sign of weakness and an indication that the French would not be supporting Siraj ud-Daulah in combat, which meant that they either had
a better chance to negotiate with the nabob for peace or, if it came to a
fight, at least would not be fighting combined French and Bengali
forces.

In March 1757, the English laid siege to the French fortress at Chandernagore, north of Calcutta on the Hugli River. British ships bombarded the walls for three hours, reducing them to rubble and killing
more than two hundred French soldiers, after which Clive's ground
forces attacked. Clive's army was unscathed in the operation, but the
two British ships took casualties and damage, thirty-two dead and
ninety-nine wounded, from the fort's return fire. Clive boasted that his
troops had dealt "an inexpressible blow to the French Company."

After this victory, the nabob responded cordially, albeit insincerely,
to British peace overtures, and he continued his march south with his
huge army toward Hugli, which stood between his main body of troops
and Calcutta, where he intended to crush and plunder the British. At
the same time, his advance guard entered Calcutta, which prompted
Clive to commit part of his force to defense there. But Clive also decided to march toward Siraj ud-Daulah's camp rather than wait to
defend an indefensible position—a bold, perhaps foolhardy plan as he
had with him at this point 470 European troops, 800 sepoys, and 70
artillerymen with one howitzer and six field cannon to engage the nabob's 50,000 men (more or less), which included 18,000 cavalry, forty
cannon, and fifty armored elephants. However, Clive was also counting on about one-third of the enemy troops to betray the nabob, either
by remaining neutral or joining the English side, though he could not
be sure that his main coconspirator, Mir J'afar, the Nabob of Bengal,
would not double-cross him.

Clive polled his officers, who by a vote of thirteen to seven advised
returning from Chandernagore to Calcutta; instead, he attacked the
nabob's army. After a forced night march of fifteen miles and a difficult

crossing of a stream that swelled to a waist-deep river during an unfortunately timed deluge, the English marched through the tiny village of Palasi and bivouacked in a mango grove at 1:00 a.m. They were about one mile from the nabob's camp, close enough to hear martial music playing through the night. At daybreak, Siraj ud-Daulah's army arrayed itself in a semicircle that backed Clive's troops up to the river, thereby blocking a quick retreat. Worse yet, the French arrayed their cannons directly in front of the English, which was ominous because Clive's small force might then lose the battle even if it inflicted catastrophic losses on the enemy.

What the combat array did not reveal, however, was that the approximately forty-five thousand Bengali troops flanking Clive's forces were under the command of three officers who had conspired with the English against the nabob. The remaining three divisions stationed behind the French cannon were under leaders who remained loyal to Siraj ud-Daulah. At about 8:00 a.m., the French opened fire—the signal for the nabob's united forces to engage the English. Early in the battle, Clive took casualties. He ordered his troops to retreat and take cover in the mango grove, which substantially reduced the effectiveness of the enemy's fire while giving the English mercenaries cover from which to aim more carefully. After three hours exchanging fire, there was no decisive progress for either side.

Then the rains came, which put the French cannon out of commission and soaked the weapons and ammunition of Siraj ud-Daulah's troops as well. Figuring that the English guns were equally useless, one of the nabob's loyal commanders mounted a cavalry charge with swords drawn. But the English had used tarpaulins to keep their powder dry and fired with telling effect on the horsemen. In the course of this exchange, the nabob's captain, Mir Mudin, fell, mortally wounded. The collapse of Mir Mudin's cavalry left the French troops unprotected, and when they retreated, one Major Kilpatrick ordered an attack on the abandoned French redoubt, apparently while Clive was taking a nap. Clive awoke just in time to reprimand Kilpatrick for acting on his own initiative, order him to the rear, and take command of the operation himself, thereby eliminating any competition for battlefield glory.

With Clive in an advanced position, with three of Siraj ud-Daulah's generals and their armies sitting out the battle, and first one and then the second of his two best, most loyal commanders dead on the field, the nabob's fortune turned. By 5:00 p.m., the East India Company's men had captured what was left of his camp. Clive had only twenty-three men killed, among whom he distinguished between the loss of seven Europeans and sixteen indigenous mercenaries; thirteen Europeans and thirty-six sepoys were wounded. The English estimated that the nabob had lost five hundred men, but it is unclear how accurate the estimate was and whether it included both dead and wounded. It is probably safe to assume that the English estimate of enemy dead inflated the victory. The combined losses were small as eighteenth-century warfare went, and this was undoubtedly because more than three-quarters of the nabob's army declined to fight. If Siraj ud-Daulah had had loyal supporters that day, they could have crushed the English easily. Instead, the nabob's countrymen betrayed him, thereby sealing both the military outcome and his personal fate—first exile and then assassination.

The Louisbourg campaign had given Britain one of three major victories over the French in North America in 1758. The fall of Fort Duquesne in western Pennsylvania was the second, and Fort Frontenac—at the eastern end of Lake Ontario, where it empties into the St. Lawrence River—the third. The campaign against Frontenac was the inspiration of one man, Lieutenant Colonel John Bradstreet, who had served in New England's triumphant siege of Louisbourg in 1745. Bradstreet, the son of an Acadian mother and a British army lieutenant, conceived a plan for the attack against the fort, and he had agitated for the assignment for three years before securing permission from London on terms that reflected his passion if not his good sense: Bradstreet would pay all expenses and would be reimbursed by the government only if the campaign was a success.*

The plan hinged on misdirection and surprise. In July, Bradstreet led his more than three thousand men from Schenectady up the Mohawk River, west and north, to Lake Ontario, which they crossed,

---

* The arrangement broke down when Lord Loudoun was dismissed as commander in chief of the British forces in North America, and Bradstreet's victory would have gotten him off the financial hook in any event.

landing without opposition about a mile from the fort on August 25. After desultory firing on both sides the next day, on August 27 Bradstreet's men seized the high ground and fired cannons at a point-blank range of about 150 yards. The French commander surrendered within a few hours: He had only 110 soldiers to defend the breastworks, along with women and children who had been left behind when most of the garrison's soldiers went to defend a different fort that they thought was the British objective. Since Frontenac had been the supply point for France's forts and fur trade in the Ohio Valley, the booty was immense and the blow to French defense and trade catastrophic.

While Bradstreet was closing in on Frontenac, a British brigadier general, John Forbes, was negotiating peace with Ohio Valley Indians and trying to break their alliance with the French so that he could march on Fort Duquesne unmolested. The Indians had no illusions: "It is plain that you white people are the cause of this war; why do not you and the French fight in the old country, and on the sea? Why do you come to fight on our land? This makes every body believe, you want to take the land from us by force, and settle it." The British denied having such intentions, but the Indians wanted peace, too, and saw French power dwindling.

Forbes also spent the summer supervising the construction of a road across Pennsylvania, which was needed for his assault on Fort Duquesne to succeed. His colonial laborers were "beyond all description," he complained, and the "many, many impediments that I meet with in this wilderness, with this hand full of men, would take a Volume, and that filled with the villainy and Rascality of the Inhabitants, who to a man seem rather bent upon our ruin, and destruction, than give the smallest assistance, which if at last extorted is so infamously charged as shews the disposition of the people in its full Glare." Virginia's colonels Washington and William Byrd encouraged Forbes to abandon the new road and take instead a southern route along the path that Braddock's men had cleared through Virginia. But he declined: He shrewdly recognized that the Virginians were giving him advice intended to promote the interests of Ohio Company land speculators, and he thought this showed the two men's "weakness," "jealousies," and the provincial interests that they indulged above "the good of the service."

There were other bumps along the Forbes Road to Fort Duquesne.

Besides the hard labor and slow pace—"I am ruined and undone by Rain," Forbes wrote—there was another defeat very like Braddock's but on a smaller scale. On September 14, French and Indians surrounded Major James Grant and eight hundred infantrymen whom Lieutenant Colonel Henry Bouquet had sent to reconnoiter the fort, contrary to Forbes's orders. The French took Grant and others to Canada as prisoners; about one-third of Grant's force was killed, captured, or wounded. Many of the rest abandoned their weapons and escaped into the woods.

On November 7, Forbes learned the details of the Easton Conference, which had concluded on October 26, where the Iroquois had successfully asserted their claim to dominance over both the eastern Delaware and Ohio Valley tribes. The Iroquois representatives had accomplished this feat by exploiting the weakness of the eastern Delaware and divisions among the Pennsylvania delegates, who had splintered into factions, one representing the Penn family's proprietary interests in the colony and others taking the positions of the Penns' political opponents, including the assembly and various Quaker reformers sympathetic to the Delaware Indians' plight. As always, those with purely commercial ambitions, with no strong political allegiances, and with loyalties that followed only land speculation and the fur trade were the wild cards.

Forbes was elated; he saw that the treaty would make it possible to weaken the French. "I must strongly recommend to you," he told the Indian delegates, "to send immediate Notice to any of your People, who may be at the French fort, to return forthwith to your Towns; where you may sit by yr Fires, wth yr Wives and Children, quiet and undisturbed, and smoke your Pipes in safety. Let the French fight their own Battles, as they were the first Cause of the War." Indian neutrality would be a major gain for the British. The Indians' price was agreement that English settlers "would draw back over the mountain," an assurance that British officials tried, and failed, to honor after the war with the Proclamation Line of 1763.

When Captain François-Marie Lignery, the French commander at Fort Duquesne, learned that his Indian allies were going home, he ordered his troops to evacuate before the Forbes expedition might arrive. By November 23, the French had loaded their cannons onto riverboats, shipped off the last two hundred men, and detonated fifty barrels of gunpowder, which reduced the fort to rubble, thereby keeping it from the enemy. Ten miles away, Forbes's troops heard the explosion. A hastily constructed barricade became the winter quarters for the two hundred Pennsylvanians whom Forbes left behind to guard the strategically essential forks of the Alleghany, Monongahela, and Ohio Rivers.

After these victories, Prime Minister Pitt decided that the conquest of Quebec was now Britain's single most important war goal. Having already determined to fight a war for empire—the Great War for the Empire, as historians would later call it—across the globe rather than on the European continent, the taking of India and North America were his primary focuses. In 1759, with India apparently secure, he considered Quebec the logical next place to challenge the French. It was not that Pitt believed Canada worth having; he did not, but it was strategically the place to press the French again with a high chance of success and the most to gain, though from an economic perspective— and the empire was all about economic ambitions at this point—the West Indies, West Africa, and India were more valuable than Canada. Anglo-Americans, of course, saw it differently. In attacking Quebec, they were fighting a war for Canada, a French and Indian war to protect themselves from the Gallic threat and to further their own ambitions in North America.

The British advantages in fighting a global war included the government's ability to raise more money than the French state could, which allowed Pitt to choose battle locations where the enemy's resources would be stretched thin, with long supply lines and multiple fronts. Another advantage was Britain's naval dominance, which had emerged in the last decade, while the European land war had played to French military strengths. The British had more ships—275 with an additional 49 under construction, compared to the 72 seaworthy French vessels—and design advantages, which included double-deck, seventy-four-gun vessels that packed more firepower and were more maneuverable than their French counterparts. By 1755, the British had captured three hundred French merchantmen and more than eight thousand sailors. (Intercepting sixteen provision ships bound for Quebec during the war also helped to weaken Canada.) Under these circumstances, the French strategy was to focus on major victories over Britain in Europe, while simply keeping the war alive in North America.

New Englanders had attempted before to invade Quebec; the first time was in 1690, with a force of twenty-five hundred men. But they had embarked too late in the season, and the disorganized three-pronged attack had ended in a debacle. The winter weather, which arrived in October, and their own lack of military experience defeated them. The British tried again in 1711, this time without the colonists and with a fleet of sixty vessels and 12,500 soldiers, a force about half the size of the total population of French Canada. Again, the weather won and the British lost. New Englanders' plans for yet another invasion in 1746, on the heels of their victory at Louisbourg, had foundered for lack of support from London, and the Treaty of Aix-la-Chapelle in 1748 had brought such plans to a temporary end.

A decade later, the French government had decided that Quebec, where about one-eighth of all French Canadians lived, was worth defending, but this was a position that could be second-guessed. From an economic perspective, holding Quebec was not worth the expense in lives or livres. In good years, of which there were few, the colony produced enough grain both to supply its own population of sixty or seventy thousand and to service the French Caribbean. Since the collapse of the beaver market in the 1690s, the fur trade had never again been sufficiently lucrative to justify government subsidies to keep New France afloat.

From a strategic perspective, though, keeping Quebec was essential to checking the British presence in North America: It assured that the defense of British North America would not come cheaply and it restrained the expansion of British colonies on the mainland and in the Caribbean. The loss of Louisbourg had been strategically more devastating than a defeat might be at Quebec, given the port's utility as a launching and supply point for defense of the North Atlantic fisheries, the entrance to the St. Lawrence River, and the French Caribbean. Now, however, without Louisbourg, Quebec had become strategically significant as the sole defensive entrepôt for French interests in the North American interior and the western Atlantic. Without it, the line of forts that sustained supply lines and protected French interests in the Ohio Valley would tumble, French naval and commercial vessels would have no safe haven on the continent, and the potential for developing markets and producing natural resources (crops, furs, and perhaps minerals) in North America would be lost.

So the French decided they had to make a stand, both to keep the English fighting in North America rather than concentrating their navy on Europe, and to defend their strategic interests. When French sentries posted along the St. Lawrence River reported the arrival of a British fleet on May 23, 1759, the decisive moment had come.

With thirty thousand regular troops in North America in addition to the colonial militias, a substantial number of ships, and experience in combined land and sea assaults as well as amphibious landings, the British had many advantages. If their expedition down the St. Lawrence faltered for any reason, there were also two land forces available to press the assault. The high command had promised General Wolfe, leading the principal force, twelve thousand British troops, but he got about eight thousand. He anticipated defense by French forces of that number, but in the end twelve thousand soldiers defended Quebec along with about two thousand Indians, principally Ottawa and Iroquois but also Micmac from Nova Scotia and others from Illinois and the Great Lakes region. He hoped, though, that the appearance of Lord Amherst with the colonists' troops would force Montcalm to divide his men, which would considerably weaken France's defensive position. Wolfe still thought of the colonists as "the worst soldiers in the universe," just as he had at the battle of Louisbourg, so he was glad that he himself commanded none but regular British battalions. He preferred to field fewer troops rather than depend on American reinforcements.

The British flew French flags on their ships to gain an element of surprise as they sailed up the St. Lawrence toward Quebec in the summer of 1759. French efforts to ram these British vessels with fireships as they approached the city—a well-known tactic to frighten and confuse the enemy—foundered on the nerves of their own seamen, who set their boats on fire too soon and jumped ship too early for the ploy to be effective. The British made it up the river and moored on the south bank just opposite Quebec, but that did not do them a lot of good. The French had topography on their side, with only a few small streets providing open access from Quebec's lower town to the higher one at the top of the cliffs on which this formidable walled city had been built—cliffs and walls that were major obstacles to any land assault. The weather, which was foul, also favored the French when they fought from entrenched, sheltered positions.

The initial British bombardment of Quebec at the end of June was loud but ineffective, though it did lead Montcalm to relocate his ammunition magazine outside the city, about six miles away, and it frayed the nerves of the besieged Quebecois. It also distracted attention from Wolfe's landing his troops upriver from Quebec, on the north bank, on July 8 and 9.

The troops on both sides were disciplined and the officers gentlemanly, particularly compared to colonists and Indians waging war. Both sides treated prisoners well, returning them and wounded combatants in short order. Officers also required the troops to return pillaged goods, and they protected women prisoners rather than allowing enlisted men to terrorize them.

The English did not advance their cause beyond Wolfe's beachhead through the month of July, and Montcalm was not so foolish as to march out to engage his enemy on an open battlefield. After a period of uncharacteristic indecisiveness, Wolfe realized that his best chance at victory would come through surprise. One attempt to engage the enemy on July 30 failed in a rainstorm that soaked their ammunition; Wolfe lost more than two hundred killed and the same number of wounded, while the French suffered comparatively light casualties (seventy killed and wounded). Worse, many of the wounded Highlanders who fought with Wolfe became the victims of the French army's Indian allies, who tortured and scalped them.

On September 4, Wolfe's troops learned that Amherst had taken the French forts at Ticonderoga and Crown Point, and that, farther west, Fort Niagara had fallen to the English as well. This was the good news; the bad news was that, as a result, Amherst's army would not be supporting the battle for Quebec. Wolfe went ahead with his preparations. Following his order to destroy any villages round about that could contribute to the French defense, British troops leveled every town within a hundred miles, creating a massive refugee problem on the French side. And the nature of the struggle for Quebec changed as retributive scalping, looting, torture, and plundering supplanted the gentlemanly rules of combat that both Montcalm and Wolfe preferred.

Montcalm's army had enough supplies to last through September 20, and Wolfe's troops were poised to attack on September 6, but severe weather handicapped the landing of more British forces upstream from the city until the night of September 12. Under cover of darkness, they scaled the cliff, and by dawn they were arrayed in battle formation on the broad plateau at the top—the Plains of Abraham—catching the French surprised and unprepared. Montcalm had around forty-five hundred troops on the field, about the same as the British, but they were not as well trained or battle hardened for what would be the decisive battle for North America.

Montcalm ordered his men into battle at about 10:00 a.m. History, with perfect hindsight, has judged the move precipitous and catastrophic, but his strategy favored aggressive engagement before the British had time to reinforce and entrench their troops on the ground. The traditional battlefield alignment here favored the classically trained British troops, however, and was to the disadvantage of the combined militia, Indians, regular army, and marines of the French, most of whom were accustomed to fighting frontier style rather than in regimented formations. Within only a few minutes of their first two volleys, the British had the French soldiers in hasty, chaotic retreat; in less than a half hour, the French capitulated, with twelve hundred wounded and two hundred dead; the British had about sixty killed and six hundred wounded in their victory.

Gunfire had struck Wolfe three times—once at the very start of the battle by a sniper; in the groin, during the first minutes of the French assault; and finally in the chest in the last moments of the British victory, at which point aides carried him from the field and he died shortly thereafter. Montcalm, too, suffered a mortal wound—during the French retreat, toward the end of the battle—but lingered into the next day. French Canadian nationalists still mourn *La Guerre de la Conquête*, the War of the Conquest, and recall the battle's place in the subjugation of the Quebecois, the day they lost their independence. The English immediately elevated the battle to iconic status, and it remains one of the most celebrated military victories in British history, right alongside the Battle of Plassey.

Quebec was a turning point in the history of the British Empire, as Plassey had been three years earlier. In India, the French lost by not entering the fight and then by abandoning the competition for commercial, military, and political supremacy in Bengal. In the Battle of Quebec, they were simply outspent, outgunned, and outmanned. The Battle of Plassey allowed the British a vision of empire centered on India, not North America—which ironically, thanks in part to their decisive victory at Quebec, would soon be lost.

New Englanders were ecstatic when they heard of Wolfe's great victory; Jonathan Mayhew, a young Congregationalist minister in Boston, was among the more exuberant celebrants of its significance, predicting that it had created conditions under which the Anglo-American colonies, "with the continued blessing of Heaven . . . will become, in another century or two, a mighty empire."

The British had not yet won the war, however, and the nature of any subsequent peace depended on the outcome of additional battles. In 1759 alone, the British failed to take their primary Caribbean objective of Martinique despite the nine thousand men Pitt sent to achieve this, and succeeded in winning only the secondary goal of Guadeloupe, an island of strategic significance with about fifty thousand people, the vast majority of them slaves who worked the lucrative sugar, cotton, and coffee plantations. The Royal Navy also won a decisive battle off the coast of Portugal in Lagos Bay, taking five French ships and inflicting losses of about five hundred, while suffering only half that many deaths; this significantly undermined any chance the French had to invade the British Isles.

Also in the summer of 1759, in western Germany, the British supported their Hanoverian and Prussian allies in a victory at Minden, made all the more significant by France's known strategic decision to focus its resources on the continental land war. Then finally, if less decisively, on November 20, Admiral Edward Hawke's fleet outmaneuvered that of Admiral Hubert de Brienne, Marquis de Conflans, in Quiberon Bay, south of Brest, during a fierce storm. The English lost two ships and between three and four hundred men. The French lost five ships, had four others disabled, and had twenty-five hundred dead, most of them by drowning.

Imperial apologists would write effusively about the significance of Clive's victory at Plassey for another two centuries. Wolfe's death at Quebec was considered epic, and it was famously preserved in a fanciful painting by Benjamin West. Orme called Clive's victory the "revolution" of Plassey. Thomas Babington Macaulay, the most imperial of England's nineteenth-century imperial historians, preened patriotically:

"With the loss of twenty-two soldiers killed and fifty wounded, Clive had scattered an army of nearly sixty thousand men, and subdued an empire larger and more populous than Great Britain." "There never was a battle in which the consequences were so vast, so immediate, and so permanent," wrote the military historian G. B. Malleson in the late nineteenth century. "Yes! As a victory, Plassey was, in its consequences, perhaps the greatest ever gained." In light of later, bloodier, and more decisive battles between the British and French, these exaggerations lay too much meaning on this one event, but the paeans to Plassey illustrate the enduring psychological effect of the victory on British politics and popular culture, and the confidence with which Britons marched through India and then into America after Clive's and Wolfe's celebrated victories.*

---

* Pondicherry did not fall until four years after Plassey, in 1761, and the Mogul Empire expired at England's feet in 1765, eight years after the battle.

6

✦

HEARTS AND MINDS

WITH THE MILITARY VICTORIES in Bengal strengthening the British position in Asia, some British leaders imagined that ousting France from North America might actually increase the dangers to their empire. Colonel James Murray, who became military governor of Quebec district in 1760, wondered whether Canada should be returned to France at the end of the war as "a guarantee for the good behaviour of its neighbouring colonies." In a similar vein, the Duke of Bedford wrote to Lord Newcastle, "I don't know whether the neighbourhood of the French to our Northern American colonies was not the greatest security of their dependence on their Mother Country, who I fear will be slighted by them when their apprehensions of the French are removed." In 1760, William Burke, a political pamphleteer and, by 1763, a member of Parliament and secretary and register of the island of Guadeloupe, also argued for the return of Canada to France: "If, Sir, the People of our Colonies find no Check from Canada . . . what the Consequences will be . . . I leave to your own reflections . . . The Possession of Canada, far from being necessary to our Safety, may in its Consequence be even dangerous. A Neighbour that keeps us in some Awe, is not always the worst of Neighbours."

Obviously, with a position in Guadeloupe at stake, Burke had an interest in British retention of the island, and it was universally recognized that either it or Canada would have to be returned to France in the peace negotiations then beginning. The argument for keeping the Caribbean islands over the mainland was less persuasive in 1759 than it had been in 1748, when Great Britain returned Cape Breton to France, because the British now recognized that their colonists in North America could be more valuable as consumers of English products than as providers of raw materials, an economic logic that inverted the values of the sugar islands and mainland colonies. It had become obvious that more consumer goods could be sold to the mainland colonists, whose numbers were growing exponentially, than to the much smaller number of island planters.

It was this kind of logic, at once hopeful, strategic, prophetic, and parochial, that inspired transatlantic distrust, ideological fixations, and political relations over the next fifteen years. From London's perspective, it was time to plot the war's endgame, to strategize negotiations for a peace treaty, and to plan the postwar administration of the sprawling British Empire with much more than the American colonies in mind. The colonists, in strong contrast, thought it was time to assert their standing, to take their place beside, not beneath, Britons on the other side of the Atlantic. The year 1759, like 1748, was a watershed in the British Empire's history, and both landmarks reinforced the colonists' convictions about the value of their enterprise. There was real continuity in their ambitions, which dated back in some cases to the seventeenth century, and the victories of the 1740s and 1750s only reinvigorated them.

For the British, victory over France would enable Parliament to enact, and the government to enforce, Britain's imperial plans without wartime distractions. It would raise administrative control over the colonies to a higher priority. The colonies now had the empire's attention, which meant that the age of salutary neglect had passed and latent conflict would become actual. The mainland American colonies were now both of greater importance and lower standing in the imperial scheme than only a few decades before. They were not the sole link, nor always the most important one, in the chain that bound the empire's periphery to its center in London.

Neither the death of King George II in 1760 and the accession of his grandson as King George III, nor the changes of ministers and ministries during the turbulent decade to follow fully explains the policies that Britain began to impose on the colonies.* Parochial perspectives

---

* George III, the third of Great Britain's Hanover kings, was the first to be born in England and to speak English as his first language.

and simple misunderstandings were common on both sides, and frequently led to mistaken conjectures about motives. Political foes would identify patterns where their opponents had never imagined them, identify change where their enemies intended continuity, lay blame and assess motives in ignorance, with bad faith, or in honest fulfillment of an ideological expectation. Irresolvable conflicts of interest and ambition marked Britons on either side of the Atlantic.

Several conflicts in imperial-colonial relations that developed at the time of the British victories of 1759 illustrate this well: Colonists saw new and threatening policy turns when the king's ministers believed they were stressing continuity in their attempt to bring order to the governance of disorderly subjects. The Parsons' Cause, a legal case in Virginia over payments to the clergy; disputes over writs of assistance in Massachusetts; and attempts to enforce long-standing policies on the governors' right to "suspend" certain legal clauses in those two colonies and South Carolina show a heightened sensitivity to (or paranoia about) imperial authority rearing its head time and again over the next quarter century. In each case, the roots of the conflict ran deeply into the seventeenth century, to the Navigation Acts, to Bacon's Rebellion and Coode's Rebellion, and to the Glorious Revolution of 1689. Events in Maryland revealed that its internal history was even less stable than that of Virginia, New York, or Massachusetts, and displayed an even more contested relationship with the imperial overseers.

Maryland's Glorious Revolution in 1689–1692 had been less bloody and more successful than those of New York and Massachusetts, although certainly there were tensions between the residents and the colony's "proprietor," Cecil Calvert, the 2nd Lord Baltimore. King Charles I had granted the colony to George Calvert, the 1st Lord Baltimore, as a fiefdom, along with broad executive and judicial authority to govern, tax, sell land, and establish institutions as he saw fit. The Calverts were Catholics, and Lord Baltimore envisioned the colony as a haven for members of his faith. The colony received its charter in 1632 and settlement began in 1634, though Calvert himself never left England. He appointed a governor—the first was his son—a council of mostly Catholics, and magistrates; he established courts, and all writs were in his name; he authorized the creation of ports of entry, required all adult males to serve in militias, exercised martial law as he saw fit, and was free to impose ordinances as long as they were not repugnant to English law and did not trample property rights.

The three main checks on the proprietor's power were that he could pass laws only with the consent of an assembly, laws had to be consistent with the laws of England, and the colonists' rights, which included "all privileges, franchises and liberties of this our kingdom of England," were to be respected. There was no imperial review of Maryland's laws, and the decisions of its courts could not be appealed to English courts. But this was where the contest for power began, not where it ended. The General Assembly asserted the right to initiate legislation and by 1649 claimed the authority to levy all taxes. The counties' courts likewise accrued power at the expense of the proprietor's authority, becoming significant units of local government that handled much more than routine civil and criminal suits. During the 1660s and 1670s, the courts took responsibility for building and maintaining roads, licensing inns, inspecting scales, supervising master-servant relations, appointing and supervising guardians for orphans, building courthouses and jails, assessing taxes, and supervising elections of assemblymen. And in 1671, the courts asserted their authority to levy local taxes.

The colonists in Maryland had divided early on into pro- and anti-proprietary factions, and many of them resisted paying taxes to a government run by Catholics, whom they suspected of conspiring with the French and the Indians, as well as with the pope. Maryland had had revolts in 1659, 1676, when Virginia did, too, and 1681. The struggle over power was not simply between local magistrates and the assembly on one side and the proprietor on the other. The largely Catholic council appointed by Lord Baltimore was constantly in conflict with the Protestant assembly. Threats from the Iroquois Five Nations (known to Marylanders as "Cinnagoes" or "Senecas") exacerbated the constitutional struggles when taxes were increased in the 1670s to pay for the colony's defense. The assembly, magistrates, and some Protestants agitated for the funds to be allocated county by county, while the proprietor, the council, and most Catholics favored storing weapons in a central magazine under proprietary control.

In 1676, a list of grievances titled "Complaint from Heaven" was addressed to King Charles II with a preface full of anti-Catholic invective and conspiracy theories. "It is high time," the Marylanders wrote, "that the originall Cause of the late and former distractions should be inquired into: the Berklieu [Governor Berkeley of Virginia] and Baltimore Partys will tell a great many over smothed Contraries." According to the authors of this list, "Pope Jesuit determined to over terne Engl^d, with feyer, sword and distractions, within themselves, and by the Maryland Papists, to drive us Protestants to Purgatory within our selves in America, with the help of the French spirits from Canada."

With the "French spirits from Canada" never far from their minds, the petitioners specified their grievances, which included an unnamed "Popish Divell" inciting Maryland's Piscataway Indians to violence in order to further the murderous ends of the French: "These Pope's messengers, hould a secret correspondence with the French pater nostres, that com now a days from Canada or Nova Franciae over the lake into the sinniko Indian Country amongst the Indians . . . and eversince this 3 or 4 years robbed divers plantations in Maryland, and killed cattle and hoghs." They considered Lord Baltimore personally "guilty of the Mischief done by the Sinnico [Seneca] Indian[s], that com now every year downe and robb the Country." He had also "raysed the People in Armes for his privat gaine and Interest, only to oppress the king's subjects with great taxes in his and [his] own creatures pocket," had provoked the Indians as an excuse to raise taxes, had profiteered in arms for his own financial benefit and that of his Catholic allies, and generally advanced the French Catholic cause against the Protestant subjects of Maryland. Further, he had embezzled some of these funds and doctored accounts to hide the thefts, had ordered troops to burn the homes of subjects who lived in isolated areas of the frontier, then confiscated these properties, and others, too, in manipulated court procedures, and had then assigned the estates either to himself or to his Catholic supporters. In consultation with the "secret Councell of Priests," kinsmen, and "stronge Catholics," Lord Baltimore had conspired to reduce the size of the assembly by half and to gouge taxpayers for his personal benefit and that of his coconspirators.

According to the petitioners, when Lord Baltimore exercised his monarchical prerogative, vetoing laws adopted by the elected assembly, he did so in defiance of Marylanders' rights as Englishmen: The "Lord proprietary assums and attracts more Royall Power to himselfe over his Tennants then owr gratious Kinge over his subjects in Engl^d." He had effectively set himself up as King of Maryland, which they saw as treason, since no man may effect an equality with the monarch, when he required all his subjects to "swear Alleagiance and supremacy under the Tittle of Fidelity to the Lord proprietary and his Hyres and Successors for ever" or suffer banishment.

The proprietor had, arbitrarily in the petitioners' opinion, introduced a property qualification for voting in 1670, and he had increased taxes. Then, in 1676, the 2nd Lord Baltimore called only two of the four representatives from each county to a session of the assembly, which the petitioners viewed as another plot against their rights as Englishmen. And there was more: His aggrieved subjects believed that Lord Baltimore was in the service of the pope, was a sponsor of priests and, worse, Jesuits, who "wander up and down in England appareled as Tradsmen and some otherwise." (This was very similar to the charge of New York's Leislerian rebels a few years later and those who discovered a slave conspiracy in 1741, who saw in every immigrant dance teacher, tutor, or itinerant tradesman a Catholic spy, a Jesuit in disguise.) In short, he was a rebel, "traytor," usurper of the king's prerogative, and he was stamping on the rights of the monarch's loyal Protestant subjects.

Unlike the Massachusetts colonists who petitioned to have their charter restored, the Marylanders wanted the king to revoke their charter, take the government of their colony out of the hands of the proprietor, and appoint a Protestant governor and council in place of the Catholics, who they believed conspired with Lord Baltimore. They were eager to swear allegiance to the king rather than to the proprietor, and to be ruled "according to the custome of England." They wanted their taxes directed entirely to their defense rather than to lining the pockets of the proprietor and his cronies. They wanted the Church of England to be the established church in Maryland and to have ministers supplied for parishes yet to be constructed.* And, finally, they

---

* Fifteen years later, there were, at most, only six Anglican priests and three Presbyterian ministers in Maryland. Likewise in Virginia during the 1670s, there were between five and ten Anglican priests at any one time for a population of thirty thousand.

needed the monarch "to send or cause to com over 6. Or 700 good resolute Scotts Highlanders, to seat on the head of rivers and the Baye, beeinge men supposed onely fitt to encounter with the Indians, and keep the French robbers at a distance."

Of course, Lord Baltimore contested all the accusations, but he found the contrary cases difficult to prove and resisted any changes that would limit his profits or authority. Economic conditions were worsening for the colonists, and they laid at least some of the hardship at his door. Declining tobacco prices in the 1680s had created a depression, and attempts made by the governor and council to collect taxes in coin rather than in the traditional medium of tobacco had compounded the decline. It was growing increasingly difficult to obtain credit, which limited the ability of recently freed servants to build a fledgling plantation. Lord Culpeper, governor of Virginia, reported to the Lords of Trade in 1681, during another Maryland revolt, that the colony was "now in torment, and not only troubled with our disease, poverty, but in very great danger of falling in pieces; whether it be that old Lord Baltimore's politic maxims are not pursued or that they are unsuited to his age." Two years later, Lord Baltimore revoked his policy of granting fifty acres of land to every colonist who paid for his own, or a servant's, transatlantic voyage, and he exacerbated the economic distress and class unrest by requiring that each colonist who wanted to claim the fifty acres pay 100 pounds of weight in tobacco, a price he raised to 120 pounds in 1684.

The absence of any provision in the Maryland charter for British review of the colony's governance contributed to chronic constitutional conflict during the 1680s. And the proprietor's Catholicism kept the fire of conspiracy theories hot when the economy plunged and those at the bottom of Maryland's society despaired of ever climbing out of the impoverished and into the propertied classes. Thus all the issues that had been raised in 1659, 1676, and 1681 were still present and contributing factors in Maryland's Glorious Revolution: taxes, tax collectors, efforts to collect taxes in coins (rare in the cash-poor economy) rather than tobacco, government fees, and the proprietor's assertion of monarchical authority, which inspired legislators to refuse to swear an "oath of fidelity" to the proprietor. Chronic poverty, intolerance of Indians, French, and Catholics (whom the Protestants outnumbered twenty to one), fluctuations in the tobacco crop and its value, and a general rowdiness continued to define life in Maryland.

The first rumblings of Maryland's Glorious Revolution came in March 1689, with news from England of the exile of King James and the arrival of William of Orange. (It appears that news of Leisler's revolt in New York that very spring did not arrive until Maryland's uprising was already in motion.) Maryland's Catholic councilors probably did favor James over the invading Protestant, and their efforts to gain central control over the colony's arms were, understandably, interpreted in light of their suspected loyalties.

The trigger for an uprising was the rumor of an Indian invasion, which the antiproprietary faction fabricated in order to enlist support for a revolt. According to the sworn deposition of one John Atkey, "he did heare Fyffe say, that he did heare Sharpe say, that he did heare the Easterne shoare Indians when they were drunk saye, that they were hired by Coll Darnall to fight against the English. But being asked when they were sober, they would not say any such thing." This seems slim hearsay evidence now as it did then—more of a pretense than an explanation for what followed. As a report to Lord Baltimore put it, "Such was the buisie spirits of some ill designeing men that when there was noe such thing as any Indians landed at the mouth of the Patuxen[t] River," as initially rumored, the reported location changed and the rumored number of Indians leaped from nine thousand to ten thousand warriors.

John Coode, an immigrant from England, a former Anglican priest, and perhaps Lord Baltimore's most vociferous opponent, led the rebellion. The leaders had in common that they were English gentry who had immigrated to Maryland because in England they had become immiserated and hoped to restore their standing and means in America. They had achieved that goal in Maryland, but they had not gained the political power they believed was appropriate for people of their rank. So their actions were, in part, a bald attempt to seize that power from those, generally Catholics, who benefited from Lord Baltimore's patronage. Coode appealed to the people of Maryland against the councilors, who could muster only 160 militiamen to their cause. Leading a force of seven to eight hundred men, he laid siege to the councilors' garrison and, without bloodshed, secured their surrender.

In mid-August 1689, Coode called for the election of a new assembly. As one of its first actions in September, it ordered an investigation of the rumored Catholic-French-Indian conspiracy. Not surprisingly, no evidence was found. The assembly did not introduce or pass new laws, and local institutions, principally the county courts and sheriffs, maintained the essential services of government.

Instructions to the rebels in Maryland did not arrive from England until late May 1690, when they were authorized to "continue in our name your care in the administration of the Government and preservation of the peace and properties of our Subjects," which they did over the next two years. Still, grievances—the same as those expressed in 1676, 1681, and 1689—were addressed to the new monarchs, and they largely focused on ousting the proprietor for abuse of power. In the spring of 1691, almost two full years after seizing governance, the rebels had their answer from the Crown, and it was exactly what they had asked for: "Having heard what your deputies and Agents have offered to us, Wee have thought fitt to take our Province of Maryland under our immediate Care and Protection."

One year later, in April 1692, Maryland's first Protestant governor arrived in the New World. (The new royal charter excluded Catholics and Quakers from office.) The first assembly under the charter made the Church of England the established church in the colony but otherwise did not change the essential structures of government. Maryland continued under royal control until 1715, when a Protestant proprietor to whom the family title had descended was able to reassert his charter rights and regain most of the original proprietors' governing powers. The fear of internal Catholic conspiracies and insecure property rights having diminished, Maryland was no longer ripe for revolution. Its colonists had not expressed anti-monarchical or anti-imperial sympathies in the previous century, but their long-cherished ideas about independence, their essential understandings of their rights as Englishmen, and their belief that their assembly had sovereignty in local governance only solidified over time.

Virginia's revolution against the Crown of England, known as Bacon's Rebellion, preceded the Glorious Revolution by more than a decade. As in Maryland, the revolt was occasioned by difficulties with the Indians and led by immigrants from England's gentry classes, who aimed to recover lost status, to profit financially, and to exercise political power. As in Massachusetts and New York, the uprising directly engaged the governor and also questioned the larger imperial structure that regulated the colony. Bacon's Rebellion failed to achieve its immediate goals, but it did affect the colony's social structure, labor system, and political alignments.

The founders of Virginia, in 1607, had utopian ambitions for Jamestown, where they hoped impoverished Englishmen would find worthy livelihoods and where they wanted to civilize the Indians, but the colony was always, like Dutch New York, a business enterprise. Although the founders intended to form a biracial society of Indians and Englishmen, neither group was prepared to accept the other. Since the Virginia Company was a joint-stock venture, its investors expected large and quick returns on their capital. Initially, all the Virginia settlers were employees of the company, which had a monopoly on their time and owned all the land. But when plots of land for private gardens were assigned in 1609, it was an early recognition that the corporate culture could not enforce the company's monopoly control of the colonists' livelihoods. In 1617, ten years after the founding, the first shipment of tobacco to England was the start of a process that saved Virginia financially but also assured that exploitation of unfree labor would continue to define its culture. Tobacco was a savior and a curse; the fortunes of Virginians rose and fell with its production and price, and farmers of the colonial era never found a staple crop to supplant it.

Indian-settler relations were tense from the beginning, given the preexisting distrust and mutual disdain, and given the colonists' apparently unquenchable thirst for land and natural resources, principally fish and game. The Powhattan Indians, dominant in the region, could have finished off the colony at any time in its first decade by simply leaving the place and letting the English fend for themselves, but the Indians vacillated as the settler population grew (very slowly at first). By 1621, just under forty-three hundred immigrants had landed in Virginia, but only twelve hundred had survived; malnutrition and disease carried off the rest. Nonetheless, the Indians feared the apparently limitless number of replacements arriving from England. In March 1622, the Powhattans attacked the colony and, if it hadn't been for the tip-off given to the English by a baptized Indian, would have destroyed it. As it was, 347 settlers died in the "massacre" and relations went from bad to worse. Even before this, George Thorpe, a former member of Parliament who was on Virginia's Council, reported, "There is scarce any man amongst us that doth soe much as afforde them [Indians] a good thought in his hart and most men wth their mouthes give them nothinge but maledictions and bitter execrations."

King James I dissolved the Virginia Company in 1624, at which point the colony came under his direct authority. Most Virginians enjoyed fewer civil and political rights at that point than they would have in England, but unlike the New England Puritans, Pennsylvania Quakers, or Maryland Catholics, they had not immigrated to secure anything but financial independence. And new statutes provided them some economic freedom—requiring the consent of the House of Burgesses (the colony's elected assembly) to any taxes the governor and council imposed. Virginians were already experienced in resisting the edicts of the Virginia Company, and they applied the same spirit to their relationships with governors and kings.

In the crapshoot that was life in Virginia, some settlers hit the jackpot. If they could stay alive, if the tobacco crop prospered, if they could also manage to keep a few field hands to help with its planting, harvesting, and processing, and if tobacco prices were high, they could make fortunes. But they always had a labor shortage—there were never enough immigrants to meet the demand—and Virginia endured a catastrophic death rate through the middle of the seventeenth century. Indians were no solution to the labor shortage, and African slaves, who first became available for purchase in 1619, did not, on average, live long enough to return a profit on the cost of purchase.

In 1644, Indians killed five hundred settlers in another surprise attack on the Virginia colony, which led Governor William Berkeley to launch reprisals that reduced the Indians' capacity to mount a further attack and opened the frontier to a rapid expansion of settlements. Labor shortages persisted, and in 1650 there were still no more than five hundred black servants or slaves in Virginia in a population of about nineteen thousand settlers, and their precise status is unclear. At midcentury, the mortality rate was falling, for reasons that are also not entirely clear—possibly better nutrition, improved and safer transatlantic travel, fewer habitations near swamps, and fewer Indians—but it took thirty-seven years for Virginia to reach a population of eight thousand (by 1644); then the number doubled in fewer than five more years, and doubled again between 1650 and 1670 to about thirty-five thousand.

The Virginia colony was always oriented along traditional north–south Indian trade paths that connected Detroit and Canada, the Hurons and Seneca, with the Chesapeake Indians, including the Piscataway, Patuxent, and Powhattans. These Indian trading routes also connected Virginians south to the Catawba and Cherokee living in what later became the Carolinas and Georgia. The colony looked east to London for the tobacco trade, of course, but also south to the Caribbean thanks to Dutch traders who bought their livestock and sold them rum, molasses, sugar, and slaves. Virginians were significant trading partners with Barbados by about 1650, and later with Bermuda. Merchant ships sailing on both African and European routes connected Virginia to the Atlantic world and to other mainland colonies to the north.

By the 1670s, Virginians were shipping ten million pounds of tobacco a year to London, and they shipped to other English ports as well, but they were receiving about half the price they had gotten at the beginning of the tobacco boom fifty years earlier. To grow that much tobacco, and to keep their heads above the waterline of debt, they needed laborers. The declining death rate and servants' preference for independence after working off the cost of their transportation had two significant consequences for Virginia society: The former servants became competitors for land and tobacco production with their former masters; and when, as increasingly was the case, those servants were unable to secure land for themselves, they became part of a permanent white underclass that threatened the tranquility of the landowners.

The planters who dominated the Virginia assembly addressed the social problems created by this increasing number of masterless men with laws that added an average of three years of service, from four to seven, for those who came to the New World without a preexisting labor contract. They also imposed higher penalties on indentured workers who were captured after fleeing service: The runaways' remaining term of service was doubled, and they had to pay with their own labor the cost of any rewards paid to apprehend them—and at a rate about half that of free-market workers. In the 1670s, the assembly added a new penalty on top of the others—having to pay compensation for labor lost during an absconder's flight. Six months of freedom could cost an additional three years of service.

Other crimes also increased the terms of indentured service: two years for pregnancy, one year for stealing a master's hog, and an additional year owed to the informer. Killing three hogs cost one man six more years of service. Nonetheless, the number of servants who survived their indenture rose sharply after 1650, as did the number who would never own land. By the end of the century, it appears that at least a third of the population in Virginia's older counties were tenants, and the percentage continued to rise after 1700. Free land was disappearing, and cheap land was to be found only out on the frontier—too remote to transport tobacco to market profitably, and where Indians remained a threat. It is no surprise, then, that the shortage of servants and cheap land, along with the high cost of earning one's freedom, created ever greater tensions within the white community. King James II made matters worse in 1674 by bestowing Virginia's public lands, those not yet granted and patented, on two of his friends, the Earl of Arlington and Baron Thomas Culpeper, and their heirs for a period of thirty-one years. Two years later, he also appointed Culpeper as governor when the seventy-one-year-old Berkeley died.

Berkeley had had a talent for keeping the lid on his unruly subjects with a combination of swagger, shrewd distribution of patronage, and infrequent elections, which kept in office men he had already cajoled and compensated, and kept out those who were most angry with his regime and with the king's selective generosity. The growing class conflict played into his hands for a time: He was able to crush two mutinies led by minor social figures and at the same time keep men of wealth, who had the most to lose from class warfare, in line.

A group of Doeg Indians triggered Bacon's Rebellion when, in 1675, they crossed the Potomac River from Maryland to trade with neighboring farmers, got into a dispute over some hogs, which the Indians said they had collected as settlement of a debt and a settler said they had stolen, and came to blows: At least one settler and one Indian died in the ensuing conflict. A party of Virginians crossed the river to avenge the death, and they killed fourteen Indians who were flying a flag of truce—Indians who were not even Doegs but Susquehannahs. The Piscataways also got involved, and Governor Berkeley authorized perhaps as many as a thousand Maryland and Virginia militiamen (out of the thirteen thousand in the colony) to cross over into the treaty-protected Indian country; these men, too, murdered five chiefs under a flag of truce. Of the roughly seven hundred Susquehannah warriors, about a hundred now crossed into Virginia to seek revenge.

Berkeley considered and then rejected a full-scale invasion of the Susquehannah settlements in Maryland and instead supported the construction of forts along the major rivers to defend the colony against further reprisals. The small planters thought these forts were both useless and an excuse for profiteering by Berkeley and his rich supporters. The high salaries that aggrandized government officials and members of the House of Burgesses were another grievance for the poorer planters whose tax money was going to Berkeley's minions. Armed settlers among them refused to disband and requested that Berkeley commission someone to lead them against the Indians, which he declined to do. To be sure, there were many competing parties and interests involved. There were wars with Indians and unrest all along the frontier, and it was a delicate situation for Berkeley to handle, since he believed that the enraged settlers, who already had a long record of indiscriminate killing of Indians, would do more harm than good if unleashed; he generally favored having harmonious relations with the Indian tribes. Into these fraught circumstances burst Nathaniel Bacon, a young gentry immigrant and a member of the Virginia Council. He seized command of the angry settlers in defiance of Berkeley.

Bacon's rebels acted as Berkeley feared: They accepted the help of friendly Occaneechee Indians, who captured Susquehannahs and turned them over to the rebels, who killed the prisoners and then killed the Occaneechees, too. Berkeley was nonetheless conciliatory in the face of what was becoming more than a minor insurrection. He called for a new election, invited the airing of grievances, and offered Bacon a full pardon, restoration of his seat on the council, and the militia commission he had sought—in return for a signed confession of his offenses against governor, colony, and king once he had returned from massacring Indians. Bacon agreed and returned to Jamestown with the governor's permission. Under Berkeley's direction, the newly elected House of Burgesses extended the vote to hitherto disenfranchised freemen who owned no land, removed councilors' exemption from taxes, instituted a cap on collection of public fees, and limited the term for sheriffs to one year—all in the name of placating those excluded from Berkeley's patronage.

Berkeley and Bacon went on jockeying for power, however, the governor giving way enough to retain his and Bacon trying to ensure that Berkeley did not buy off the freemen under his influence with token reforms. Their mutual distrust became so great that Bacon made an armed demand for the military commission Berkeley had promised him and then withheld, and strong-armed the General Assembly into financing his next raid on Indian country for plunder and conquest. Bacon returned to Jamestown from that foray with forty-five peaceful Pamunkey prisoners, and made further trouble by offering freedom to the servants and slaves of masters who were loyal to Berkeley. His success against the Indians, his championing of independence for the unfree, and his call for the redistribution of wealth among property-less freemen inspired a large following. Bacon's forces soon outnumbered Berkeley's, whereupon the governor and his closest associates abandoned Jamestown before Bacon burned it to the ground on September 19.

Bacon died of dysentery in October 1676. Soon thereafter, armed ships arrived from England to retake the colony. By January 1677, Governor Berkeley was back in control, well on his way to executing the rebel leaders, and engaged in a process of (legally) plundering the estates of those who had opposed him. Bacon and his army had never proposed a revolutionary manifesto or a fundamental principle that they could cite as their reason for revolt, and their rebellion brought about no enduring reforms. Bacon had simply exploited the colonists' hatred of Indians, their resentment of those in power, and the class fissures in Virginia society to challenge those at the top. With the military support of the English government, Berkeley and his loyalists easily put down the unraveling mutiny after its leader's death.

The resolution of Bacon's Rebellion was part of a long-term social process, not the result of enacted reforms. As slavery became more entrenched in Virginia, the demand for servants decreased, whether indentured or slave or free. And with the Indians, both friendly and hostile, driven deeper into the continent (except for a new reservation for some of them in the Tidewater), there was more room to expand the colonial settlements, thus reducing the pressure on land that had deprived the lower classes of that important resource. The formula was now in place for a democratization of society with a social division based on race rather than class, and so long as poor and middling-class whites welcomed it, this worked brilliantly for those at the top.

A wide franchise of white male Virginians, based on a broad distribution of land and a shared fear of a slave rebellion, brought them together in a common republican identity that had them thinking of the colony as their "country." This view of independence worked as long as Virginia's frontier was stable and while the British facilitated its economic success and tacitly tolerated local sovereignty. These were the accommodations at stake in 1754, when Virginia militiamen under George Washington triggered the French and Indian War. The Anglo-American victories over the French and their Indian allies culminating in the fall of Quebec in 1759 helped to sustain Virginia's independence, but they also enabled England's political leaders to clarify a robust imperial vision, which they were determined to pursue with less distraction and the dedication of additional resources.

There were signs pointing to Virginia's instability in the mid-eighteenth century. An important one was the dispute over what were called the Two-Penny Acts of 1755 and 1758. The General Assembly adopted these during wartime turmoil, when refugees from the frontier were crowding the roads over the Blue Ridge Mountains, "flying as if every moment was death," when the boundary between settlement and wilderness was contracting eastward 150 miles and more, when there were not enough militia to meet the prescribed quotas for Indian fighters, and when taxes had been increased to fight the war. Virginians felt they were suffering under the demands of government. The Reverend James Maury explained sympathetically to an English correspondent in August 1755, "Our people are loaded with debt and taxes. Money is much scarcer than it has been for many years. Our spring crops of wheat, barley, oats, and rye, have been ruined by an early drought . . . Some of our neighboring colonies have likewise suffered in the same manner and cannot assist us." On top of it all, the tobacco crop that summer, which was "the only medium of raising money," failed as well.

In order to provide some debt and tax relief, the General Assembly in October 1755 adopted "An Act to enable the inhabitants to discharge their tobacco debts in money, for this present year." Tobacco debts of all kinds could therefore be paid in (depreciating) paper currency for ten months, until the next crop came in. For example, the annual salaries paid to Anglican ministers—effectively a tax administered through the vestries of local churches—had been set by law in 1748 at sixteen thousand pounds of tobacco. (The law of 1748 was not implemented until 1751, due to its requisite "suspending" clause, which delayed, or suspended, its enforcement until the Crown had approved the measure.) Now this new act fixed the price of tobacco at two pence per pound, considerably less than the usual amount. Maury explained, "In my own case, who am entitled to upwards of seventeen thousand weight of tobacco per annum, the difference amounts to a considerable sum. However, each individual must expect to share in the misfortunes of the community to which he belongs."

The second Two-Penny Act, of 1755, which contained no suspending clause, was short-term debt relief in a colony where the highest spenders and biggest debtors were the great planters who controlled the General Assembly. There was also widespread anticlerical sentiment in Virginia and a tradition of lax religious practice and resentment of established religion. In other words, Virginians were being taxed to pay for clerics they had not chosen and might not want. Perhaps other Anglican clergy in Virginia accepted the 1755 Two-Penny Act for much the same reasons as Maury, but there was resentment, the more so since other legislation, which accompanied the law, issued £20,000 in paper money and another £40,000 five years later, causing an inflation and the further devaluation of clerical salaries.

Since the Crown had confirmed the 1751 act, it could be amended only with the king's consent. The governor and General Assembly agreed, though, that a "suspending" clause in the 1755 act would have obviated its whole point, which was to provide short-term relief to planters until the next harvest; by the time authorization could have been secured, the crisis would have passed. In any case, there was no imperial rebuke to this breach in 1755, because even though the clergy grumbled, they made no formal protest.

In 1758, another act addressed the same problem again. This time, the clergy did file a formal complaint, which led to an eight-year battle in the courts and a five-year pamphlet war about the Parsons' Cause.

The 1758 Two-Penny Act was, like the first one, a response to pleas for tax relief. One petition, from Prince George County in September 1758, noted that "by reason of the short crops of tobacco made this year, it will be impossible . . . to discharge . . . public dues and taxes that are to be paid in tobacco." Again, as in 1755, the petitioners sought tax relief, not an overthrow of established religion or the monarch's prerogative. The act passed the House of Burgesses on September 23 and received the endorsement of the governor and the council.

In the letter accompanying the law, Governor Francis Fauquier explained why he signed it even though royal instructions forbade him to endorse any law that repealed or modified legislation the king had approved unless it had a suspending clause. The people were beleaguered by war and drought, which created a burden too great for them to bear, he wrote. The law offered only temporary relief because tobacco was scarce, and the General Assembly and the people it represented were virtually unanimous in supporting it. He thought it would be a mistake for him, "an entire stranger to the distress of the country," to stand against the people he governed, and the law had a precedent in the one of 1755, about which there had been no official reprimand.

Clergy formally protested both acts after the passage of the second one, first in a petition to the Lords of Trade and Plantations: "By these several acts the condition of the clergy is rendered most distressful, various, and uncertain." They argued further, to Bishop Thomas Sherlock of London, that "it is not in the power of the assembly to break through the laws confirmed by His Majesty's royal authority," and attributed sly, if not rebellious, motives to the Virginia legislators, since the two acts "are made to commence immediately, and contain no suspending clause to wait the royal judgment and pleasure; and . . . are short temporary acts, made only for 10 or 12 months so as to prevent the possibility of the royal consideration of them whilst in continuance: the better to effect which purpose the same are either not sent over at all or at best not until very near the expiration of the same."

When Bishop Sherlock forwarded the clergy's petition to the Board of Trade along with his own letter, he was even blunter in assessing the General Assembly's motives: "It seems to be the Work of Men, conscious to themselves that they were doing wrong . . . To make an act to suspend the operations of the Royal Act, is an attempt which in some times would have been called Treason, and I do not know any other name for it in our Law." Virginia may once have been a "very orderly and well regulated colony," but now the colonists "seem to have nothing more at Heart than to lessen the influence of the Crown and the maintenance of the Clergy both which ends will be effectually served by the act now under consideration." From his perspective, the Virginians' rebellious "spirit" had first revealed itself in a 1748 act, "by which the patronage of all the livings in the Colony were taken from the Crown and given to the Vestry in the several parishes, and yet this act received the Royal assent." This was an assault on the royal prerogative rather than on the established Church of England, but also an entering wedge in the colonists' efforts to reduce the clergy's salaries.

After taking testimony and reviewing the case, the Lords of Trade supported the clergy and the royal prerogative. They judged the Virginia Two-Penny Acts "very unjust in the principles and effects," and signed by the governor in "direct contradiction" of royal instructions. They recommended disallowance of both laws and ordered the governor "for the future strictly to observe and obey" his royal instructions. The king in Council ruled accordingly in August 1759, but the simple disallowance was beside the point, because the laws had already expired, having accomplished the General Assembly's short-term goals. And the clergy lost their bid to have the laws ruled null, which would have meant that their salaries were fully recoverable.

There was a precedent, going back to the seventeenth century, that a disallowance, the equivalent of repeal, was effective only from the moment it was announced officially in the colony, which would be months after its issuance. But the planters interpreted this toothless imperial intervention as a policy change, a threat to constitutional liberties and local governance. From a more dispassionate viewpoint, the dispute was not at all a contest between Britain and its colony but a legal conflict between the clergy of Virginia and its planter-politicians, and the clergy were defeated both in England and in Virginia's courts. The "change" in policy was in the eyes of the planters, and in that sense the dispute was simply a product of higher financial stakes in 1758 than in 1755, which made the clergy press the constitutional point, and which expressed heightened sensitivities born of new and larger political contexts.

The king's ruling was followed by some of the clerics bringing lawsuits against their vestries for back wages and by a pamphlet war that raged in Virginia over the next five years. Landon Carter, one of the colony's wealthiest planters, struck the first blow in December 1759. In a response to Bishop Sherlock's letter to the Board of Trade, he denied his premises, accused him of getting the facts wrong, and diagnosed a hostile intent in Sherlock's inflammatory language, intending to alienate the "affections of the Throne from the Subject." The bishop had "misconstrued everything into an attack on the Royal authority," but on the contrary, Carter argued, the Two-Penny Act "was never intended to affect the Royal Act in any manner at all for any longer term than that in which the calamity subsisted." The Virginians had not repealed or revised a law that had received a royal consent; rather, they had suspended it for only a brief time in response to a natural catastrophe. This, Carter thought, was simply "common sense," a perspective shared by Lieutenant Governor Dinwiddie, who was otherwise no great friend of the colonists and hardly someone likely to betray the monarch's prerogative. Dinwiddie believed that Virginia's conduct was consistent with a "rational Constitution" rather than an abrogation of it, and a reflection of "a light which reason and justice dictate."

Richard Bland, another wealthy planter, asked what the bishop would have had the House of Burgesses do in the face of drought, crop failures, war, and the petitions of the colony's leading citizens. Not to provide relief in such circumstances "would have been treason indeed." Where necessity dictated, even royal instructions must be suspended to deal with the emergency: "This is so evident to reason, and so clear and fundamental a rule in the English Constitution, that it would be losing of time to produce instances of it." Bland expressed reverence for the British constitution but insisted that it was "rational," that it recognized reason, justice, common sense, and flexibility in the face of exceptional circumstances. There was no attack on royal authority, no suspension of the prerogative, and no treason by loyal subjects, simply a plea for the "tenderness and compassion" of a benign monarch.

Writing against these two was John Camm, rector of York-Hampton Parish in Williamsburg, whose salary had been cut by two-thirds in 1758. He mocked the planters as men of wealth and leisure who suffered significant financial losses only at "voracious and insatiable gaming-tables." But in court his arguments were overshadowed by the oratory of Patrick Henry, a young lawyer joining the defense against Maury, who had sued for recovery of his salary. Henry struck an inflammatory pose, and he had a sympathetic jury of New Light Dissenters "with not a Gentleman among them," as Maury put it. Fashioning himself in the rhetorical style of the evangelical preachers who stirred up crowds throughout the colonies, Henry played to the jurors' emotions rather than to the law. Maury reported that Henry said, "excepting they [the jury] were disposed to rivet the chains of bondage on their own necks, he hoped they would not let slip the opportunity which now offered, of making such an example of him [Maury] as might, hereafter, be a warning to himself and his brethren, not to have the temerity, for the future, to dispute the validity of such laws."

Maury thought Henry's harangue went over the brink of treason when he asserted that "a King, by annulling or disallowing acts of so salutary a nature [as the Two-Penny Acts], from being the Father of his people degenerated into a Tyrant, and forfeits all right to his subjects' obedience." If Henry actually spoke such words, he was taking a stronger stand for local rights and for Virginians' control over their own governance than others had yet done publicly, and he was at least poised for conflict and set on burning transatlantic bridges behind him.

The clergy lost their suits, but the planters felt beleaguered nonetheless. They were not, at least not yet, under assault by British officials, but people live, and arguments in politics are made, by perceptions, not undisputed facts. When economic self-interest is at stake, the contending parties can call on many constitutional, legal, and ideological rationalizations.

Similar debates about suspending clauses, prerogatives, the rights of Englishmen, and the independent authority of colonial legislatures were occurring in Massachusetts at about the same time as in Virginia. To the colonists the timing was no mere coincidence but, rather, a sign of an emerging pattern. The resolution of both cases in their favor encouraged the colonists not only to call for vigilance and warn against complacence but also to suspect that British officials were plotting against American independence, just as their predecessors had in the seventeenth century. They knew the histories of the risings in Maryland, Virginia, New York, and Massachusetts to defend the colonies' liberties against Indians, Catholics, and royal prerogatives.

In 1759, in anticipation of an end to the war against France, British officials shifted their focus away from strategy to administration of the empire as a commercial entity. As always, they valued the colonies most for their contribution to the empire's economy. Foundational laws of the 1660s, the Navigation Acts, which laid out the limits of legitimate colonial trade, included prohibitions on the colonies' export of certain goods to foreign nations and on the transatlantic transport of goods on any but English-owned and manned ships. For many decades, the only changes had been additions to the list of protected goods; Parliament added molasses, rice, furs, and copper to indigo, sugar, tobacco, ginger, cotton, and some dyes. To protect British manufacturing, Parliament also forbade colonists to transport woolens, hats, and iron. The Molasses Act (1733) helped British sugar planters by setting high tariffs on rum, sugar, and molasses brought into the colonies from foreign ports. Tobacco producers were also the beneficiaries of protective legislation.

Seventeenth-century acts had also established a customs service in America and laid out the law under which customs officers worked. Reforms in the 1760s generally aimed to enforce existing regulations by the tried-and-true methods of customs collection in England in order to raise revenue and fight fraud. This was the regulatory context— which included long-term administrative ambitions that had been thwarted by ineffective enforcement, a low priority on customs policies, and the distractions of an overburdened bureaucracy repeatedly challenged by war—for a conflict that broke out in Massachusetts over suspending clauses and general writs of assistance (open-ended warrants for the search and seizure of contraband goods).

Unlike Virginia, Massachusetts still had its seventeenth-century charter in the mid-eighteenth century. When the Lords Commissioners for Trade and Plantations objected in 1760 to a new Massachusetts act that regulated official fees, they did so on the grounds that it would require the suspension of a permanent law that the king had endorsed. The colony's agent in London, William Bollan, argued that it was simply a necessary response to wartime conditions. Moreover, the

> Province now, and at all times since their constitution, was formed by their present Charter, conceived the General Court was well entitled to the free exercise of their Authority, in making such proper laws as

the welfare of the province . . . in their judgment required, which laws
were to take immediate effect, that the power of repealing their own
laws, was likewise unrestrained, and that there had never yet been an
instance of a suspending clause being inserted in any Act.

In 1762, a committee of its legislature, the General Court, gave the
colony's new London agent, Jasper Mauduit, instructions on how to
address the issue, which was a deep constitutional one, not a matter of
merely one law or one set of regulations. They reached back more than
seventy years to John Locke's explanation of the transition from a state
of nature in which men were governed only by natural law, to a civil
society in which "the Liberty of all Men in society is to be under no
other legislative power but that established by Consent in the Commonwealth, nor under the Dominion of any Will or Restraint of any
Law, but what such legislative shall enact, according to the trust put in
it." A direct line led from Magna Carta to the charter of Massachusetts
Bay, which articulated the rights of Englishmen in the clear and consistent terms of common law. "No Reason can be given why a man
should be abridg'd in his Liberty, by removing from London to Dover,
or from one side of a street to the other. So long as he remains a British
Subject, so long must he be intitled to all the privileges of one."

The very nature of liberty and of an Englishman's rights were thus
embodied in his person and not in his place of residence. When a nation founds colonies, the committeemen argued, those "naturally" become "part of the State, equally with its antient possessions." How odd,
how unprecedented it would be if three centuries after the discovery of
America, ten generations after the founding of the British colonies, the
descendants of those who had established, cleared, and defended them,
those who had sacrificed and contributed so much to the wealth of the
British Empire, should have their liberties snatched away on the pretense that they were dependents rather than the civic equals of Englishmen who lived on the other side of the Atlantic. How unjust that
in a time of war, which was "protracted beyond what was expected," in
which Massachusetts had "readily complied with every Requisition
made for his Majesty's service," the empire they had bled to protect
might reduce its citizens to the standing of "slaves." "Nothing," the
committee argued, "tends more to the destruction of both" Great Britain and the colonies "than sowing seeds of Dissention between them."

The committee made it clear that it believed the power and right of legislating for Massachusetts "immediately derived from the Charter of King William and Queen Mary." By this charter, "it is granted, or-dained, and established" that all the inhabitants thereof "shall have and enjoy all the Liberties and Immunities, of free and natural sub-jects, within any of the dominions, to all intents, and Constructions and purposes, whatsoever, as if they had, and every of them were born within the Realm of England." The general case and the specific ap-plications seemed to them incontrovertible under the Massachusetts Charter, the common law, traditional rights, and contract theory—the four gospels of English governance.

Their governor had a "negative voice" under the principles of the charter. The Privy Council—a committee of the monarch's closest advisers—had three years to overturn a colonial law, but the king's ap-probation, expressed in the vehicle of suspending clauses, had no standing in Massachusetts, because the charter neither asserted nor implied that he had such authority. Traditional practice reaching back for a century had never introduced the principle, and in any case laws for assessments, rates, and taxes, such as the one in question, were by their very nature annual and thus could not, as a practical matter, be suspended until such a time as the colony submitted them and heard back from London. "If these are not to take effect until they have re-ceived the royal Sanction," said the committee, "they would often not take effect at all, for the time of their continuance, or the greatest part of it would be ordinarily elapsed before such sanction could possibly be obtained." In a time of war, as in the current case, suspending clauses would be not only inconvenient and impractical but also dangerous, bringing the funding of local military operations to a halt.

The Lords Commissioners apparently dropped the matter, as Mas-sachusetts appears to have implemented the law and there is no further correspondence on the subject. The committee, the General Court, and the men in Massachusetts who focused on the issue could reason-ably assume, then, a cause-and-effect relationship between the com-mittee's argument and the British officials' silence. But this assumption would have been mistaken, as subsequent events revealed. The com-mittee's argument and others like it were unconvincing to the king, successive ministries, and a majority in Parliament. The British impe-rial vision was of colonists as dependents, not equals. The logic that seemed so incontrovertible in Massachusetts and Virginia was, but for an absence of focused attention, dismissed out of hand in London, where a different calculus of authority was respected, which, the British believed, had been resolved in the seventeenth century in favor of a rebalanced constitutional relationship between Parliament and king. The locus of sovereignty was in London, and divided sovereignty, with local legislatures sovereign over what the colonists called "internal" governance and taxes, was an oxymoron in British constitutional theory.

The foundation of misunderstanding upon which amicable relations between the colonies and the empire were built had endured through the distractions of the Seven Years War. In London, there was no time for and no interest in the colonists' theories, and no comprehension of the constitutional gulf yawning at the heart of Britain's relationship with the colonies. In retrospect, we can see cracks in the structure, as the colonists themselves would soon begin to perceive. It did not take long for the foundation to crumble, but very few felt the rumbling underfoot in 1760, which seemed no more jarring than the tumblers that had rattled imperial relations from time to time throughout the colonial period. But by 1763, more people could feel the quaking.

Another, more serious controversy, which put Massachusetts colonists in conflict with each other as well as with British officials, arose in 1760. General writs of assistance that authorized customs officials to make searches for contraband goods without a warrant specifying the items suspected of being smuggled or evidence of their location had been issued during the war with France, and they were set to expire six months after the death of King George II. After his death in October 1760, sixty-three Boston merchants presented a united front against petitions for the issuance of new writs. An obvious inference was that they did not want customs officers snooping around in their warehouses, but they claimed it as a question of principle and rights. If British officials issued new writs, they would remain operative long after the war, expiring only upon the death of King George III, who was twenty-two years old.

The law case about these writs was complicated by the recent appointment of Thomas Hutchinson, already Massachusetts' lieutenant governor, as chief justice, an office to which James Otis Jr., the attorney representing the merchants, aspired. He blamed Hutchinson, not knowing that had Hutchinson declined the office, it still would not have gone to him. The case raised questions about law, about the merchants' trafficking with the enemy in particular and smuggling in general, and about the customs officers' methods of law enforcement. Jealousy, self-interest, and local politics stoked the flames. John Adams, at least, believed that the personal animosity between Otis and Hutchinson "produced a dissention . . . which had consequences of great moment." Hutchinson thought so, too: "Upon the Governor's nominating me to Office, one of the Gentleman's sons who was solicitous for it swore revenge."

Otis, arguing for the plaintiffs, claimed that the Massachusetts Superior Court lacked authority to authorize general writs or warrants, and that it would be an unconstitutional act even if Parliament had legislated it. General writs allowed any citizen, acting as a self-interested informant, accompanied by a sheriff and constable, to enter the home or business of any other, and this, he contended, was "against the fundamental principles of law," and that an act of Parliament "against the Constitution is void." Looking back on the case fifty years later, Adams recalled, "Then and there, was the first scene of the first act of opposition to the arbitrary claims of Great Britain. Then and there the child Independence was born."

Hutchinson ruled that if Otis were correct, the remedy was an appeal to the Court of High Admiralty in England rather than a civil suit in a Massachusetts court. He also noted that the Massachusetts court had issued general writs in 1755, 1758, 1759, and 1760 without challenge, and the practice had a long tradition in English law. He did not consider formally whether such an open authority to search, which the colony denied to its own law enforcers, should nonetheless be extended to customs agents.

Otis was arguing for a local nullification of unconstitutional acts, for the Massachusetts court to have at once a circumscribed and an enhanced authority. He believed it had no constitutional authority to issue writs, no matter what authorization Parliament and past practice provided, although it had the authority to rule parliamentary acts and traditional practice unconstitutional and thus void. This radical reading of the law, asserting local rights over the authority of imperial officials and Parliament, was neither sound nor consistent. According to Adams, Otis "asserted, that every man, merely natural, was an independent sovereign, subject to no law, but the law written on his heart and revealed to him by his Maker, in the constitution of his nature, and the inspiration of his understanding and his conscience."

When Hutchinson instructed the jury, he rejected Otis's novel reading of the law, his revolutionary doctrines, and his inflammatory rhetoric, and the jury ruled against the merchants. But this was a very unpopular verdict that did Hutchinson and the customs collectors no good in the eyes of the public. The merchants lost in the courtroom but won on the streets. Despite the restatement of the authority of general writs, the devices had become difficult to use in Massachusetts and were resisted by threats and violence that the courts and Parliament were powerless to stop. Otis's specific challenge to the sovereignty of Parliament in matters of Massachusetts law enforcement, no matter the nature of the alleged breach, was a novel public position that would become commonplace over the next decade.

In South Carolina, the opening volley in a heated dispute between empire and colony came at about the same time as those in Virginia and Massachusetts, and it too concerned suspending clauses and royal prerogative.* A new governor, Thomas Boone, arrived in 1761 with news that the Privy Council had voided the colony's election act of 1759 on the grounds that the authorizing legislation lacked a suspending clause. Since voters had elected the sitting legislature under the now disallowed act, Boone dissolved it. But when the legislature reconvened in March 1762, it declined the governor's demand to adopt a new election law that was more specific about forms, less "loose and general," and contained the requisite suspending clause. Boone retaliated by refusing to swear into office Christopher Gadsden, a member of the legislature who had been chosen at a special election, and in September he dissolved the legislature again.

Voters reelected nearly all of the same legislators, including Gadsden,

---

* "Royal prerogative" refers to the administrative powers of the monarch, which include the customary authority, privileges, and immunities recognized by the common law.

and when they convened anew in November, they adopted a resolution denouncing Boone for his "precipitate, unadvised and prejudiced procedure." He replied that he had absolute power "of adjourning, proroguing or dissolving an assembly, abruptly, precipitately, unadvisedly, for a good, insufficient or no reason at all." After a further exchange of hostile messages, the assembly voted in December to have nothing more to do with the governor. Nonetheless, the feud continued through May 1764, when Boone sailed to England, purportedly on a leave of absence but in fact never to return. The final shot came from the assembly—it refused to authorize payment of the governor's back salary.

The confluence of multiple challenges to laws with no suspending clauses suggests a decision, made by we don't know whom, to assert Britain's imperial authority more strongly and less flexibly. But the architects of the policy evidently underestimated the will of the North American colonists, or at the least they misjudged the colonists' sense of independence, if that even crossed their minds. They simply saw gains to be made by bringing enforcement into line with policy and regulations and did not consider the American colonists' opinions any more seriously than those of the Hindus of Bengal or West Indian slaves. The British Empire clearly had authority, sovereignty unquestionably lay in Parliament, and the bureaucracy was responsible for administering what now, in light of the victories of the 1740s and 1750s, was going to be the largest, most powerful, and geographically most extensive empire in the world.

Before the victories at Plassey and Quebec, North America had been a locus of Britain's military and territorial competition with France that had secondary commercial dimensions. India had been principally a site of commercial contestation between two companies backed by their state patrons; after Clive's victory at Plassey, it was but one focal point in a global struggle for dominance between two heavily militarized nations prodded by mercantile interests. Competition that had once been all about profits now had political goals as well; the two empires focused on the conquest of India and on territorial aggrandizement under state control. The contest was still about profits, but now also about state sovereignty over territory and indigenous peoples. By

1763, there was no European power to challenge the British Empire in North America, and India was ripe for the plucking. On his deathbed in 1763, the Earl of Granville could say with pride, "This [the Seven Years War] has been the most glorious war and the most triumphant peace that England ever knew." Had he lived past 1763, he would not have basked in the peace.

Britain's comparative wealth and strength was as decisive as its military victories over France in India and North America. France could not match England's naval interventions in Bengal and on the Coromandel Coast during the 1750s or its ability to govern the territories under its jurisdiction in the 1760s. Once British leaders decided to administer India and regulate the East India Company, they filled the political void created by the disintegration of the Mogul Empire and France's withdrawal. Making a reinvestment in India that neither France nor the Compagnie des Indes could afford, Britain left no opening for France's return. After a half century of commercial warfare waged both on the battlefield and in the marketplace, Bengal became the uncontested base of the British Empire's operations in India.

Within five years (1756–1761), Robert Clive had led the East India Company from a comparatively weak position to dominance over its European and Indian rivals. In 1763, it seemed to be entering a new phase of prosperity, with tea as the principal commodity sold in England and North America. But the company's tea quickly saturated the market, and it responded ineffectually to the changing market conditions; internal bickering became endemic. By 1765, the company's finances and the value of its stock were volatile, and Britain itself was deeply in war-induced debt. The East India Company was so essential to Britain's imperial economy as a source of state revenue and loans, as a stable refuge for investors, as an anchor for the new Indian empire, and as a spur to the economy that parliamentary leaders in three different administrations—those of Charles Townshend, Lord North, and the Duke of Portland—believed that intervention was necessary to keep it afloat. It was simply too big to fail. Parliament made three attempts (in 1767, 1773, and 1784) to reform the company's administration and return it to profitability, and the first two contributed significantly to the coming of the American Revolution.

Montreal fell to the English in 1760, the French failed to retake Quebec, and New France formally surrendered in September. In India, the British won at Wandiwash in the same year and the French surrendered Pondicherry in 1761. The British took Martinique in 1762, as well as Havana and Manila. By 1763, English political leaders aimed to conquer all of India, an even more ambitious goal than those they had for North America and the Caribbean.

The expulsion of French traders and settlers from North America emboldened the Anglo-American colonists at precisely the time they were beginning to feel constrained by Britain's policy toward them. They felt underappreciated in the imperial context, and at the same time they overvalued their own military prowess and mercantile potential. They could imagine being independent and separated from the empire at some vague time in the future, although a few radicals such as Patrick Henry and James Otis envisioned a quick transition. They began to interpret imperial policies through an ideological lens that made more robust governance seem like a plot to take away their liberties, rather than as the logical next step in a project, dating back at least to 1748, to bring coherence to a sprawling empire with profitable colonies in India and the West Indies.

If the Revolution was a battle for hearts and minds, as in John Adams's definition, the minds were at odds already and trust was half-hearted at best. This means that what Adams saw as a revolutionary process starting in 1763 was actually nearing its end. The colonists' century-long struggle to maintain their independence within the empire was on the brink of failure, which few politically active men on either side of the Atlantic anticipated in the short term but more and more of them imagined as likely at some point.

✦ PART TWO ✦

◆

Fits and Stops

7

✦

THE SPIRIT OF 1763

"Put us, say some, on the footing we were in sixty-three," Thomas Paine would write in *Common Sense* (1776), but he insisted that was not possible. The British had broken trust and could not heal the breach, no matter what a conciliatory Parliament might do: "To be on the footing of sixty-three, it is not sufficient, that the laws only be put on the same state, but, that our circumstances, likewise, be put on the same state; Our burnt and destroyed towns repaired or built up, our private losses made good, our public debts (contracted for defence) discharged; otherwise, we shall be millions worse than we were at that enviable period."

Paine argued for "Independence"—always with an uppercase *I*—and favored "independency" for the colonies, a status to which he believed the colonists had not aspired in 1763 and were still slow to support at the beginning of 1776. His characterization of the Revolution's beginnings was consistent with John Adams's idea that independence was a process that began in the 1760s and was completed irreversibly by 1776; Paine and Adams also agreed that Americans' ancestors had always acted independently and had risen up from time to time to assert their independence within the imperial structure. They both knew that the difference between independence and separation from Britain was clear to the colonists but too subtle for British officials and misunderstood by them over the century preceding 1763.

Paine believed that separation from the British Empire had made sense even in 1763, given the changed circumstances in the colonies.

Adams, on the other hand, thought it made sense in 1776 because Parliament and the monarch had imposed significant changes on the colonies from the outside. They may well have both been right, because both internal and external forces were driving toward separation. Long before 1763, many colonists presumed that they would one day be independent, but there was strong disagreement about the timing. "I have never met with a man, in either England or America," Paine wrote, "who hath not confessed his opinion, that a separation between the countries, would take place one time or other."

Paine may have been correct, personally and historically, but prior to 1763 most Anglo-Americans typically imagined that their national independence would come on some distant day, to be lamented or celebrated by subsequent generations. Separation from Britain was not the defining characteristic of the independence that they prided themselves on—and that British political leaders found such an unattractive feature of Anglo-colonial culture. To the British, the colonists' independence was an attitude, a swagger, a presumption, a way of life that had always colored relations between London and its colonial peripheries on the North American continent. They thought that at its center was an oppositional attitude that denied the realities of America's inferior standing and dependency, and the time had long since come to discipline the colonists in order to restore respect for sovereign British authority.

Richard Coote, 1st Earl of Bellomont, had experienced the colonists' independence when he served as governor of New York from 1698 to 1701. He faced the same defiance endured by his predecessor there, Governor Andros, by Lord Baltimore in Maryland, by Governor Berkeley in Virginia, and by other British officials who had dealt with the Americans over the previous century. In 1699, Bellomont lectured the assembly on New Yorkers' "Independance from the Crown of England": "You need not be told to what degree Faction and Sedition have taken Root in this Town, 'tis a thing so generally known." According to him, New Yorkers were pirates and smugglers whose behavior was the product of "Irreligion and Immorality," which produced a "long Habit of breaking Laws, which has introduced Lisentious and Dissolute Living."

Bellomont believed that evil men had seduced New Yorkers by spreading lies disguised as constitutional arguments against Parliament's authority to impose duties and limitations on trade. The colonists needed to understand that Parliament ruled for the entire empire, and these limitations benefited Britons on both sides of the Atlantic in a coordinated policy of protection for producers of raw materials and manufacturers of processed goods. In return for their obedience and the revenue provided by the duties on trade, the colonists received the "Protection of the Crown, and are under the best Construction of Laws, and . . . in fellowship with the best and bravest People in the World, the People of England; and they must be obedient to English Laws, 'tis their Duty and Interest so to be." Defense of the colonies during King William's War (1688–1697) had cost the empire dearly, and it was only reasonable that the colonists contribute through customs duties to defray those expenses.

During the eighteenth century, imperial authorities continued to make arguments similar to Bellomont's to indict the perceived lawlessness of the American colonists and their self-righteous beliefs that they were independent of the laws of England. Whether the issue was smuggling to avoid customs duties or opposing Anglican regulation of its outposts in America, the logic was much the same. As a pamphleteer wrote on the subject of "well ordering the interest of the churches" in 1713, "every one that breaks the Law, breaks from the Rule of his Duty and Trust, and in a degree violates the Power of the Nation, and Usurps the whole Legislation."

Resistance or recalcitrance in the name of freedom actually undermined the independence of the whole, he argued, and the colonists' thinking reflected a narrow, shortsighted view. The penalties of the law must be enforced, because "in the Execution of these Direful Sanctions and Penalties affixed to the Statutes, the Omnipotent Power of the Nation Revenges the Glory of its own Independence and Unaccountableness upon its Insolent Subjects." Contrary to the arguments of those who justified selective lawlessness, independence emanated from the imperial center and, rather than being defended by colonists on the peripheries of the empire, was actually undermined by those who claimed to act in its name.

A similar issue evoked the same logic in 1754, when New York's Anglican party sought to bring King's College (later Columbia University) under the control of the Church of England. The lawyer William Livingston argued the contrary side as "The Independent Reflector"—the inflated language being typical of the age. His was a call to resist the "open attempts of every cabal that would enslave the Province, or in any degree, abridge the civil or religious rights of the people." And naturally, if any religious denomination dominated government, the people could bid "Adieu then to liberty and peace! Adieu to private freedom and public independence!" Again, Livingston's ideal was that of independence defended and enjoyed on the provincial level. England was neither the font nor the threat but, rather, the seat of sovereign authority to which local Anglicans could appeal in their maneuvers for power.

Charles Bowler, an attorney writing from Newport, Rhode Island, saw nothing but danger in the spirit of independence, which he laid at the feet of Quakers in 1758. "Many of these people think themselves Independent," he wrote, and here he quoted Rhode Island's governor Stephen Hopkins, "'that the King and Parliament of Great-Britain, have no more Right to make Laws for us, than the Mohawks.'" Bowler believed it was important, "since this pernicious Notion prevails too much in this Part of the World," to distinguish between independence and liberty. "Independence is a Power to do what we please," he wrote. "Liberty is only a Right to do what the Laws permit." Wanton pursuit of independence could lead, in Bowler's opinion, only to "Anarchy and Confusion."

British officials could not have agreed more. A radical devotion to American independence could only undermine the rule of law in an imperial structure with the sovereign in London. The logic of Americans' independence was grounded in radical dissenters' devotion to liberty of conscience, which bound no one to any act of government inconsistent with his personal beliefs. This was not the logic of a constitution by which to rule an empire. And yet Americans such as John Douglas, writing from Boston in 1760, believed in it passionately; he argued against maintaining a large British military presence in North America after the Seven Years War because it would constitute a "Military Encroachment on our Constitutional Independence." This concept made no sense at all to officials in London.

Benjamin Franklin, always a prescient observer, understood the problem embedded in discussions of independence that did not distinguish between separation from the British Empire on the one hand and, on the other, limited autonomy within Britain's imperial structure. He also comprehended the material stakes in play when these constitutional abstractions were applied to theoretical cases. In 1760, Franklin put all his cards on the table, something he did rarely and warily, when he entered the debate over restoring Canada to France in trade for Guadeloupe, the prospect that William Burke, among others, had endorsed. "If the visionary Danger of Independence in our Colonies is to be feared," Franklin wrote, and here he was equating independence with separation, "Nothing is more likely to render it substantial than the Neighbourhood of Foreigners at Enmity with the sovereign Government, capable of giving either Aid or an Asylum as the Event shall require." If the British feared that the Anglo-American colonists might wage a war for independence, they ought not to leave France in control of Canada, where it would be in a position to support the rebels, who otherwise would be too weak to secure their separation from such a formidable military power as Great Britain.

What Franklin's sensitive ear heard was a distinction that others either missed or simply glossed over, which was that when Americans spoke of independence they meant freedom *within the empire*; when the British heard or used the word, they understood it to be synonymous with separation. And, he argued in his American way, "Independence of each other, and separate Interests, though among a People united by common Manners, Language, and I may say Religion, inferior neither in Wisdom, Bravery, nor their Love of Liberty to the Romans themselves, was all the Security the Sovereigns wished for their Sovereignty."

For Franklin, it was not the laws or the enforcement of them that kept Americans connected to Great Britain. The "spirit of sixty-three" was not an agreement or even an accommodation. He was right: The connection was principally cultural and traditional, but that was not a perspective taken on either side in past political struggles or one that would inform the conflicts to come. The relationship had also been partly defined by a common enemy, and that was no longer a danger once the British had wrested Canada from the French. As the colonists knew, the British Empire's military power could intimidate as well as protect, as it had, on the one hand, in Louisbourg in 1745 and Quebec in 1759, and, on the other hand, in responding to Bacon's and Leisler's rebellions at an even earlier time.

The disagreements were deep-seated and of long standing, back to the very founding of the colonies in North America. Relations had always been strained, and the British sense of them had not changed. The colonists' independence had always tested them, and the colonists' interpretation of the relationship rested on a uniquely American constitutional argument that was never taken seriously in England. The bond remained intact because the disagreements were tacit and the misunderstandings perennial, the relationship depending on the absence of overt constitutional conflict, which usually provoked direct responses in which the two sides drew lines in the sand. Paine and Adams romanticized the spirit of sixty-three, minimizing how greatly it was based on habit, idealization, and the presence of the French on the northern border. Change would bring theory and practice into closer alignment, but the changes were themselves misunderstood, and this helped hold the empire together for another decade.

Contrary to the retrospective constructions of Paine and Adams, transatlantic imperial relations were already tense when 1763 began and worsened in the course of the year. In October, the British decreed that beyond a certain line in the Appalachian Mountains the land was reserved to the Indians.* Then, in April of the following year, Parliament passed the American Duties Act, popularly called the Sugar Act, which challenged American independence by its renewed attempt to enforce old laws. What colonists saw as liberty-threatening changes, and imperial policy makers intended as law enforcement, simply exacerbated the old conflicts in new circumstances.

From the colonists' perspective, the record of British military oppression of them may have been exceeded in degree, but certainly not in kind, during the Seven Years War. Indeed, if it were not for the victory over France in 1763 and social developments over the previous century, the empire might have floated on the high tide of animosity that ran for decades after Bacon's Rebellion in 1676 and the revolts accompanying the Glorious Revolution. In Virginia, the British force that responded to Bacon's Rebellion should, the colonists thought,

---

* The line was determined by the location of the headwaters of rivers that flowed into the Atlantic on the east, and, on the west, those that flowed into the Mississippi.

have defended them against Governor Berkeley's heavy hand and corruption. The resentful colonists treated the soldiers as an occupying force, refused to quarter them, and displayed other signs of hostility. The last two companies of regulars had stayed until 1682 but in growing desperation, given how infrequently they were paid and provisioned from England, and given the Virginians' refusal to supply them unless they paid cash on the barrelhead.

And in the years leading up to the Glorious Revolution in Massachusetts, the British troops stationed by Governor Andros in Boston had caused major flash points in the imperial relationship. "*Standing Forces!*" complained Increase Mather. "A word not so very grateful to the palate of English Parliaments. *Standing Forces!* . . . Do they mean those that were brought a thousand Leagues to Drab [associate with prostitutes], Drink, Blaspheme, Curse and Damm. A crew that were every foot moving Tumults and Committing Insufferable Riots amongst a quiet and peacible people, and that without Redress upon frequent Complaints. These were the *Standing Forces.*" New Yorkers' experiences with British troops that put down Leisler's Rebellion were no better.

The harsh military discipline they witnessed and experienced led New Yorkers and New Englanders to insist, after 1689, on having their own officers, elected by the militiamen themselves, before agreeing to support British regulars in military operations. As New York governor Benjamin Fletcher explained during King William's War (1689–1697), "If you do not concede this to us you will find our soldiers very unwilling to march to Albany." Generally, it was brutal whippings administered in hundreds of lashes that inflamed the Americans' sensibilities, but even worse and more sadistic punishments were delivered on a whim. One lieutenant ordered a soldier who had committed an unnamed offense to be suspended "by the hand with a cod line clear from the ground only bearing one foote upon a sharp stake a long time, and afterwards tied neck and heels, and after that tyed up by the other hand as before, with his other hand and foote tyed cross behind him, and after that bound down with his back upon a sharp rayle or stake, saying that he would so punish him that he should not be able to earn his liveing if he lived but begg from Dore to Dore."

In the spring of 1709, the British committed to an invasion of Canada, which the colonists planned at substantial expense, and the

British then called off without notice. The slow ship that delivered the news of Great Britain's cancellation without explanation did not arrive until October, long after second thoughts had led the British down another path. Had it seemed urgent to tell the colonists the plans had changed, a ship could have reached North America with the news by July, but the message did not even leave London until late August. With no knowledge of the Earl of Admiralty's decision to redirect the fleet to Europe, for four months the Americans were left equipped, trained, and uncompensated by military strategists who clearly had priorities higher than they. The misspent funds would be recovered by higher taxes on the colonists, who resented them as much as they did the initial slight.

The following year, New Englanders had joined the successful British attack on Port Royal in a spirit of distrust and recrimination. And by June 1711, the Anglo-American force left behind to defend Annapolis Royal had long since succumbed to bad feelings as it lost more than a hundred men to disease and desertion. The remaining regulars and militiamen fell "verry often into disputes about command precedency and other nicietys, which creates a great many heats amongst both officers and souldiers."

When, after their Canadian victory, the British had planned anew for an assault on Quebec, the northern colonies were still eager to join them but considerably more wary in light of their recent experiences. They responded less cooperatively to recruitment quotas, and enlisted men were more obstinate in response to orders. In June 1711, when Admiral Sir Hoveden Walker's fleet of a dozen men-of-war and forty transports made port in Boston, he had about eighty-five hundred hungry men to feed and Boston was itself suffering from poor harvests and widespread hunger. A French spy who had spread a false rumor that a huge French fleet was on the way had also undermined the Bostonians' enthusiasm for the Canadian expedition. As a result, Admiral Walker had fewer supporters than he had counted on—and more enemies.

Bostonians were understandably reluctant to advance the admiral credit, and demanded cash before they would slaughter cattle to feed his men. The British found such behavior churlish and "a very great Mystery," but the Americans were calculating the British army's creditworthiness based on past experience. Only a preliminary loan backed by the Massachusetts Council broke the impasse before the food short-age resulted in violence. The loan was only a first step, but a rate of ex-change (sterling for local paper currency) agreeable to both sides was as elusive as the food.

Desertions from the British force were high, and its officers sus-pected that Bostonians harbored runaways out of hostility to British military discipline. The New Englanders were delaying every stage of the preparation, which led one officer to complain about the "ill nature and sowerness of these people, whose government, doctrine, and man-ners, whose hypocrisy and canting [complaining] are insupportable. Till they are all settled under one government . . . they will grow every day more stiff and disobedient more burthensume than advantageous to Great Britain."

Admiral Walker was prepared to blame the colonists if the Cana-dian invasion failed, and he did blame them for its late start. The flo-tilla of seventy ships with twelve thousand men sailed from Boston for Quebec on July 30, 1711. At about the same time, more than two thou-sand troops left Albany for an assault on Montreal. Upon entering the St. Lawrence River, Walker's fleet got lost in a thick fog, and during the night of August 23–24 the eight forward ships ran aground, with a loss of nine hundred men, almost all British regulars. At this point, Walker decided to abort the invasion and return to England with his surviving ships and men. Rather than blame the fog, he blamed the disaster on the New Englanders, who of course placed the blame elsewhere. They noted the arrogance and incompetence of the command, and the un-reasonable demands made by a military establishment with only a lukewarm commitment to an action that risked the lives of New En-gland's men and devoured its resources.

The first charge the British made against New England was that all along the colonists had been dragging their feet, because they made so much money in the smuggling trade with the enemy that it was in their interest to undermine the invasion. The second charge was that the expedition had to be abandoned because the colonists would stop sup-plying it after the losses sustained in the fog. Third, Walker reported, the New Englanders lured enlisted men to desert and then concealed them in their homes.

The colonists vigorously disagreed. According to Jeremiah Dum-mer, the Massachusetts agent in London, who published a reply to

Admiral Walker's accusations in 1712, never had a people more desired the elimination of such a threat as the one French Canada posed to New England, which cost New Englanders countless lives and much of their fortunes to defend against. "Never [had] any People fell into any matter with greater Alacrity and Application than these Colonies did into this, nor made a braver Dispatch. They heartily and instantly comply'd with all her Majesty's Directions, and perform'd even more than she demanded." Also, the colonists reckoned that the taking of Canada, and particularly Nova Scotia, would pay a windfall return to both Crown and colonies. So the charges against them were simply an attempt to shift blame for the misfortune away from the incompetence of the British army and naval officers to colonists who were not in London to defend themselves.

It was not only in New England that colonists and British military forces were finding fault with each other. Long before, and building toward, the Seven Years War, was a history of mutual bad experiences, which, as usual, each side interpreted differently. Americans who had ample contact with British military men found them bureaucratic, inept, arrogant, brutal, and stubbornly inattentive to good advice from people who had experience on the ground. The British soldiers thought the Americans were cowardly, disorderly, unpatriotic, impecunious, and provincial. The class prejudices of their officer corps encouraged them to belittle American officers and enlisted men, and the officers' sense of professionalism contributed to their utter disdain for Americans as fighting men or military commanders.

A striking example of this was occasioned by the experience of South Carolinians and Georgians when England went to war with Spain in 1739. The colony of Georgia had been in existence for only six years, one rationale for founding it being to put a protective buffer between the English colonies of North and South Carolina and Spanish-held territory to the south of them. Its founding governor, the former general James Oglethorpe, held that the best defense against Spain was offense, so for him the war offered a perfect excuse for an invasion of Spanish Florida, which he had wanted all along. In early 1740, he began to organize troops and to solicit men and supplies from the Carolinas. South Carolina agreed to help, but only if its troops remained independent contingents under their own officers, the only persons authorized to sentence and punish the colony's enlisted men, and only if South Carolina's officers had equal voting rights with Oglethorpe's officers on command decisions. There also had to be an accommodation on the division of plunder, and an agreement that the South Carolinians were free to return home after four months in the field.

From the start, there were tensions. The South Carolinians were appalled when Oglethorpe forbade them to slaughter the cattle of Spanish settlers without compensating the owners. Experienced frontier fighters among the South Carolina officer corps scouted the fort at St. Augustine and found its defenders in disarray and its ramparts in a shambles, so they favored a quick assault on it. Oglethorpe favored caution, consulted only with his own officers, and even denied South Carolina officers refuge under his roof during a rainstorm.

A fever weakened Oglethorpe over the summer, but his physical condition was the least of his problems during the siege of St. Augustine in June and July. He also lost naval support in rough seas, his provincial and regular officers squabbled, and militiamen were disgruntled because he had denied them permission to plunder. All this led Oglethorpe to order what became a disorderly retreat at the end of July. The argument became one over assignment of blame, and the candidates were the Royal Navy, the commanders, and the provincial militiamen and their officers. The recriminations were bitter and the campaign for blameless high ground was intense.

In the fall of 1740, a combined force under British command began an assault on Spain's possessions in the Caribbean. William Gooch, lieutenant governor of Virginia and himself, like Oglethorpe, a former British officer, led a contingent of thirty-five hundred colonists recruited once again with promises of plunder to be shared all around. Gooch's American Foot, as the force was known, was composed of thirty-six companies, each maintaining an independent identity and serving under its own officers; there was a company for each of the participating colonies and also subdivisions by county, city, and region for some of them. So it was not, in one sense, a united force but rather a combination of independent units that, by the standards of British military discipline, was unruly and ill trained.

The American Foot left Virginia for the British colony of Jamaica in October 1740. When they arrived at the staging site there, the British were not prepared to supply the men with tents and food or to integrate them with the regular forces that had already arrived. Instead, the British command confined the Americans to the ships they arrived in, where they had to subsist on short rations and live in tight quarters in blazing heat—a thriving environment for disease and disorder. The men languished "quite disheartened" and "dying like rotten Sheep"; a hundred of them succumbed during November and December. Quartermasters denied provisions to the colonial troops whether by requisition or on credit, mirroring how the colonists had treated British regulars in the mainland colonies.

The British command did not include Gooch in their council of war, and British officers disdained his men as low class and irregular, as mere "Blacksmiths, Taylors, Barbers, Shoemakers, and all the Banditry the colonies afford: insomuch that the other part of the Army held them at Scorn." For two months, until the royal fleet arrived in January, the American soldiers waited to get off the ships and to be integrated into the force, which was dormant in any event. Then it was decided to use them as deckhands on the undermanned British ships, so they were separated from their units and conducted under armed guard to their new assignments, which were certainly not those for which they had enlisted.

In March 1741, the despairing American militiamen sailed from Jamaica on the invasion of Cartagena, in New Granada (now Colombia), as de facto members of the Royal Navy under Admiral Edward Vernon; this was the largest amphibious assault in British history until the invasion of Normandy in 1944. About a thousand of them landed, but as bearers of supplies rather than as the fighting troops they had enlisted to be. Yet when the attack failed miserably, they were put high on the list of blameworthy participants. A report to the admiralty described "the wretched Behaviour of the Americans, who had the Charge of the Scaling Ladders, working Tools, etc., which they threw down on the first Approach of Danger, and thereby occasioned the loss of the greatest part of 'em." Another report discussed "the Americans in whom nobody had any Confidence, [who] run away as was expected. It must be allowed that hardly anybody, except the Americans who were without Arms, ever shewed the least Disposition to turn their Backs till they had Orders for it."

The contingent from Massachusetts lost well over half of its men to disease. A majority of the American troops never returned, being kept as conscripted sailors on the ships to which they had been abducted. For example, when HMS *Dunkirk* left the Caribbean for England in 1742, it had on board fifty-two colonists from sixteen different companies. Reports suggested that the Americans impressed in this fashion were subject to systematic abuse, given the prejudices against them among the English sailors and officers. Such treatment would not be forgotten, making it harder to recruit Americans for subsequent military operations, "especially, if, as I am told, we are not to expect any of those men, who were on the last Expedition, they not having digested the hard Usage of being Broke in Jamaica, and sent Home without a farthing in their Pockets." Although it is not known how many of the thirty-five hundred Americans returned home from the Caribbean expedition, anecdotal evidence suggests that it was far less than half, which is the way it was widely reported throughout the colonies. In October 1742, seventeen American officers, 130 able-bodied enlisted men, and 268 ill soldiers returned from Jamaica to the mainland colonies on four transport ships, one to New York, two to Virginia, and one to North Carolina. According to Dr. William Douglass, in his history of the *British Settlements in North-America* in 1748, of the five hundred men sent from Massachusetts to the Caribbean in 1740, only fifty had returned.

Americans recognized painfully the limitations put on their ability to work with the British regulars. "The strength of our colonies is divided," wrote one. "Jealous are they of each other—some ill-constituted—others shaken with intestine divisions—and . . . parsimonious even to prodigality. Our assemblies . . . mutually misrepresent each other to the Court of Great Britain . . . Without a general constitution for warlike operations, we can neither plan nor execute." A British officer stationed in Pennsylvania complained about the "villainy and Rascality of the Inhabitants, who to a man seem rather bent upon our ruin . . . than give the smallest assistance, which if at last extorted is so infamously charged as shews the disposition of the people in its full Glare." Another said, "It is the constant Study of every Province here to throw every Expence on the Crown, and bear no part of the Expence of this War on themselves," and yet another said that he "never saw such a sett

of people, obstinate, and perverse to the last degree." One British officer saw the colonists as a "Sett of people whose Sole pleasure seems to
be that of thwarting every Measure of Government, tho ever So beneficial to themselves." Lord Loudoun* complained that "they will give
you, not one Shilling, to carry on the War. They will give you not one
thing, but for double the Money it ought to cost." To Massachusetts
governor Thomas Pownall, Loudoun summarized: "'Tis the Nature of
the People to do all in their Power to pull down every legal Authority."

Colonists generally viewed recruiting officers as seducers of servants and slaves. "The whole Country Are Against the Regulars," a
British officer reported during the French and Indian War. "And in
Stead of Assisting a Recruiting Officer, Are at all times Ready to Lay
Stumbling Blocks in His way." Another, recruiting in New Hampshire,
reported, "I have had my party out in the Country but they generally
get Mob[b]ed; one of them was beat in the Streets the other Evening by
five Sailors."

Outright defiance included mass desertion when circumstances
seemed to the Americans to warrant it. The colonists also left the battlefield when their enlistments ran out even if in the midst of a campaign; after all, at home there were fields to till and crops to harvest,
barrels, beer, and shoes to make. And, from their perspective, they had
the right to do this: A deal was a deal. According to Loudoun, the provincial forces were "the lowest dregs of the People, on which no dependance can be had, for the defence of any particular Post by themselves."
Lieutenant Alexander Johnson described Americans and their militia
as "Naturely an Obstinate and Ungovernable People, and Uterly Un-
aquainted with the Nature of Subordination in Generall." Brigadier
General James Wolfe believed the "Americans are in general the dirtiest most contemptible cowardly dogs that you can conceive. There is no
depending on them in action. They fall down dead in their own dirt
and desert by battalions, officers and all. Such rascals as those are
rather an encumbrance than any real strength to an army." According
to General John Forbes, the provincials were "a gathering from the
scum of the worst of people." Countless other British officers had even
worse opinions of the Americans long before the French and Indian War.

---

* Major General John Campbell, the 4th Earl of Loudoun, commander in chief of
British forces in North America and governor-general of Virginia, 1756–1759.

By the mid-eighteenth century, news spread more quickly in America, and reports on the abuses of the British military were closely read and never forgotten. For example, William Ricketts, of Elizabethtown, New Jersey, was sailing his sloop home from Manhattan on June 7, 1750, with several members of his household on board, including a servant named Abigail Stibbins. As they sailed, they passed the HMS *Greyhound*, anchored between the Battery and Governor's Island. Its captain was on shore, having left in charge Lieutenant John How, who, with Gunner's Mate James Parks, stood watch. As the sloop passed, Parks, on How's order, leveled the swivel gun on it, waiting to see if Ricketts would lower his pennant in salute, as was the naval tradition when passing a royal ship. When the pennant remained aloft, the lieutenant viewed it as a hostile act "in Contempt of the Kings Colours." He fired a warning shot, which Ricketts undoubtedly heard but may not have understood, and seeing that the pennant was still flying, Parks fired a second shot on How's order. By this time Ricketts was a mile or more past the *Greyhound*, so it was a fluke that the cannonball tore through the mainsail and smashed Abigail's skull above her right eye, killing her.

The colonists, unwilling to accept the claim that the homicide was an accident, wanted a criminal trial. At a minimum, they believed that the fatal shot was another example of the British military's total lack of regard for civilians. How escaped such a trial, though, having been returned on another naval vessel to England, where he was tried and acquitted of the murder charge due to lack of evidence that anyone had actually died. It was in a context set by events like these that Americans experienced the impressment controversies of the 1750s as other examples of military callousness toward civilian lives and rights. When a naval vessel was shorthanded, it seemed as though the impressment gangs were just as glad to take able-bodied civilians as to search for deserters. The Knowles Riot* and others like it were battles in a century-long war between the British military and Anglo-American colonists that was heating up in the 1750s.

---

* In 1747, British commodore Charles Knowles impressed forty-six civilians in Boston. A riot ensued, the protesters ultimately numbering in the thousands. After three days, Governor Shirley negotiated the release of the men and Knowles left empty-handed.

All the same problems, all the same prejudices, and all the same recriminations continued through the French and Indian War as they had through previous ones. The colonists' endemic war profiteering and supplying of the enemy focused the conflict between the British political and military authorities and the colonists, the former viewing such practices as treasonous, the latter as resourceful entrepreneurship. The principal suppliers of French Canada during the war were the colonies close to Canada—Pennsylvania, New York, Rhode Island, and Massachusetts—which were also the ones most directly threatened by the French war effort. When the Royal Navy intervened to stop this trade, colonial merchants shifted their business to neutral ports and engaged in less direct smuggling with Cape Breton and Quebec.

In Loudoun's opinion, the Rhode Islanders were "a lawless set of smugglers" who continued, despite his best efforts, to find avenues for trade with the enemy. When Parliament adopted a law in 1757 to prohibit the colonies from trading to anyplace but Great Britain, Ireland, or another British colony, colonial merchants adjusted their practices to circumvent the new regulations. One strategy involved transshipping goods to Ireland and the West Indies;* others either skirted or ignored the law in various accommodations to wartime conditions. Not only were the merchants selling supplies to the enemy, but they also were opening markets for French produce. The French did not seize Anglo-American ships during the war, according to Lord Loudoun, because the colonists generally carried "lycences from the French Governors who refused them to none that applied for them."

The British governors of American colonies opened another avenue for trade by issuing licenses ostensibly to allow ships to exchange prisoners, a practice called "flag-trucing." Merchant ships could then carry one or more prisoners of war under a flag of truce for the alleged purpose of repatriation or exchange, but this was a cover for trading with French vessels and evading British customs duties. Governor William Denny of Pennsylvania openly sold such licenses, at first in small numbers for high prices, but as the value fell and the numbers increased, he finally "scrupled not to set his name to, & dispose of great

---

* Transshipping involved making port legally and then, often without even unloading a cargo, proceeding to a prohibited port.

numbers of blank flags of Truce, at the low price of twenty pounds sterling or under," some of which circulated as currency and were sold "from hand to hand at advanced prices."

This trade in blank licenses, with no names or dates, gave the owner maximum flexibility, including the opportunity to use them on a later voyage if his crew was not challenged on the one for which he intended it. When approached by a British naval vessel, the captain simply retired to his quarters, filled in the blanks on the form, and had it ready when his ship was boarded. In this manner, Rhode Islanders transported lumber and dry goods to French Caribbean islands, along with a few prisoners of war, and returned with molasses and sugar.

Another avenue was, of course, simply to sneak through Britain's porous imperial enforcement "under the pretence of being bound to Jamaica" but actually landing in a French Caribbean port and then returning with goods the crew falsely claimed to have brought from a British one. Forgery, purchased licenses, secret landings out of reach of British customs officials in American ports, and transshipment through neutral sites were customary practices honed in peacetime and adapted in time of war.

The merchants of New York, Boston, Newport, and Philadelphia all plied the flag-trucing trade at least as early as the 1740s, during King George's War, and simply continued the successful practice when the French and Indian War broke out in 1754. "Scarce a week passes," one patriotic New Yorker noted in 1748, "without an illicit trader's going out or coming into this port, under the specious name of flags of truce, who are continually supplying and supporting our most avowed enemies, to the great loss and damage of all honest traders and true-hearted subjects, and in direct violation of all law and good policy."

Smuggling and trade with the enemy were traditional practices of the colonists reaching back to the seventeenth century. They were not confined to a few renegades but reached across the entire mercantile community to include public officials, including the mayor and aldermen of New York City, New York's assemblymen, members of the governor's council, and the families of supreme court justices, lieutenant governors, and other public officers. The behavior was not predictive of a revolutionary-war disposition; just as many smugglers remained loyal to the Crown as there were patriots among them. Since merchants had always smuggled to avoid customs duties and to get around restrictions on trade, and since they had traded with the enemy in previous wars, they were well practiced in the cat-and-mouse game they played with the Royal Navy and the French fleet.

When French privateers or military vessels on the high seas took Anglo-American ships as prizes, the colonists considered it the unfortunate cost of doing business during wartime, but the danger was often avoided by one or another ruse. When the Royal Navy did the same, as happened with increasing frequency over the course of the Seven Years War, the merchants saw it as an unwarranted interruption of trade that punished individuals for practices that were universal among them. They expected the protection of the Royal Navy and resented its military enforcement of maritime law. Since their competitors, including the Dutch and Spanish, ignored the rules of war, they felt seriously handicapped when their British protectors turned into pursuers. The French were also more open to trading vessels from Anglo-American colonists during the war, when they were painfully undersupplied, than they had been in peacetime, when French regulations forbade trade with foreigners just as British maritime laws did.

By the time of the Seven Years War, the economies of England's colonies and those of France were closely linked, their patterns of trade were deeply established, and practices of wartime trade with the enemy were as long-standing in North America as they were in the Caribbean and India. As one New Englander wrote before the Seven Years War, "It is certain that the inhabitants of Canada do at no time raise Provisions sufficient to their Support, and that were it not for the great Supplies thrown in from several Neighbouring English Colonies . . . the King [of France] could not maintain his Troops in that wretched Country so that these People in their Marches to destroy one English Province, are actually supported by the Bread raised in another." And a British admiral observed during the war that the "vile Illicit Trade that has been carried on here ever since the commencement of the present War is really and still remains infamous and barefaced."

Another ploy was to use Spanish sites in the Caribbean, which were neutral in the war, for transshipment to the enemy. The tiny port town of San Fernando de Monte Cristi in Santo Domingo, on the Spanish half of Hispaniola, for example, was an infamous entrepôt where crews either loaded cargo directly onto French ships or transshipped it to

Saint-Domingue (present-day Haiti), France's port on the other half of the island. This was a bald challenge to the Royal Navy, as Monte Cristi and its Spanish environs produced nothing the colonial merchants wanted and had so few people that it would hardly pay to sell produce to them. All of the goods landed there were transported to French ports. In fact, even more brazenly over time, crews often transferred goods directly between Anglo-American and French ships in the harbor without ever landing in the Spanish port at all. At times in 1759 and 1760, there were more than a hundred Anglo-American vessels in the port; in 1760, between four and five hundred American vessels took on French sugar and molasses there. From Monte Cristi, American ships sometimes even carried cargo directly to London with forged papers authenticating their origin in British Caribbean ports.

Five years into the war, France was hard-pressed to supply its North American and Caribbean possessions. The British navy had largely succeeded in blockading French ports and capturing prizes that left Europe for the colonies. By the end of 1759, the "iniquitous" trade by Anglo-American "Traitors to their Country" was virtually the sole supplier of the French Caribbean, since British sailors estimated that not one French vessel had reached its destination there in more than eight months. Without American goods, the French could not have equipped the privateers that harassed British trade with North America. In August 1760, Prime Minister William Pitt issued a dispatch to colonial governors in North America about this "illegal and most pernicious Trade, carried on by the king's Subjects, in North America, and the West Indies, as well to the French Islands, as to the French Settlements" in Canada. By means of this illicit trade "principally, if not alone," Pitt believed that France was "enabled to sustain, and protract, this long and expensive War."

The French West Indies was helpless. Relief from France was impossible, according to Pitt, and Guadeloupe had already fallen to the English. Without American aid, Martinique, Dominica, and the rest of the French islands would fall in short order. As a result, the principal focus of the British Atlantic fleet was on intercepting American vessels rather than French ones. New Jersey governor Thomas Boone, who would soon be reassigned as governor of South Carolina, believed by the end of 1760 that "the Kind of Civil War" waged by the British navy against American shipping had largely crushed the illegal trade. By early

1761, Admiral Charles Holmes reported to Pitt that ships under his command had ended the practice. Both were wrong and underestimated the resourcefulness of American smugglers, who no longer even bothered to adopt the ruse of shipping to neutral ports but sailed boldly into French ones. The Royal Navy had failed to stop the smuggling. Evasions had simply become more complex, as one case showed: A commercial vessel out of New York met up on the high seas with a French vessel that had disguised its identity by flying a British flag. In response to the flag, the American captain hid his French pass—and then produced it when the French boarded his vessel and he learned the identity of his captors.

In frustration, General Amherst, commander of British forces in North America, emphasized that "there is the greatest Reason imaginable, to think that without Supplys from this Continent the Enemy could not Subsist their Fleets in the West Indies." Lieutenant Governor Cadwallader Colden of New York agreed that the merchants of his colony "consider nothing but their private profit." New York was not unique in this regard. Amherst made the same complaints about Connecticut and Rhode Island, as well he might have of Pennsylvania. It was particularly frustrating in light of his difficulty throughout the war in getting the Americans to supply British troops and support the British war effort in North America. The spirit of sixty-three was partly outrage, mutual disdain, and ongoing conflict in colonial American ports and on the high seas.

During the Seven Years War, the British government continued its efforts to bring the colonial governments under tighter imperial control. Defense of the royal prerogative was one dimension of invigorated law enforcement, insisting on suspending clauses in colonial legislation was a second, and a third affected judicial appointments. Colonists perceived these movements on multiple legal, political, maritime, and military fronts as a coordinated assault on American independence. And this interpretation contributed to their viewing other contentious matters through a filter of conspiracy theories that explained their pattern plausibly and that showed the connections among policies the British imposed after the war.

As of 1739 in New Jersey and 1744 in New York, royal instructions had authorized the traditional appointment of supreme court justices "during good behavior," which was effectively for life. But in 1754, instructions to the governors of royal colonies dictated appointments "during pleasure only"—an attempt to manage the colonies' courts from London. When acting governor of New York Cadwallader Colden sought to clarify the policy in 1761, the Board of Trade replied that good-behavior tenures would be "Subversive of all true Policy, destructive to the Interests of Your Majesty's Subjects and tending to Lessen that just dependance which the Colonies ought to have upon the Government of the mother country." In November 1761, the Privy Council issued a circular instruction to all the governors of royal colonies to grant judicial commissions "during pleasure only" and threatened to dismiss any governor who ignored the instructions.

In March 1762, the new royally appointed chief justice of the New York Supreme Court, Benjamin Pratt, petitioned the colony's legislature on the question of judicial salaries. Pratt pointed out that the assembly, having made allocation of the justices' salaries contingent on appointments to serve under "good behavior," was at odds with the governors' instructions from the Privy Council and thereby put the justices in danger of having to serve without pay. William Nicoll, Speaker of the New York House, replied that legislators were well aware of the danger that the justices would refuse to serve without pay and the judicial system would fail, but were also "sensible of the value of the essential Rights and security of the People."

The assembly buckled first, authorizing pay to the justices appointed "at pleasure" to go forward while it petitioned the king for redress. The Privy Council denied the petition, and the new appointment guidelines remained in force until the American Revolution. Simultaneously Governor Josiah Hardy of New Jersey defied the instructions and made his colony's supreme court appointments conditional on the traditional "good behavior" terms; the Board of Trade recommended his dismissal "as a necessary example to deter others in the same situation from like Acts of Disobedience." In January 1763, Great Britain's attorney general Charles York advised the Privy Council that instructions to the governors "regulated the mode of their [the royal colonies'] Constitution"—in other words, the governors' commissions and London's instructions to them had a force of law superior to that of laws passed by the colonial legislatures.

Another contentious matter concerned the long-standing British ambition to establish a bishopric for the Anglican church in America. The heterogeneous population in the American colonies and the animosity to that church of the Dissenters among them, whose ancestors had after all emigrated to escape it, doomed the effort to bring Anglican orthodoxy to the New World and thereby to curtail the colonists' "independency," but the enduring hostility did not stop monarchs and bishops from trying. In 1637, King Charles I had issued a fierce edict that put a clear limit on the colonists' autonomy in matters of religion:

> The king being informed that great numbers of his subjects are yearly transported into New England, with their families and whole estates, that they might be out of reach of ecclesiastical authority, his Majesty therefore commands that his officers of the several ports should suffer none to pass without license from the commissioners of the plantations, and a testimonial from their ministers of their conformity to the order and discipline of the Church.

The plan to have an American bishop of the Anglican church was another approach to the same end, and also as old as the colonies themselves, reaching back at least to Archbishop of Canterbury William Laud in 1638, who had thought to impose a bishop on the New England Puritans. In the early 1650s, there was an attempt to establish a bishop in Virginia and, in 1664, another effort to bring one to New England.

When King Charles II appointed Henry Compton bishop of London in 1675, the new bishop let it be known that he took a particular interest in the colonies: "As the care of your churches, with the rest of the plantations, lies upon me as your diocesan, so to discharge that trust, I shall omit no occasions of promoting their good and interest." Compton's office did not officially carry with it the authority to appoint bishops, but he had enough political influence to secure an additional instruction to future governors of royal colonies, and it stirred the colonists' suspicions for a century:

> That God be duly served, *The Book of Common Prayer as is now established, read each Sunday and Holy Day, and the Blessed Sacrament*

administered according to the rules of the Church of England . . . And our will and pleasure is that no Minister be preferr'd by you, to any Ecclesiastical Benefice in that Our Colony without a Certificate from the Lord Bp. of London, of his being conformable to the Doctrine of the Church of England.

It took much less than this for New England's Puritans to perceive an assault on their religious liberties. Pilgrims had fled the Church of England in the 1620s and the founders of Massachusetts in the next decade. At a time when they thought the Massachusetts Charter was under siege, and when Maryland and Virginia were on the edge of rebellion, Bishop Compton's interest in their souls was sufficient grounds for detecting a conspiracy between the king's government and his established Church of England to undermine the colonies' independence.

This unresolved issue continued to fester for the next century in New England, New York, and Pennsylvania, where there were few Anglican clergy or parishioners. From Virginia and Maryland, where there was a significant Anglican presence, Compton and his successors received complaints that colonists offended ecclesiastical law, had lax morals, resisted paying to support ministers, and exercised a chronic independence that defied church, social, and political hierarchy. That is why the Lords of Trade and Plantations had issued an edict in 1680 instructing every official in the governments of the royal colonies to serve as a vestryman in his parish, adding that "no vestry be held without him except in case of sickness, or that after notice of a vestry summoned he absent himself."

Outside Maryland and Virginia, the church's problem was invisibility rather than troubled administration. According to Governor Andros, in New England he had "not heard of any Church or Assembly according to ye Church of England in any [of] the Collonyes; their Ecclesiasticall government is as in their law bookes and practice most or wholly independant." In 1680, there was only one Anglican clergyman in all of New England and only four in all the Anglo-American colonies outside of Maryland and Virginia. Maryland had about forty parishes and half that many Anglican ministers; in Virginia, approximately twenty-six parishes were served by thirteen ministers.

But Compton had succeeded in establishing the authority of the bishop of London in the colonies and in recruiting imperial power to support his efforts. By 1700, the number of Anglican clergy in America had increased to sixty, of which forty served in Maryland and Virginia, but that was still an insignificant number for the Church of England in its colonial outposts. Archbishop of Canterbury Thomas Tenison and Bishop Compton petitioned the king to charter a missionary society to the colonies, and this was incorporated under the royal seal in June 1701 as the Society for Propagating the Gospel in Foreign Parts (SPG). Although its founding ideals were spiritual, its early actions took a political turn, and the SPG became, among other things, a lobbying group for the establishment of an American bishop. The missionaries' efforts, ineffectual on all fronts, were noticed by colonists wary of the society's real purpose, who suspected they might have the Anglican equivalent of Jesuit spies in their midst. The missionaries did more harm than good to their cause in this way, and colonists had good reasons to wonder what the governors were up to, since they supported the missionaries and obeyed instructions that the Anglican bishops had dictated.

For about fifty years, though, the persistent distrust did not blossom into outright opposition; there were only occasional bumps caused by overly ambitious or exceptionally ineffectual individuals. Between 1712 and 1715, Britain made a concerted effort to establish a bishop in the Middle Colonies, with agitation coming from Anglican clergy in both America and England, but after the death of Queen Anne in 1715 there was little sympathy from either monarchs or British officials for challenging the status quo. In 1728, when Edmund Gibson became bishop of London, he found, as his predecessors had, that his authority over the colonies was inadequate to enforce administration of the church there, so he petitioned the king to enhance his power. Convinced that any attempt to exercise jurisdiction over the whole body of the laity would be resisted "or would at least occasion great dissatisfaction," Gibson requested that the king and Council grant him a commission under the great seal, the direct authority of the king, to support such ends. The monarch granted his request, and on April 29, 1728, Gibson received "A Royal Commission for exercising Spiritual and Ecclesiastical Jurisdiction in the American Plantations" in order "to exercise Spiritual and Ecclesiastical Jurisdiction in the special causes and matters hereinafter expressed and specified, within our several Colonies, Plantations, and other Dominions in America."

Petitioners in the colonies who supported the appointment of an American bishop regularly alluded to the "mobbish" behaviors and antimonarchical sympathies that grew from influential dissenting principles. In 1725, shortly after the successful Anglo-American assault on Cape Breton, the Reverend Samuel Johnson of Connecticut petitioned the bishop of London on the subject of an American bishopric for his colony, perhaps with himself in mind as its first occupant:

> There is nothing apparently more evident, than that a regular Episcopal Settlement would be so far from promoting a spirit of Independency, that it would be the most effectual means that could be devised to secure a Dependence on our Mother Country; especially at this Juncture when we are so puffed up with our late success at Cape Breton, that our Enthusiasts are almost apt to think themselves omnipotent.

In 1741, Thomas Secker, archbishop of Oxford, adopted the same political logic to make his plea for strengthening the Church of England in the colonies: "Nor would such an establishment [of an American bishop] encroach at all on the Present rights of the Civil Government in our Colonies or bring their dependence to any degree of that Danger." On the contrary, he argued, the real threat of American "independency" came from the colonists who "reject Religion itself." For him, "dependence" on the British government was absolutely tied to ecclesiastical conformity within the established church.

Gibson's successor, Thomas Sherlock, bishop of London in 1748–1761, thought his predecessor's commission was too vague and in any event would have expired with Gibson's death. Sherlock argued that the only adequate resolution of the problem was to have the king and his minister support the establishment of an American bishop. What he got, though, was another commission and stronger instructions to the colonial governors to support the bishop of London and his representatives "in the legal exercise of such Ecclesiastical jurisdiction according to the laws of the province under your government," which included the specific injunction "that all laws against blasphemy, adultery, drunkenness, swearing, etc., be vigorously put in force."

For the colonists, this commission was another intrusion, another step, though it fell far short of its stated goal. In any case, it helped to create the environment in which Virginia's Anglican clergy appealed to the bishop of London and the archbishop of Canterbury to support them in the Parsons' Cause in 1760–1765. Bishop Sherlock's defense of suspending clauses and his argument in civil law against the Two-Penny Acts of 1755 and 1758 demonstrated the link between ecclesiastical and imperial authority that both Anglican Virginians and Congregationalist New Englanders feared. It was evidence of the very mix of church and state that led Virginians to trumpet the larger political implications of the Parsons' Cause, and that colonists in New England discerned in the actions of the SPG closer to home. As John Adams understood, this possible attack on the colonists' independence actually predated 1763, and the plan to appoint an American bishop had "spread an universal alarm against the authority of Parliament . . . If Parliament could tax us, they could establish the Church of England, with all its creeds, articles, tests, ceremonies, and tithes, and prohibit all other churches, as conventicles and schism shops."

Viewed in isolation, the American reaction to rumors about a bishop for them can seem overblown. But the political context, the temper of the times, and typical habits of mind assembled the news into patterns that supported conspiracy theories. The theories escalated the rhetoric, which raised the stakes of every successive conflict. Each conflict seemed more serious than the one before because it reinforced the theories, not necessarily because of its inherent qualities. The ability of the colonies to bump along in the empire was diminishing, as the molehills grew into a mountain, as the problems accumulated in changed circumstances that militated against compromise. Trust, faith, and connections frayed, leaving weakened ties, which could be broken by slighter tugs than it would once have taken to break an imperial bond.

8

✦

1763

THE COLONISTS NEED NOT HAVE feared that the British Empire would betray them yet again by restoring Canada to the defeated French. Prime Minister Pitt had endorsed the invasion of Quebec in 1759 in order "to avert all future Dangers to His Majesty's Subjects in Nº. America." In London, Benjamin Franklin had heard an economic argument for that course of action: "In Case of another War, if we keep Possession of Canada, the Nation will save two or three Millions a Year, now spent in defending the American Colonies, and be so much the stronger in Europe, by the Addition of the Troops now employ'd on that Side of the Water."

The British retention of Canada in the Treaty of Paris did indeed have a strategic and economic rationale, since it would, as King George III put it, help maintain the "security of our colonies in North America." Lord Shelburne, president of the Board of Trade in the spring and summer of 1763, dismissed the idea of trading Canada back to the French for Guadeloupe, which was "a trifling object" from a commercial perspective while North America opened "new fields" for commerce. According to him, "The northern colonies encrease population, and of course the consumption of our manufactures, pay us for them by their trade with foreigners, and thereby giving employment to millions of inhabitants in Great Britain and Ireland."

To be sure, France was not the British Empire's only problem in North America, but Britons on both sides of the Atlantic Ocean genuinely hoped that relations between Crown and colonies would improve;

they simply disagreed about what would constitute improvement. As Benjamin Franklin had expected, throwing the French out of North America did not bring peace to the continent. The Anglo-American colonists there were still surrounded, he wrote, by "wide extended forests . . . inhabited by barbarous tribes of savages that delight in war and take pride in murder, subjects properly neither of the French nor English." But at least the French Catholic "art and indefatigable industry of priests, similarity of superstitions, and frequent family alliances" would no longer influence the Indians. They would not be "continually instigated to fall upon and massacre our planters, even in times of full peace between the two crowns, to the certain diminution of our people and the contraction of our settlements."

Dr. William Clarke, a Boston physician and pamphleteer, shared Franklin's view, writing that the Indians had been "instigated by their priests, who have generally the chief management of their public councils, to acts of hostility against the English . . . The French not only excite the Indians to acts of hostility, but reward them for it by buying the English prisoners of them; for the ransom of each of which they afterwards demand of us the price that is usually given for a slave in these colonies." Both Clarke and Franklin thought that while the French were holding Canada, the Indians could "get more by hunting the English than by hunting wild-beasts."

Wary as they were, Clarke and Franklin were unduly optimistic about the greater potential for peace on the frontier without the French in the mix. Representatives of neither Indians nor Anglo-American colonists participated in the negotiations that brought the Seven Years War to a close in February 1763. Both groups had expectations, though, fears and dreams, and more issues unresolved than settled by the war or the peace. The Indians hoped that the French would quickly return to renew their battle for North America and that, in the meantime, the British would show them respect through the generous distribution of presents, as the French had; restrain their land-hungry, brutal, Indian-hating colonists; and close the frontier to further settlement. The tribes also had scores to settle with one another and competing claims they wanted to sort out on their own.

The colonists assumed that peace would bring them relief from the taxes they had paid their colonial governments to sustain the war effort. They also anticipated an unbridled opening of the frontier for settlement of lands west of the Appalachian Mountains. Speculators wanted a return to the British policy of giving large grants to favored land companies, and settlers wanted free land, with clear titles if possible, which they were eager to invest their lives and labor to farm. Both speculators and settlers expected that the British troops still stationed on the frontier under the command of General Amherst would clear their path of Indians.

Instead of reducing costs, the postwar settlement increased them to support Britain's expanded military presence in North America and to pay the interest on the huge wartime debt that had been the result of massive deficit spending. Instead of lowering the colonists' tax burden, Britain tried to add external taxes levied by Parliament to the costs of local governance. Instead of reducing the number of British regulars stationed in North America or devoting most of them to defense of the frontier, the size of the force more than doubled from prewar levels to seventy-five hundred after the war, many of them stationed in coastal cities. Instead of increasing trade, there was a postwar recession. Instead of the defeat of France reducing conflict on the frontier, another war with the Indians began even as the ink dried on the peace treaty.

There was no way to please everyone, but the British managed to provoke all sides. In April 1761, General Amherst had irked the Iroquois by issuing a permit for settlement at Niagara without consulting the Senecas. Then he had ordered the building of a blockhouse at Sandusky, a strategic location on the southern shore of Lake Erie, again without consulting local Indians. In August, Amherst reported proudly that soldiers under Colonel James Grant had destroyed fifteen Cherokee towns, "but also 1400 Acres of Corne, pease, & Beans, & has driven near 5000 Men, Women, & Children, into the Woods, where, if they do not make a proper Submission, they cannot fail of starving in the Winter."

By the end of 1761, the king had signed instructions that forbade further land purchases in New York, New Hampshire, Nova Scotia, North Carolina, South Carolina, and Georgia without specific permission in each case; the next year, the Privy Council voided Amherst's permit for Niagara. But the damage to Indian relations had already been done. The colonists were hopeful that the restrictions were simply war measures. The Indians hoped that closing the frontier to land grants and settlement was an enlightened policy for the long term.

Before he was relieved of his command, Amherst helped to bring another war to the frontier by his heavy-handed treatment of Indians throughout the backcountry. He had decided that with the French gone, it was unnecessary to facilitate Indian diplomacy by delivering gifts and supplying weapons and ammunition to the tribes, as the English, but especially the French, had done for so long. He favored "punishment" over diplomacy and "bribes." It was no wonder that the Iroquois were "uneasy at the coolness and indifference which they think is shewed towards them," as William Johnson observed. Johnson, who had been New York's commissioner of Indian affairs until 1756, when the British gave him that assignment for all the colonies, reporting directly to London, was an experienced frontier diplomat with good channels of communication. Now, he feared, "something not right is abrewing."

The British committed additional troops to North America for various reasons, one of which was to help forestall an expected French attempt to retake Canada and the Ohio Valley. As Johnson had explained in 1762, "Altho' our frontier Forts . . . may prove a means of retarding the progress of an Army, or oppose an European force, they can in no wise prevent the Incursions of the Indians, who need not approach them in any of their inroads, and can destroy the inhabitants and their Dwellings with very little risque." Since forts could not do the job, there would have to be another approach to bringing peace on the frontier and extending the imperial reach into the new territories that Britain had acquired by the peace treaty.

The Privy Council, consistently shortsighted and dismissive of American views, had not even consulted Amherst about troop allocations for defending the frontier against Indians, and it underestimated the general's arrogance and ability to provoke all parties in a frontier dispute. He never did take seriously the warnings that trouble was "abrewing" among the Indians and described reported plots among them as "Meer *Bugbears*, and can never have any other Effect than that of hurting themselves by making Us Treat them as Enemies and Withdraw Our Friendship from them." Amherst simply reasoned according to his own logic, without consulting anyone else's, that "whatever idle notions they may entertain in regard to the cessions made by the French Crown can be of very little consequence, as it is their interest to behave peaceably." He minimized the potential for war on the frontier, and the Privy Council continued to give a higher priority to other concerns right up until they heard that about three hundred warriors, including an Ottawa Indian called Chief Pontiac by the English or Obwandiyag by his people, had wiped out a British military detachment near Detroit and laid siege to its fort from May 7 to October 31, 1763. The war that ensued came to be known by Pontiac's name, although his role was likely more local and limited than the attribution implies. The number of Indians from various tribes participating in the siege of Detroit reached nine hundred during the fall. A letter published in the *London Chronicle* on January 14, 1764, describing Amherst as "the sole cause of the cruel war, which inflicts horror and desolation on our suffering colonies," was an exaggeration, but it was based on plenty of evidence. William Livingston of New York blamed that war on Amherst's "blundering and disdainful Conduct towards the distant Tribes." He was far from alone in that belief.

The colonists were no happier than the Indians. They suspected—rightly—that the British intended the hugely increased number of troops to protect the Indians from them; the Privy Council and Southern Department wanted to keep settlers from moving ever farther into the interior, where they would be beyond the reach of imperial authority and become more self-reliant and less dependent on British manufactures. They hoped to forestall potential rebellions in the colonies, which they believed were more likely now, and they wanted more outlets for military patronage appointments. North America was an ideal place to station officers at the rank of colonel, and the proliferating appointments there gave King George additional influence with members of Parliament. Stationing these officers in North America also minimized the likelihood of domestic protests against the size of the standing army, which British subjects traditionally considered a threat to their liberty. Of course, the price paid was that those same objections now arose among the colonists, who had the same fears and made the same claims to their rights as Englishmen. But members of Parliament and ministers in charge of imperial business did not take the possibility of protests in North America as seriously as they did potential unrest at home, and the king and his advisers did not bestow patronage appointments on any colonists, none of whom would have been deemed fit to lead British soldiers.

The job of drafting policy for North America fell to Shelburne, who drew from a number of sources—ideas espoused by Lord Egremont, secretary of state for the Southern Department; earlier conversations in which various commonplace approaches had been discussed; and consultations with other Board of Trade members. One of these was Maurice Morgann, who believed the colonists were "merely factors for the purpose of trade," and therefore the Privy Council should revoke their charters, and taxes on colonial trade should provide the revenue to administer them. Shelburne also relied, perhaps most of all, on "hints" drafted by Henry Ellis, previously governor of Georgia. This important figure, Egremont's closest adviser on colonial affairs, was now absentee governor of Nova Scotia, secretary and clerk of the Council of Canada, provost marshal of Grenada, Dominica, and Tobago, and likely the author of the first draft of the Proclamation of 1763.

The confluence of goals advocated by these policy makers was sometimes publicly expressed and sometimes reserved for private communications. There were those who believed, as one army officer did, that without the French in Canada it was imperative that garrisons in America "check" the British colonists. The colonists suspected as much. John Dickinson of Pennsylvania theorized that Great Britain "seems determined to fix upon us a large Number of regular Troops under pretence for our Defence; but rather designed as a rod & Check over us." Morgann advised Lord Shelburne that the French had

> already marked the proper Places for the stationing of Troops in order to awe the British Colonies. The Lines of Forts so much talked of before the war will restrain the colonies at present as well as formerly. The Pretences for this regulation, must be, the keeping of the Indians in subjection, and making of Roads, in which last Work the Troops ought actually to be employed, that they may be kept disciplined, and Hardy.

Morgann drafted for Shelburne's attention a "Plan for securing the future Dependance of the Provinces on the Continent of America," in which he recommended, first, that "the Military Force on that Continent be increased and stationed in East Florida, Nova Scotia, Canada and in Posts the whole Length of the Navigation between Montreal and the Mouths of the Mississippi, so that with the aid of a Naval Force, the whole of the Provinces shall be surrounded." Second, that "under Pretence of regulating the Indian Trade, a very straight line be suddenly drawn on the Back of the Provinces and the Country beyond that Line thrown, for the present, under the Dominion of the Indians, and the Indians be everywhere encouraged to support their own Sovereignty." And finally, "the Provinces being now surrounded by an Army, a Navy and by hostile Tribes of Indians . . . it may be time (not to oppress or injure them in any Shape but) to exact a due obedience to the just and equitable regulations of a British Parliament."

John Pownall, permanent secretary of the Board of Trade, drew on Morgann's hints and plan, Shelburne's memoranda, and other sources for his report on how Britain must dispose of its newly acquired colonies (Canada, East and West Florida, and the West Indian islands) and make an integrated plan for North America and the Caribbean. He proposed that, for the present, the land between the "ridge of the Apalachian mountains and the river Mississippi" should become an Indian reservation under the administration of the British army. The reservation should be open to trade, and any new colonies established in the acquired region "are not, nor will they for some time, be in a capacity to receive the full impression of this free constitution to its full extent, for either they are not inhabited at all, or by such as are under a legal disability of being admitted efficient members of the community so as to act in any judicial or legislative capacity. The form of government for the present therefore must of necessity be oligarchical." The plan was temporary and imagined a long-term evolution toward colonies that supplanted the Indians, who would, for now, be subject to British military discipline without being harassed by colonists flooding over the mountains.

This attempt to design and implement a rational policy governing Britain's newly acquired territories foundered on three intervening events. The first was news that war had broken out on the frontier in May 1763 and that the army was doing its best to subdue the Indians and control the violence. The second and third events, in August of that year, were the death of Egremont and Shelburne's resignation, with consequent discontinuity in the Southern Department, given the canceled meetings and the uncertainty attached to personnel changes. Lord Hillsborough replaced Egremont and appointed the Earl of Halifax to head the department.

There were no policy disagreements in the transition, but there was a perceived need for dispatch and movement on all fronts simultaneously. A rational plan was reduced to an executive order and a royal proclamation—the intended temporary nature of which got lost in the implementation and further distractions. As usual, the thought of communicating these policies to the colonists never occurred to anyone in London, so the colonists were left to imagine London's intent. From the policy makers' perspective, there was nothing surprising or controversial here, nothing that seemed to them a change in policy. If there had not been a change in personnel or if different people had replaced Egremont and Shelburne, there is no reason to believe that policies would have differed.

On October 7, the royal proclamation declared the form of government and rule of law for the colonies acquired in the war, dictated that there be free trade with the temporary Indian reserve west of the Appalachian Mountains, commissioned a military commander of the new territory, and empowered the British army to seize fugitive criminals (including escaped slaves and indentured servants) and turn them over to civil authorities in the colonies from which they had escaped. It would have been reasonable to expect that bringing all the new policies under the umbrella of one proclamation would clarify, simplify, and thus speed up the creation of new settlements and independent colonies. But the policy makers failed to mention the Illinois territory that Britain had acquired from France, probably because they did not know where and what it was; and in declaring that the law of England should prevail, they also failed to consider that Canada already had a legal system and that there would be contradictions between the two—leading, most seriously, to contested land claims.

As Shelburne had explained, and as the Board of Trade continued to believe, the overriding goal of these policies was the "true interest and policy of this kingdom, in reference to its colonies, either as that interest and policy arises from their nature and situation in general, or relatively to our commerce and political connections with the various nations and tribes of Indians now under your Majesty's dominion and protection." Within such boundaries, it was essential that governance of the old colonies and the new ones be guided by the same policies and principles.

The first copies of King George's Proclamation arrived in North America by December 1763. Its most famous clause, establishing a line down the crest of the Appalachian chain as Shelburne had suggested, aimed but failed to stem the tide of settlement west of it into Indian country. The line was not a new policy or intended to be a permanent one, but "fore the present" and an acknowledgment of part of the treaty agreement reached with the Indians at Easton, Pennsylvania, in 1757. It distinguished between the king's white "subjects" and the empire's Indian allies, who had sovereignty over their internal affairs but would ultimately become conquered peoples; until such a time, the line was meant to provide a mechanism for keeping the peace. But, as usual, the policy makers were ignorant of conditions on the ground and overly optimistic about their ability to govern across an ocean.

Terror had already replaced the seventy-five years of peace that preceded 1755 in Pennsylvania. Dreams of cleared land—"improved" and "productive" in the colonists' eyes—had already succumbed to waking nightmares of bloody harvests. Lightning strikes by vengeful Indian warriors could take out an entire family before their neighbors saw the smoke and responded only to find ashes and corpses. Not surprisingly, panic and frustration led to the murder of innocents, and racial bigotry infected all sides.

"No nation that has carried on a war with disadvantage, and is unable to continue it, can be said, under such circumstances, to be *independent*," Franklin had observed several years earlier. Pontiac's War (1763–1765) now showed that the treaty ending the French and Indian War had resolved nothing among the various groups—German, Scots-Irish, Delaware, Conestoga, Tuscarora, Seneca/Mingo, and various combinations of Iroquoian peoples—that contended for the backcountry. Indeed, the goal now was to terrorize, not just kill, enemies. Butchered, not simply dead, bodies littered the frontier. Warriors posed scalped and dissected children in the crotch of trees. They left behind the smashed skulls of babies, tiny arms and legs torn from torsos and strewn across landscapes, and naked, mangled corpses that they dragged into the middle of roads for maximum effect.

The Susquehanna and Wyoming valleys of Pennsylvania were home to Conestoga, Shawnee, and Delaware Indians—the last having been displaced from the counties surrounding Philadelphia. German and Scots-Irish settlers contended with these Indians, the Scots-Irish being more inclined to seize land without purchasing or even consulting absentee titleholders or Indians who also had claims. The colony's land office estimated that about half of Pennsylvania's quarter million whites had settled on land illegally. This is likely an exaggeration, but the figure expresses contemporary beliefs about the degree of the problem.

Pennsylvania settlers felt beleaguered on all sides—by sheriffs, Quakers, the governor and assembly, absentee titleholders, and Indians. They were not even sure that the British army was on their side, and they had no confidence that Parliament had their best interests in mind. Many lacked the requisite £50 freehold that secured the right to vote, because it was generally achieved by clear land titles, which they lacked, and they thought their region was underrepresented in the assembly in any event. Even in an honest distribution of representation by population, their interests would lose out every time to representatives from Philadelphia, Chester, and Bucks, the original and most heavily populated counties in Pennsylvania.

Different interest groups were all working, often at cross-purposes, to bring peace to the frontier. The Indians were even less united in their goals and methods than they had been in the past. In 1756, 1757, and, most decisively, at Easton in 1758, significant efforts had been made to achieve peace through diplomacy even as raids continued on all sides. In this last treaty, Pennsylvania had ceded the Ohio Valley to the Iroquois, thereby enraging the Delaware and Shawnee who lived there. The competing claims of Connecticut and Pennsylvania to the Wyoming Valley remained unresolved and a source of ongoing violence. Pontiac's War, which started as a response to the heavy hand of the British imperial administration, inflamed Detroit first, and its sparks spread the conflagration to Pennsylvania.

Measured by either body counts or terror, the Indians already appeared to be winning before the fall of 1763, when they took the war east from Detroit. The question for settlers was whom to blame for the violence on the frontier. Obviously, the "savages," but more generally the usual white suspects as well: Quakers, even though they no longer dominated Pennsylvania's government; the French, although they no longer ruled Canada; and British military and imperial officials who were responsible, so they believed, for protecting the Indians.

The settlers were capable of seeing any representative of authority as a "traitor to his country." It was not a rational response; they were lashing out against authorities who were as elusive as the warriors who disappeared into the forests before they could be engaged. Settlers in Lancaster County burned a Catholic chapel to the ground, insisting that "Papists" fomented Indian raids. In Reading, "The people exclaim against the Quakers, & some are scarce restrained from burning the Houses of those few who are in This Town." Like Catholics, French or otherwise, Jesuit or not, Quakers appeared to have a special relationship with Indians when they should have been acting "white" by helping to exterminate them.

As divisive as the rhetoric of blame might seem, it was actually unifying—against Quakers, Catholics, Indians, and, ultimately, the imperial authorities who were unable or unwilling to protect them. Settlers who once had been divided by ethnicity and religion became unified by race and region against a racial other, a traditional enemy, and against authorities who were remote abstractions, their remoteness being part of the problem. All these were restraining the freedom that the settlers had risked everything to secure. It was now, during the 1760s, as an aspect of their Indian hating, that colonists began to identify themselves as "white people."

As a political or cultural category, initially not so much a racial one, whiteness was fungible. Questions, inconsistencies, and tensions surrounded it. Were captives of the Indians, especially those who declined to be rescued, white? Were Catholics, especially French Catholics, white? What did it mean to be British if the empire did not protect white people from savages? If the racial loyalty of British officials or Quakers was questionable, was their identity as white liminal as well? Once a category like "white" was used to redefine identities, colonists began to reconsider relationships that had previously been clear to them if only because they were traditional and unexamined. Among these, what it meant to be British—or even to be American as a separate identity, rather than as a subcategory of British identity—was now unclear and subject to debate.

During the French and Indian War, killing Indian prisoners had become official policy. In 1758, Pennsylvania governor Robert Hunter Morris had offered bounties on Indian scalps. Famously, the garrison at Fort Pitt presented smallpox-infected blankets to Delaware Indians; "out of our Regard to them . . . I hope it will have the desired effect," an officer wrote. Also toward the end of the war, General Amherst told his subordinates, "I Wish to Hear of *no Prisoners*," by which he meant no Indian prisoners.

There *were* prisoners, however, because the settlers needed living Indians to trade for white captives. Difficult issues abounded here, too, because many of the Indians' white captives did not want to be repatriated. Those taken as children had grown attached to their Indian families, who also loved their adopted children as their own. Wyandots insisted that they would return only those who did not "have a mind" to stay. At the end of the French and Indian War, the Shawnees held scores of captives. Indians also believed that the captives gave them some insulation from whites who would otherwise attack them viciously and indiscriminately.

Pontiac was a respected man among the Ottawa Indians, perhaps a shaman, quite possibly a leader, but not the clear holder of a particular office or status among his people. He was a man of influence, but he neither caused nor led, in any strict senses of the words, the war that bears his name. He belonged to a group of people among whom authority was decentralized and whose identity was evolving as clear tribal groupings became increasingly muddied, given the pressure of settlement and the migration west and north of Delaware, Conestoga, Tuscarora, and Seneca/Mingo peoples. As many as one hundred thousand Scots-Irish and the same number of German immigrants pushed west during the first three-quarters of the eighteenth century; more than thirty-five thousand of the Germans had arrived during the five-year period preceding the French and Indian War.

Pontiac's War was deeply connected to all these changes—the bloodshed of the previous decade, the Indians' bitterness about France having abandoned the continent, and their anger at British stinginess with gifts and the provision of ammunition, blacksmith services, and medical care. Instead, the British "had treated the Indians like Slaves," according to the translated statement of one of them, and indeed the Senecas expected the British to "attempt inslaving them." Ohio Indians complained to British officers that "as soon as you conquered the French, you did not care how you treated us, as you did not think us worth your notice. We request that you may not treat us again in the same manner." Shawnees told a departing French officer that the British "tell us that they regard us as dogs, that they are masters of all the

Land, that they have overthrown our French father and they regard him as a dog."

In short, from the Indians' perspective, the British treated them with disrespect and starved them of needed supplies and services once provided by the French. The settlers confiscated scarce resources and repeatedly attempted to throw them off their land. The Indians came to believe that they would have to take what they needed, fight for what was theirs, and try to drive the greedy, disrespectful British soldiers and colonists back across the mountains. When the British commander of Detroit had a female Indian slave hanged in "the most Exemplary and publick manner," the insult damaged relations there permanently.

The British treated living Indians as conquered people who were fortunate to be spared. General Amherst had understood the insult he delivered when he withheld supplies to them in 1763. The Indians were "greatly surprised" and "disappointed" that the British "sett so little store by thire friendshipe." They understood that the British had conquered the French in war—but not that the British had conquered them.

In the summer of 1763, Indians launched a series of attacks on British garrisons—Forts Venango, LeBoeuf, and Presque Isle—and laid siege to Forts Ligonier and Bedford, then Fort Pitt, proving that they were not a subject people. In mid-July, warriors invaded the river valleys of Juniata, Tuscarora, Cumberland, and Sherman. Settlers fled the western edge of Pennsylvania to what they hoped would be the comparative safety of the central and eastern regions, and then ultimately back to the Susquehanna River and Lancaster County. From there, Edward Shippen, a prominent lawyer and judge from Philadelphia, wrote to his son in July that the refugees and residents of Paxton "must be in great Terror, night and day, and the Poor Familys that are come thither from Juniata & other Places, in great want of the Necessarys of Life." The British efforts to economize in their North American operations after an expensive war, coupled with the unbridled arrogance of their officers, backfired. It would now cost more, in every way, to master the frontier.

Instead of diplomacy, Amherst favored a war of annihilation. He instructed Captain James Dalyell:

It is my intention that you should act with the Corps under your Command offensively against the Indians, and, that No opportunity may be lost of Punishing them in the most effectual manner for the Enormous Cruelties committed by them, You have, by these Instructions, a Latitude . . . in Attacking the Savages and Destroying their Hutts and Plantations, [to treat them] Not as a Generous Enemy but as the Vilest Race of Beings that Ever Infested the Earth and whose Riddance from it, must be Esteemed a Meritorious Act, for the good of Mankind.

Dalyell and about sixty of his men died trying to follow these orders with a surprise attack on Indians who were not surprised.

Also in 1763, a wagon train carrying supplies to beleaguered Fort Detroit fell under attack near Niagara. The sergeant leading it died in the battle, and the Indians nearly wiped out the force of twenty-eight and the additional troops who heard the firing and attempted a rescue. Of these, about eighty officers and men died and twenty were wounded. Troops under Colonel Henry Bouquet suffered similar losses, forty-nine dead and sixty wounded, at Bushy Run, on their way to reinforce Fort Pitt. The relief parties eventually did bolster the forces at Forts Detroit and Pitt, and the stalemate in the war continued.

The British leaders' casual assumption of French influence on the frontier had some validity, but the influence was indirect and long-term. The Jesuits had had some success in converting Ottawas in the seventeenth century, and at least some of those conversions must have endured over time. At most, though, it was a Catholic influence, not a French one, that one could discern in the revitalized, syncretic faith to which Pontiac called his people. Similarly, the teachings of Calvinists, Catholics, Quakers, and Moravians influenced the "Delaware Prophet," Neolin, whose "Great Creator" resembled English ideas of a king. The "holy war" to which Pontiac called his people had any number of causes and appealed to any number of Indian groups with different religious traditions. As always, there was no Indian "side," no centralized Indian leadership, and undoubtedly as many perspectives and agendas as there were groupings that "followed" Pontiac or anyone else. The goal was to terrorize and kill white people, which Indian warriors did, except in the French settlements.

The British strategy was to secure the major forts—Pitt, Detroit, and Niagara; this would help to protect major routes from the North to Virginia, eastern Pennsylvania, Montreal, and Albany. General Amherst had no more than two thousand men to fight, as the rest of the seventy-five hundred he had in North America were tied down elsewhere, and there may have been a total of thirty-five hundred warriors fighting against the colonists, though not all at the same time. By the end of 1763, the war was deadlocked along the line between Detroit and Niagara; the British naval presence in Lake Erie was decisive in saving those forts. But small bands of between about six and fifty Indians continued to terrorize settlers across the frontier. According to an article in the *Pennsylvania Gazette*, "Never was Panic more general . . . than that of the Back Inhabitants, whose Terrors, at this Time, exceed what followed on the Defeat of General Braddock" in 1755. It is unclear how many settlers died at the hands of Indians in 1763—one estimate put the number at two thousand, a wild guess and likely high—but it was the psychological scars to the living that had the greater impact than the raw numbers of settlers the Indians killed.

Late in the year, Thomas Gage, now a major general, replaced Amherst as commander of British forces in North America. Gage was more open to advice and less disdainful of both colonists and Indians, and thus more effective in the transition, but the Indians had already fixed on an anti-British strategy and banked on return of the French to help them regain control of the frontier. In 1764, the British seized the initiative in the Great Lakes and Ohio regions. The Indians safeguarded their villages successfully but were now on the defensive. A contingent of soldiers under Colonel Bouquet recovered two hundred captives from Delaware, Mingo, and Shawnee tribes in the Ohio Valley and marched them triumphantly to Fort Pitt in November. The British congratulated themselves on having "reduced and humbled" the Indians, thereby preparing them for "proper Management," but the "victory" was more in the minds of the British than it was a military reality. Still, it showed there was movement from open warfare to negotiations as 1765 began. The war was still effectively stalemated: The British were unable to dominate the continent's interior and the Indians were unable to drive the colonists and the soldiers out of the backcountry.

A negotiated peace ended Pontiac's War in 1765. The Indians surrendered their captives in return for promises of peace. But the vengeful colonists did not feel bound by a peace negotiated with the British army, and they continued to kill Indians whenever they could. Virginia governor Francis Fauquier "found by experience that it is impossible to bring anybody to Justice for the murder of an Indian." In Pennsylvania and New York, settlers broke out of jail anyone charged with such a crime. All across the frontier, no authority could keep settlers from taking revenge against Indians. According to Edward Shippen, hundreds of colonists at any one time "appear daily in Arms, and seem to be in an actual State of Rebellion" against all lawful authority standing in the way of their single-minded efforts to exterminate Indians. There were not enough soldiers or sheriffs to protect the Indians or to enforce the law. Settlers along the Susquehanna River were convinced that no Indians were peaceful, that even those living with the pacifist Moravian missionaries, the Society of the Brethren, according to an official report commissioned by the Pennsylvania assembly, "have been, and still are, secretly supplied by the Brethren with Arms and Ammunition, which they the said Indians having an Intercourse with our Enemies on the Frontiers, do barter and exchange with them . . . and that there is much Reason to suspect the said Moravian Indians have also been principally concerned in the late Murders committed near Bethlehem, in the County of Northampton."

News of the Proclamation Line had incensed the already furious settlers when it reached them in December 1763. That same month, a contingent of about fifty Scots-Irish rangers rode into Conestoga Manor, near Paxton, and murdered the six Indians who were living there under the protection of Pennsylvania's government. Two weeks later, these Paxton Boys attacked the workhouse in Lancaster and executed the remaining Conestoga Indians whom authorities had moved there for protection. The settlers' goal was to annihilate these Indians and, with them, the frontier policies of the Pennsylvania government and the empire. According to the sheriff responsible for protecting the Indians from just this sort of attack, "A number of Persons to the amount (by their appearance), of fifty or Sixty, armed with Rifles, Tomahawks, &c . . . broke open the Work House, and have killed all the Indians there." It was, by all accounts, a bloody affair. According to William Henry, of Lancaster,

> Near the back door of the prison lay an old Indian and his squaw, particularly well known and esteemed by the people of the town on

account of his placid and friendly conduct. His name was Will Sock; across him and squaw lay two children, of about the age of three years, whose heads were split with the tomahawk, and their scalps taken off . . . In this manner lay the whole of them, men, women and children spread about the prison yard; shot, scalped, hacked and cut to pieces.

In 1763, there was strife in the forests of New England as well, but of a different kind. The Indians had been neutralized there, close to wiped out, and the withdrawal of French and Indian combatants resulted in a security that the region had not previously known during its century and a half as an English settlement. No longer was the region a borderland and no longer was it under siege. But the siege mentality was deeply ingrained in New England culture, since the Puritans had brought it with them from England and then amplified it with Indians, the French, and the devil on their doorsteps. It may not be an exaggeration to say that the Puritans, now the New Englanders, needed a formidable enemy to feed their apocalyptic ideology, their sense of themselves as a Chosen People, beleaguered but vigilant in anticipation of the Second Coming.

The immediate problem was trees, and the difficulty was with the empire, in which New Englanders viewed themselves as independent agents sharing the rights of Englishmen and profiting from the protection of the Royal Navy. Imperial officials had always intended the colonies to provide natural resources in traded exchange for British manufactured goods, and among the natural resources, white pines that could make ship's masts, pitch, and tar for the navy were high on the list of New England's potential contributions. (The other main source of wood for masts—the countries bordering on the Baltic Sea—was both inadequate and subject to wartime interruptions.) The first sawmill appeared in 1631, on the Piscataqua River, now forming part of the Maine–New Hampshire border, and the first oceangoing ship built by settlers, at Malden, Massachusetts, set sail in the same year. New Englanders shipped their first white pines to England in 1634.

British officials' expectation, which had been set out in the Navigation Acts of 1660 and again in 1676, was that the colonies' naval stores would be sold exclusively to the British government. But New England merchants, who by the 1660s were gaining control of lumbering and shipbuilding operations, did not abide by either the spirit or the letter of these laws. They pursued their usual independent course of selling to the best market, seeking the highest profit, and balancing exports with imports from their customers, principally in the Caribbean but also globally, from whom they purchased the commodities their customers valued most highly. According to correspondence received by the Board of Trade, in the 1670s that meant sending masts to "Guinea, Madagaskar, and Scanderoon [an Ottoman port in what is today Turkey]," among other far-flung places outside the empire, and to France even in wartime, whenever they got a better price there than from the Royal Navy, or whenever they could obtain more prized products than from British merchants.

The Massachusetts Charter of 1691 had addressed a number of the issues that always caused friction with British officials and that hadn't been dealt with in the original charter of 1629, revoked in 1684. It specifically addressed the central subject of New England trade: "For the better providing and furnishing of Masts for our Royal Navy wee do hereby reserve to us, our heirs and successors, all trees of the diameter of twenty-four inches and upwards at twelve inches from the ground, growing upon any Soils or Tract of Land within our said Province or Territory not heretofore granted to any private Persons." This white pines clause had seemed to its drafters clear, precise, and inclusive. At first New Englanders appeared not even to notice it, and they continued to cut and sell the trees just as they always had. The colonists were deeply involved in King William's War (1688–1697), the first of six colonial wars fought between New France and New England, and in any event there was no attempt to enforce the clause.

When the price of Baltic masts began to rise a few years later and recurrent European wars interrupted deliveries in the late seventeenth and early eighteenth centuries, New England's pine trees became even more important to the Royal Navy. Breaches of the law began to be noticed officially, but by then New England's merchants had already identified ways to make a greater profit from trees that were either marked for the king's masts or should have been: Before they were claimed by the subcontractors licensed by the navy to mark, cut, and ship masts, they could be sawed into lumber for the Caribbean trade and shipped off. Also, exceptions to the law were allowed for trees that grew in "townships"—trees that would become a town's shade trees—

and soon enough, fictitious "paper" townships arose in forests far from any colonial habitation. Timber merchants, with the complicity of the New Hampshire Council, which they controlled, and the Massachusetts General Court routinely established vast acreages of forest "townships."

In 1704, British officials had recognized that, lacking adequate sticks to enforce the law deep in New England's forests, they needed to offer carrots. So the navy introduced new incentives to support the trade in naval stores by purchasing them in bullion and subsidizing the prices. An "Act for encouraging the Importation of Naval Stores from Her Majesty's Plantations in America" also added sanctions—£5 for each offense and £10 for setting fire to protected trees—and tried to eliminate loopholes through which the New England merchants had always traded.

The 1705 naval stores act added rice to the list of enumerated products that colonists could ship only to British ports, and appointed a surveyor general to police the forests. The position fell to Jonathan Bridger, who sailed for Boston in 1706. He contracted out the mast trade to men with political connections in England, who, in turn, subcontracted the work to New England lumbermen. Ralph Gulston, a turkey merchant, was one of the first contractors. Although the price varied, a mast with a thirty-six-inch diameter would fetch about £150 in London but always more in Lisbon, for example.

About forty-five hundred of these massive poles reached the Royal Navy from New England between 1694 and 1775. As demand increased and evasions continued, Parliament adopted a series of laws to tighten the gaps through which the smugglers sailed. A 1722 law, for example, prohibited the felling of *any* pine tree except under contract and license of the Royal Navy. Nonetheless, New Englanders still sold masts in Canada, where they were undoubtedly "used in the service of the French king" during subsequent wars.

In 1708, New Hampshire adopted its own white pines act, which provided stiff penalties, but it was for show, not enforcement, as every member of the colony's council owned a sawmill, and no one could successfully patrol the colony's vast stretches of forest; arrests were random acts and a woodsman's bad luck. Judges and juries in the lumbering districts were themselves concerned in the business, so the surveyor general and his deputies were repeatedly frustrated in their attempts to make examples of those they did catch in the act of pilfering what were, after all, the king's masts. According to the surveyor general, New England judges "acted more like attorneys against the Crown." As the lumber industry expanded, stretching into what later became Vermont and continuing strong in Massachusetts (which still included what are now Maine and New Hampshire), the capacity of the Board of Trade to enforce policy diminished even more.

It was not clear that the Lords of Trade were even paying attention. Their institutional lethargy, frequent turnovers in personnel, and ignorance of geography, pertinent laws, and the industry they were supposed to be regulating all contributed to a situation that New Englanders could easily interpret as independence for them, no matter the letter of the law. The impotency of officials on the ground also facilitated the disregard for laws. Enforcement was a game of hide-and-seek that the colonists generally won even when they were caught. As Bridger had explained in a letter of March 29, 1709, to the Earl of Sunderland, secretary of state to Queen Anne, "There is a great spoyle made in her Majties: Woods by the Inhabitants and tis out of my power singly to restraine it having noe Deputies to Assist me. The Woods are large and of great extent. Neither can I be at two places together . . . My salary is but two hundred a year my Travailing Charges is but little less, for I cannot move from one place to another without a guard." If Bridger survived the Indians, "who Daily Committ Murders, Ravages, and take Captives," juries "accquited them for, all the People here are Equally guilty."

A persistent feud between Surveyor General David Dunbar and New Hampshire and Massachusetts governor Jonathan Belcher came to a head in 1734, when Dunbar seized a half million board feet of planking at a mill in Exeter (now in New Hampshire). According to James Pittman, one of the fifteen deputies hired to guard the seized lumber, he and some of the others were preparing for bed when "about thirty men broke into the Room . . . & did then & there Beat us & Dragged us about, & . . . pulled us out then with a clubb did knock him down upon the Ground giving him several blows with wch was in great danger of his life having rec^d several wounds, & lost a great deal of blood." The entire male population of Exeter turned out to take the deputies prisoner, thrash them, and drive them into the woods. Dunbar demanded that Governor Belcher support him against the people of Exeter, so

Belcher published announcements in Boston and Portsmouth news-papers offering amnesty to anyone "concern'd in the Tumult" if he swore under oath to the circumstances that provoked the riot. Not surprisingly, no one came forward.

Colonists continued to adopt ingenious interpretations of the Mas-sachusetts Charter and the successive laws proscribing the harvesting of white pines except for the British Navy. For example, vice-admiralty judge Robert Auchmuty interpreted the Massachusetts Charter to ap-ply only to pines that were at least twenty-four inches in diameter *in 1690*, before the charter's adoption, and not to ones that reached that size later. This outrageous reading well demonstrated the sharp deal-ing for which New Englanders were already infamous. Everyone who had business experience with them knew that you had to frame a con-tract with a New Englander very carefully.

In the same year as the failed seizure of white boards in Exeter, the famous case of *Frost v. Leighton* displayed just how independent New Englanders were. In 1730, the Crown had licensed Ralph Gulston to cut and deliver a stated number of white pine masts from the colonies. Gulston sent his license to Samuel Waldo of Boston, who hired Wil-liam Leighton to cut down the trees and convey the masts to shore for transport. But before that happened, Surveyor Dunbar had to approve and mark trees that conformed to the contract and to existing law. In apparent compliance with these regulations, Leighton felled six great white pines on the land of John Frost during the winter of 1733–1734, but he did so without Frost's consent and without offering to pay for these trees or for the other ninety-one that had to be cut down to make a path for dragging the six masts out of the forest. In March 1734, Frost brought suit against Leighton in York County, Massachusetts, alleging these facts.

Leighton pleaded in defense that the six trees belonged to the Crown under the white pines provision of the Massachusetts Charter of 1691, that he had a valid license to fell them, that the Crown's ownership in-cluded the right to cut down as many trees as were necessary to clear a path, and that he had felled only the absolute minimum necessary to comply with the contract and the law. The court awarded Frost £121 damages, a judgment the Massachusetts Superior Court sustained on appeal, at which point Leighton, the subcontractor, appealed to the Privy Council in England.

The Privy Council ordered a refund of the damages and costs, and a retrial in which written records were kept that would enable it to review the facts and the law in the case. But Frost refused to repay Leighton the £121 and the Superior Court declined to enforce this, even after a second order from the Privy Council in 1739. In October 1743, nine years after the events and original action, and in response to a third order from the Privy Council, the Superior Court ordered its clerk to deliver to Frost a copy of the summons that had ordered him to refund the damages and costs to Leighton.* The question of law remained unsettled, so the lesson learned was that any such removal of trees even in compliance with the letter of the law could result in a decade of litigation, court costs, and no profit for the efforts of a licensed subcontractor. The case also demonstrated the willingness of New England officials to ignore the authority of Britain's highest judicial and legislative bodies.

Over the remaining thirty years before the Revolution, few serious attempts were made to enforce the White Pines Acts. Sometimes people burned the logs before deputies could ship or sell them. In 1753, Daniel Black of Middletown, Connecticut, was commissioned to "seize all White pine trees that you may find Cutt within the said Coleny also all Logs or other timber into which the said trees or Masts may be Cut." But when he tried to exercise this authority, he got tossed into a millpond and, he claimed, nearly drowned. Parties unknown stole logs on the Merrimack River in 1756, apparently sawed some into boards, and floated the rest out to sea. In 1763, the attempted seizure of logs in Connecticut and New Hampshire failed when local people threatened the deputies, who then resigned their posts.

In October 1763, the Lords of the Treasury recommended several changes in enforcement of the Navigation Acts and the various amendments that had accrued over the past century, and reviewed the general problem of administration of customs collection in North America. The Privy Council put these policy changes into effect with an order in council, an executive order issued in the name of the king. The fundamental issue was the revenue raised in customs duties, but the unen-

---

* There is no surviving evidence of repayment or that Frost was again served with a summons, though it does appear that Frost ultimately refunded the damages he had been awarded and did not ask for a new trial, as was his right at this point.

forceability of the White Pines Acts and Sugar Act of 1733 were also very much in the picture.

> We find, that the Revenue arising therefrom is very small and inconsiderable having in no degree increased with the Commerce of those Countries, and is not yet sufficient to defray a fourth Part of the Expence necessary for collecting it. We observe with concern that through Neglect, Connivance and Fraud, not only the Revenue is impaired, but the Commerce of the Colonies is diverted from its natural Course and the salutary Provisions of many wise Laws to secure it to the Mother Country are in great Measure defeated.

Smuggling and tax evasion had rendered ineffectual every effort to raise revenue and enforce the law. The tradition of disregard was by this time so embedded in relations between London and the colonies that it would take invigorated enforcement to reverse things, and that alone would undoubtedly provoke resistance.

Part of the problem was the poorly trained, unprofessional, corrupt, and woefully outmanned customs agents, who could expect no support from hostile officers of the law, and who could not possibly make a living without the bribes they solicited. The Privy Council recognized that "these our Regulations will not fully answer the end for which they are designed, unless, in consequence of your Majestys Commands, the other Departments of Your Government afford their utmost Assistance in support of them." This included governors, sheriffs, judges, and, most significantly, the British army and navy. It was ordered, therefore, that the

> Commanders in Chief of Your Majestys Ships and Troops in America and the West Indies are directed to attend to this object with the utmost care, and to make such a Disposition of the Force under their respective Commands as will be most serviceable in suppressing these dangerous Practices, and in protecting the Officers of the Revenue from the violence of any desperate and lawless Persons, who shall attempt to resist the due execution of the Laws in the same manner as is practiced in England.

Finally, the Privy Council announced its intention to design and implement a "uniform plan" for the admiralty courts that would free them from abuses and secure their independence from local interference.

The British Empire had periodically imposed other restrictions on colonial trade, including the Sugar Act of 1733, which levied duties of up to 100 percent on foreign molasses, sugar, and rum, the goal being to establish a monopoly on these products for Britain's politically influential West Indian planters. The duty on foreign molasses would have doubled its retail price, but as with other regulatory legislation, the customs service was able to enforce the Sugar Act only partially, intermittently, and differentially. In Boston, for example, it was traditionally collected at one-tenth of the legislated rate, while New York and Salem had significantly lower rates, reflecting what the customs agents, in their eccentric judgment, believed the market would bear. The total amount collected in North America in any one year before 1760 was never more than £1,000 and was sometimes as low as £100.

Foreign molasses was valuable as a barter item for the English colonists' own products, as their principal sweetener and the source for the cheap rum they distilled. Rhode Islanders found a ready market for their horses, foodstuffs, and tobacco in Dutch Guiana, which they traded for molasses. Molasses was cheap in the French Caribbean ports, even with the fraction of import duties that merchants paid in their home ports, because the French government restricted rum distillation as a protection for its brandy producers. The mainland colonies apparently imported each year somewhere in the range of three million gallons of foreign molasses in at least technical violation of the Sugar Act. If the British government tightened enforcement of its customs collections, it would undermine a flourishing, well-established trade that it had effectively subsidized by negligence. This changed in 1763.

In 1757, Governor Charles Hardy and Lieutenant Governor James DeLancey of New York had become concerned about smuggling and trade with the enemy, and when the Board of Trade investigated, it turned up no fewer than twenty-six reports over the previous twenty years. The reports confirmed the well-established patterns of illegal conduct but were less clear on the cure. Significantly, the reports had been saved and were easy to obtain, which suggests the seriousness with which lower clerks dealt with them, and also the impotence of the bureaucrats even to address enforcement. A 1750 *Memorial of the Sugar Planters* summarized: "Every Law must prove ineffectual, where the carrying it into execution depends upon those who are interested in the breach of it." As Governor George Clinton of New York had written in frustration a decade earlier, there was an "entire disregard of the Laws of Trade," which had been the case for the entire history of the colony.*

In 1759, having reviewed all these reports, the commissioners of customs argued somewhat defensively that "so long as the high Duty on Foreign Rum, Sugar, and Molasses . . . continues, the running of those goods . . . will be unavoidable." The implication was clear: Any effort to collect duties must be accompanied by a reduction in rates to a level that the market and international competition would bear. Their second point was that bonds on "the legal discharge of cargoes" must be vacated within eighteen months of sailing, but enforcement would remain ineffectual as long as "these prosecutions must be carried on in the ordinary course of proceeding in the Colonies, where it is apprehended, that Verdicts, upon points of this Nature, are not so impartial as in England." In other words, independent admiralty courts would be essential.

This 1759 report was close at hand when a proposal for lower rates on sugar and molasses came before Parliament in March 1763. In April, Parliament authorized use of the Royal Navy as an enforcement arm of the customs service. Eight warships and twelve armed sloops would support the tax collectors in North America, their captains empowered "to seize and proceed to condemnation of all such Ships and Vessels as you shall find offending against the said Laws," and to seize any illicit goods found on board. In November, the Customs Board sent a notice to all its officers in North America, warning of summary dismissal for failure to perform their offices in full—that is, for failure to collect the entire legislated duty on every shipment in all ports. General Amherst also received instructions to support vigorous customs collection with his troops.

* This is Admiral of the Fleet the Hon. George Clinton, who was governor of New York 1743–1753. He was no relation to and should not be confused with the American George Clinton, who was governor of New York 1777–1795 and 1801–1804, and the uncle of DeWitt Clinton, a later New York governor.

On February 23, 1763, Richard Rigby, an MP from Tavistock, wrote to the Duke of Bedford with news from London, and noted in passing: "I understand part of the plan of the army is, and which I very much approve, to make North America pay its own army." And indeed, in May Lord Egremont inquired of the Board of Trade, "In what Mode, least Burthensome and most palatable to the Colonies can they contribute towards the Support of the Additional Expence, which must attend their Civil and Military establishment?"

There is no record of an answer given at that time, but there are hints that the general point was already decided without dissent in London and that taxation of the North American colonies for the purposes of raising revenue was on the horizon. In September, the Treasury Board instructed the commissioners of the British stamp duties to draft a bill for submission to Parliament that would extend stamp taxes—fixed-sum taxes on enumerated goods, legal transactions, and services that required an official stamp—to the colonies.

9

✦

TAXES

ETTLERS IN EASTERN PENNSYLVANIA, who controlled the colony's assembly, favored low taxes and government support of the
Indian trade, from which they profited. Their main thought about Indians was that they were producers or suppliers, principally of animal
furs for the European market, and customers of manufactured products. The backcountry settlers favored higher taxes, which would inevitably fall disproportionately on the wealthier East, to help pay for a
vigorous defense of the frontier along with a vigorous killing of Indians, whom they thought of as murderous savages whose extermination
was an important step in opening up the frontier. After the two massacres of Indians by Paxton rangers at Conestoga Manor and Lancaster
in December 1763, this east-west conflict in Pennsylvania was hotter
than ever. Despite such deep disagreements about provincial taxes and
the nature of Indians, though, the colonists could be driven to agreement, and even to collaboration, by British policies on Indians and by
British taxes to raise revenue in the colonies. And this is precisely what
imperial taxes and policies would do after the French and Indian
War—drive the colonists to unite against a common enemy.

On January 2, 1764, Pennsylvania governor John Penn, a grandson
of William Penn and the last colonial governor of Pennsylvania, issued
a second proclamation having to do with the massacres of peaceful
Conestoga Indians, offering a reward of £200 for the arrest and prosecution of the killers. This effort to get local sheriffs to do their duty
failed, for the power of central authority on either side of the Atlantic

in the backcountry was weak. The next day, Penn showed the council an anonymous letter warning that "Many of the Inhabitants of the Townships of Lebanon, Paxton & Hanover, are Voluntarily forming themselves in a Company to March to Philadelphia, with a Design to kill the Indians that Harbour there."

In response, the council applied to the assembly for funds to defend Philadelphia and decided to send the 140 Indians the colony held to New York, where, it believed, the Indians would be safer and would become somebody else's problem. On January 10, Governor Cadwallader Colden of New York wrote back declining to accept Pennsylvania's Indians, saying that they were the "most obnoxious to the People of this Province of any, having done the most mischief. They consist of a number of rogues and thieves, runaways from the other Nations, and for that reason [are] not to be trusted." Having been marched up and down New Jersey while awaiting the dueling edicts of the two governors, the prisoners were returned to Philadelphia's barracks.

On January 25, the council received a report from Lancaster that fifteen hundred men from the backcountry were marching on Philadelphia to kill the Indians still in the government's custody. On January 29, the governor ordered the Carlisle regiment to stand ready to repel this force. The assembly adopted and the governor signed a riot act, which authorized firing on British subjects in the event of a rebellion. On February 5, carpenters began to build a defensive fortification and the Philadelphia militia hauled several cannons into place.

Rumors flooded the city. Conflicting reports had the Paxton rangers attacking from the west or north. The invaders had crossed the Schuylkill River into Germantown, or they had not yet arrived. Different witnesses reported five hundred, two thousand, and three thousand armed frontiersmen. Merchants barred their shop doors and boarded up the windows. In a panic, the Philadelphia militia almost blew to bits a contingent of German butchers arriving to support the defense. Even some Quakers took up arms, which was an occasion for more ridicule than thanks from their fellow Pennsylvanians. Henry Muhlenberg, a German minister, was one of many who noted what they saw as bald hypocrisy: "What increased the wonder was, that the pious lambs in the long French, Spanish, and Indian wars had such tender consciences, and would sooner die than raise a hand in defence against these dangerous enemies, and now at once like Zedekiah, the son of

Chenaanah [1 Kings 22], with iron horns rushing upon a handful of our poor distressed and ruined fellow citizens and inhabitants of the frontiers."

The governor and council noted that "few or none of the German church people had attended to take up arms against the rioters." This widely observed fact led to rumors that the Germans sympathized with the Paxton Boys, which was largely true. According to Muhlenberg, the German Lutherans were angered by the Quakers' and Moravians' gentle treatment of the Indians and their giving of gifts despite the Indians' savage acts; and they were pleased that "the authorities required of our German citizens to fight with their own flesh and blood, their fellow citizens and fellow Christians, to keep them off or even kill them, and to defend the Bethlehem Indians."

Not only was there disagreement about the numbers, identity, and intentions of the invaders of Philadelphia, but reports of their actual behavior varied wildly. One German minister, Paul Brycelius, wrote, "They appeared resolute, warlike, and at the same time steady and decent." David Rittenhouse, an internationally known astronomer and clockmaker, described them as "scoundrels," who marauded through the streets of Philadelphia "frightening women, by running the muzzles of guns through windows, swearing and hallooing; attacking men without the least provocation; dragging them by their hair to the ground, and pretending to scalp them; shooting a number of dogs and fowls;— these are some of their exploits."

An anonymous Quaker described the Paxton invaders as property-less men dressed in blanket coats and moccasins, armed with rifles and tomahawks, who were rough, naïve, ignorant, but well-meaning, and had been "hired or persuaded to the undertaking, by persons, whose views and designs may, perhaps, in time, be disclosed." This observer thought "they behaved with great civility to those they conversed with— were surprised to hear that the citizens had taken up arms to oppose them—declared that they had no intention of injuring any one, and only wanted satisfaction of the Indians, as some of them had been concerned in the murder of their friends and relations."

Another panic swept Philadelphia on February 7, in reaction to new unsubstantiated rumors about the Paxton men. Negotiations ensued, and after long discussions between representatives of the two sides, the Paxton men agreed to go home and "the Philadelphians promised to give speedy consideration to all grievances, if laid before the assembly and governor in proper form." On February 14, the Paxton group submitted their Declaration and Remonstrance: "Nothing but Necessity itself could induce us to, or justify us in . . . an Appearance of flying in the Face of Authority." The Indians they had executed were "known to be firmly connected in Friendship with our openly avowed imbittered Enemies; and some of whom have, by several Oaths, been proved to be Murderers."

Yet, they went on, their own government continued to supply and protect their bitter enemies, which "were tedious beyond the Patience of a Job to endure." The Paxton men declared that these indignities derived from an underrepresentation of the backcountry settlers' interests in the assembly, which had allowed, in turn, an invasion of their rights as Englishmen. They cited a special law that denied them trial by a jury of their peers in their home county when any of them were accused of murdering Indians. The law had been drafted after it became clear that no jury in the western counties would under any circumstances convict a white man of murdering an Indian. Actually, as the government was finding, neither would any sheriff in the western counties arrest and transport a settler accused of murdering an Indian to the eastern counties for trial.

The ungovernable violence on the frontier and the colony's response to it revealed alternative regional interests, and the alternative views of justice and rights that rationalized them. The backcountry settlers would continue to believe that the Quakers, the Philadelphians, and the merchants of the older, eastern counties were sacrificing the settlers' lives, rights, and interests so as to defend the settlers' mortal enemies, the Indians, and therefore they had no choice but to act in self-defense. The opposite view was equally clear. A letter from Joseph Read, acting chief justice of New Jersey, captured much of the emotion felt by the easterners: "To have fallen on a Town of the Enemy *Indians* and to have destroyed them and it, might have terrified the *Indians*, and lessened the Number of our Enemies; but such an inhuman Murder as that at *Lancaster*, can only serve to convince the World, that there are among us persons more savage than *Indians* themselves."

The Paxton Rebellion became a popular revolt against authority, and when the settlers' demands were not met, their resolve was only strengthened. The Paxton men's seizure of the initiative united the backcountry and revealed fissures in the eastern establishment. Pennsylvania was now more vulnerable internally than it ever had been, and the fault lines along which established coalitions might crumble and new ones might govern had begun to clarify. The desire for social and political change aimed in two directions, against Indians and against the political status quo. If British imperial power were to step between the populist rebels and their targets, the internal revolt could become a revolution against Great Britain, which would be a common enemy to both sides.

Colonial charters dating back to 1606 had guaranteed that the subjects living in Virginia "shall have and enjoy all Liberties, Franchises, and Immunities . . . as if they had been abiding and born within this our Realm of England." The British colonial Naturalization Act of 1740 had extended the same rights and privileges to naturalized subjects living in the colonies. So colonists staked their general claims to independence within the empire on such specific guarantees of their rights as Englishmen and on their historical experience.

Before the English Revolution, it was plausible to argue that the monarch alone governed the colonies exclusively through his royal prerogative. In 1649, though, the revolutionary Rump Parliament had declared that "the People of England, and of all the Dominions and Territories thereunto belonging . . . shall from henceforth be Governed . . . by the Supreme Authority of this Nation, The Representatives of the People in Parliament." Laws followed in the 1650s, 1660s, and 1670s regulating trade, navigation, and manufacturing within the empire. Parliament was clearly asserting its authority over the colonies, and it was confirmed by the settlement associated with the Glorious Revolution in 1689 and the succession of William and Mary.

In 1764, Lord Grenville acknowledged that Parliament had, as a matter of policy, never attempted to raise revenue from the colonies. Customs duties, for example, had never returned as much as £2,000 from the colonies in any one year and cost between £7,000 and £8,000 yearly to enforce. In fact if not in theory, Parliament had drawn the line of its authority short of taxing Ireland and the colonies. There was also little love lost on the somewhat disregarded colonies in North America. The popular view was that the Americans had traitorously traded with the enemy during the recent war and had, by and large, declined to contribute to their own defense. Nor was there any doubt that sovereignty over the colonies resided in London and that the government had absolute authority to tax and govern the colonies as it saw fit. Benjamin Franklin later noted, "Every man in England seems to consider himself as a piece of a sovereign over America, seems to jostle himself into the Throne with the king, and talks of OUR *subjects in the colonies.*"

The American lobby in London was weak at best: Part-time agents of the colonial legislatures were usually either Americans in London on business or English merchants with American interests. The agents represented the assemblies mainly to the king's ministers and not to Parliament, but the lobbies to both were less organized and effective than the West Indies lobby, with which North American interests were generally in conflict. In any event, authority was diffusely distributed, so lobbying was complicated. Army commanders reported to the secretary of state for the Southern Department; naval commanders to the admiralty office; colonial governors and other civil administrators to either the secretary of state or the Board of Trade; and revenue officers to the Customs Board or the Treasury. New efforts were being made to rationalize the administration of the colonies, but they were still at a preliminary stage.

In March 1764, the House of Commons resolved that "it may be proper to charge certain Stamp Duties in the said Colonies and Plantations," but the budget Lord Grenville presented on March 9 contained no such recommendation. The idea of taxing the colonies for revenue was not new to the MPs and ministers, for they had made numerous proposals for decades. Sixty years earlier, when Robert Quary, surveyor general of the Customs, reported to the Lords of Trade on conditions in New York, he had lobbied for giving up all the old colonial charters and trying again, like the failed efforts of the 1670s and 1680s, to bring them under one uniform "Constitution of Government."

The "ill management" of revenue was a core problem in New York, as Quary had seen, and required an act of Parliament to ensure a revenue-sharing plan to administer the colonies centrally. He had advised swift action, as the colonists' "sour temper which hath already possessed them in opposition to Government" would only grow, because their "commonwealth notions improve daily and if it be not checked in time, the rights and privileges of English subjects will be thought by them too narrow." In Connecticut, Quary had found "nothing but confusion and Roguery" in the customhouses, and Rhode Island, Massachusetts, and New York were no better.

After Quary's day, the illegal sugar and molasses trade had grown. And New Englanders were pilfering white pines that rightly belonged to the Royal Navy, building ships with them, and then trading the ships to the French, even during wars, for molasses they smuggled into the colonies. Quary was not the first and was far from the last imperial official to observe that enforcement of existing customs laws would produce revenue to cover the salaries of colonial officials, the costs of government, and protection of the North American coastline.

In 1716, Archibald Cumings, surveyor of the Customs and searcher at the port of Boston, explained the facts on the ground to the Board of Trade: "It would seem highly reasonable these foreign Commodities should pay the 4½ p Ct. [pence per hundredweight] to his Majesty upon the Importation here or more to putt the Importer upon Levell in trade with those trading to our own Islands and make a revenue of 800 or 1000 pounds p[er] annum this money which would ease the Crown of Charges here or the defraying of other Expences." But the British were facing the same "sour temper" that Quary had noted. In 1710, New York governor Robert Hunter could extract no more than half the cost of government from the assembly, which argued that Queen Anne "hath no power to appointe Salaries" and should pay the governor's salary out of the funds allocated by Parliament to run her government. Hunter recommended "an effectual and speedy" remedy: Parliament should level revenue-raising taxes on all goods imported to and exported from New York, and an excise tax on the retail sale of all "Strong liquors."

Caleb Heathcote, a customs official and judge in the admiralty courts of New York, agreed. He wanted to see a revocation of the original colonial charters, consolidation of their governments, and a uniform system of customs and excises over the whole continent, modeled on that in England. This, Heathcote believed, would finance administration of the colonies and the costs of ships to guard the port cities. Six years after Hunter had sent his stillborn proposals to London, Heathcote wrote to the Treasury in 1716: "I have My Lords oft wondered why measures had not long ere this been taken, to settle a Revenue & not only on this Coast but in all other parts of His Majesty's Dominions abroad, who having the happinesse to enjoy the like benefits & privelidge, in all the Acts of Trade, & Commerce, with His Majesty's subjects in Great Brittan."

In 1728, Sir William Keith, former governor of Pennsylvania, had presented to the Lords of Trade "A Short Discourse on the present State of the Colonies in America with Respect to the Interest of Great Britain." Keith too advocated a centralization of colonial administration, but he recognized that any "improvement" would "signify very little, unless a sufficient revenue can be raised to support the needful expense. In order to which, it is humbly submitted whether the duties of stamps upon parchments and paper in England, may not with good reason be extended by Act of Parliament to all American plantations." Keith tried again to convince London of the immediate need for centralized administration in several pamphlets written between 1739 and 1742, but they too had no immediate impact on policy, though they apparently circulated privately before being published in the 1760s.

Keith's other concern had been the colonies' vulnerability to attack from Indians and Great Britain's European enemies and, because they lacked coordinated policies, their inability to defend themselves. His proposed solution was a uniform tax for common defense under a unified military command:

> There is good Reason to expect the British Subjects in America, for whose immediate Advantage and particular Service this Scheme is chiefly designed, would on that account chearfully comply with an moderate and easy Tax that could be laid on them for so good and necessary a Purpose; on Condition however that all the Money to be so levied amongst them should be punctually and strictly applied to this Service, and no other.

And in 1749, William Shirley, an experienced administrator intimately knowledgeable about conditions in New England, used the same logic to advise a similar plan. It was necessary to fortify the frontier against French and Indian threats, and a tax for the construction and maintenance of fortifications

> should be lay'd by Parliament upon the Colonies . . . The reasonableness of doing this for the common Protection of the Inhabitants

against their Enemies, and the Security of his Majesty's Government among 'em, seems to be as clear a point as the Reasonableness of the Parliament's making Acts for securing the Benefit of the Trade of the Colonies to their Mother Country, and creating a Dependency of 'em upon her.

In other words, for both these officials, taxing the colonies for their common defense seemed entirely consistent with existing imperial policies and no more likely to arouse resistance than previous laws had, which is not to say that there would be none or that the taxes would be easy to collect. But by the time the Board of Trade asked Shirley for more specific advice in the 1760s, he was having second thoughts. Now he advised a general fund to which the colonies would contribute voluntarily: "For the general Satisfaction of the People in each Colony, it would be advisable to leave it to their Choice to raise the Sum assessed upon them according to their own discretion." In the event that one of them refused to comply, he thought the ministry should hit the recalcitrant colony with a poll tax—a fixed tax on the heads of households, also known as a head or capitation tax. This was a traditional form in the colonies and hence least likely to be resisted on grounds of novelty or contrived principle.

It made sense that this knowledgeable and experienced man backed off the direct-tax idea rather than accept responsibility for the consequences of its implementation. As Shirley was well aware, the colonists had resisted the White Pines Acts, the Molasses Act, the Navigation Acts, and other legislation to regulate trade, so the only persuasive logic that Shirley and Keith thought would assure compliance with a new tax was to make a direct link between revenues and colonial defense. What little evidence exists, however, suggests that the administrators in London had little confidence that the colonists would pay a stamp tax or revenue-raising customs duties, given their long-standing resistance. A new law would be an invitation to trouble and not worth the effort.

George Clinton, governor of New York in 1750, was not sanguine about the colonists' willingness to pay taxes or duties even when the funds were clearly being dedicated to their own defense. He wrote to the Board of Trade, "Though it be very just and natural for His Majesty's Ministers to think, that the people in this Colony will do every thing in their power, to preserve and secure themselves; yet in reality it is far otherwise, for nothing is in good earnest thought of, but the forming of factions in the assembly, and of converting the Publick money to private uses." Clinton believed that Parliament had to seize the financial reins and grant its governors and other public servants in the colonies incomes independent of the whims of the colonial assemblies. He recommended increased duties on West Indian commodities such as molasses and rum to finance the proposal, but he did not say how the customs service could collect the duties more successfully than in the past.

Robert Hunter Morris, chief justice of New Jersey and later lieutenant governor of Pennsylvania, shared these views about the problems and solutions, and he painted an even bleaker view of the future. In 1752, Morris had warned the Board of Trade that the window was closing on the empire's ability to enforce its edicts in North America, as the colonists "are now striking at the very right of government itself, and are in a fair way of taking from the British officers the very frame & shadows of government having long ago seized the substance."

In 1754, when Maryland governor Horatio Sharpe faced an assembly unwilling to authorize funds for the defense of the frontier, he, too, had recommended that Parliament impose a uniform tax on the colonies, and suggested a poll tax or, in lieu of that, customs duties on imported liquors and wine: "An Excise on such as may be either imported to or made on the continent which indeed I think the most preferable; or By a Stamp Duty or something similar to it on Deeds and Writings" would be fair and sufficient. A uniform tax imposed on all the colonies would also obviate resistance on the grounds of differential treatment.

Three years later, Sharpe was still locked in conflict with Maryland's assembly over these issues; moreover, "they talk of disbanding all our Troops & leaving it to the Frontier Inhabitants to defend themselves." And when the assembly did authorize taxes, it was a bluff intended to provoke conflict with Maryland's proprietor rather than actually to raise funds. It imposed a land tax, which they knew the council would never approve, the governor would never sign, it being contrary to his instructions, the proprietor would never tolerate, it being against his self-interest, the Board of Trade would never authorize, and the colony could never collect. Just as the Pennsylvania assembly had, the Maryland legislators insisted that such a tax be equally assessed on the proprietor's "personal & real Estate," which, if executed, would have the effect of overthrowing the colony's proprietary government and opening vast acreages of free land. The requisition bill proposed in 1757 contained "so many exceptionable Clauses that there is not the least Probability of its passing the Upper House," Governor Sharpe said, which was exactly what the legislators intended. "There is scarcely a Person of Common Sense among us," Governor Sharpe told Lord Loudoun, head of the Board of Trade, "but laments that no Act of Parliament has been yet made for that purpose, for my own part I am of Opinion that nothing else can effectually preserve these Colonies from Ruin."

In 1755, Virginia's lieutenant governor Robert Dinwiddie had hoped that he would be more successful in raising funds from his assembly than the governors of Maryland and Pennsylvania had been, but he was not optimistic. "I shall do all in my Power to raise in our People a proper Spirit, and, if possible, to get a Supply," he wrote to Sir Thomas Robinson, secretary of state for the Southern Department, "but really, with't [without] a British Act of Parliament to oblige all the Colonies to a mutual Supply, I dread the Gov'rs will hardly be able to perswade them." To Lord Halifax, president of the Board of Trade, he had echoed the advice the other governors were giving: "An Union of the Colonies is greatly to be desired, but even then these Colonies will continue obstinate and fractious, unless a general Tax is laid on all the colonies by a British Act of Parliament." He too suggested a poll tax or land tax, but anticipated that any tax would be resisted. "I know our People will be inflam'd if they hear of my making y's [this] Proposal, as they are averse to all Taxes, but," he continued, "in my Duty, and in Obedience to Your Com'ds [commands], I cannot but think it is the most eligible [desirable], and will remain as long [as] the Land, but as before, if not done by a British Parliament, I may venture to affirm no Gov'rs on y's Cont't [continent] will be able to prevail with Y'r Assemblies to pass Laws for the above Purpose." He agreed with the other governors that all the colonies would resist any tax levied by Parliament, but it was the only option remaining to finance the governments.

After meeting with the governors at the Albany Conference in 1754, General Braddock had accepted their assessment. "I cannot but take the liberty to represent to you the necessity of laying a tax upon all his Majesty's dominions in America," he wrote to the secretary of state for the Southern Department. When John Campbell, 4th Earl of Loudoun, arrived in North America in 1756 as commander in chief and governor-general of Virginia, he assessed the situation in much the same way. It seemed to Lord Loudoun that the governors had already forfeited leadership to the assemblies, on which they depended for their salaries, but since seats in the assemblies were highly prized and avidly competed for, the assemblymen tended to forfeit their power when currying favor with this or that sector of the electorate. This resulted in a lack of leadership overall, "from whence there is no Law prevailing at present here, that I have met with, but the Rule every man pleases to lay down to himself." He thought the situation was desperate, requiring an immediate intervention from England supported by the troops already in North America, because "if you delay it till a peace, you will not have a force to exert any Brittish Acts of Parliament here." Make no mistake about it, Loudoun argued, by the 1750s it would have taken Parliament's intervention supported by military force to bring order to the colonies.

Colonel Thomas Gage saw the military and civil failures as connected. The colonists first underfunded and then only begrudgingly supported the army. In 1756, he wrote to Lord Albemarle, at this point a major general, "If they expect at home success in America, a General must be sent to us; acts of Parliament made to tax the provinces, in proportion to what each is able to bear; to make one common fund, and pursue one general, uniform plan for America . . . in short, all affairs here, both military and civil, want a thorough reformation."

In 1757, William Pitt, by then leader of the House of Commons, got the same advice, some of it from the same men. "The Taxes which the people pay in this Country, are really so trifling that they do not deserve the Name," wrote Loudoun. "So that if some Method is not found out of laying on a Tax, for the Support of a War in America, by a Brittish Act of Parliament, it appears to me, that you will continue to have no Assistance from them in Money, and will have very little Assistance in Men."

In 1763, with the war over, Pitt and his successor, Lord Bute, were both out of power, and George Grenville headed the ministry, which seized the opportunity to implement these long-anticipated changes. Grenville's ministers had before them the reports from governors, military leaders, and customs officials in North America, each with a useful and often complementary perspective on some part or parts of the problem. Massachusetts governor Francis Bernard wrote in 1764 that the discussions of rights and representation, which had reared their heads occasionally to justify defiance of executive orders, instructions to governors, and laws passed by Parliament, were irrelevant to administration of the empire. The locus of sovereignty was clearly "the king in Parliament," the constitutional expression of the monarch and the Houses of Commons and Lords acting in concert: "The *King in Parliament* has the sole right of legislation, and the supreme superintendency of the government; and, in this plenitude of power, is absolute, uncontrollable, and accountable to none; and therefore, in a political sense, can do no wrong." So the British colonies were, therefore, "subordinate to and dependent upon the Kingdom of Great Britain, and must derive from thence all their powers of legislation and jurisdiction."

The concept of divided sovereignty or spheres of external and internal sovereignty was, according to Bernard, a non sequitur, because a separate legislation "is not necessary to an external and dependent government . . . A separate Legislation is not an absolute right of British subjects residing out of the seat of Empire." Sovereignty could not be divided logically or legally. It resided in the absolute authority of the king in Parliament, and the colonies were dependencies. That was the obvious and unquestionable meaning of the concepts, law, and constitutional settlement of the Glorious Revolution in 1689. There would be, could be, no debate.

Beyond the law, however, Bernard saw issues of policy that were open for debate. The first of these was a question of responsibility: He believed that "the Colonies ought, so far as they are able, to pay the charge of the support of their own Governments, and of their own defence." He thought it only logical that since the principal site of defense of the colonies was the open seas, where the Royal Navy protected the colonists' trading vessels, "duties upon imports and exports, make the most proper funds for the expenses of such defence." And it was clearly Parliament's right and duty to regulate trade and set duties to raise sufficient revenue to pay for this protection. But other taxes, what Bernard called internal taxes, on domestic products and transactions, such as excises, poll taxes, and stamp taxes, would be "more agreeable to the people" if they were "raised by the Provincial Legislatures; as they will be most able to consult the particular convenience of their respective provinces. Whereas, it may be difficult to form a general Parliamentary tax, so as to make it equally suitable to all Provinces." It was Bernard's view that Parliament should impose internal taxes only if the colonial legislatures refused to levy and collect their own.

Bernard also favored revocation of the colonial charters, realignment and centralization of the colonies, "in some places to unite and consolidate; in others to separate and transfer; and in general to divide by natural boundaries instead of imaginary lines," and a top-to-bottom reform of the various eccentric governments that had evolved over the previous century. He concluded: "This is therefore the proper and critical time to reform the American governments upon a general, constitution[al], firm, and durable plan; and if it is not done now, it will probably every day grow more difficult, till at last it becomes impracticable."

Raising revenue and enforcing the rule of law were, then, the next steps in reformation of imperial relationships. When Grenville became First Lord of the Treasury in April 1763, he faced a national debt that had grown from £73 million in 1755 to £137 million; the annual interest alone was £5 million and growing, out of an annual budget of £8 million. His government simply had to find other sources of revenue. The landed interests that controlled Parliament had borne a large share of the increased wartime taxation and were unwilling to bear more. Grenville imposed a domestic cider tax, which evoked howls of protest from the opposition about the abuses of "personal liberties." Mobs roiled the streets of London.

The Treasury determined, after ample research, that if the present government were to remain in power, it would have to secure some of the increased funds from the colonies. The customs commissioners made three suggestions in September 1763, all of which the ministry implemented along with other reforms introduced in 1764. First, absentee customs collectors would have to take up their posts in the colonies or lose them; there would be no farming out to subordinates. Second, collectors would henceforth be paid only from what they collected; their livings would not be supplemented by fees (or bribes). Third, duties on molasses and sugar would have to be lowered in order to make them enforceable; the Molasses Act of 1733 had been "for the most part either wholly evaded or fraudulently compounded."

After additional research over the winter of 1763–1764, the commissioners recommended lowering the rate from six pence per gallon to three on a barrel of molasses, and this provision was contained in the Sugar Act adopted in April 1764. They predicted that a rate of three pence would raise more funds than either two or four, because it would lower the incentive to smuggle without affecting demand; they anticipated a return of £77,775 versus £66,667 on a rate of two pence. This sum could be applied directly to support the army in North America but would not even fully fund that.

When Grenville introduced the bill as part of his budget, there was no organized opposition. The Sugar Act of 1764 passed both houses of Parliament, and the king signed it in April. No colonial assembly instructed its London agent to protest. Jasper Mauduit, agent for Massachusetts, did not "find the least disposition in the other agents to oppose it." Richard Jackson, agent for the Pennsylvania and Connecticut assemblies, actually expressed support for a revenue-raising duty on molasses and sugar as long as it was low. When printed copies of the act arrived in the colonies, no protests against taxation without representation were made, despite the clear articulation of intent in the preamble to the act "for improving the revenue of this kingdom, and for extending and securing the navigation and commerce between Great Britain and your Majesty's dominions in America . . . for defraying the expences of defending, protecting, and securing the same."

The colonists eventually figured out, on close reading of the long and complex measure, that the devil was in the details of enforcement, not in the rates and continuation of business as usual. Most of the act concerned reform of the customs service and tightening loopholes in tax collection, which included shifting onto the accused the burden of proof that a cargo was not smuggled. At the discretion of the customs agents, prosecution could be in a new admiralty court in Halifax, which was independent of the colonists and inconvenient for merchants based in New England or farther south. It turned out to be inconvenient for the tax collectors as well, who would have to abandon their posts for days or weeks and suffer costs similar to those of the accused; those accused of smuggling had to pay for transportation of witnesses, evidence, and legal representation, and they could not recover their defense costs under the new law. Offering or accepting bribes was now a serious crime, so previous arrangements with informers who expected payment could not continue. If this invigorated customs service supported by the Royal Navy actually enforced the law, the profits of colonial merchants were bound to decrease.

In this stressful new environment, colonists feared for their rights and traditional constitutional relationships. The Boston lawyer and politician James Otis wrote a widely circulated pamphlet in response to the Sugar Act, titled *The Rights of the British Colonies Asserted and Proved*—first published in Boston in 1764 and then reprinted in London later in the year, where it was advertised as "universally approved" of in the colonies, which it was not. Otis's pamphlet is best read as a brief by a talented lawyer in support of his clients, American colonists defending traditional imperial relationships, rather than as a work of systematic political philosophy.

Governor Bernard was correct: The ascendance of Parliament and the locus of sovereignty in the king in Parliament were the hard-won givens of British constitutional law and domestic politics. Otis's pamphlet looked at these givens from a colonial perspective and through the lens of John Locke's political philosophy. Otis believed that a contract or compact existed between rulers and those they governed; Locke said that the people surrendered their sovereignty in return for governments that defended their best interests and gave them security of life, liberty, and property. "There is no one act, which a government can have a *right* to make," Otis argued, "that does not tend to the advancement of the security, tranquility, and prosperity of the people." In other words, the sovereignty of a governmental institution exists only as long as it serves the best interests of those it governs. Sovereignty must, according to this reading of Locke, reside in the legislative arm of the government, the one in which the people and their interests are represented. And "yet the legislative being only a fiduciary power, to act for certain ends, there remains still '*in the people, a supream power to remove, or alter, the legislative when they find the legislative act contrary to the trust reposed in them.*'" If the king in Parliament should break the compact, sovereignty reverts to the people.

The people, then, are always the supreme power even though sovereignty rests in the legislative branch of their government. A challenge to a government's legitimacy could arise, as Otis quotes Locke, with the legislature "invading the *property* of the subject and making themselves arbitrary disposers of the lives, liberties, and fortunes of the people." Specifically, the colonists had long labored at great risk to support themselves and profit the empire in an imperial system whose officials were ignorant of their living conditions and, therefore, could not plausibly govern them. "There is a man now living or but lately dead," wrote Otis, "who once was a secretary of state, during whose *wonderful* conduct of national affairs, without knowing whether *Jamaica* lay in the Mediterranean, the Baltic, or in the moon, letters were often received directed to the governor of the *island* of New England."

In such circumstances, the colonies had to fend for themselves and repose their sovereignty in their own legislatures. It could be no other way. By definition, "a plantation or colony is a settlement of subjects in a territory *disjoined* or *remote* from the mother country," in which the "colonists are entitled to as *ample* rights, liberties, and privileges as the subjects of the mother country are, and in some respects *to more*." In the specific case of the North American colonies over the previous 150 years, they had experienced an exception to parliamentary sovereignty, a split sovereignty due to the impossibility of taxing them or governing their internal affairs from afar.

Governor Bernard and the political classes in London believed that divided sovereignty was an oxymoron constructed to justify smuggling and tax evasion. Whether one thought that Otis's position was principled or merely rationalized lawlessness obviously depended on one's perspective and perception of self-interest. Otis imagined a time when British imperial officials might revoke colonial charters "without fault or forfeiture, without trial or notice . . . when instead of a process at common law the Parliament shall give a decisive blow to every charter in America, and declare them all void." In such an event, he argued, Parliament would not be sovereign in America, as "no act of Parliament can deprive them of the liberties of such, unless any will contend that an act of Parliament can make slaves not only of one but of two millions of the commonwealth." Nor would token representation in Parliament, a possibility suggested from time to time, "be equivalent to a subordinate legislative among themselves . . . It would be impossible for the Parliament to judge so well of their abilities to bear taxes, impositions on trade, and other duties and burdens, or of the local laws that might be really needful, as a legislative here."

Otis argued for a fundamental right that "in a state of nature no man can take my property from me without my consent: if he does, he deprives me of my liberty and makes me a slave. If such a proceeding is a breach of the law of nature, no law of society can make it just." A right to property cannot be partial or compromised, for the basic principle applies across all forms of property. If Parliament had authority to tax trade, it had the authority to take anything and everything that the colonists possessed without their consent: "Why may not the Parliament lay stamps, land taxes, establish tithes to the Church of England, and so indefinitely? I know of no bounds." Indeed. The only plausible solution in an empire that recognized the basic rights of Englishmen was taxation levied only by the legislatures that represented the colonists.

Given the intensity of resistance to just the entering wedge of reform, given the utterly conflicting readings of rights, tradition, and law, and given the colonists' understanding of responsibilities and interests, there is ample evidence to suggest that it was already too difficult, already too late to change the imperial relationships. Narratives were too deeply imbedded, reached back too far in time, and revealed incompatible interpretations of what had already happened and why. What seemed obvious to Governor Bernard and British policy makers and what was clear to colonists such as Otis were so utterly at odds as to preclude the possibility of dialogue, never mind understanding and compromise.

It was not clear when colonists might decide that they no longer could be both independent *and* subjects in the British Empire, but it was certain that by 1763 British officials believed they had to enforce the rule of law and establish colonial sources of revenue. The colonists had a tradition of independence and an ideological vision that supported their interpretation of rights; the paths they would take were contingent on actions and perceptions on both sides of the Atlantic, but they were not going to surrender independence or relinquish sovereignty over their internal affairs. Actions over the next decade were not mistakes in the perspectives of those who took them but were based on their interests, profoundly different on either side of the Atlantic. Nobody fully comprehended the situation, but the British officials in North America were perhaps the first to understand the impossibility of it, and they ended up frustrated with everyone.

In 1764, all parties assumed that they shared a language, but soon enough they came to see that this was correct only in the narrowest linguistic sense. Given the differing interpretations of law, history, and self-interest, and in light of the extent of ideological differences, the issues were irresolvable, even had there been universal goodwill and a shared desire to preserve the empire. And the events of 1765 were to undermine dramatically the goodwill that remained in 1764.

10

✦

STAMPS

EVENTS IN 1765 SHOWED CLEARLY that there was no united colonial perspective. A sizable and influential number of colonists whom Governor Horatio Sharpe of Maryland called "Person[s] of Common Sense," people of substance and influence, opposed the interpretation of imperial relationships that James Otis had proposed in his 1764 pamphlet. And it was unclear how many politicians had the "little wisdom, common sense, and integrity" that Sharpe believed it took to avoid the "unhappy revolutions, which for ages have distressed the human race."

Most colonists would have liked to sit out the burgeoning conflict over the proposed Stamp Act, hoping it would pass as others had before it, and to go about their lives without such unsettled and unsettling politics. These were the colonists who remained either loyal but passive subjects or alienated from both sides, people who had emigrated to escape conflict, to find peace and land, who were busy raising families, clearing trees, planting and fencing fields, making barrels or shoes or candles, who had their eyes more on the kingdom of God than on the British Empire, and/or who had little time for politicians and were uninterested in political literature or debate. Politically active people continued to disagree about how many colonists fell on either side of the political divide and which side could count on the less committed if it came to an irreconcilable conflict. In 1764, the British Empire could still rely on habits of mind, affection for the king, and cultural attachments that kept most colonists loyal. One year later, the solid core of habituated subjects was shrinking.

Henry McCulloh (or McCulloch), sometimes called the father of the Stamp Act, was an Ulster Scot who became a successful London merchant and used his political connections to speculate heavily in North Carolina land. An initial grant of 1.2 million acres from King George II in 1738 was contingent on the settlement of six thousand Ulster Scots on the tract, and there were numerous twists, gains and losses, struggles over the payment of quitrents, a form of land tax, and contested claims over the years. He was collector of North Carolina quitrents in 1738 and Crown secretary of the colony in 1756–1761.

During the 1750s and 1760s, McCulloh submitted to imperial officials a series of advisory plans for reforming colonial policies that were based on his experiences in North Carolina (and sometimes promoting his investments there). All of these were closely read in London, and some of them influenced policy, including the decision to levy a stamp tax on the colonies. Although he is often credited with the idea for the Stamp Act, and although he was there at the birth of the Grenville ministry's plan for it, he predicted that the final form of the law would be strongly resisted among colonists, and would fail.

In 1751, McCulloh had proposed to Lord Halifax a tax for the colonies that would require official stamps on all "Writings, Deeds, Instruments or other matters relating to the law in the said Provinces." He advised that funds raised by the stamp taxes should be dedicated to the costs of the colonies' security and government. In *A Miscellaneous Essay* of 1755, he advocated "fixt and certain" policies to bring order to the chaos of governance in the colonies. "It is the Want of System in the Conduct of our Affairs," he wrote, "which is the Bane and Ruin of our American Colonies, and must in the End prove destructive to our Trade and Commerce." Since administration of the colonies fell under the prerogative of the Crown, there should be but one clear avenue for conducting business, and that was the Board of Trade. Division of authority among a number of agencies contributed, in McCulloh's view, to the disarray. And the absence of a tax on the colonies administered from London and dedicated to financing their governance exacerbated the muddle. He also advised licensing ships that traded to the French and Spanish Caribbean to replace the existing policy of impotently banning the trade entirely and thus collecting no revenue on the unstoppable smuggling.

In 1761, McCulloh was back with *Miscellaneous Representations*, which repeated his recommendation that "particular Care ought to be taken to have all the Colonies act upon one system." And once again he advocated a stamp tax and the enforcement of a lower tax on rum and molasses, the incomes from which should be dedicated to colonial administration and defense. He reemphasized the need for currency regulation, for channeling all communication with the colonies through the Board of Trade, and for vigorous defense of the royal prerogative. All of these synchronized well with the ambitions of King George III and his successive ministries.

England first had stamp taxes in 1671, and had them continuously in the eighteenth century. During the Seven Years War, they had raised the considerable sum of £260,000. Proposals had been made to extend stamp taxes to the colonies in 1722, 1726, 1728, 1742, and repeatedly after 1755. Timely changes in the Treasury, higher priorities, a lack of enforcement mechanisms, and a belief that it was not worth the effort all help to explain why none of these proposals was implemented. The dramatically increased debt resulting from the Seven Years War, the presence of large numbers of British troops in the colonies after the war, and Americans' challenge to Parliament's authority to levy taxes on them assured that this time the stamp tax would become law. The Grenville ministry's belief that it had to raise funds without provoking domestic protest, and had to face down the Americans' defiance if it were to stay in power, contributed to the timing of the Stamp Act's passage.

Grenville's intimation in March 1764 that stamp taxes were on the horizon was enough to evoke protests from the colonies, and he felt compelled to rebut them. New York's petition to the House of Commons of October 18 claimed that it was an "indispensible Duty, to trouble you with a seasonable Representation of the Claim of our Constituents, to an Exemption from the Burthen of all Taxes not granted by themselves, and their Foresight of the tragical Consequences of an Adoption of the contrary Principle, to the Crown, the Mother Country, themselves and their Posterity." The New Yorkers believed that, as a matter of long-standing rights, governments could not take property from citizens without the citizens' consent as expressed through representatives to the legislature that levied the taxes. The New Yorkers took care to explain that their opposition to taxes levied by Parliament did not "arise from a Desire of Independency upon the supreme Power of the Parliament," but submission to taxes without representation would sacrifice "the most essential of all the Rights to which they are intitled . . . since all Impositions, whether they be internal Taxes, or Duties paid, for what we consume, equally diminish the Estates upon which they are charged."

The New York assembly perceived an even larger problem in the pattern of legislation that had begun in the 1764 session of Parliament. Perhaps most disturbingly, the Sugar Act prohibited trade to the "foreign Sugar Colonies," which meant eliminating customers for the New Yorkers' otherwise unmarketable products, including furs, timber, foodstuffs, cattle, horses, beer, flour, flax, and iron bars, "which being there converted into Cash and Merchandize, made necessary Remittances for the *British* Manufactures we consumed." Parliament had then compounded the loss of income and currency through trade by adopting another law during the same session that "renders our Paper Money no legal Tender." Together, this Currency Act and the Sugar Act created unmeasurable distress in New York, as it did in other colonies. The Sugar Act also deprived New York of the Irish market for lumber, which in turn would damage the Irish linen trade, "and, when we consider the Wisdom of our Ancestors in contriving Trials by Juries, we cannot stifle our Regret, that the Laws of Trade in general, change the Current of Justice from the common Law, and subject Controversies of the utmost Importance to the Decisions of the Vice-Admiralty Courts, who proceed not according [to] the wholesom Laws of the Land."

The Virginia House of Burgesses adopted separate petitions to the king, the House of Lords, and the House of Commons in December 1764. To the king the legislators insisted on their "ancient and inestimable Right of being governed by such Laws respecting their internal Polity and Taxation as are derived from their own Consent." To the House of Lords they asked for "Protection of their just and undoubted Rights as *Britons*," insisting that their ancestors had brought across the ocean with them "every Right and Privilege they could with Justice claim in their Mother Kingdom," among which, they believed, was a "fundamental Principle of the *British* Constitution, without which

Freedom can no Where exist, that the People are not subject to any Taxes but such as are laid on them by their own Consent, or by those who are legally appointed to represent them." And to the House of Commons the Virginians noted their dismay that Parliament had declared "it may be proper to charge certain Stamp Duties in the said Colonies and Plantations," since it was "essential to *British* Liberty that Laws imposing Taxes on the People ought not to be made without the Consent of Representatives chosen by themselves." They hoped Parliament would reconsider its plans, recognizing that "*British* Patriots will never consent to the Exercise of anticonstitutional Power."

The imperial response was predictable: The king in Parliament is sovereign, and sovereignty is indivisible. As Thomas Whately, member of Parliament and commissioner of the Board of Trade, put it in *The Regulations lately Made concerning the Colonies*, published after adoption of the Stamp Act in 1765, "the Reasonableness, and even the Necessity of requiring an *American* Revenue being admitted, the Right of the Mother Country to impose such a Duty upon her Colonies, if duly considered, cannot be questioned." Yes, the principle of no taxation without representation was valid—"No new Law whatever can bind us that is made without the Concurrence of our Representatives"—and a tax law was no different. But equally, an exception to the sovereignty of Parliament would nullify it, and Parliament had the undeniable and sovereign right to legislate for the empire and all its subjects.

In the past, Whately observed, the colonists had "acquiesced under several parliamentary Taxes," among them the Molasses Act of 1733 and the Navigation Acts going back to 1660. All were laws that established taxes or duties (synonymous terms in this usage). As he wrote, "Duties laid for these Purposes, as well as for the Purposes of Revenue, are still Levies of Money upon the People. The Constitution again knows no Distinction between Impost Duties and internal Taxation; and if some speculative Difference should be attempted to be made, it certainly is contradicted by Fact; for an internal Tax also was laid on the Colonies by the Establishment of a Post Office there." The fact that colonists were also represented in their assemblies was irrelevant, Whately explained, because "so are the Citizens of *London* in their Common Council; and yet so far from excluding them from the national Representation, it does not impeach their Right to chuse Members of Parliament."

Grenville had given the colonists notice on the Stamp Act. The colonial agents met with Grenville on May 17, 1764, to receive clarification of his intentions. Jasper Mauduit, from Massachusetts, understood that the minister would "certainly bring in such a Bill" but was open to hearing "their requests about any particular modification of it as they should think fit." Charles Garth, South Carolina's agent, understood that the minister was *not* open to proposals from the colonies either to tax themselves or to suggest another tax levied by Parliament. Grenville underlined that it was essential for the colonists to pay part of the costs of their defense, that there were precedents (in the post office) for parliamentary taxation of the colonies, and that he believed a stamp tax would be "the most easy and least exceptionable to the Colonies."

A rumor was circulating in America that Grenville was open to proposals from the colonies to tax themselves, but this was untrue. He had simply warned them of what was to come, given them a year to get used to it, hoped that they would, upon consideration, recognize the reasonableness of the policy, and accept the authority of Parliament to pass laws governing them. His ministry listened to the protests from the colonial legislators and agents and to protests submitted through private channels, and dismissed them. No alternative emerged and no specific recommendations arrived.

Jared Ingersoll—a Yale graduate, married into one of Connecticut's most powerful family networks—had been appointed king's attorney for New Haven County at the age of twenty-nine, and in his church was a member of the conservative Old Light opposition to Connecticut's Great Awakening. In 1758–1761, Ingersoll had been Connecticut's agent in London, which he had found enthralling; it was thrilling to come from the colonial periphery to the bustling imperial capital, the center of Britain's culture, economy, politics, and high society. On February 11, 1765, he was back in London and wrote that "the Point of the Authority of Parliament to impose such Tax I found on my Arrival here was so fully and Universally yielded [accepted], that there was not the least hopes of making any impressions that way." He reported the widely shared view among MPs that the House of Commons represented the "great body of the people, who are below the dignity of peers; that this house of Commons Consists of a certain number of Men Chosen by certain people of certain places, which Electors, by the way, they Insist, are not a tenth part of the people," and yet it legislated for all Britons.

In the course of debating the Stamp Act, MPs contended that

the only reason why America has not been heretofore taxed in the fullest Manner, has been merely on Account of their Infancy and Inability; that there have been, however, not wanting Instances of the Exercise of this Power, in the various regulations of the American trade, the Establishment of the post Office &c, and they deny any Distinction between what is called an internal & external Tax as to the point of the Authority imposing such taxes.

Supporters of the Stamp Act pointed out that nothing in any of the colonial charters exempted the colonists "from the Authority of one of the branches of the great body of Legislation." The Pennsylvania Charter expressly mentioned Parliament's authority to impose taxes. "In short," Ingersoll heard during the debates, "they say a Power to tax is a necessary part of every Supreme Legislative Authority, and that if they have not that Power over America, they have none, & then America is at once a kingdom of itself."

Opponents of the Stamp Act in Parliament, and there were a few, argued that even though Parliament had the "supreme unlimited Authority" to make laws, yet they doubted whether it would ever be "prudent" to tax Ireland or the colonies. They also thought the argument that Americans were represented in Parliament was a "construction" that ignored the real difference between the actual relationships that Englishmen had with their MPs and the lack of such for the Americans: "Here in England the Member of Parliament is equally known to the Neighbour who elects & to him who does not . . . The taxes are laid equally by one Rule and fall as well on the Member himself as on the people."

Lord Camden, speaking in the House of Lords in 1766, was to agree with the colonists that they were not represented in Parliament and that therefore Parliament had no authority to tax them. The "British parliament have no right to tax the Americans . . . [because] taxation and representation are coeval with and essential to this constitution," he said. And the claim that colonists enjoyed "virtual" representation in Parliament implied the opposite, he argued, for it was ipso facto acknowledgment that they were not represented: Either the colonists were represented or they were not. But only a very small number of the members of Parliament shared Camden's views. Most who opposed the Stamp Act did so as a matter of policy rather than of rights, and not many opposed it at all.

The bill Parliament voted into law on March 22, 1765, asserted that it was "just and necessary" to adopt measures "towards further defraying the expences of defending, protecting, and securing" the colonies. With only a handful of stated exceptions, all official documents, everything from probated wills to ecclesiastical documents, land transfers, lawsuits, legal pleadings—"every skin or piece of vellum or parchment, or sheet or piece of paper, on [which] shall be ingrossed, written, or printed . . . of any record or proceeding in any court whatsoever within the said colonies and plantations"—would require a fee and stamp. Any grant of office, bond, government appointment, apprenticeship, mortgage, deed, or notarized document must bear a stamp to be paid at specific rates for each. Every pack of playing cards, dice, newspaper, pamphlet, almanac, calendar, and advertisement printed in a newspaper had to be officially stamped. And all the duties had to be paid in the "sterling money of *Great Britain.*"

When news of the Stamp Act arrived in the colonies in late May, it provoked heated debate. Virginia's governor Fauquier reported to the Lords of Trade that he felt obliged to dissolve the House of Burgesses in light of its irregular proceedings when, "on *Wednesday* the 29th of May, just at the end of the Session when most of the members had left the town, there being but 39 present out of 116 of which the House of Burgesses now consists, a motion was made to take into consideration the Stamp Act, a copy of which had crept into the House, and in a Committee of the whole House five resolutions were proposed and agreed to, all by very small majorities." In the governor's view, a few young hotheads spearheaded the debate, among whom a new member, Patrick Henry, was the most offensive.

The assembly's journal recorded four resolutions. The first two asserted that the original colonists arrived with "all the Liberties, Privileges, Franchises, and Immunities, that have at any Time been held, enjoyed, and possessed, by the people of *Great Britain*," and that two royal charters granted by King James I had confirmed these rights. The third resolution insisted that the Taxation of the People by themselves, or by Persons chosen by themselves to represent them, who can only know what Taxes the People are able to bear, or the easiest Method of raising them, and must themselves be affected by every Tax laid on the People, is the only Security against a burthensome Taxation, and the distinguishing Characteristick of *British* Freedom, without which the ancient Constitution cannot exist.

The fourth affirmed that Virginians had always "enjoyed the inestimable Right of being governed by such Laws, respecting their internal Polity and Taxation, as are derived from their own Consent," and that they had never yielded that right, which the sovereigns and people of Great Britain had acknowledged.

By the time Rhode Island's *Newport Mercury* reported on the Virginia resolutions on June 24, they had multiplied in the retelling to six, and the language of the first four had been radicalized. The rewritten fourth asserted that the Virginia assembly had "the only exclusive Right and Power to lay Taxes and Imposts upon the Inhabitants of this Colony. And that every Attempt to vest such Power in any other Person or Persons whatever, than the General Assembly aforesaid, is illegal, unconstitutional and unjust, and have a manifest Tendency to destroy British as well as American Liberty." A fabricated fifth resolution, probably composed from a draft that was never presented to the Virginia assembly, also challenged Parliament directly: "The Inhabitants of this Colony, are not bound to yield Obedience to any Law or Ordinance whatever, designed to impose any Taxation whatsoever upon them, other than the Laws or Ordinances of the General Assembly." And the sixth announced that "any Person, who shall, by speaking or writing, assert or maintain, that any Person or Persons, other than the General Assembly of this Colony, have any Right or Power to impose or lay any Taxation on the People here, shall be deemed an Enemy to this his Majesty's Colony."

This was the version, published in the newspapers, rather than the actual Virginia resolutions adopted by the rump meeting, that informed the debate in the colonies and got reported back to Parliament. What was almost certainly the view of a very small number of the most radical members of the Virginia House of Burgesses inspired representatives in other colonies to adopt more provocative proposals. The newspaper resolutions became a template that assemblymen in other colonies embellished and altered to suit their political goals.

The anonymous author of "A Letter from a Plain Yeoman," which had appeared in the *Providence Gazette* in May, responded to the charge that colonists were "*aiming at independance*":

> If by *independance* be intended our maintenance of argument against the levying taxes upon us without our own consent, then it is so far true that we do *aim at independance*. Such *independance* is the main pillar of our happy frame of government, and hath ever been claimed and enjoyed, from the times of the *Saxons* down to this day, by our fellow-subjects in *Britain* . . . How then, my lord, can it be deemed as *aiming at independance*, in the worst sense of the words, *i. e.* an effort to cast off our allegiance, for the dominions in *America* to assert and claim that as a right, which all the rest of the king's subjects have ever claimed and enjoyed.

The subtlety of the Yeoman's insistence on independence for subjects who nonetheless pledged allegiance to the king was not likely to be credited in England, if indeed it was noticed. The point was as significant, though, as the arguments about taxation and representation, all of them examples of the claim to "independance." Parliament had never before "imposed an internal Tax upon the Colonies for *the single Purpose of Revenue*," but this was now one in a lengthening string of novel challenges to their independence over the past decade. If they could not be independent, the colonists would want to be free of the empire, but separation was not their goal.

The resolves adopted by Pennsylvania's assembly, in September, also declared the Stamp Act an unconstitutional subversion of the colonists' "most valuable Rights." The laying of taxes by any other body than their own assembly was "manifestly subversive of public Liberty" and "utterly destructive of public Happiness." In Maryland, the legislature noted that the colony's specific charter rights included freedom from taxation except by their own representatives, and added that trial by jury "is the Grand Bulwark of Liberty, the undoubted Birthright of every Englishman and Consequently of every British Subject in America."

The Connecticut Resolves agreed on all points, noting that its legislature had sole jurisdiction over "taxing and internal Police." The Massachusetts assembly's resolves of October similarly traced its constituents' rights to the British constitution, their royal charter, the "Law of God and Nature," and the "common Rights of Mankind": "Resolved, That the Inhabitants of this Province are *unalienably* entitled to those essential Rights in common with all Men: And that no Law of Society can consistent with the Law of God and Nature divest them of those Rights." They believed that Magna Carta, their charter, previous acts of Parliament, and "Reason and common Sense" created an entitlement "to the same Extent of Liberty with His Majesty's Subjects in *Britain*," and agreed that inhabitants of Massachusetts "are not, and never have been, represented in the Parliament of *Great Britain*; And that such a Representation *there*, as the Subjects in *Britain* do actually and rightfully enjoy, is *impracticable* for the subjects *in America*."

The South Carolina assembly adopted eighteen resolutions covering much the same ground on November 29, and New Jersey endorsed eleven the next day. New York's assembly complained about the Sugar Act, which its colony found "grievous and burthensome," and delivered a dire prediction if Parliament ignored the protests of the colonial legislatures:

> *Resolved, Nemine Contradicente,*
> That if the honourable House of Commons insist on their Power of Taxing this Colony, and by that means deprive its Inhabitants of what they have always looked upon as an undoubted Right, though this Power should be exerted in the mildest Manner, it will teach them to consider the People of *Great-Britain*, as vested with absolute Power to dispose of all their Property, and tend to weaken that Affection for the Mother Country, which this Colony *ever had*, and is *extremely* desirous of retaining.

Protests against the Stamp Act were not, of course, confined to the legislative resolutions and petitions sent to the king, the House of Commons, and the House of Lords. Parliament declined to receive petitions that challenged its sovereignty, which eliminated any possibility for discussions or formal negotiations to settle the taxation and representation questions, but the colonists themselves loudly protested in poetry and prose.

The *American Country Almanac* published a poem attributed to "Poor Roger" (actually written by the deceased English poet James Thomson) that warned readers:

> . . . *[as] soon as independence stoops the head,*
> *To vice-enslaved, and vice-created wants,*
> *Then to some foul corrupting-hand, whose waste*
> *Their craving lusts with fatal bounty feeds,*
> *They fall a willing, undefended prize;*
> *From man to man th' infectious softness runs,*
> *Till the whole state unnerved in slavery sinks.*

At about the same time, the Rhode Islander Dr. Benjamin Church published "The Times, a Poem," entreating his fellow colonists "to independence bend the filial knee / and kiss her sister sage economy"—hardly an aggressive pose—but also advocating fidelity to the king. Likewise, the Pennsylvania assembly, in a letter to the king protesting the Stamp Act, reminded him that the colonists had a "warm sense of the honour, freedom, and independance of the subjects of a patriot King." Even Martin Howard, a Rhode Island merchant and lawyer who publicly opposed the Stamp Act yet accepted appointment as a stamp distributor, acknowledged the limited scope of the colonists' arguments, seeing in them no ambition for separation from the empire. But he rejected any "high pretensions to independence," advocating greater modesty and "dutiful submission."

In early 1766, Richard Bland, a Virginia planter, argued that when the colonies' founders had immigrated to the New World, they had recovered "their natural Freedom and Independence" even while remaining subjects of the monarch. He believed that each colony was a "sovereign State, independent of the State from which they separated." And Nicholas Ray, a New Yorker living in London, cautioned the English against driving the colonists to rebellion by being insensitive to the "Desire of Independence," which he believed was "inherent in all Men" and no threat to the imperial relationship. If the British did not practice "Lenity and Mildness" toward the colonies, there would be trouble, for "few will long bear even imaginary Grievances, with the Means in their Hands, however desperate, of shaking them off."

Giving the colonists token representation in Parliament would not address the problem, and Americans did not advocate it. Such a "scheme, if adopted, would not only be grievously expensive to the colonies," explained an anonymous contributor to the *Pennsylvania Journal*, but also could do them no good. "To allow the colonies such a number of members in the house of commons," he continued, "as would enable them to carry points against the mother country, when a competition of interests arises, would be in effect to resign her own independency, which we may be assured she never will do."

Not a single colony supported its stamp collectors. None considered the option of compliance with the law along with writing petitions to correct specific articles in it. Everyone suffered or encouraged active rebellion—or, at least, that is how it seemed from England. The colonists based their claims to exemption from taxes on their charters, but Englishmen knew the charters were subject to the sovereignty of Parliament and could be revoked at any time. "The question now is," a contributor to the *London General Evening Post* wrote in the winter of 1765–1766, "Whether those American subjects are, or are not, bound by the resolutions of a British parliament? If they are *not*, they are entirely a separate people from us." Another, signed "Anti-Sejanus," wrote in the *London Chronicle* in January 1866, "The Mother-country is entitled to the support of her colonies, as a parent to the obedience of her children." "Pacificus" believed the Virginians were "immersed in Libertinism; and the New-Englanders swell with the stiff Tenets of Independency. The latter are a crabbed Race, not very unlike their Half Brothers, the Indians, for unsocial Principles, and an unrelenting Cruelty." These were not debating points on the English constitution but screeds delivered across an ocean.

In July 1765, King George dismissed Prime Minister Grenville, whom he disliked and whose support in Parliament was weakening, and appointed the Marquis of Rockingham in his place. Rockingham had no stake in enforcing the Stamp Act, and, after his one year as prime minister, was to become a staunch supporter of the colonists' constitutional rights. But repeal of the Stamp Act was difficult in the short term, given the colonists' challenge to Parliament's sovereignty over them. When riots, public defiance, and physical assaults on stamp collectors came on top of the resolves, petitions, pamphlets, and newspaper articles, MPs were in no mood to back down, even when it became clear that the tax would not produce the revenue they had expected.

As Anti-Sejanus, the English writer who opposed repeal of the Stamp Act, argued, "it is not for the paltry sum of one hundred thousand pounds a year that we are contending; but for the honour of the Crown, the dignity of P[arliament], the credit and welfare of the nation, together with the very essence of our excellent constitution." It was the colonists' "disposition to shake off all dependance and subjection" that the opponents of repeal believed was the real problem. Anti-Sejanus thought the colonists wished "for nothing more than to be sever'd from the mother trunk . . . The Americans imbibe notions of independance and liberty with their very milk, and will some time or other shake off all subjection. If we yield to them in this particular, by repealing the Stamp-Act, it is all over; they will from that moment assert their freedom."

What the colonists had done—as opposed to what they had argued—to arouse such animus was to make agreements in town meetings, merchant associations, and legislative assemblies to boycott British manufactures as long as the Stamp Act remained in force, to go on with business as usual in defiance of the law, to intimidate the men who had accepted positions as stamp agents, and to destroy the property and threaten others in authority whether or not they had any relationship to the hated tax. Publication of the inflammatory, inaccurate versions of the Virginia Resolves had been "an Alarm bell to the disaffected"—not simply those disaffected from the tax but also those dissatisfied with other authority and for other reasons.

In Boston, a crowd hanged Andrew Oliver in effigy because he had agreed to administer the Stamp Act in Massachusetts; he rightly interpreted this as a personal threat. Sheriff's officers trying to cut down the effigy were put "in imminent danger of their lives," or so they believed. After dark on the next evening, August 15, a "mob" carried Oliver's effigy to shops in a commercial building that he had recently had constructed, which "they called the Stamp Office, and pulled it down to the Ground in five minutes." From there, they walked to Oliver's house, where they beheaded the effigy and "broke all the Windows next the Street; then they carried the Effigy to Fort Hill near Mr. Oliver's House, where they burnt the Effigy in a Bonfire made of the Timber they had pulled down from the Building." Returning to his home, from which Oliver and his family had fled, the mob found "the Doors barricaded, broke down the whole fence of the Garden towards Fort Hill, and coming on beat in all the doors and Windows of the garden front, and entered the House." They searched everywhere for Oliver, "declaring they would kill him," and then searched other houses nearby. When Lieutenant Governor Thomas Hutchinson (who was Oliver's brother-in-law) came with the sheriff to address the crowd at Oliver's house, a "Ringleader cried out, The Governor and the Sheriff! To your Arms, my boys." The "boys" unleashed a volley of stones, and the two bruised men only narrowly escaped. An attempt to raise the militia was unsuccessful, apparently because the militiamen who were not part of the mob either supported or feared it.

Ten days later, another Boston mob planned to attack Hutchinson's home, even though Hutchinson had actually opposed the Stamp Act, advocated its repeal, and indeed believed that he "was become rather Popular." When he got word that a mob was descending on his home, Hutchinson closed it and fled with his family. By the next morning, "one of the best finished houses in the Province had nothing remaining but the bare walls and floors." Then the crowd tore down the walls and took the slate and boards from the roof. "Such ruins were never seen in America," Hutchinson lamented. The crowd had taken everything it had not destroyed, leaving him and his family without even their clothes. Hutchinson believed that the men who had encouraged the first mob to attack Oliver "never intended matters should go this length and the people in general express the utmost detestation of this unparalleled outrage and I wish they could be convinced what infinite hazard there is of the most terrible consequences from such daemons when they are let loose in a government where there is not constant authority at hand sufficient to suppress them."

In despair at his losses—which included the manuscript of his history of Massachusetts and many public papers—but hopeful that he would at least be reimbursed for them, Hutchinson was unclear on what the British response to the mayhem should be: "On the one hand it will be said if concessions be made the parliament endanger the loss of their authority over the colonies on the other hand if external force should be used there seems to be danger of a total lasting alienation of affection. Is there no alternative? May the infinitely wise God direct you."

During the same week, in Newport, Rhode Island, crowds dismantled the houses of Martin Howard and Dr. Thomas Moffat, two writers of anonymous progovernment newspaper essays. They too had nothing directly to do with the Stamp Act, and neither of them was in a position of authority in the government. But Moffat was told by a leader of the crowd that "it was notorious in New England that I had on many occasions and even to Himself asserted and maintaind the uncontroulable authority and jurisdiction of Parliament over America and that I had perswaded others to embrace and profess the same opinion." Some time after, rioters returned to destroy the houses and chop down the giant elms on the properties. The two men, in fear for their lives and having lost all they valued, sought refuge on a Royal Navy vessel, from which they eventually transferred to a commercial ship sailing to Bristol, England.

In 1764, Jared Ingersoll had joined the other colonial agents in London in last-ditch efforts to convince Lord Grenville to abandon his stamp tax proposal. When it became clear that the proposal was moving forward nonetheless, Ingersoll used his influence to help persuade the Treasury to set duties at a lower rate than initially planned. In his own eyes, Ingersoll had served his colony well and to the best of his abilities.

With this self-satisfied view, which Ingersoll expected would earn him gratitude from his countrymen, he accepted the office of stamp distributor for Connecticut in 1765, but when he returned to New Haven in August, he discovered how wrong he was. Rather than accepting the Stamp Act with resignation, his fellow colonists were angrily resisting it and blamed him for selling out their interests for his own advancement. A letter in the *Connecticut Gazette* asked rhetorically, "Have three hundred Pounds a Year, or even a more trifling Consideration been found sufficient to debauch from their Interest those who have been entrusted with the most important concerns by the Colonies?" A sharp reply was imagined: "*No* you'll say, *I don't delight in the Ruin of my Country, but, since 'tis decreed she must fall, who can blame me for taking a Part in the Plunder?* Tenderly said! Why did you not rather say—*If my Father must die, who can accuse me as defective in filial Duty, in becoming his Executioner, that so much of the Estate, at least, as goes to the Hangman, may be retained in the Family?*"

Angry colonists hanged Ingersoll's effigy, his "virtual representative," from trees in at least six different towns and then marched on New Haven, where he lived. He rode toward Hartford in the hope of turning the case over to the legislature there, but before he reached the capital he met up with an advance party of five hundred protesters; they called themselves the Sons of Liberty, thereby linking their efforts with those in other colonies. Their threats led Ingersoll to resign as stamp distributor on the spot, hoping by that action to avoid violence to himself and his property.

The divisions in Connecticut over the Stamp Act ran along preexisting lines of dispute. The Sons of Liberty and other like-minded radical resisters were generally from the eastern part of the colony, were associated with the New Light evangelical movement, and had interests in the land speculations of the Susquehanna Company, founded in 1753 to develop land claims in Pennsylvania. The Old Light Anglicans associated with Ingersoll tended to be deferential to authority and were either disinterested in or opposed to the Susquehanna Company's efforts to annex the Wyoming Valley, which Pennsylvania also claimed. Ingersoll had once been a minor investor himself, but his years in England had convinced him that efforts to enlist imperial support for the venture would fail, and when he returned he discouraged its champions, which made them think he was hostile to the Susquehanna Company and had opposed it while in England.

Ingersoll could do nothing to redeem himself in his fellow colonists' minds. They read letters of his in which he had encouraged the Rockingham ministry at least to lower rates if they were not prepared to repeal the Stamp Act. His political career was ruined. His place in society was destroyed. Ingersoll had become the most hated man in Connecticut by virtue of his prominent place on the increasingly unfashionable side of moderation and restraint. His association with the opponents of movements that swept all before them was to cast him, an ultimate insider, as an outsider for the rest of his life.

In Maryland, when Zachariah Hood declined to resign his position as stamp distributor, a mob tore down his house on September 2, and he fled for his life with only the clothes on his back. George Meserve, distributor for New Hampshire, was warned that it would not be safe to disembark from the ship on which he was returning from England until he resigned his office, which he did. John Hughes, distributor for Pennsylvania and Delaware, resigned under duress, as did George

Mercer of Virginia. Residents of Charleston, South Carolina, forced the resignation of the colony's distributor and of the inspector of stamps for North Carolina, South Carolina, and Bermuda, both of whom lived in the town. In Georgia, the story was much the same.

In response to a call by the Massachusetts assembly to plan a united protest against the Stamp Act, which was scheduled to go into effect on November 1, twenty-seven delegates representing nine colonies met in New York on October 7, calling themselves the Stamp Act Congress. They deliberated for twelve days before reaching agreement on fourteen declarations, and adjourned on October 24. The governors of Virginia, North Carolina, and Georgia had stymied plans to send delegates from their jurisdictions by refusing to convene their respective assemblies; New Hampshire also declined to send delegates. (New Hampshire and Georgia did, however, later approve the proceedings.) The congress's declarations summarized the arguments on the colonies' historical relationship with the British Empire, and their positions on representation and taxation, the abridgment of trial by jury, and the burden imposed by the novel tax, especially its provision for collection in specie rather than colonial paper money. In sum, the delegates called for "Repeal of . . . the Stamp Duties, of all Clauses of any other Acts of Parliament, whereby the Jurisdiction of the Admiralty is extended as aforesaid, and of the other late Acts for the Restriction of *American* Commerce."

By November 1, official notice of the Stamp Act had not, in fact, reached all the colonies; the stamps were unavailable; stamp distributors and inspectors had for the most part resigned; and ports and courts closed in major cities rather than comply with the law. The strategies varied, but eventually ports and courts were prepared to open in defiance of the law. Colonists hoped that Parliament and English merchants would buckle before the closures wreaked havoc with the colonial economy and food supplies.

On December 21, John Dickinson, a Pennsylvania lawyer and politician, wrote to William Pitt from Philadelphia, "I mean not, sir, to exaggerate things: but beyond all Question it is certain, that an unexampled and universal jealousy, Grief and Indignation have been excited in the Colonists by the Conduct of their Mother Country since the Conclusion of the last War." Like other colonists, he regarded the accusation that they sought independence from the empire "with inexpressible Detestation and Abhorrence." It showed a total misunderstanding of the principles upon which they refused to be taxed without representation. "Not that I doubt in the least that the Attempt [to separate from the empire] may be executed whenever it is made," he went on. "The Strength of the Colonies, their Distance, the Wealth that woud pour into them on opening their Ports to all Nations, the Jealousy entertained of Great Britain by some European Powers, and the peculiar Circumstances of that Kingdom, woud insure Success." The colonies' allegiance could be preserved, he thought, only "by preserving their Affections." The British were effectively driving them out of the empire despite their loyalty.

Consistent efforts over the previous two decades to tighten the grip of the royal prerogative had also taken a toll on the colonies' attachment to Great Britain. "It seems to have been the constant Intention of the Administration," Dickinson wrote, "except in some short and shining Periods, to establish a Prerogative in America quite different from that in Great Britain. In short, to give the Crown a Power here, that if aimed at there, would rouse the whole Nation in Vindication of its Rights." There were two ways for the British Empire to exercise its authority in the colonies. One was by heavy-handed attempts to seize their internal governance; this was the case with extension of the prerogative, with inflexible instructions to the governors, and with the exaction of internal taxes. The other, more benevolent and traditional, was to regulate their commerce just as Parliament regulated the commerce in the rest of the empire. It was the assaults on their "internal Government" that had the colonists up in arms. "A People is never fond of plunging into the horrors of War without great Temptations or Provocations," Dickinson wrote, "and these with prudent Management may be utterly removd from the Colonies."

According to Thomas Hutchinson, still reeling from the mob's destruction of his home and confiscation of his property, the problem was bigger than the Stamp Act; collectively, the protests constituted a broad assault on authority in Massachusetts. At this point, the only way to enforce the Stamp Act would be with "superior force," Hutchinson believed, though—even if Parliament repealed the law and enacted no other of its kind—"we shall still be in a deplorable condition." In Boston and other American cities, "the authority is in the populace, no law can be carried into execution against their mind. I am not sure that the acts of trade will not be considered as grievous as the stamp act."

When Parliament convened in January 1766, the Rockingham ministry had been searching for six months for a way out of the crisis and a way to rid itself of the burden of Grenville's misbegotten tax, and it had not gotten very far. Then William Pitt rose to deliver a speech, which would gain him credit for the Stamp Act's repeal. Pitt advocated the Americans' distinction between taxation and legislation:

> It is my opinion that this kingdom has no right to lay a tax upon the colonies. At the same time, I assert the authority of this kingdom over the colonies, to be sovereign and supreme, in every circumstance of government and legislation whatsoever . . . Taxation is no part of the governing or legislative power . . . The distinction between legislation and taxation is essentially necessary to liberty.

The concept of "virtual" representation was, to Pitt, of no merit, and the American colonists were not represented in Parliament.

London merchants were by now greatly concerned about the closed ports and the overstocked and spoiling products they had hoped to sell in the colonies. And in England their voices carried significantly more weight than those of the Sons of Liberty, the colonial assemblies, or the Stamp Act Congress. The merchants petitioned England's lord mayors to support their efforts in pursuit of the "best Interests of Great Britain . . . it being our Opinion that conclusive Arguments for granting every Ease or Advantage the North-Americans can with Propriety desire, may be fairly deduced from that principle only." This was a practical dollars-and-cents, and only peripherally political, approach.

The merchants lobbied Parliament directly to think in economic terms about the issue. On January 16, 1766, it received their petition, which asked MPs to consider the "Nature of this Trade, consisting of *British* Manufactures exported, and of the Import of raw Materials from *America*, many of them used in our Manufactures, and all of them tending to lessen our Dependence on neighbouring States." The merchants anticipated the "utter Ruin" of commerce unless Parliament repealed all the stamp taxes. Indeed, without open ports the Americans would be in no position to pay their debts, which would bring the whole commercial empire crumbling down.

Nonetheless, Rockingham was in a delicate spot, caught between the colonists' challenge to Parliament's sovereignty and the empire's economy and perhaps its very survival. The British public was certainly in no mood to fight another expensive war, to give the nation's enemies an opening to support its colonists if they were to bid for independence, or to concede that Britain was without power and authority to rule its colonies. Rockingham came up with a formula that conceded the tax while retaining the principle and, he hoped, would keep his ministry in power.

His idea was a repeal accompanied by a Declaratory Act asserting Parliament's authority: "Resolved, that it appears to this Committee that the most dangerous tumults and insurrections have been raised and carried on in several of the North American colonies, in open defiance of the powers and dignity of his Majesty's government there, and in manifest violation of the laws and legislative authority of this kingdom." This was not a conciliatory view of the case. It continued: "Resolved, that the said tumults have been *greatly* encouraged and inflamed by *sundry* votes and resolutions passed in several assemblies of the said provinces, *greatly derogatory* to the honour and dignity of his Majesty's Government, destructive of the legal and constitutional dependency of the said Colonies on the Imperial Crown and Parliament of Great Britain."

The Declaratory Act then called for an investigation to identify and, presumably, to prosecute the "authors, abettors, and perpetrators of the said riots and *insurrections*." It also directed the colonial assemblies to compensate victims of the mobs. Finally, Parliament stood its ground: "Resolved, that the Parliament of Great Britain had, hath, and of a right ought to have, full power and authority to make laws and statutes of sufficient force and validity to bind the Colonies and people of America *in all cases whatsoever*." It is hard to imagine that anyone thought this would end the conflict. It is doubtful that anyone saw compromise of principles or interests as the way out.

In March 1766, meanwhile, before anyone in America knew that Parliament was repealing the Stamp Act, thirty black-faced men attacked the house and store of Richard King, who was one of the richest merchants and leading creditors in Scarborough, Maine, and therefore heartily disliked by some of his neighbors. The public rationale for the strike against him was the false rumor that he supported the Stamp Act and had stamps in his house. A public declaration explained that King was a "bad man, who will ruin us all if he goes on at this rate . . . if he is not humbled." The crowd gutted the interior of the house, tore out doors and paneling, smashed furniture, broke windows, and stole account books. The last made the crowd's anger especially clear. A note left behind threatened to burn down the house and barn and to slice King to pieces if he tried to have anyone prosecuted for these acts. When King defied the warning, a mob set fire to the barn, routed his tenant from the house and burned it down, mutilated livestock, stole tools, broke the remaining windows, spread excrement on his door, and assaulted him. King eventually secured a judgment in court for a fraction of the damages but was unable to collect a penny of it before he died in 1775.

In August, another mob, this one in Falmouth (now Portland, Maine), stole a cargo of smuggled sugar and rum that customs collectors had seized from one Enoch Ilsey. This kind of action was called a "rescue" of the cargo from the hands of the customs men. For good measure the crowd also stormed the inn where the customs collectors were spending the night and roughed them up. In his report on these events to the Board of Trade, Governor Bernard observed that "formerly a rescue was an accidental or occasional Affair; now it is the natural & certain Consequences of a seizure, & the effect of a predetermined Resolution that the Laws of Trade shall not be executed."

Governor Bernard was correct in saying that resistance to customs collection had increased in both frequency and violence. But that was only half the story and gives a truncated view of the situation. Increased resistance was a response to tightened enforcement with less flexibility than in the past and fewer accommodations to local custom and tradition—no longer any discounts on the taxes legally due, a harsher approach to enforcement, and a refusal to make the sorts of arrangements by bribery that had become standard practice.

11

✦

RESISTANCE

For more than a century, American colonists had been smuggling to mitigate the effects of British restrictions on their trade, but they largely ignored restrictions on their manufacturing, which Parliament had imposed in order to subsidize British-made goods. The commercial advantages of being protected by the Royal Navy had outweighed the costs of trade restrictions, which the toothless customs service enforced laxly up until the mid-1760s. But the Sugar Act of 1764 changed the rules of the game, using the navy as the strong arm of the empire and giving ship captains a financial stake in the seizure of suspected contraband goods.* The Royal Navy, being after all a disciplined military organization, enforced the commercial restrictions in a military manner—severely. Parliament had not intended and, given their historical experience, the colonists certainly did not expect revenue laws to be enforced literally, but the navy knew no other way.

For ten years the Sugar Act was the single most effective revenue-raising measure enacted by Parliament and enforced in Britain's North American colonies, realizing £306,000. The Navigation Acts—which

---

* Half of the value of goods seized went to crews of ships making the seizures and half to the Treasury. In cases enforced by the customs service without naval support, one-third went to the governor of the colony, one-third to an informer where there was one, and one-third to the customs service. Between 1768 and 1774, the value of the customs officers' seizures exceeded £30,000, and the navy seized goods valued in the same range.

listed principally export duties on enumerated products shipped to other colonies, particularly indigo, rice, fustic (a yellow dye made from trees), and tobacco—brought in much less, £25,000, and returns on the Stamp Act had been minimal at about £3,000. The Revenue Act of 1767 (also known as the Townshend Duties, named for the prime minister who proposed them) imposed import duties on a short list of British manufactures—glass, lead used in paint, painters' colors, and some grades of paper—which brought in £33,000, about one-tenth of what the Treasury collected from the Sugar Act.

But the total taxes collected, about £367,000, were only half the financial story. Several other factors must be weighed in the balance. First, the taxes fell most heavily on four cities—Boston, New York, Philadelphia, and Charleston, where resistance to the imperial program was to catch fire—and on four colonies—Massachusetts, New York, Pennsylvania, and Virginia—where support for the opposition grew most quickly. Second, the costs for customs collection legally imposed on the colonists were to be almost double that of the taxes themselves, about £607,000, including seizures and authorized fees. Finally, the total cost to the colonists went even higher—no one could calculate how much higher—given the bribes and unwarranted seizures made by corrupt customs officers in collusion with British naval officers. Thus the considerable cost to the colonists was a factor in their resistance. The costs affected the economies of major cities in particular and united the interests of wealthy merchants, ships' crews, shopkeepers, consumers, and producers.

The same day that Parliament passed the Revenue Act in June 1767, it also created an American Board of Customs Commissioners, which would be headquartered in Boston. The commissioners themselves, rather than simply the taxes, contributed mightily to the tensions growing in the next years, as did the enforcement clauses of the revenue acts of 1764 and the new Revenue Act of 1767. They became a flash point of the Revolution.

The laws required the payment of bonds before loading goods onto ships. This gave the collectors power to delay commerce and created an opening for selective enforcement, leveraging bribes, and exacting retribution. Likewise, any vessel carrying more than twenty tons that British naval authorities sighted more than two leagues (five miles) from shore could be seized if it lacked bonds and other clearance papers.

This meant that vessels trading domestically were subject to regulations previously enforceable only on transatlantic and international trade. The penalty was confiscation of the ship and its contents.

A ship sailing from Charleston, South Carolina, to Newport, Rhode Island, for example, that was caught in a storm or sent off course by a combination of strong winds and currents and therefore made a routine stop at Martha's Vineyard for repairs—perhaps also to dispose of some spoiled provisions and to barter a small part of its cargo to pay for the repairs—was now in technical violation of the law for unauthorized and undocumented "breaking bulk." The ship was thus subject to seizure—on the Vineyard, on the high seas, or at its ultimate destination—for discrepancies between the cocket, which listed every item on board, and the goods found on the ship. The burden of proof in a seizure prosecuted in admiralty court fell entirely on the vessel's owner. This included owners of the many small lumber boats that traded locally in New England.

Perhaps the most resented practice of all was the customs service's selective enforcement of provisions of the Sugar Act that affected intra-colonial traffic, even after admiralty court rulings and legal opinions of the attorneys general of Massachusetts and England went against what were deemed unwarranted seizures. The customs men were not merely cracking down on smuggling and fraud; they were also harassing small-time traders, who may have had their entire equity in one small vessel and could not afford court costs even if the law was on their side. Customs agents also confiscated the goods and possessions of ordinary seamen, who by tradition engaged in their own petty trade to supplement their salaries, whenever the captain failed to enter their goods on the manifests.

On top of it all, unpredictability, the bane of business enterprise, became another tool that customs collectors used to increase their leverage against traders, whether fair or foul, who did not accept the new rules of the game. Collectors would overlook minor infractions of the law for a time, as bait, and then hook the unwary with an unannounced inflexibility that maximized the value of what they seized. Collectively, the literal and malicious enforcement of apparently minor provisions of the revenue acts altered the nature of business in the colonies and drove competitors and people of different class, professional, and regional interests together against a common enemy.

In 1767, Charles Lloyd, a member of the Birmingham and Pennsylvania banking family, published a pamphlet in London that offered the opinion that the ministry had to give colonial governors more guidance on how to manage the colonists, who were so different from the English. According to him, it was the governors "whose conduct was to determine, whether the empire of North America should be retained in obedience, or thrown into an independance fatal to themselves and dangerous to Great-Britain." Again—and typically—the idea of separation came from fearful London officials or British ones in North America rather than being a stated ambition of the colonists themselves. Lloyd's pamphlet included several reprinted circular letters to the governors that expressed this British view.

The resolutions from colonial assemblies against the Stamp Act, on the other hand, asserted "an independence upon England . . . meant to be not merely verbal assertions, but principles of action." The Virginia assembly avowed "the principles of independence on England," which included repudiation of the "many outrages" committed in "open defiance" of Parliament, which themselves could be interpreted only as "seditious." Lloyd "had been repeatedly informed that the schemes of independence were formed and guided by the lawyers, and supported by the principals of the provinces," which, he believed, "encreased the danger of the insurrections."

The Privy Council claimed that it had "authentic and particular intelligence, that the principles of resistance and independence, which had been unchecked, had produced their natural consequences, tumult and rebellion" in the colonists' response to the Townshend Duties. The resolutions passed by the Stamp Act Congress "were designed to establish the claim of an absolute independence on the British parliament . . . To enable them to maintain this independence . . . an unprecedented, illegal and dangerous meeting, of committees from all the provinces was assembled at New York." Asserting the colonies' independence in "popular publications, provincial assemblies, and the still more dangerous step of open resistance; they had looked on, while to maintain this independence, an American senate was formed, which might receive the reverence due to the parliament of England," and the colonies had also raised an army "to support their pretensions." It is unclear from whom the ministry was gathering this intelligence, but its reactions were undoubtedly more in response to inflammatory rumors than to any clear realities on the ground.

The Treasury had not expected resistance to the Townshend Duties, as they were the same sort of external taxes the colonists were paying, with grumbling partial compliance, under the Sugar Act. Nor had ministers anticipated opposition to the Quartering Act of 1765, which had the colonists paying for British troops' room and board, even after the end of the war with the French and Indians. They certainly had not expected that colonists would read the Quartering Act as an indirect tax and thus unconstitutional for the same reasons they believed the Stamp Act to be unconstitutional: a Parliament in which they were not and could not be represented authorizing the taking of their property. In some colonists' view, the Quartering Act effectively imposed *direct* costs. The law mandated that military personnel barracked in warehouses, "or in hired uninhabited houses, out-houses, barns, or other buildings, shall, from time to time, be furnished and supplied . . . with fire, candles, vinegar, and salt, bedding, utensils for dressing their victuals, and small beer or cyder, not exceeding five pints, or half a pint of rum mixed with a quart of water, to each man, without paying any thing for the same." The colonies were to bear the cost. In December 1766, the New York assembly explicitly refused to comply with the act, and on July 2, 1767, Parliament suspended the legislature "until provision shall have been made by the said assembly of *New York* for furnishing his Majesty's troops within the said province with all such necessaries as are required by the said acts of parliament."

In a similar assertion of Parliament's authority in the face of increasing challenges from the colonial assemblies, the colonial governors received instructions in 1767 "not upon any pretense whatever [to] give your assent to any law" passed by the assemblies "by which the number of the assembly shall be enlarged or diminished, the duration of it ascertained, the qualification of the electors or the elected fixed or altered, or by which any regulations shall be established with respect thereto" until the Privy Council reviewed and approved the bill. Not surprisingly, colonists saw this instruction as an unwarranted intrusion on their internal governance; now the ministry was attacking their representative institutions. From London, of course, the government saw itself as simply administering the empire more diligently than it had in the past and in the face of repeated challenges to its authority by lawless colonists.

As always, the ministry assumed that only a few malcontents and rabble-rousers led the protests. One of these, according to the Boston customs collector Joseph Harrison, was John Dickinson, the Philadelphia lawyer whose influential pamphlet *Letters from a Farmer in Pennsylvania* was "one of the most dangerous" of a "vast number of inflaming and seditious Publications tending to poison and incense the Minds of the People and alienate them from all regard and obedience to the Legislature of the Mother Country." The *Letters* first appeared serially in newspapers between November 1767 and January 1768, and were then collected in a very popular pamphlet. Dickinson addressed specifically the Quartering Act and the suspension of the New York assembly. By compelling the support of troops in the colonies, Parliament had, according to Dickinson in the first of his letters, taxed the colonists. "If the people of *New-York* cannot be legally taxed but by their own representatives," he argued, "they cannot be legally deprived of the privilege of legislation, only for insisting on that exclusive privilege of taxation. If they may be legally deprived in such a case, of the privilege of legislation, why may they not, with equal reason, be deprived of every other privilege?"

In his second letter, Dickinson aimed the same logic at the Townshend Duties, which seemed to him "unconstitutional, and as destructive of the liberty of these colonies, as that mentioned in my last letter." He did not question Parliament's authority to regulate trade in the empire, which included levying duties so as to "preserve and promote a mutually beneficial intercourse between the several constituent parts of the empire." The attempt to raise revenue in this way was, however, unprecedented, according to Dickinson, whether by internal taxes such as the Stamp Act, external taxes such as the Townshend Duties, or indirect taxes like the Quartering Act, which took the colonists' property without their being represented in Parliament. Never before the Sugar Act, he argued, had Parliament even thought "of imposing duties in *America*, FOR THE PURPOSE OF RAISING A REVENUE."*

---

* Dickinson discussed the distinction between internal and external taxes in the fourth letter but considered them all "duties," which Parliament intended to raise revenue.

A rousing summary in the twelfth letter caught the attention of readers who believed that Americans were aiming for separation from Britain. The logic of the linked steps taken in London dictated a resistance, wrote Dickinson, and the ministry construed this as rebellion; imperial logic imagined only limited options. As the king and his ministers saw it, they had either to crush the rebellion or to succumb to the dissolution of the empire. The "farmer" concluded:

> Let these *truths* be indelibly impressed on our minds, *that we cannot be* HAPPY, WITHOUT *being* FREE—that we cannot be free, *without being secure in our property*—that *we* cannot be secure in our property, *if, without our consent, others may, as by right, take it away*—that *taxes* imposed on us by parliament, *do thus take it away*—that *duties laid for the sole purpose of raising money*, are taxes—that *attempts* to lay such duties *should be instantly and firmly opposed.*

From the imperial perspective, events in the spring of 1768 followed Dickinson's lead. From the perspective of many colonists, the events fulfilled their worst fears about imperial motives as suggested by writers like Dickinson, who had warned them to unite in defense of their traditional independence. On May 9, a small sloop called *Liberty* arrived at dusk in the port of Boston, loaded with a shipment of wine from the island of Madeira. The ship belonged to John Hancock, one of Boston's richest merchants and also a representative of Boston in the colony's assembly. Since it was drawing toward nightfall, the customs inspection would take place the next morning. On board, there was one tidewaiter, as customs collectors who boarded ships in the harbor were called. The next morning, when Joseph Harrison, another customs collector, and Benjamin Hallowell, comptroller of customs, boarded the *Liberty*, they discovered that the ship held only a fraction of its cargo capacity. Nonetheless, after consulting with the tidewaiter, they certified the ship for unloading.

One month later, under oath, the tidewaiter, Thomas Kirk, repudiated his earlier testimony. Harrison reported his new story: "In the Night a large number of People being collected together, they seized and confined the Tideswaiter that was on board, broke open the Hatches, and took out the greatest part of the Cargo of Wines. When the business was finished they released the Tidesman but with such Threats and Denunciations of Vengeance Death and Destruction in Case he divulged the Affair." It is unclear how Kirk found the courage to change his story, but he was under pressure from Governor Bernard and the customs officers, who wanted to make an example of Hancock as retribution for his political activities. The commissioners now seized the sloop and had it towed into the harbor, where it anchored under the guns of the *Romney*, a British man-of-war. As Harrison later said, smuggling remained rampant, and he and other collectors were trying to run a fine line between "the Commissioners on one Side requiring (as in duty bound) the Exaction of all Customs, and the People on the other disputing the payment of any and even objecting to the legality of them."

Having secured the *Liberty* and put it under the protection of the Royal Navy, Harrison, Hallowell, and Harrison's eighteen-year-old son debarked, left the wharf, and were walking down the street when a mob pursued them. "The onset was begun by throwing Dirt at me," Harrison later testified, "which was presently succeeded by Volleys of Stones, Brickbatts, Sticks or anything that came to hand: In this man-ner I run the Gauntlet near 200 Yards, my poor Son . . . was knocked down and then laid hold of by the Legs, Arms and hair of his Head, and in the manner dragged along the Kennel [gutter] in a most barba-rous and cruel manner." Eventually the three men escaped from the crowd with bumps, bruises, and contusions, but nothing worse. Once having reached a safe haven, they believed the incident had ended and the mob had spent its fury.

Two hours later, though, at about 9:00 p.m., the crowd reassembled and bore down on the houses of several members of the customs ser-vice, breaking windows and trying, without success, to find the ten-ants. Then the crowd pulled a pleasure boat owned by Harrison from the water and dragged it through the streets to the Liberty Tree—the famous elm that stood near Boston Common and had become a rally-ing point for protests against the British occupation—where they con-demned it in a mockery of the customs process used against smugglers and then burned it to ashes. The next day, the parties negotiated a truce, which returned the *Liberty* to Hancock pending the outcome of the prosecution. On Monday, still in fear for their lives, Harrison and his family received passage to Castle William, the harbor fortress con-trolled by Governor Bernard and protected by troops.

Harrison reported to his superiors that between the demands made by the commissioners, who were "not very friendly (on account of my being an Advocate for temporate Measures till such Time as the Hands of Government shall be strengthened) and the Temper of the People as to render it unsafe for me to be ashore," he suffered a nervous disorder that ruined his health. The prosecutor dropped the suit against Hancock in the fall, no doubt to accommodate the inflamed tempers of Bostonians. Several months later, Harrison returned to England. Hancock, however, felt persecuted by the customs service and accepted his role as a popular symbol of British oppression. The *Liberty* affair was a heady moment for him, and he was being swept up by events rather than by decisions of his own.

Henry Laurens was a merchant in Charleston, South Carolina, and probably the wealthiest resident of the southern colonies. A conservative in politics, he had played no part in opposition to the Stamp Act and had opposed sending delegates from South Carolina to the Stamp Act Congress. His business operations were so large and complex—transatlantic partnerships, international credit relationships, and an empire-wide customer base—that he valued highly the protection of the Royal Navy and considered smuggling a threat to his business rather than an opportunity for profit. He judged the risks of noncompliance with customs regulations too high and was constitutionally inclined to obey the law in any event.

For all these reasons, the customs service made a mistake when it singled out Laurens, an error that was to have empire-wide repercussions. Initially, it was simply a particular agent who focused on Laurens's operations: Daniel Moore, a customs collector from London who arrived in Charleston in March 1767. Immediately and unilaterally he increased the fees for execution of official documents, inspections, and certificates that authorized exports of indigo. He would make the merchants "sweat . . . at law with their own money," he was reported as saying, and challenged them to fight him in the admiralty courts if they dared.

Moore's efforts to require bonds on ships engaged in intracolonial trade were largely unsuccessful. But even when he lost suits over his seizures, provisions in recent laws generally allowed him to collect fees and costs, which were sometimes greater than the value of the small boats in question. Three of his first seizures were of ships owned by Laurens. One of them, the *Wambaw*, cleared Charleston for Laurens's plantation in Georgia with the full knowledge of customs officers, who expressed no objections since the goods on board were for transport, not sale, and none were on their list of enumerated goods. But on the return leg of its trip, the *Wambaw*'s captain took on shingles as ballast to keep the vessel stable in the wind and waves. Laurens was alert to the legal vulnerability of this load, and, unable to reach a customs office from his Georgia plantation, he secured bonds from two magistrates. Nonetheless, Moore ordered the ship seized when it entered the port at Charleston on the grounds that it lacked a lumber bond.

Laurens received notice that the ship would be released for a "fee," but he declined to bribe Moore. In admiralty proceedings, the court condemned the *Wambaw* and its cargo, and levied the costs of prosecution on Laurens. These included a hefty "fee" of £277 for the judge, who allowed Laurens to repurchase his sloop for £175. In the meantime, agents seized another of Laurens's boats under similar circumstances. In this case, the ballast was logs of no commercial value that could serve only as firewood, but it still fell under the letter of the law requiring a lumber bond. The judge dismissed the charges on the grounds that the trip had not been a commercial venture and there had been no attempt to circumvent the law. Still, the court assessed Laurens £216 in costs, but since there was no probable cause for the seizure, Laurens successfully filed a civil suit for £1,400 damages, which were paid out of customs revenues, thereby ensuring the enmity of the collectors, who personally lost income from the settlement.

When soon thereafter customs agents seized Laurens's ship *Ann* on similar dubious technicalities, their prosecution became a cause similar to that of Hancock and the *Liberty* in Boston. Agents had now seized three of Laurens's ships in one year for practices identical to those of other merchants whom they had not harassed. At risk in this last case was more than £1,000 in enumerated goods, plus the ship and court costs. Laurens owned only one-quarter of the enterprise, so his credibility as an investment partner was also at stake. If his fellow investors suffered for doing business with him, he might well be marginalized in mercantile circles.

Again, the customs agents proposed a deal that struck Laurens as the solicitation of a bribe. Laurens published his defense in the *South*

Carolina Gazette on July 11, 1768, and it created a public uproar; the case was dismissed. According to Laurens, "We consider that no part of the money so wrested from us, does, or could be expected to go into the treasury. On the contrary it is wholly swallowed up by a set of Revenue Officers ever formidable to liberty, the numbers of whom was before much too great for safety of the constitution." Along with other newspapers throughout the colonies, the *Pennsylvania Journal* took note of the Laurens case: "Our property is thereby not only taken from us without our consent, but when thus taken, is applied still further to oppress and ruin us."

The customs service had driven another colonist of wealth and influence into popular politics. From the summer of 1768 on, Laurens became the recognized leader of the opposition movement in South Carolina. Reforms that resulted from the protests empowered these popular leaders and gave further credibility to their cause. Several of the most corrupt customs collectors in Charleston lost their jobs, as did the admiralty judge who had profited from the seizures of Laurens's ships. The British Treasury Office put admiralty judges on salary to eliminate the conflict of interest from seizures, but the loyalty that had bound colonists to the empire suffered additional damage and, as it turned out, would not be repaired.

The many changes in the colonies' relationship to Britain in the 1740s, 1750s, and 1760s would have been hard to bear under any circumstances. From the colonists' perspective, threats to their independence within the empire came from new rules and enhanced enforcement of old ones, as well as from the huge increases in the numbers of imperial troops, customs collectors, and naval patrols of the coastline. More troops meant more conflict and greater demands on their resources. More naval patrols required more impressment, which otherwise might have abated after the war. The power of the British Empire was recognized in the corrupt customs service, the rigorous defense of the royal prerogative, the rigid instructions to governors, the eagerness to impose an Anglican bishop, the regulation of paper money, the requirements that taxes be paid in hard money (specie), and the efforts to wring from the colonists more taxes, fees, and the indirect costs of imperial administration.

Much worse, though, were the circumstances in which these changes were effected. A postwar recession, which began in 1763, undermined the economy, reduced the amount of coin in circulation, increased unemployment, and enlarged a permanent underclass, especially in the cities. Shifts in the structure of the colonial social world exacerbated population pressure and made for more and more interregional conflict—principally coastal versus backcountry—and continued violence on the frontier. Economic development, immigration, and unemployment brought about class conflict in the cities, which well-to-do elites tried to redirect into a campaign that blamed the empire, plausibly enough, for what were largely domestic and transnational problems. Across the colonies, from the northern districts of Maine and New Hampshire to Connecticut, New York, Pennsylvania, New Jersey, Virginia, and the Carolinas, the contest for ownership of land with clear titles escalated. Imperial restraints and internal constraints contributed to volatility, as social processes across the colonies, rather than the willed actions of individuals in any one place, propelled events.

In the case of New Jersey, volatile struggles over land titles were a century old. Settlers in the 1660s, who insisted they had purchased their land from Indians and done the work of clearing it, challenged the claims of the proprietor of East Jersey, whose rights rested on royal grants. The conflict exploded in riots during the 1740s and 1750s, and naturally enough the issue was to affect the way New Jerseyans chose sides in the Revolution; the disputes continued in the courts and fields well beyond the colonial period.

Many Puritan farmers had left New England—principally from New Haven, when that colony was absorbed by Connecticut in 1664—to move to East Jersey, where they ran up against land grants made by King Charles II through the Duke of York (later James II) to the courtiers Sir George Carteret and Lord John Berkeley, the original proprietors there. King James had empowered the two men to form a government, sell land, and collect quitrents, which would, in theory, bring them great wealth. But like William Penn and the Lords Baltimore, Carteret and Berkeley found the riches elusive and their authority difficult to enforce.

New York governor Richard Nicolls, following orders from King

James to fill the area with settlers as quickly as possible, and in ignorance of the king's conflicting grants to Carteret and Berkeley, made large grants to the migrating Puritans in the 1660s. But when agents for the proprietors began to rent and sell land, title disputes turned violent; this rebellion against the proprietors persisted from 1667 through 1675. The problem became even more complex when a group of Quakers purchased Berkeley's half of the grant in 1674 and called their new colony West Jersey, separate from East Jersey, the original Carteret grant. This division of the colony introduced a boundary dispute on top of the existing conflicts over titles and over the proprietors' efforts to collect quitrents—annual taxes, or rents, on lands that fell within their royal grants. Conflict among squatters, agents of absentee proprietors, and Scottish and Quaker owners stirred the cauldron of political and social turmoil.

At least fifteen times between 1698 and 1701 alone, antiproprietary mobs in East Jersey attacked courts, jails, and government officials who challenged their titles, or tried to eject them from land they considered theirs, and/or tried to collect quitrents. This chronic instability inspired Queen Anne's decision to reunite the two Jerseys into the royal colony of New Jersey in 1702. But this of course solved nothing. As the population grew, demographic pressures raised property values, created a perceived shortage of unclaimed acreage, and increased the financial stakes in the land disputes.

At that point, Puritan immigrants and their descendants made up about 70 percent of the East Jersey (now north New Jersey) white population. These Puritans were antiproprietary from the start and remained so throughout the colonial period. In their new setting, they became Presbyterians, which was not a theological move—both New England Congregationalists and Presbyterians were Calvinist—but a change in church structure: The congregations in New England were independent while the Presbyterian churches were organized into synods.

The Presbyterian and Dutch Reformed churches in northern Jersey were deeply affected in the 1740s by the Great Awakening, when George Whitefield and other New Light preachers—about whom the colonial Old Light Anglican gentry had always been deeply suspicious—swept through the region. Religious controversy pitted Old Light Anglicans, attached to the imperial administration through the government-authorized patronage system that benefited their churches, against the New Light Presbyterian and Dutch Reformed parishes, excluded from the patronage network and with land titles that conflicted with those of the richer Anglican insiders.*

This new religious conflict—in some cases inspired and in others exacerbated by the Great Awakening—corresponded to preexisting conflicts over land, but it now gave a moral dimension to questions of politics and law. The antiproprietary land claimants and their New Light pastors seized the moral high ground against established authority. If, as the New Light preachers avowed, all souls are equal in the eyes of God, so, too, are all people, regardless of social rank or political position, equal to each other and in relation to the government. With God as the claimants' highest authority, no governor, sheriff, or judge could stand in the way of their claims to rightful possession of their land. In 1746, a pamphlet titled *A Brief Vindication of the Purchasers Against the Proprietors in a Christian Manner* accused claimants to proprietary land grants of the sin of avarice, which escalated the controversy into the spiritual realm. Responding in kind, the proprietary party predicted that those who challenged authority would "bring Destruction on themselves, both to Soul and Body."

The challenges to governance in New Jersey became a crisis quite apart from the other controversies that roiled British-American relations in the 1750s and 1760s. Between 1735 and 1763, New Jersey's institutions, which had never been strong, crumbled. Demographic growth certainly affected the timing of the social disintegration: Between 1700 and 1745, the population quadrupled, from 15,000 to more than 61,000. The population growth accelerated lumber harvesting, a greater demand for lumber made the price of lumber rise, which in turn increased the value of the land from which it was harvested. Higher property values raised the stakes in the land disputes, which became more violent.

Rich proprietors and their clients used the courts to reassert their land claims, while farmers used their saws and strength in numbers to defend theirs. The discovery of iron and copper dates back to seventeenth-century Dutch settlers, but the earliest iron mines started around 1710. Competition for the minerals contributed to violence during the eighteenth century. There were class dimensions to the

---

* Whitefield was a New Light Anglican.

conflicts, but not of agrarian conservatives intent on defending tradi-tional land uses against capitalist developers. In this case, both sides wanted to exploit natural resources for profit.

By 1745, disorder ruled New Jersey. On the political front, royally appointed governors and their appointed councils and judiciary were at continual odds with the elected assembly. While the assembly was mostly made up of comparatively wealthy men, the assemblymen played to the crowds challenging the proprietary interests represented by the council. Control of patronage enabled the governor, councilors, and other influential men to appoint judges prejudiced in their favor, which only undermined the credibility of the courts and encouraged a repu-diation of government and institutions. A first line of struggle pitted judges against juries, but the conflict did not stop there. As one propri-etor wrote in 1742, "I am well assured that no jury can be found in Bergen County that will give it [a verdict] in favour of the Proprietors." The same was true in five other East Jersey counties as well.

Between 1735 and 1742, there were at least five acts of collective vio-lence against surveyors (agents of the proprietors) and eleven others in response to court-ordered evictions of antiproprietary claimants. The violence continued sporadically well into the 1750s. On July 17, 1747, two hundred "rioters" marched into Perth Amboy, "armed with Clubs . . . to the Great terrour of the inhabitants . . . a party of them upwards of a Hundred in Number, marched on foot in a Warlike manner to the King's Gaol." The sheriff and deputies who warned the crowds off "were assaulted by the mob with staves and clubs." Rioters broke open the jail and released John Bainbridge, who had been arrested for resist-ing a sheriff trying to execute a court order. After freeing Bainbridge, the crowd "marched through town with fiddles playing before them, threatening Death and Destruction to all that should oppose them." By the end of the year, six more jailbreaks freed popular leaders who had resisted court-ordered land seizures.

As in Boston in the 1760s, crowds and committees ruled New Jer-sey in opposition to the formal institutions authorized by Great Brit-ain. The number of patronage positions in the latter could not satisfy all the comparatively wealthy men with political aspirations in the colony, and they noted the correspondence between exclusion from the patronage network and their own antiproprietary allegiance. A new class of alienated elites was arising, which united with the small farmers against the entrenched privileged class; their support of the extra-legal committees and crowds gave the protests credibility and provided a savvy leadership. It also made outright class conflict unlikely. Committee leaders were empowered from below and by evangelicals, as against Anglicans empowered by imperial patronage and upper-class associations. And the political outsiders came to outnumber the insiders and their clients. When some of the independent committees began to ally across town and county lines, the alliance included about nine thousand white men over the age of sixteen. In 1748, East Jersey's Board of Proprietors reported, "The great Majority . . . are Favourers of the Rioters." The following year, the Essex County sheriff estimated that one-third of the men in the county had participated in riots and that 80–90 percent supported the extralegal actions. In 1745, the committees had even established an extralegal assembly that collected taxes and issued its own currency. And in the same year, a crowd of about 150 men stormed the Newark jail.

At root, the dispute was about economic interests, but it was also about independence and the source of property rights. The proprietors had a point when they wondered, as one did rhetorically in 1746, whether "to pretend to hold Lands by an Indian Deed only, is not . . . declaring the Indian Grantor to be the Superior Lord of that Land, and disowning the Crown of England to be so?" Another proprietary supporter argued to the (official) assembly that if the rioters' ownership by right of Indian purchase was confirmed, the "purchases . . . obtained by the Proprietors from the Crown of England, must be Void and Unjust, Bad and Unlawful, and of Course a royal fraud." Robert Hunter Morris played out the implications at about the same time: "If the people settling . . . the British Dominions in America can Derive property in soil or powers of Government from any other source than the Crown which by the Laws of England is the fountain of Powers, and properly then are they as much independent of the Crown & nation of Britain as any people whatever." This was fifteen years before the revenue-raising acts, the strictly enforced customs regulations, and the corrupt customs agents undermined British authority.

Settlers had started moving into the South Carolina backcountry in the 1730s, but it was during the 1740s and 1750s that there was significant expansion into the pine forests that began fifty miles from the coast. Scots-Irish settlers moving down from western Pennsylvania, Virginia, and North Carolina predominated, but Germans, Welsh Baptists, French Huguenots, and Irish Quakers could be found, too, and together these disparate people outnumbered the settlers moving in from the coast. As the settlements pressed westward, they intruded on lands traditionally hunted and occupied by the Cherokee nation. Relations between the Cherokee and the British settlers deteriorated in the 1750s for many reasons—pressure from the French and from the settlers themselves, and from the frontier-wide war that began in 1754.

By this time, the Cherokees occupied about sixty towns at the southern end of the Appalachian range, scattered over an area of about seventy-five hundred square miles. In the early eighteenth century, there were about twenty thousand Cherokees in the region, six thousand of whom were warriors. (The white population of South Carolina was about twelve thousand in 1720 and fifteen thousand in 1740.) A smallpox epidemic killed about half the Cherokees in 1738, reducing them to about ten thousand, three thousand of them warriors, still a formidable force but nowhere near as powerful in proportion to the whites as they had been earlier in the century. And they also had to take a defensive posture against the Choctaws, who outnumbered them, and the French to the southwest.

Cherokees had accompanied General John Forbes's troops in their assault on Fort Duquesne in 1758, but they deserted in the face of what seemed to them an ill-planned and likely disastrous campaign, clashing with settlers as they went south to return home; the whites were incapable of discerning a homeward-bound Cherokee from an attacking Indian of any tribe. Skirmishes continued through 1759. The ongoing issues were the same ones common to the rest of the frontier—the expansion of the white population into territory the Cherokee considered their own and the Indians' reliance on the British to restrain this expansion; the fragility of Cherokee independence in the face of so many potential enemies, both Indian and white; their increasing dependence on European trade goods; their complicated attempts to navigate a diplomatic position among the English and French empires, American settlers, and the Indian tribes that surrounded them; and the weakening of France as a makeweight to English power.

The Cherokee War in the South Carolina backcountry grew from skirmishes that well displayed the region's underlying instability and culminated in systematic campaigns by both sides to eradicate the other and in the virtual collapse of the settlers' frontier society. In 1760, about 100 Cherokees attacked a wagon train of 250 Scots-Irish settlers trying to evacuate the frontier. Forty of the settlers, mostly women and children, either died or were captured. Two days later, there was another "massacre" of twenty-three fleeing women and children. Ultimately, hundreds of South Carolina settlers abandoned their farms and huddled in ramshackle forts, living in conditions that contributed to a smallpox epidemic that swept the region. Both Indians and whites committed atrocities, which included the taking of scalps from the wounded and dead. At one point, militia surrounded a house where forty Indians had taken refuge and burned it to the ground; as the Cherokees fled the flames, militiamen picked them off.

The Cherokees depended on trade with the settlers to survive, and it was this pattern—rather than their losses in combat—that led them to surrender after the hard winter of 1760–1761 starved them out; by the end of the year they agreed to peace terms. The settlers fared no better, for many of those who had escaped the violence succumbed to disease. Much of the South Carolina assembly's funding for relief never reached the refugees, and their belongings and food were plundered by the very military and civilian officials charged with supporting them; militia rangers recruited to fight Indians found robbing the settlers a more lucrative proposition. "These rangers," one settler observed, "instead of Annoying the enemy, fell to plundering of, and living at free quarter on the poor scatter'd Inhabitants. The forts into which they retired were fill'd with Whores and Prostitutes and there maintain'd at the Public Expence." The rangers lived "in an open, scandalous, debauch'd Manner . . . instead of going on Duty." Given this exploitation by their purported defenders, it is no wonder that the refugees said "they sustain'd more damage from their Protectors than from the Enemy, as they stript them of the little the other had left."

After the peace treaty that ended the Cherokee War was signed in 1762, the South Carolina backcountry was "very slowly resettled," according to the "Remonstrance of the Back Country" published in November 1767. The depopulation, trauma, and dissolution of society had left the region in a shambles. Many now found lives of crime both easier and more profitable than the hard work of starting over from scratch. The "Remonstrance" observed that "for many Years past, the Back Parts of this Province hath been infested with an infernal Gang of Villains, who have committed such horrid Depredations on our Properties and Estates—Such Insults on the Persons of many Settlers and perpetrated such shocking Outrages thro-out the Back Settlements, as is past Description." A petition to the assembly in 1769 pleaded that "since the Cessation of the Cherokee War . . . these back settlements have been in a state of anarchy, disorder, and confusion."

By the mid-eighteenth century, settlement of the North Carolina back-country was also under way. There had been only a few hundred settlers in the Piedmont in the 1740s, but by 1767 there were thirty-nine thousand of European descent and three thousand African-Americans. About fifteen hundred Catawbas also made it their home, but a smallpox epidemic in 1759 reduced the Indian population to about five hundred, too few to resist the waves of settlers moving south and west onto their land. The Cherokee War spilled over from South Carolina, but it was less devastating farther north. And Moravians, members of a German Lutheran Pietist sect, arrived shortly after 1750 to settle the large tract of land they had purchased in Wachovia. The basic mix of ethnicities and the geographic origins of the settlers was much the same as in South Carolina.

North Carolina as a whole had about 175,000 inhabitants by 1767, of which about 20 percent were slaves. (In some of the coastal Tidewater counties where labor-intensive crops such as rice and indigo were grown, slaves composed about 40 percent of the population, while less than 10 percent of the population in the wheat-growing backcountry was enslaved.) And there were other significant contrasts between the two regions. One was in religious affiliation. The Church of England was the established church in the colony, and most North Carolina Anglicans lived in the east, while dissenters, who resented paying taxes to support the Anglican church, predominated in the backcountry, where more land was available and it was less expensive than in either the East or the northern colonies from which most of the settlers had emigrated. It was difficult to secure clear land titles, and the immigrants found themselves struggling against easterners, absentee speculators, and local elites who claimed vast tracts of land themselves or enforced the claims of absentee owners. British officials had intended the open land to be a magnet for settlement and the establishment of clear title to be straightforward and relatively inexpensive. The men who had authority over the processes, however, tried to profit exorbitantly not just from the land but also from the fees for land transfers and title registry. "Land matters in North Carolina are . . . in unbelievable confusion," wrote a Moravian leader, "and I do not see how endless law-suits are to be avoided."

Some land agents and owners also tried to profit by ignoring squatters until after they had cleared and plowed the land, which greatly enhanced its value, at which point the agents would try either to evict the occupants or sell the land to them. When one land agent intended to have a tract surveyed so as to establish clear boundaries before a sale, he was met by a crowd of more than a hundred settlers who intimidated him, asking "whether he thought he would have as many Men attend him to his Grave or not." Some of the men broke his surveyor's chain, confiscated his compass, and sent him on his way, but he was determined to make "examples of some of the Ringleaders." Protests against the Stamp Act closed down some of the colony's courts, so the squatters couldn't be prosecuted at that time; the conflicts continued and were bound to be caught up in the other complex relationships that held the colony and the empire together.

The corruption of speculators and local officials naturally added to the settlers' economic burden, especially when tax collectors and some creditors expected to be paid in coin rather than in crops or depreciated paper currency, which continued to circulate illegally. Farmers generally borrowed annually to see themselves and their families through to harvest, but that pattern jeopardized their property and livelihood in years with poor crop yields. When they diversified production— corn, wheat, and animal skins—to meet market demands in addition to providing for their own needs, they were tied to the international network of trade and credit. Companies that established stores on the frontier speculated in credit as well as in crop futures and deerskins, and the mounting uncollectible debt was passed on in the price of the manufactured goods they sold to farmers and the interest they charged on credit accounts. Since, as creditors, they had first claim on farmers' crops, they were also able to pay low prices, squeezing the farmers economically from yet another direction.

Not surprisingly in such a system, the settlers felt victimized by everyone from absentee landlords, whose agents blamed them for the high rents, sale prices, and mortgage interest; to colonial officials, who blamed London for their policies; to shopkeepers, who blamed their employers and international market forces for the high prices they charged and the interest on their credit accounts. Parliament's Currency Acts of 1751, which prohibited the issue of new bills of credit in the New England colonies, and 1764, which extended the prohibition to all the mainland colonies, also worked against the settlers' interests, since debtors had been favored by the colonies' paper money when it depreciated in value against hard currency. Disallowing payments in paper of debts, court fees, and some taxes created a currency contraction, and economic hardship followed for those at the periphery of the imperial and international financial networks. The farther from the center—for most purposes London, but also the Netherlands and wherever else London merchants borrowed money—the greater the burden and the less control people had of their own lives. Few were farther from the center than the settlers who lived on the frontiers in North America, where there was no one but Indians and a few slaves to exploit.

The decade of the 1760s was precisely the time that the frontiersmen's ability to meet their financial obligations reached a nadir while their taxes increased. In North Carolina, there were the efforts to retire paper currency and at the same time to raise poll taxes, government fees, duties on liquor, parish taxes for the Anglican churches, and quitrents. Compulsory militia service also took men away from their fields, and the consequent drop in crop production was, effectively, another tax. Corruption made everything worse; the sheriffs collecting the taxes did not always turn the money over to the colony's authorities, so the revenues provided few or no benefits to the taxpayers.

With the small amount of hard currency in circulation accumulating in the hands of a few well-positioned men, class tensions increased, as did resentment of the politicians in the Tidewater region of North Carolina, who usually passed laws in support of their own interests. The Piedmont was ripe for vigilante action against merchants, big landowners and their agents, and court and colonial officials on whom farmers could lay their hands. Farmers rightly thought that the magistrates and sheriffs they encountered were agents of the colony's rich

and powerful families, and rightly believed the merchants were responsible for their economic plight. So they attacked the sheriffs and
deputies charged with enforcing court orders, and they burned down
stores to which they were indebted. As the 1760s wore on, spontaneous
individual violence became organized crowd action. By the end of the
decade a "Regulator" movement had sprung up—a paramilitary organization of these desperate and angry men, who intended to bring justice to the civil and economic relations that had so badly deteriorated,
and to protect their farms, now threatened by forces outside their
control.*

The ideological underpinnings of the Regulator movement blended
evangelical theology and the political contract theory that was so popular in the colonies. The religious ferment of the era, along with the
dissenting theology shared by many or most backcountry settlers, gave
them a formula for judging government by their own moral standards
and rebelling against injustice. They followed the "spirit within" on a
path that allowed them to question the authority of both church and
state. Many of them, believing they were in direct spiritual communion with the Holy Ghost, considered ministers, like magistrates, as
lesser authorities who had no authority at all when they acted contrary
to higher law. For the Regulators, the government, whether in Charleston or London, had broken the contract that bound settlers in loyalty
and obedience; in their corrupt, self-interested enforcement of law, local officials had acted as agents of an immoral economy and state; they
had thereby abdicated authority under God's law. Their religion encouraged the Regulators to believe that all souls were equal before
God, that social class carried no innate authority, and that they owed
deference to no man because of his worldly status. There were profound theological differences among them—Regulators included so-
called Separate Baptists and the German Baptists known as Dunkers
as well as Presbyterians, Moravians, and Quakers—but they shared

---

* The word "Regulator" emerged during the English Revolution, apparently used for
the first time in 1655 to describe a man appointed by officers of the state to inquire
into complaints about governmental malfunction or misfeasance. Reformers on the
South Carolina frontier adopted the term. As North Carolina governor William Tryon
observed, the Regulators he faced were self-appointed, a considerable alteration from
the original usage.

core principles and their opposition to the Anglicans, who they believed ruled the colony and indeed the British Empire corruptly.

The Regulators wanted civic institutions that were spiritually pure and that would tighten the regulation of public and private morality. The movement was about not just taxes and economic policy but also values and community-imposed norms. They hoped to eradicate drunkenness, dancing, card playing, gambling, rumormongering, and the use of profane language. They elevated community and consensus over individual rights and democratic processes.

In August 1766, members of the Sandy Creek Association—a network of Separate Baptist churches spread over the hills of North Carolina—traveled twenty miles or more to the county seat of Hillsborough, where the court was in session. There they read out a manifesto about western North Carolina's problems, caused, they said, by corruption of the government and individuals representing authority on the frontier, and offered as a solution the farmers' active participation in the political process. The association got nowhere and dissolved the following year, but this was the beginning of the farmers' more radical approach to dealing with the local power elites, and ultimately with the colony itself and the British Empire.

Had the Regulators been successful, the North Carolina frontier might have come to resemble New England's villages in the seventeenth century rather than the bustling market towns that had succeeded them. Like the Puritans and the founding generation of Quakers, the Regulators preached simplicity, frugality, plain speech and dress, and the abolition of wigs, frills, and fashion. They discouraged indebtedness as a way to transact business or to live one's life. In sum, the Regulators sought conformity and the measurement of public and private behavior by the same rule: that of God as they knew Him. According to Herman Husband, one of their leaders, "When the Opposition to the Stamp Act began, I was early convinced that the Authors who Wrote in favour of Liberty was Generally Inspired by the same Spirit that we Relegeous Professors Called Christ."

North Carolina's Regulators initially hoped for the reform of existing political institutions. They nominated candidates for the assembly and did their best to "purify" the election process by abolishing the custom of "treating" voters with liquor during campaigns and at the polls. They believed that representatives with real integrity and the confidence of the voters could make the case for reform to the governor, council, and assembly, all of which they suspected were ignorant of conditions on the frontier. But they had overestimated the goodwill of the men in power, who were unwilling to surrender their control of patronage to backcountry farmers who lacked political connections or social standing. Nor were they willing to forgo the patronage network that selected sheriffs and magistrates based on loyalty and influence.

In response to the Regulators' challenges, the backcountry sheriffs' behavior only got worse. "Encouraged as we imagine by the imperious Carriage of their Superiors," a committee of Regulators wrote, they "now grew more and more insulting, taking unusual Distresses for Levies: taking Double, Treble, and four times the value" when they repossessed property of defendants in lawsuits for collection of debts or accused of being in arrears on their taxes. The sheriffs and their deputies then sold the confiscated property at a fraction of its value to rich men who had hard currency that circulated locally, pocketed the cash, taking exorbitant fees along with the magistrates and embezzling the tax money, too, which was never returned to the colony's coffers.

The backcountry representatives to the assembly exerted no influence on the governor or on the legislative process. The courts and sheriffs remained corrupt and became more abusive. The local economy was in a shambles and the farmers' property was obviously vulnerable to a system over which they had no influence or control. With no institutional recourse, the Regulators determined to take matters into their own hands. They would use extra-institutional, even illegal means to secure justice and their independence from an immoral system.

The Regulator movement was a moral cause with political reform as its goal. In elevating politics to the spiritual realm, and by harkening back to lost values rather than forward to new principles, the Regulators and those like them in other colonies advocated conservative reforms, but with a radical moral edge. They defined independence as a collective obligation rather than an individual right, and set themselves against the market values of a secularizing world. Communal purification would require that self-discipline replace self-indulgence and self-interest. In other colonies there were those who wanted people to renounce the imported products the British Empire now taxed; the Regulators went further, rejecting the modern marketplace of new goods and the debt that went with them. They rejected new ideas—the

Old Testament was the best source they had for solutions to their problems. For them, independence meant being left alone to worship and govern themselves without interference from external forces—colonial governments, land speculators and landlords, taxes, the established Anglican church (even if it had an American bishop), and imperial regulations.

In March 1768, the North Carolina Regulators took a more aggressive approach in their protests. They were enraged to learn that the assembly had allocated the phenomenal sum of £15,000 to build Governor Tryon a "palace" and began to use the language of Stamp Act protests in their objections to the colony's government. The Regulators wanted accountability in the allocation of their taxes, with accessible paper trails that showed them where their tax money went. They expressed reluctance, though not outright refusal to pay taxes, and they vowed in the language of dissenting Protestants to "bear witness against" the corruption that affected tax assessments and collections.

A flash point came when a sheriff seized the horse of a Regulator who owed back taxes. About a hundred men armed with "Clubs, Staves & cloven Musquets" grabbed the sheriff, tied him up, and carried him off. Eventually they recovered the horse and released the sheriff, humiliated but not seriously injured. And when he called out the militia to arrest the ringleaders, most of the militiamen failed to report and many of the rest "chose to stand neutral." In other actions, about forty armed Regulators delayed the opening of one court and others disrupted proceedings at another, telling the court clerk that they were there "to Settle some matters in the County, for which they wanted the use of the Court House." They confronted magistrates with the question of "what they were taxed for." They must have been dissatisfied with the answers, because they debated among themselves whether to tear down the jail, finally deciding against it.

In the southwest corner of North Carolina, more than five hundred men agreed to mass together to protect their liberty, which "we were almost deprived of by our Leading Men," whom they described as "oppressors." In the northwestern corner, settlers "signed a Contract against the Public Taxes and other grievances." Other groups calling themselves Regulators planned to have periodic "conventions" to discuss their grievances and to consider remedies for them.

When hundreds of Regulators gathered at Hillsborough in March

1768 to protest the arrest of two of their leaders and to petition for redress of grievances, Governor Tryon's private secretary, seeing a real threat in the crowd of angry farmers, promised them that if they dispersed peacefully, the governor would accept their petition and address their complaints. Herman Husband later remembered that "the whole Multitude, as with one Voice, cried out, Agreed. That is all we want; Liberty to Make our grievances known." The Regulators believed this might begin a fruitful dialogue that would lead to reform.

It did not. The Regulators had simply scared the local officials, the very ones who embezzled their taxes, extracted exorbitant fees from them, exploited the lack of specie, increased their indebtedness in order to repossess property, foreclosed on mortgages, and raised interest rates in a noncompetitive market. The farmers were still at the mercy of these men who monopolized land, cash, privilege, and patronage in a closed system that was corrupt to its core and largely unregulated by its patrons in the Tidewater part of the colony. The two sides in the backcountry—debtors and creditors, the outs and the ins—vied for the attention of the governor and council; one side had lawful authority and connections, and the other had the force of numbers, an ability to act collectively, and the belief that God and Justice were on their side.

Governor Tryon's response to the Regulators' petitions in the summer of 1768 showed that he had no sympathy for their position and that they could expect no reforms from him. As far as he was concerned, "the Grievances complained of by no means Warrant the extraordinary steps" they had taken. He rejected their claim that they had acted in defense of the constitution, believing instead that their resistance "tended to the subversion of the Constitution of this Government." He even objected to what they called themselves, as the name implied criticism of his administration and suggested that the group was legally constituted. The Regulators now began to believe that what they had interpreted as local corruption might in fact be an arm of a larger conspiracy perpetrated from the very top of North Carolina's government, or even from London.

Governor Tryon was now aware that local sheriffs had been embezzling a very high percentage of taxes collected when the colony's paper currency was supposed to be retired as the Currency Act of 1764 required. There was much more paper money in circulation than there should have been if the amount collected had actually been destroyed.

But the assembly was reluctant to legislate any reforms that might undermine the very profitable network of connections to which its members were party. Tryon now understood that "by not suing the sheriffs in Arrears they [assembly members] obtain a considerable weight of interest among the Connections of these Delinquent Sheriffs and which generally secures them a re-election in their Offices." The patronage network connected assemblymen, sheriffs, magistrates, and elite, influential men in a system that operated against both the law and the interests of backcountry farmers.

Tryon decided that no matter how unlawfully the authorities behaved, he must reestablish "order" on the frontier to ensure submission to lawful authority. So he responded to the Regulator movement with the threat of force, which only emboldened the already bold sheriffs and magistrates, who increased their already unlawfully high fees and expanded their brazenly corrupt practices. Tryon feared that the residual popular anger over the Stamp Act, and the sense of empowerment that had grown from the success of the protests against it, might link the Regulators' grievances to those in the movement that resisted imperial taxation. And indeed, in the minds of the backcountry dissenters who made up the Regulator movement, the British Vestry Act of 1703, which taxed the colonists to pay an Anglican clergyman, was also taxation without representation. Although they had representation in the assembly, their representatives were too few, and the assembly always voted the interests of eastern Anglicans.

Despite the governor's opposite interpretation, the Regulators were out to reform the government, not to overthrow it. They were not radicals or intent on violence; indeed, their goals were modest and their inclinations conservative. It was not true, as Governor Tryon claimed, that they sought the "abolition of taxes and debts."

When the Regulators next met to decide their plan of action, the governor responded with a military invasion of the frontier. In early September 1768, he led troops into the backcountry. To the Regulators, these regularized militia were the colony's standing army marching against its citizenry—another ideological offense, in addition to those about corruption and representation. Governor Tryon and his troops created an explosive situation in North Carolina, much as British troops did in their occupation of Boston in the same year and in much the same way.

The city of Boston had a longer tradition of more violent collective action than the Carolinas had experienced. It was really a town by European standards, with a population of about sixteen thousand.* As in London, street brawls could have political significance, express class conflict, be festive, territorial, or sporting. They could also be quite violent: In 1764, a boy died during the annual Pope's Day celebration.†

The lesson that Bostonians took from the success of the riots protesting the Stamp Act was that their power was irresistible. In an environment in which many or most Bostonians were coming to believe that legally constituted authority was corrupt and thus illegitimate, mob rule appeared morally appropriate. The political struggle that pitted the people against judges intent on enforcing the Stamp Act cost the judiciary the traditional respect accorded its decisions. As John Adams asked rhetorically in his diary, "Can we be sufficiently amazed at the Chickanery, the Finesse, the Prevarication, and Insincerity, the simulation, nay the Lyes and Falsehoods of the Judges of the Superior Court? These are harsh Words, but true."

Although the crowds could appear raucous and their violence random, those of the 1760s and 1770s were actually highly disciplined when under the leadership of such men as Ebenezer McIntosh, a shoemaker and volunteer firefighter from the South End. On one occasion, according to an unsympathetic witness, McIntosh

> paraded the Town with a Mob of 2,000 Men in two Files, & passed by
> the Stadthouse, when the general Assembly were sitting, to display his
> Power: if a Whisper was heard among his Followers, the holding up of
> his Finger hushed it in a Moment: and when he had fully displayed his
> Authority, he marched his Men to the first Rendezvous, & Order'd them
> to retire peacably to their several Homes; & was punctually obeyed.

---

* Manchester had a population of 30,000; Edinburgh, 50,000; and London, 750,000 in the 1760s.

† On November 5 there was an annual celebration of the discovery in 1606 of the Catholic conspiracy (hence pope) called the Gunpowder Plot to blow up Parliament; it was also known as Guy Fawkes Day, for the conspirator captured and executed for the crime.

Men like McIntosh were political leaders, the equivalent of modern ward bosses, who could organize their followers to fight a fire, campaign or vote, or simply fight. Patronage, blood, ethnicity, and neighborhood bound men into a network with an array of social and political functions. When the shadowy Sons of Liberty, also known as the Loyal Nine, emerged in the 1760s and 1770s from the smoke-filled rooms where Samuel Adams operated so effectively, they relied on alliances with these existing networks to focus on a common enemy: the British troops that occupied Boston in the fall of 1768.

Governor Francis Bernard had requested the troops in July, telling Secretary of War William Barrington that they were needed not "to quell a Riot or a Tumult, but to rescue the Government out of the hands of a trained mob, & to restore the Activity of the Civil Power, which is now entirely obstructed." Two regiments and one company of artillery with five cannons from Halifax began to debark for Boston on October 1; the last troops arrived in early December, by which time progress had finally been made to secure housing for them.

The rank-and-file troops endured almost daily insults, but there were no mass demonstrations of hostility through the winter and spring of 1769. Indeed, by June the military command had grown complacent and ordered some troop reductions. By July, half of the men had withdrawn to Halifax. On August 1, Governor Bernard felt justified in acting on his long-planned resignation and embarked with his family on the return trip to England. Even before his ship sailed, the local populace was celebrating the departure of the unpopular governor and their success in meeting the challenges of imposed military and civilian authority.

General Thomas Gage, commander of imperial troops in North America, was confident that the contingent occupying Boston had achieved its goals. The local populace appeared cowed, and removing some of the troops would, he thought, achieve amicable relations between Bostonians and the smaller force remaining. He reported to Lord Hillsborough, secretary of state for the colonies and president of the Board of Trade: "I should be glad to relieve the Troops from the oppression they are said to suffer where they are, and save a deal of vexatious trouble, by removing them to places where they would be less obnoxious, amongst people better disposed and less turbulent."

Bostonians' interactions with the soldiers included encouraging deserters, hiding them, and defending them from attempts to recapture them. Enlisted men deserted individually and in groups of up to eight. Black-faced mobs "in very great numbers" would surround the search parties assigned to recover them and would rescue their prisoners. Captain William Mackay felt defeated by the deserters and their civilian accomplices: "How far we can ever retake them or get them back but by voluntary surrendering is more than I can say."

Troops that did not desert faced constant harassment from civilians, who claimed rights that the British denied to natives in India or on islands that were part of their far-flung empire. Sentries who challenged suspicious-looking Bostonians often got roughed up by gangs or found themselves in court on civil charges of trespass or assault. To make military duty in Boston even worse, local juries would not convict a Bostonian accused of a crime against a soldier, no matter what the charge or the evidence. There was no way for the soldiers to win and many ways for the occupying force to lose men. Captain Mackay observed the irony of being "ordered here to Aid & assist the Civill Magistrate in preserving the peace & protecting his Majestys Subjects, when those very majistrates are our Opressors."

In 1765, Benjamin Franklin had predicted that although British soldiers sent to America "will not find a rebellion; they may indeed make one." Five years later, an occupying army in Boston evoked precisely the response he had predicted. Over weeks of occupation that became months and then years, irritations between the military men and civilians multiplied, and nerves frayed. When commanders drew down the occupying force, hostility toward the army actually increased. The remaining troops felt more vulnerable than ever and sensed that they had fewer and fewer options. The civilians became convinced over time that they could win a test of wills and even of arms with the soldiers.

12

✦

MASSACRE

THE ANGLO-IRISH POET GEORGE CANNING'S *Letter to the Right Honourable the Earl of Hillsborough,* published in Boston in 1769, made an eloquent case for the enduring "independence" of the American colonies within the British Empire. He saw clearly that their founders had left England in pursuit of religious freedom, "which they were denied within the jurisdiction of parliament, availing themselves of a natural right, which is notoriously invested in every member of society; to abandon a disagreeable or oppressive government, and thereby recover his natural freedom and independence, and annihilate the sovereignty and jurisdiction of the abandoned society." And in America, the colonists had "reverted to their natural freedom and independance" under the British monarch.

In colonial Massachusetts, a judge could assess a convicted thief the court costs plus triple damages payable to the victim. If the convict could not pay the restitution, the victim could, with the court's authorization, sell the convict's labor to recover the fine. In 1769, for the first time, a Boston judge imposed such a sentence on a British soldier. "They have Indented him as a Slave & sold him for a term of years," Captain William Mackay reported to General Gage. A financial settlement between the military and the victim averted a conflict, but another case soon followed. This time, the court convicted Private John Moyse of breaking and entering a shop and stealing £26 in goods.

Moyse being unable to pay the treble damages, the plaintiff sold his labor for three years. This time the price was too steep for Captain Mackay, but the shopkeeper was unwilling to compromise. Gage exploded in frustration when Mackay reported the details to him. "Such an infamous piece of Tyranny savours more of the Meridian of Turkey than a British Province," Gage wrote in reply. "It is a trite Remark, that these bawlers against Government under the pretence of Liberty, are always the greatest Tyrants. It is not Tyranny they dislike, they only Squabble for the Power to become Tyrants."

Mackay and Gage eventually learned that the case was even worse than it had first appeared. Apparently the whole thing was a ruse; there had been no robbery. The plaintiff and defendant had conspired to free Moyse from his military service, which was for life. The shopkeeper kept the money he received for Moyse's indenture, and Moyse realized his freedom in return for three years' labor, about half what indentured servants were paying for their passage to the New World. The military officers felt powerless to affect this civilian administration of justice, and so they steamed. According to Mackay, the case had been "a connivance . . . in order to secure him his Discharge, or in other words a sort of Legall Dismission from the regiment."

In New Hampshire and Maine, squatters were contesting the patents of absentee landowners. Pennsylvania laws intended to enforce landlords' deeds against Scots-Irish squatters failed, and Connecticut colonists continued to contest Pennsylvania's claim to the Wyoming Valley in northeastern Pennsylvania, bordering New York and New Jersey. Farmers in Maryland still refused to pay quitrents to the colony's proprietors. Landlords had problems with their tenants on vast estates in the Hudson Valley of New York. Squatters, Indians, and imperial restrictions challenged Virginia speculators in frontier land.

The social fabric of New Jersey, which was always tattered, remained badly torn after the violence of the previous decades. Class resentments, contested land claims (including conflicts over church lands between Presbyterians and Anglicans), and a debt crisis primed by the contraction of the supply of paper money affected New Jerseyans of all classes. The population of some northern counties doubled during the third quarter of the century, which reflected the extreme process that was shrinking the colony's average farm size by about half. More than 90 percent of cases in the courts of common pleas concerned debts owed by farmers affected by economic decline. Tenancy was on the rise, and the lower percentage of men who owned enough property to vote confined suffrage by the 1770s to about half of New Jersey's adult men.

In July 1769, farmers in Monmouth County blockaded the courthouse as a way to deter debt cases that might result in court-ordered seizure of their land. Within only a few months the crowds were calling themselves Sons of Liberty and linking their cause to that of the protesters in Boston. In Newark, farmers set up their own local government after arbitrators made decisions against them and in favor of gentry claims to the contested lands. Men calling themselves "Liberty Boys" marched on the Newark courthouse to prevent evictions. Other rioters adapted the rhetoric of radicals elsewhere to fit local conditions. The contraction of suffrage had led to a change in the makeup of the assembly, which showed little sympathy for the rioters. Most of the assemblymen were now Anglicans, Quakers, and Dutch Reformed, conservative men who disliked disorder and people taking extralegal action. New Jersey's problems had started long before, and they were often only tangentially related to the current crisis in the colonies' relations with Britain. But in these changed times, old scores and new grievances combined to heighten political conflict and social resentments across class lines.

When, in the summer of 1768, North Carolina governor Tryon had declared the frontier Regulators revolutionaries and had dispatched troops to quell them, his characterization was inaccurate. True, the backcountry farmers believed they were "Continually Squez'd and oppressed by our Publick Officers both with Regard to their fees as also in the Laying on of Taxes as well as in collecting [them,] together with Iniquitious Appropriations, and Wrong Applications of the same," but they were "ready to comply with, and be obedient to the laws of the Government." The North Carolina government, however, declined to establish small-claims courts that would better suit circumstances on the frontier. It refused to remove even the most corrupt sheriffs whose tax-collection methods and seizures of property inflamed the Regulators, since they were so far in excess of the delinquent taxes or debts. At the same time, though, and apparently perceiving no inconsistency, the assembly endorsed the circular letter from Massachusetts opposing the 1767 Townshend Acts on the grounds that Britain had taxed them without their consent. The Regulators pointed out the hypocrisy of this position.

When Governor Tryon dissolved the assembly in the spring of 1769, the Regulators hoped they could affect the makeup of a new one by campaigning to replace the "Lawyers, clerks, and others in Connection with them" who ran the corrupt patronage system. They succeeded both in ousting some of their most bitter enemies and in electing some of their own leaders. The new assemblymen introduced bills to reform the political process, including secret ballots and the exclusion of lawyers and court clerks from the assembly. They proposed salaries for clerks and judges, hoping this would help to eliminate their extortionate fees, and tax reform by replacing the regressive poll taxes with income taxes, "each person to pay in proportion to the Profitts arising from his Estate." The new assemblymen representing the Piedmont also wanted to reform the system that administered land grants and purchases contrary to imperial regulations and the colonial laws that benefited well-connected absentee speculators over the farmers who tilled the fields. They also wanted repeal of recent legislation that had aggressively favored the established Church of England by denying dissenting ministers the authority to conduct marriages "according to the Decretals, Rites and Ceremonys, of their Respective Churches," a right "granted even to the very Catholics in Ireland, and the Protestants in France."

This thoroughgoing program of agrarian reform went nowhere in the assembly, and if it had, Governor Tryon would certainly have vetoed it. By December 1769, after another eighteen months of insider corruption and government unresponsiveness to requests for reform, the frontier farmers were becoming radicalized. They had all but given up on achieving justice through the legal system or from government officials. According to Herman Husband, "as Hypocrisy in Religion is a gross Affront and Mockery of God, so good Forms kept up in any State, are, when turned to bad Uses, a gross Affront and Mockery of the People."

In September 1770, an angry crowd in Hillsborough claiming to speak "for the whole Body of the People called Regulators" declared that they intended "to see Justice done, and Justice They would have." They did not keep the court from opening, but they did attack the deputy attorney for the Hillsborough District who sought shelter in a nearby store, and they beat up the store's owner. They dragged a sheriff from the courthouse, spat on him, and roughed him up. They pummeled two justices of the peace, the county clerk, and a few others who had something to do with judgments against farmers associated with them. Then they chased from town a protégé of the governor's named Edmund Fanning, hated for his promotion to associate justice of the colony in 1765 apparently as a reward for his support of the Stamp Act, his central place in the patronage network as a Crown attorney and militia colonel, and his profiting from the farmers' debts. They broke into his home, destroyed his furniture, and carried away clothes and household items before leveling the house.

In Granville County, the barn and stables of Judge Richard Henderson burned to the ground in November; two days later, fire destroyed his house. On December 5, Governor Tryon addressed the new session of the assembly and called to its attention "the Abuses in the Conduct of the Public Funds; the General Complaints against Offices and Officers; The Evils arising from the Circulation of Counterfeit Money; and the Injuries offered to His Majesty's Government and its Subjects at and since the last Hillsborough Superior Court." Among the injuries, he considered the worst to be the "Seditious Mob" that had "torn down Justice from Her Tribunal, and renounced all Legislative Authority." Immediate action was necessary, he believed, to check the "contagion" of unrest that challenged public institutions, officials, and order.

On December 15, 1770, Samuel Johnson, a lawyer and merchant (he later became a representative to the Continental Congress), introduced a riot act in the assembly. It declared felonious any gathering of ten or more that refused to disperse within an hour after receiving orders from a justice of the peace or sheriff. A person convicted of participating in such a gathering "unlawfully, tumultuously and riotously" was subject to execution for the crime. The act applied retroactively to participants in the recent assault on the Hillsborough courthouse. Those accused of participating and who did not surrender within sixty days were outlaws, who could be hunted down and killed on sight. The act also permitted the governor to raise militia regiments to enforce the law and authorized unlimited funds for the purpose.

Governor Tryon signed this law on January 15, 1771, and it remained in force for one year, plenty of time for the governor and his troops to put down the threat to political order posed by the backcountry Regulators. At the same time, though, the assembly also addressed some of the farmers' principal grievances by establishing small-claims courts, which would help in the "speedy recovery of small debts" of under £5. But nothing was done to reform the regressive tax system or the corruption in its enforcement, and the assembly did not address any of the settlers' other grievances.

The combination of repressive action reflected in the Riot Act and inaction on all but one of the Regulators' grievances inflamed the anger of those associated with the movement and radicalized farmers who had thus far remained neutral in the petitioning, campaigning, and collective action. When Governor Tryon arrived in May 1771 at a field on Alamance Creek at the head of eleven hundred militiamen, almost all from the eastern regions of the colony, an army about twice its size met his forces. Some members of the Regulator army dispersed when Tryon had the Riot Act read; others left because of their religious convictions against violence. But there was a battle, and in it about 20 Regulators and 10 militiamen died and 150 were wounded. The governor ordered two summary executions, one by firing squad and the other by hanging, and offered a pardon to men who swore an oath of allegiance; about 6,400 men, 75 percent of the male population of the Piedmont, took the oath. Right after the battle, fourteen prisoners were tried under the Riot Act; twelve were convicted and Tryon pardoned six, ordering the execution by hanging of the six others. He then left and was soon sailing off to his new post as the governor of New York, where Edmund Fanning would join him as his personal secretary.

The violence on the battlefield and the judicial violence effectively ended the North Carolina Regulator movement. But outside the colony, radicals recognized the cause of the Regulators as their own, and they blamed Governor Tryon, the British appointee, for repressing a legitimate independence movement. A striking irony here is that among the soldiers who followed Tryon into battle, the sheriffs who embezzled taxes and enforced the law to benefit their patronage network, and the assemblymen who legislated against the interests of the settlers were men who would join the Revolutionary movement. Despite their efforts over the next few years to appease the Regulators with additional reforms, the Revolutionaries could not gain support from the North Carolina backcountry, and thus the Revolution was to change nothing there. One farmer lamented in the 1780s, "I have fought for my country, and fought for my king; and have been whipped both times."

Relations among Regulators in South Carolina, the colony's governor, and the eastern or Tidewater region remained throughout the 1760s significantly better than they were in North Carolina. The issues in South Carolina were the lack of access to patronage appointments in both regions and an inadequate court system on the frontier. In 1768, the assembly passed an act "for establishing Courts, Building Goals [jails], and appointing Sheriffs and other Officers for the more convenient administration of Justice in this Province," which would help to alleviate the disorder about which the backcountry Regulators complained. The council ratified this bill, the governor, Lord Montagu, signed it— and the British government disallowed it.

The offending clauses were those that authorized the service of judges "during good behavior" rather than for life, which the British interpreted as a constitutional challenge to the royal prerogative to appoint justices independent of local influence. "I stated in the strongest Manner I was able," wrote Charles Garth, the colony's agent in London, "the Distress of the back People, the Disorders committed and unpunished, the Expence of obtaining Justice civil and Criminal, and the Inconveniences" of the existing weak system. Garth felt that he and the act had been caught in the maelstrom of British politics, when his lobbying efforts were complicated by the death of Charles Townshend in September 1767; the illness and retirement of the colonists' friend William Pitt, the Earl of Chatham; the creation of a third secretary of state, which shifted responsibility for the colonies to yet another bureaucratic arm of the British government; and the appointment to that post of Lord Hillsborough, who had opposed South Carolina's judiciary bill even before it arrived on his desk.

Tidewater and Piedmont South Carolinians now drew together in common cause against the British challenges to their independence within the empire. The Regulators' originally limited aims expanded in the absence of redress by either the colonial or the British government. And when they took matters into their own hands, establishing unauthorized institutions to meet their needs, they addressed not only the problems caused by the imperial bureaucracy and their own colony's government but also the larger context for disorder in their region, the reformation of morals and family life, the collection of debts, and the labor shortages. They became more extreme in their views and aims, thereby becoming controversial locally as well.

In response, a "Moderator" movement emerged in South Carolina. The Moderators disliked the harsh corporal punishment executed by Regulators, their dispensing with formal trials and their set limits on sentences. A man named John Harvey had received five hundred lashes, ten from each of fifty Regulators, when they claimed to have found him in possession of a stolen horse. Even men of wealth and stature were not immune to floggings if they challenged the Regulators' authority. John Musgrove was one such man, who was flogged multiple times for supporting the colonial law that had voided the Regulator laws. Such conflicts led to unlikely alliances between gangs and rich men on the frontier, which alienated colonial officials, including those who were sympathetic to both the Moderators and Regulators. A March 1769 truce between the two groups saved South Carolina from the bloodshed that ended North Carolina's Regulator movement at the Battle of Alamance.

The passage of a new circuit court bill for South Carolina a few months later addressed the major grievance of backcountry settlers on both sides of the controversy. This time the assembly omitted the offending clause that granted judicial tenure during good behavior. But now the governor objected because the assembly had not also responded to other reservations expressed by the ministry when it disallowed the previous bill. Governor Montagu insisted that the patronage appointments of sheriffs were the prerogative of the governor and council, and that the salaries of South Carolina's attorney general and clerk of the Court of Common Pleas should be fixed permanently rather than annually by the assembly. The assembly agreed to these proposed amendments, and first the Grafton ministry and then King George accepted the law in November 1769.

With the new law, the South Carolina backcountry was assigned four circuit courts, and its residents secured the right to trial by jury. The law accommodated the Regulators' demand for a less expensive and faster process for settling small claims. There were also provisions to curb any exploitation of the judicial system to harass defendants. The assembly financed the building of courthouses and jails in the backcountry, which brought some jobs and an infusion of funds to the region. The first circuit courts met in 1772, and by 1774 they were functioning smoothly and completely throughout South Carolina. Lawlessness did not disappear from the backcountry, but property crime did decline and there was no class warfare of the kind that afflicted New Jersey and the North Carolina backcountry. The best evidence of the law's success, and of the restoration of peace to the backcountry, is that mention of the region disappeared from the colonies' newspapers, where its problems had previously been prominently discussed.

In 1769, the British government feared the prospect of another war against North America's Indians more than it did the alienation of its North American colonists. And it elevated continuity in constitutional principles and consistency of administration across the empire over the colonists' social stability and economic prosperity. Thus it continued to tighten enforcement of existing regulations, supplemented with new ones designed for changed circumstances—notably the acquisition of a huge swath of territory in North America, and the obligation to balance the interests of French Canadians, Indian nations, and competing colonial groups that had been part of the earlier empire. So Anglo–North American colonists faced not just internal challenges to their rule of law and deteriorating economic conditions but also rigid enforcement of edicts and regulations by Crown appointees.

One significant event in the escalating conflict was the Treaty of Hard Labor, which the British negotiated with the Cherokees in 1768, independent of the colonists. This treaty ceded southwestern Virginia and what would later become Kentucky and southern West Virginia to the Cherokees, which ran up against the interests of many Virginia land speculators, including Thomas Jefferson, George Washington, Patrick Henry, and George Mason.

One month later, however, the Iroquois sold the same land to colonial representatives whom they met at Fort Stanwix, in New York, the British fort built only ten years before to protect the key portage area between the Mohawk River and the rivers leading to Lake Ontario. The Iroquois claim to the land—based on their diplomatic position as "elder brethren" of some of the Indians who actually hunted there—was dubious, but the Virginia assembly, using the Fort Stanwix Treaty as support for its claim, petitioned the British for Kentucky. The Crown denied the petition late in the year, infuriating Virginia's land speculators.

At this point, British officials feared the very real possibility of a pan-Indian alliance, which would be stronger than the one that had propelled Pontiac's Rebellion in 1763. In August 1770, the Shawnees called a conference at Scioto, in what we know as Ohio, at which every major Indian nation north of the Ohio River agreed to make peace with the tribes south of the river. According to one Shawnee, his people feared that the British "designed to take all our Country and then destroy us." From the imperial perspective, this treaty made it all the more imperative to keep the Cherokees out of the alliance by keeping the Virginians out of the area that later would become Kentucky. So Lord Hillsborough worked for a "final settlement" of a boundary between Cherokee lands and Virginia that would leave Kentucky on the Cherokee side. From the perspective of Virginia's land speculators, at stake was as much land as had been sold in the entire century and a half of the colony's existence. Both the British fear of an even stronger pan-Indian alliance and the Virginia speculators' fear of a "final settlement" boundary line were escalating.

The Proclamation Line of 1763, which had not been intended as a "final settlement," had nonetheless succeeded in undermining the land speculators to some degree, since they could not secure imperial grants of land west of the line, but it did not stop squatters from establishing farms in Indian country. (They might have preferred to secure clear title to their farms, but as squatters they could not.) Since any institutions of colonial government west of the line were forbidden, the region became a refuge for those who had no money to buy land, or were trying to avoid paying taxes, or were in flight from authority. On balance, rich colonists who speculated in western lands were more hostile than the small farmers to the new, stiffer British policy on the frontier.

Even as the speculating planters lost out in the West, they were losing other economic opportunities as well. Retail stores run by mercantile businesses undercut their profits as middlemen between small farmers and English and Scottish merchants. The Virginia gentlemen had once been able both to inflate the price of goods and to charge interest on advances against their future tobacco crops. The importation of slaves also undermined their efforts to monopolize the domestic slave trade, since small farmers now purchased slaves directly from the traders who brought them to America, rather than buying slaves from the planters—the surplus ones resulting from the natural increase of the slave population on their plantations. Throughout the 1760s and 1770s, the planters who controlled the Virginia assembly tried hard to prevail over the transatlantic slave traders, first by doubling the import duties on slaves in 1767 and again in 1769, and then by adopting a resolution in 1772 that petitioned King George to abolish the international trade completely.

The gentlemen were experiencing what felt like a real debt crisis. They were vulnerable to demands made by their English creditors, which eroded their economic independence. And they were running up more and more debts—being thwarted in their efforts to sell land to small farmers, charge interest on advances, sell goods imported from England, or control the local market in slaves—to sustain their lavish lifestyles.

To the gentlemen planters of Virginia—Jefferson, Washington, Madison, and the others—it seemed that British merchants had influenced Parliament in its passage of all the laws of the previous decade that gave England a monopoly on American trade, sabotaged American efforts to establish manufacturing, and added new taxes on top of it all. They had long believed that they were already effectively taxed by the Navigation Acts' restriction on colonial trade and manufacturing. The new taxes and monetary policies were economically destructive and therefore ideologically offensive. As the planters saw it, they were short of cash, constrained by credit, threatened by Indians, and unable to develop other avenues of investment all because of onerous British policies they considered unconstitutional. The taxes were the last straw— "double contributions" on top of the other restrictions.

The vigorously negative response to the Townshend Duties in Massachusetts gave the Virginia men a hook to hang many of their problems on. A boycott movement emerged in 1769 that could give them what George Washington termed "a pretext to live within bounds." With lower debts thanks to new domestic manufacturing and more modest lifestyles, the planters could influence the price realized for tobacco by withholding crops from the market. Washington wrote to

George Mason, "A Scheme of this Sort will contribute more effectually than any other I can devise to immerge the Country from the distress it at present labours under."

The plan to recover economic independence from England failed, however, because the nonimportation agreement circulated by the Sons of Liberty in 1769 excluded whole categories of British goods, including cheap clothing, which was the single biggest import and effectively irreplaceable by domestic manufacturing, since it would not pay to take slaves or white men from the field to make clothes and there were not enough white women for the work. By 1772, the economy of the Chesapeake region had fallen into a deep recession because of plunging tobacco prices and a recession on the other side of the Atlantic, and this put additional pressure on the debtor economy of the upper South.

Relations between British troops and Bostonians worsened during 1769. In July, a justice of the peace fined Private John Riley five shillings when he was convicted of assaulting an innkeeper, Jonathan Winship; since Riley did not have the money, the justice of the peace sentenced him to jail. When a constable, Peter Barbour, tried to take him into custody, other soldiers fought Barbour off. The assembly ordered an investigation and a hearing and called witnesses; then a grand jury indicted the commanding officer and five soldiers for riot and "unlawful rescue." At the trial in December, the facts of the case clearly pointed to conviction. The only question concerned the actions of one Lieutenant Alexander Ross: Some witnesses testified that they heard him order the soldiers to resist the constable, others that he had ordered them to desist and return to their barracks. The court convicted Ross and four of his men and fined them each £7. Upon appeal of Ross's case, the court increased his fine to £20 at the March 1770 session.

Other cases came before the courts during the fall of 1769 and the ensuing winter. On October 23, there was a tussle between a mob armed with brickbats and soldiers at a guardhouse on Boston Neck. It started with a dispute over some firewood that Robert Pierpont accused Ensign John Ness of stealing. When Ness tried to stanch the violence by marching his squad back to their barracks, the crowd pursued them, a soldier's musket accidentally discharged, and a ball hit the wall of a blacksmith's shop. The crowd began throwing stones at the soldiers. Three soldiers joined Ness's men as they continued their retreat. One man in the angry crowd, perhaps the blacksmith whose shop absorbed the errant shot, broke through the ranks and punched a private in the face. The soldiers did not retaliate but held off the blacksmith and others with fixed bayonets.

Captain Ponsonby Molesworth, who commanded the guard on Boston Neck, took over command of Ness's men and the reinforcements. He ordered them to close ranks and "be careful not to strike any of the mob unless obliged to it in your own defense. But if any man strike you, put your bayonet through him." The soldiers reached the barracks without further incident. It had been simple good fortune, though, that no serious injuries or deaths had resulted from the confrontation. Boston was a powder keg primed to explode.

The court acquitted Ness on the charge of theft, when no witnesses testified against him. Prosecutors brought him before the magistrates a second time to answer the charge that he had ordered his men to fire on civilians in contravention of a law that banned the discharge of firearms within Boston city limits. A sergeant and Captain Molesworth also faced assault charges before three hostile justices. "Who brought you here? Who sent for you?" one of them asked rhetorically. "By what authority do you mount guard, or march in the streets with arms? It is contrary to the laws of the Province, and you should be taken up for so offending. We want none of your guards. We have arms of our own, and can protect ourselves. You are but a handful. Better take care not to provoke us. If you do, you must take the Consequences."

Ness's acquittal and the decision not to prosecute the sergeant came despite the unsympathetic hearing their cases received. Molesworth's case was different, since in ordering his men to use their bayonets in response to mere assaults, he had clearly broken the law; self-defense had to be proportionate to the threat, and only if reasonably in fear for their lives could soldiers legally kill an assailant. The jury returned a guilty verdict against Molesworth. No record survives of a sentence or final disposition of the case. Lieutenant Colonel William Dalrymple, who was Molesworth's superior, believed that this standoff between soldiers and civilians was "but a prelude to some motion more consequential. I am sure something very unpleasant is at hand."

Conflict in the civilian community was also sharpening. Nathaniel Rogers, a merchant who had declined to subscribe to the nonimportation agreement circulated by the Sons of Liberty, received a couple of warnings. "Twice my house was besmeared," he complained, "the last time with the Vilest filth of the Vilest Vault." According to a lawyer named Benjamin Kent, "Those who dar'd to Import any Goods contrary to the agreement of the Merchants were Guilty of High Treason against the Majesty of the People" and should be treated accordingly. In the fall of 1769, Samuel Adams declared that "it is too late in the day" for merchants who had not signed the nonimportation agreement to change their minds: "Their previous conduct was so highly blameable that atonement could not be made on this side of the Grave. God perhaps might possibly forgive them, but I and the rest of the People never could." Now such men as Nathaniel Rogers were "in real danger of their Lives. Their Property was actually unsafe, their Signs, Doors and Windows were daub'd over in the Night time with every kind of Filth, and one of them particularly had his Person treated in the same manner."

The nonimportation agreement was meant to end the importation and sale of British goods until Parliament repealed the Townshend Duties and "every other kind" of tax. The Boston merchants also discussed and agreed provisionally (pending support from New York and Philadelphia) to stop importing sugar and molasses from the British West Indies. This last agreement, though, achieved "very indifferent success," according to the merchants themselves.

James Otis, whose inflammatory pamphlet against the Stamp Act had attracted so much attention, made several verbal attacks on the customs commissioners, which led to a battle of walking sticks with one of them, John Robinson. The increasingly erratic Otis suffered a head injury, which he described as a "premeditated, cowardly and villanous attempt . . . to assassinate me." Some people later ascribed Otis's mental decline, and his more and more inflamed, irrational attacks on the imperial system, to this barroom brawl, but the deterioration of his mental health had preceded the conk on his head. In any event, the incident provided fodder for the ongoing newspaper war and the efforts being made to orchestrate opposition to the British customs service and occupying army. A crowd of some two thousand Bostonians gathered to watch preliminary hearings against one of the men who had supported Robinson in the brawl with Otis. Afterward, the crowd moved on to spread the contents of an outhouse on the walls of the *Boston Chronicle*'s office and a bookshop owned by John Mein, who was unsympathetic to the antimilitary and antitax movement.

One of Mein's offenses had been to publish in the *Boston Chronicle* customs-service records that documented what he considered to be the hypocrisy of the nonimportation movement: He showed that while supporters of the movement went after merchants who declined to abide by the boycott agreement, many, most, or all of the signatories continued to import British goods surreptitiously. Perhaps, he suggested, the movement was simply a way for some merchants to crush their competitors. Possibly the movement was not about independence or constitutional ideas at all. Certainly the evidence of double-dealing proved that the antitax movement was unprincipled.

Not content to publish his findings in the *Chronicle*, with its circulation of fourteen hundred, Mein printed four thousand additional copies of the customhouse manifests, which gave the names of all those in Boston who were still importing British goods. He "circulated them, gratis, over all America, from Florida to Nova Scotia," and then issued another edition as a pamphlet, which he also circulated free throughout the colonies. Along with the documentation, Mein offered his opinion that the signatories' "Patriotism was founded on Self Interest and Malice."

His opponents viewed Mein as an unwelcome outsider, since he was a Scottish immigrant who had arrived in Boston only five years earlier and who sold paper imported from England to the customs commissioners. His satirical portrayal of the movement's leaders was courageous, effective, and foolhardy. Mein had made himself a marked man, and after receiving dire threats he began to carry a pistol.

In the evening of October 29, 1769, a crowd of about twenty men surrounded Mein and a friend as they walked down a Boston street. The men started arguing with Mein, and one of them poked him hard in the stomach with a walking stick. Mein drew his pistol. There were shouts of "Knock him down! Kill him!" The editor had good reasons to fear for his life. One man swung a shovel at him, missing his head but tearing a two-inch gash in his shoulder just as Mein and his friend reached the protection of a sentry post. The crowd that drove Mein into the guardhouse had by now grown to about two hundred men and boys. In the melee, Mein's companion accidentally discharged his pistol but hit no one. Nonetheless, a rumor spread that Mein had fired with malice into the crowd, and a justice issued a warrant for his arrest on the charge that he had fired a pistol at the king's subjects, who were "lawfully and peaceably assembled together." "Their plan," Mein wrote a few days later, "was to get me into the Custody of the Officer, & it being then dark, to knock [me] on the head; & then their usual saying might have been repeated that it was done by Boys & Negroes, or by Nobody."

On the same evening that the crowd chased Mein down the street, a sailor named George Gailer suffered a worse fate at the hands of a mob. The popular belief was that Gailer was the informant who was responsible for the British seizure of a Rhode Island sloop, *Success*, which had carried a cargo of smuggled wine. A crowd lay in wait for Gailer, seized him, stripped him naked, administered a thick coat of hot tar, and then covered him in feathers. The mob of about fifteen hundred men marched him down Main Street toward the Liberty Tree. As they passed Mein's house, some tossed rocks through the windows. An apprentice inside fired an unloaded musket to frighten them, which it did, but when they broke into the house, they saw that Mein was not in and contented themselves with doing some damage and stealing two guns. They then continued on, roughing up Gailer along the way and abusing a lone sentry whose guardhouse they passed. Content that Gailer would abide an oath, they made him swear never to inform again on a customs violation and then released their prisoner and retired for the evening. Again, by good fortune alone, no one was seriously injured or killed.

In January 1770, tensions remained high, with ruffled feathers, rocks thrown through windows, excrement spread on shop signs and doors, threats, trade goods spirited from one warehouse to another during dark of night, and effigies hung from the Liberty Tree. In February, supporters of the nonimportation movement launched a campaign to eliminate "the pernicious Practice of tea-drinking" in Boston, which organizers aimed principally at women. Some believed that this non-consumption pact was a ruse, with so-called patriotic women actually serving tea from coffee or chocolate pots to disguise their behavior.

On February 22, a crowd gathered outside the office of Theophilus Lillie, a tea importer. Someone had smeared the office windows with tar and feathers and posted a warning sign that identified Lillie as an enemy of the people. He had angered the nonimportation movement's leaders not just by refusing to sign their agreement but also by ridiculing them in the *Boston News-Letter*: "It always seemed strange to me that people who contend so much for civil and religious Liberty should be so ready to deprive others of their natural liberty—that Men who are guarding against being subject to Laws [to] which they never gave their consent in person or by their representative, should at the same time make Laws . . . to which . . . I am sure I never gave my consent either in person or by my representative."

Ebenezer Richardson, a much-hated informer for the British customs office, was one of Lillie's neighbors. He seized a horse-drawn wagon and tried to knock down the warning sign in front of Lillie's establishment. The boys and men (mostly boys) who had been throwing rocks at Lillie's shop now made Richardson their target. He was chased back into his house and then reemerged in a rage. The boys were now throwing rocks at him and his house. Fruit, sticks, stones, and eggs flew through the air. A rock struck Richardson's wife. Windows were broken. Richardson again retreated into his house, but the crowd broke open the front door. Richardson appeared at an upstairs window with his musket. No one thought he would fire, but he did, hitting an eleven-year-old boy named Christopher Seider and wounding another, a nineteen-year-old, in the right hand and thigh. Seider took eleven birdshot in the chest and abdomen.

For a time, Richardson fought off the crowd with a cutlass, but men carrying a noose eventually took him prisoner, along with George Wilmot, a sailor who had helped him defend his house. Then cooler heads prevailed. One man later explained that the leaders had the crowd nominally under control, and "as they were pretty sure that they could procure a Jury for Conviction, so some of the Leaders of the Faction chose that he should be hanged by the Forms of Law, rather than suffer the Disgrace of Hangmen themselves." Nonetheless, the crowd dragged Richardson and Wilmot through the streets, abusing them along the way, until they reached justices of the peace, who heard witnesses before more than a thousand spectators. The justices committed Richardson and Wilmot to jail until the next sitting of the Superior Court, which was scheduled for March 13. The charge was "firing off & discharging a gun loaded with gun powder & swan shot at one Christopher Snyder thereby giving him a very dangerous wound," as the boy's life still hung by a thread. The authorities had to fight off another crowd bent on lynching the two men. Only the intervention of some of the leading men of the nonimportation movement saved the prisoners for a second time that day.

At 9:00 p.m., about eight hours after the shooting, Christopher Seider died. Dr. Joseph Warren, one of the movement's leaders, performed an autopsy on the spot. A coroner's jury was swiftly convened and returned a verdict of death from being "willfully and feloniously shott by Ebenezer Richardson." Three weeks hence, Richardson would stand trial for murder and Wilmot would be tried as an accessory. The trick was to keep the prisoners alive until they could be formally tried, convicted, and executed according to law. Meanwhile, the attacks on houses and offices of importers continued. Lillie moved to the country. The movement's leaders publicized the event for its full propaganda value. Nothing, not the Stamp Act, the Townshend Duties, or the occupation of Boston by the British army, had done so much to further the antitax movement. Seider's death moved neutrals to take a side. Either you were for the crowd or against it, and it was becoming harder and harder to avoid declaring loyalty either to the government or to the people, to your neighbors or to those who ruled in the name of the Crown.

Seider's funeral on February 26 was, according to newspaper reports, "the largest perhaps ever known in America." The procession stretched over half a mile. Between four and five hundred schoolboys preceded the casket, followed by about two thousand mourners and thirty horse-drawn wagons. A sign on the Liberty Tree quoted Scripture: "Thou shalt take no satisfaction for the life of a MURDERER—he shall surely be put to death." The lesson that John Adams drew from the spectacle, which was orchestrated by his cousin Sam, was that "this Shewes, there are many more Lives to spend if wanted in the Service of their Country. It Shewes, too that the Faction is not yet expiring—that the Ardor of the People is not to be quelled by the Slaughter of one Child and the Wounding of another."

As March began, people on all sides recognized that more violence lay ahead, and what a bad idea the stationing of troops in Boston had been. Even General Gage admitted, "The People were as Lawless and Licentious after the Troops arrived, as they were before. The Troops could not act by Military Authority, and no Person in Civil Authority would ask their aid." Each side believed the other was plotting the next confrontation. Of the six hundred soldiers garrisoned in Boston, only four hundred were available for duty at any one time, which meant they would be woefully outnumbered if it came to an all-out conflict. What the movement leaders believed they needed to further their cause was an event in which civilians were the clear victims and not to blame.

Just such an opportunity for a politically effective confrontation with the army arose on March 2, when the owner of a rope-manufacturing business provoked a soldier on the docks who was looking for part-time work. Since the soldiers were poorly paid but sufficiently housed and provisioned, they were willing to work for lower wages than men with families to support, and this was one reason for the bad relations between the soldiers and the working poor. On this particular day, the soldier suffered a humiliating beating at the hands of rope workers. He later returned with eight or nine soldiers to support him in a rematch with better odds. Again, though, the rope workers beat off the soldiers, who ran back to their barracks and returned fifteen minutes later with about forty men. The battle rekindled, but again the civilians drove off the soldiers.

The next day, a Saturday, saw other fights break out, but this in itself was not unusual. It was the environment after Seider's death and fu-neral, and the recognition that such random violence could be turned to political ends, that made this weekend distinctive. Civilians and soldiers were on edge, and the movement's leaders were becoming ex-perienced at exploiting the propaganda value of any mistake the sol-diers made. Predictions of trouble soon emerged—not just because tensions were high but also because people knew that plans were afoot to show the army in its worst light. The Reverend Andrew Eliot knew at least by Saturday that "many" Bostonians were looking forward to "fighting it out with the soldiers on the Monday." He and presumably many others knew that church "bells were to be rung to assemble the inhabitants together" for a confrontation with the British forces. It is unclear whether some soldiers also knew that a fight was planned.

The evening of March 5 was cold, with about a foot of snow on the ground, much of it having become icy after foot traffic during the day had turned it to slush. A quarter-moon reflecting off the snow was the only illumination of the area between the Custom House and the military headquarters. On King Street, near the Custom House, a lone private occupied a sentry post. This was Hugh White, who was ill equipped by training, experience, or age for the decisions he was going to have to make that night.

Two young men, wigmaker's apprentices, provoked young White with insults. White struck one of them on the side of the head with his musket. The ruckus drew a crowd of eight or nine men and boys. Later, one of them remembered a church bell tolling somewhere in the city. Bells were usually a fire alarm, calling men to turn out en masse to fight the flames, and normally they would arrive on the scene with buckets. This night there was no fire, though, and people appeared with clubs, sticks, and cutlasses; some picked up stones and chunks of ice, and a few had pistols. The crowd taunting Private White grew to fifty. Later, witnesses remembered White with his back up against the customhouse door and boys screaming, "Kill him, kill him, knock him down. Fire, damn you, fire, you dare not fire." White was trying to yell over the din, "Turn out, Main Guard!"

A crowd also milled outside the barracks, throwing balls of ice and snow at any soldiers who stuck out their heads. A third crowd of several hundred gathered at a market. The cry of "Fire!" continued. "It is very odd," one man recalled remarking to a companion, "to come to put out a fire with sticks and bludgeons." The three crowds came together on King Street, where Private White was now under siege. Sometime after 9:00 p.m., there was a chorus of more church bells, which drew many more people who believed that there was indeed a fire.

At the Main Guard, Captain Thomas Preston heard the din, witnessed the street scene, and contemplated for about thirty minutes what to do. He thought White was in danger for his life but knew that sending troops to relieve him could stir the crowd more. He also believed that another crowd was headed toward King Street. He knew, too, that if he delayed, the situation would worsen.

Preston decided to send six privates and a corporal to rescue White. Given his estimation of the delicacy of the situation, he also decided to go himself. When the men arrived at the sentry post, Preston ordered White to fall in, and they all tried to march back to the Main Guard, but the crowd surrounded them. The men deployed in a semicircle with the customhouse at their backs and bayonets fixed to fend off the crowd. The mob pressed so close that, according to one of the witnesses at the trial, "you could not get your hat betwixt them and the bayonets," and Preston's orders to the crowd to disperse only riled whoever could hear him.

It was all noise and confusion. The large and growing crowd mocked the soldiers and taunted them to fire. The nervous soldiers feared for their lives and were deafened by the din. Someone threw a club that struck Private Hugh Montgomery squarely, knocking him down and the musket from his hands. When he rose, he was angry, scared, humiliated, and hurt. Some witnesses heard him shout, "Damn you, fire!" and then *he* did. Miraculously, under the circumstances, he apparently hit no one. A man swung a club at Montgomery and Preston, catching the captain full on the arm; Montgomery parried with his bayonet. A man who rushed the soldiers took a stab wound to his biceps. People later remembered a pause after the first shot, but estimates of its length varied from a few seconds to a couple of minutes.

Then the soldiers started to fire, reload, and fire again. Three civilians fell dead; two died later and several others were wounded. On the face of it, the riot was not obviously a "Boston Massacre," but the Americans who told the story told it like that, and newspapers and pamphlets circulated it throughout the colonies. Not surprisingly, the British army's version circulated more influentially in London, where depositions were collected into *A Fair Account of the Late Unhappy Disturbance in Boston*, which reached the ministry and then sold as a pamphlet. *A Short Narrative of the Horrid Massacre in Boston*, which the army's enemies in Boston produced quickly for domestic readers, attributed the whole affair to a plot by customs commissioners colluding with military leaders.

It mattered little that the facts were impossible to sort out—who shot whom; who, if anyone, gave the soldiers orders to fire and to cease firing; how much of the crowd spontaneously gathered and how much was orchestrated for political effect; what was the intent of anyone in particular; and who were the true victims that night. There are strong grounds for suspicions, but only clues and contradictory testimony on which to base them. A witness who swore that he was no more than two feet from Captain Preston heard him order his men to "fire." Another swore that he heard Preston order the men to fire and then curse them for not complying more quickly. Others heard someone order the soldiers to fire but could not be sure who, whether members of the crowd, the corporal, or the captain; still others testified that Preston may have actually said "do not fire" or nothing at all.

Later that night, Governor Hutchinson addressed the huge crowd from the balcony of the State House and calmed inflamed tempers by ordering the arrest of Captain Preston and the soldiers under him. He also ordered British officers to confine their men to the barracks. The next day, when the town meeting demanded that the troops withdraw from the town, Hutchinson tried to compromise by ordering one of the two regiments to be confined to Castle William, several miles away and strongly defended. Samuel Adams, representing the town meeting, told Hutchinson that compromise was unacceptable: "It is at your peril if you refuse. The meeting is composed of three thousand people. They are become impatient. A thousand men are already arrived from the neighborhood, and the whole country is in motion. Night is approaching. An immediate answer is expected. Both regiments or none!" Governor Hutchinson and the council accepted Adams's terms in order to avoid what they called a "perfect convulsion." In June, the customs commissioners and their families moved into the fort after several more months of broken windows and threats from Boston mobs that made them fear for their lives.

The Sons of Liberty now ran Boston, and public opinion was overwhelmingly against the governor, the council, and the British soldiers. The procession and funerals of the "martyrs" made even Seider's pale in comparison. Between ten and twelve thousand of Boston's total population of thirteen thousand publicly mourned those fellow citizens who fell to the soldiers' shots. Not everyone was convinced, though. "They call me a brainless Tory," one Bostonian remarked, "but tell me, my young friend, which is better—to be ruled by one tyrant three thousand miles away, or by three thousand tyrants not one mile away?"

In Gloucester, Massachusetts, a fishing town on the shore north of Boston, on the night of March 23 a group of men, some with blackened faces and others disguised as Indians, tore Jesse Savil (called Saville in some sources), a known agent and informer, from his bed. After marching him barefoot about four miles, they carted him through town, tarred and feathered him, and forced him to swear never again to inform on his fellow citizens. Then they ordered him to thank the group for its "gentle Discipline" and released him. At best, Savil had showed himself on the side of lawful authority if forced to choose sides, and constitutionally conservative; this would have made him a "Loyalist" or "Tory," which were fungible terms. The labels could be accusations of disloyalty in communities disinclined to abide difference and dissent. Either word meant "outsider" and was used as a warning to conform or suffer the consequences of personal independence against community ideals.

The crowd created an identity for Savil and those it lumped with him for many different reasons, some of which had little to do with a Tory's politics. The radicals were trying to force the political issues by clearing the middle ground of neutrals and making clear the price for choosing the opposite side from one's neighbors. The effect was to harden lines and lead the opposing parties to coalesce, however dangerous a public position could be in some places.

In Boston, the court delayed the soldiers' trials until fall, wisely allowing time for tempers to calm. During the intervening six months, Preston and his men were confined to Boston's thoroughly unpleasant jail. It was not easy, right after the indictments were filed, to find attorneys willing to take their cases, yet the Sons of Liberty were determined to get them a fair trial. Anything less would shine a bad light on Boston and the cause of American independence. To win this round of the propaganda war, the judicial system had to be above reproach, although it is likely that no one imagined the accused could possibly be found not guilty. When asked, John Adams agreed to represent Preston, explaining, "If he thinks he cannot have a fair Tryal of that Issue without my Assistance, without hesitation he shall have it." Clearly, the Sons of Liberty orchestrated representation for the captain and enlisted men. No lawyer would have dared take the case without their sanction, because it would have been career ending, if not life threatening.

The case of Ebenezer Richardson, accused murderer of young Christopher Seider, and his alleged accomplice, George Wilmot, came before the court in April. Richardson had difficulty securing counsel, and his lawyer reported in sick when the case was called. The court appointed Josiah Quincy Jr., a reputable radical attorney, to handle the defense. The prosecutors were the king's attorney Samuel Quincy (Josiah's older brother) and Robert Treat Paine, a successful lawyer with a practice in southern Massachusetts and Rhode Island. At about the same time, the Court of General Sessions ordered the sheriff to "cause a New Gallows to be Erected on the [Boston] Neck, the old one being

gone to decay," and to increase security at the jail to "six men constantly to watch there."

The prosecution argued that there had been no threat to Richardson's life on the day in question, that it was just a gang of schoolboys
throwing rocks at his windows. Moreover, Seider had simply been bending over to pick up a stone when Richardson shot him; he was obviously not threatening Richardson's life. Since the crowd did not go into
Richardson's house until after the shooting, a claim of self-defense was
unsustainable in law. Josiah Quincy did, as the prosecution anticipated,
argue that Richardson acted in self-defense, and witnesses including
family members testified to the viciousness of the assault against him.

Three of the four judges, Edmund Trowbridge, John Cushing, and
Benjamin Lynde, in summing up the case and instructing the jury,
agreed with the defense that Richardson's actions constituted manslaughter at worst. Judge Peter Oliver went further, explaining to the
jurors that Richardson had not in fact committed any offense. In his
opinion, Seider's death was a justifiable homicide resulting from self-
defense and a tragic result of the crowd's illegal assembly. The jury left
the courtroom to deliberate amid raucous instructions from the spectators: "Blood requires blood," shouted one man. "Damn him, don't
bring it in manslaughter! Hang the dog! Hang him! Damn him, hang
him! Murder, not manslaughter," others screamed.

It took the jury a long night, from 11:00 p.m. to 8:00 a.m., to reach
its verdict. "How say you?" asked the clerk. The jury found Richardson
guilty of murder and Wilmot not guilty of complicity. The spectators
erupted with shouts of approval. The judges were in a difficult position.
Popular opinion was clear, but they and the governor believed the jury
had acted contrary to law. To buy time, the judges formally received
the verdict but postponed sentencing until May 29.

During the interim between the verdict and sentencing, news arrived in Boston that Parliament had repealed all the Townshend Duties
except the one on tea. Members of the antitax, antiarmy, anticonsump-
tion, and proindependence movement saw this as a great victory, to be
sure, but not enough for them to change course. Indeed, unless the
Sons of Liberty acted wisely, the repeal might inspire complacency and
thus weaken their movement. At least in Boston they still had the
soldiers and tea to focus their energies, and the Richardson verdict and
the soldiers' trials to highlight the ongoing dangers.

On May 29, Judge Oliver fell from his horse, on purpose some theorized, and Judge Trowbridge claimed to be sick with a bout of "nervous illness." That meant that Judges Lynde and Cushing were left to take the heat alone. They adjourned the court until May 31, buying themselves two more days.

Meanwhile, Boston was not without political theater. Lieutenant Governor Hutchinson, soon to formally replace Bernard as governor, and the assembly were locked in a quarrel that stemmed from Hutchinson's having acted on royal instructions and called the session to sit at Cambridge, across the river from the mob that ruled Boston.

The nonimportation movement had fallen apart, and this actually led to more collective violence against the merchants unprotected by the Sons of Liberty. Crowds sometimes seized their goods by force and put them into storage. They closed down the shop of three brothers whom they accused of importing banned goods, and terrorized one of them by forcing him to run a gantlet of men who spit in his face. Breaking windows, daubing excrement on doors, identifying boycotted merchants by posting warning signs outside their shops, and roughing up suspected informers continued unabated, even after the news of Parliament's repeal of all but the duty on tea. Tar and featherings were no longer confined to the dark of night. At Boston's town meetings, according to newspaper reports, "The spirit rose very high. Independence was a word much used."

George Whitefield, the revivalist preacher who had so moved colonists in the 1740s during the Great Awakening, arrived in Boston in August 1770 on his seventh American tour. Decades of travel, often preaching sixty hours a week, had taken a toll. Whitefield now wheezed asthmatically when he preached, which he did several times a day in hot, crowded churches throughout the city. Some noticed that he had a calming influence on the inflamed populace. The revivalist then headed north, preaching in Newburyport on September 29, where he died the next morning from an asthmatic seizure.

The judges continued all summer to try to avoid their fateful sentencing of Richardson. Judge Lynde tendered his resignation at least twice to Hutchinson, who persuaded him to stay in office. Judge Trowbridge remained fearful in the face of intimidation. Judge Oliver was the subject of repeated newspaper attacks. Judge Cushing seemed solid so long as Oliver was. But Governor Hutchinson had no braver replacements if these men resigned. And the four judges were not merely intimidated. They felt their hands were tied, for the law provided no remedy for their plight. Given the verdict against Richardson, they had no choice but to sentence him to death. Interviews with members of the jury in September revealed that most of them had made up their minds about the defendant's guilt before the trial began, and that all of them were influenced by the reactions of the courtroom spectators. The one initial holdout against conviction had changed his vote to create the required unanimous verdict for a capital crime, because he believed that given how the judges had instructed the jurors, they would spare Richardson's life no matter what the verdict.

When the soldiers arrested in the Boston Massacre case were arraigned on September 7, the judges still had not sentenced Richardson. The court delayed the soldiers' trial until late October, which angered everyone—the Sons of Liberty, who saw in the delay an attempt by the judiciary and government loyalists to avoid a trial altogether, and the British military officers, who hoped the soldiers would be released at the earliest possible time. When the court adjourned its September session, the judges still had not sentenced Richardson.

When the court reconvened in October, the defense in the soldiers' case had to face several problems. First of all, Captain Preston's trial had been separated from those of the soldiers, and his best defense was to argue that he had never given an order to fire, while the enlisted men's best argument was that they had fired in response to a direct order, which they had to do under pain of death. And it was impossible to link any particular soldier to the death of any particular victim. So on the prosecution side the indictments would have to be vague, thereby weakening them, or would fall under the weight of inadequate evidence linking any particular shot to any particular death. In such a situation, the best prosecution argument would be that whoever shot a given victim, all the soldiers abetted the murder, making them all equally guilty of each death.

Philip Dumaresq, a juror in the Preston trial, was known to have stated on more than one occasion that he "believed Captain Preston to be as innocent as the Child unborn," and that if he was selected for the jury he "would never convict him if he sat to all eternity." At least two others may have had similar views and have been as stubbornly devoted to the political principles that underlay them. Since the law required a unanimous jury verdict to convict in a capital case, Preston, at least, would go free.

Richard Palmes, a member of the crowd, testified that although he had been standing close enough to have his hand on Captain Preston's shoulder, he could not say who had given the order to fire. Andrew, a slave, testified that Private Montgomery fired without any order, and that when the order to fire did come he was "certain the voice came from beyond" Preston. These two witnesses gave the jury ample cause for reasonable doubt, whatever their predilections or politics. It took only three hours for them to reach a unanimous verdict of not guilty.

In light of Captain Preston's acquittal, the burden of the defense in the soldiers' case was to convince the jury that the men acted in self-defense when they fired into the crowd and killed five Bostonians. Dr. John Jeffries supported this argument by testifying that before Patrick Carr died, he "particularly said that he forgave the man whoever he was that shot him, [as] he was satisfied he had no malice, but fired to defend himself." As John Adams summarized the case for the defense, "If an assault was made to endanger their lives, the law is clear, they had a right to kill in their own defense, if it is not so severe as to endanger their lives, yet if they were assaulted at all, struck and abused by blows of any sort . . . this was a provocation, for which the law reduces the offence of killing down to manslaughter."

After deliberating for less than three hours, the jury returned a verdict of not guilty in four cases and manslaughter in the other two, Montgomery and Mathew Kilroy. The two convicted men still faced possible death sentences, but when they returned to court for sentencing on December 14, each "prayed clergy." This traditional plea for mercy, when accepted by the court, required branding the convicts on the thumb to ensure that they could not effectively make such a plea should they ever again be convicted of a capital offense. Later, Montgomery confided to his lawyer that it was he who had given the order to fire. Key witnesses were unavailable in the cases of the remaining two soldiers, so the court postponed the trials indefinitely.

In another trial, a jury acquitted four civilians accused of firing on the crowd from the customhouse balcony. These defendants did not have lawyers, and the jury members never left their courtroom seats to deliberate in private. It was a token prosecution, with the charges brought only for the propaganda value of implicating the customs service in the deaths of civilians. John Adams, looking back on all the Boston Massacre cases three years later, before the war for independence began, wrote that a death sentence in any of them "would have been as foul a Stain upon this Country as the Executions of the Quakers or Witches, anciently. As the Evidence was, the Verdict of the Jury was exactly right." Nonetheless, Adams wrote in 1815, "to this hour, my conduct in it is remembered, and is alleged against me to prove I am an enemy to my country, and always have been."

In an address to King George III published in 1770, "Junius" was one of the very few Englishmen who openly acknowledged that he was "looking forward to" the "independence" of the American colonies, at which point he anticipated that the colonists might "possibly receive you for their king." But the anonymous Junius was talking about an undefined future event rather than a contemporary plan, and even he was couching his observations in such a way as to encourage the North ministry to see the error of its ways.* In the same year, a traveler named Alexander Cluny published some observations on the colonies in which he noted that the "inhabitants enjoy a State of Independence in a Manner peculiar to themselves."

In the following year, Edward Bancroft, a physician born in Massachusetts and living in London, wrote in defense of the colonies, which, he pointed out, were growing apace in population and wealth. He could imagine a future, "perhaps in a few Years," which "may produce a People too numerous to continue Victims of Oppression and too brave not to assert their just and constitutional Rights; and if this should ever happen, that distance, which separates this Kingdom from the Colonies, might be converted to a very important Instrument for establishing the Independence of the Latter."

* The identity of "Junius" is still unknown, but the leading candidate is Sir Philip Francis, an Irish-born soldier, war office clerk, and pamphleteer who often attended Parliament when there were discussions of American questions.

✦PART THREE✦

✦

Independence

13

✦

PARTIES

THE RETREAT OF BRITISH TROOPS from the streets of Boston after the "Massacre" in March 1770 defused the violence there. And when colonists heard of Lord North's rescission of all the Townshend Duties except the one on tea in that same month, they considered the news a resounding affirmation of their independence. What was left of their nonimportation plan collapsed, given these imperial concessions, and the shared intercolonial efforts on its behalf fell into disarray. New York merchants withdrew from the boycott agreement over the summer, Philadelphia merchants in the fall. This left Boston's merchants alone and divided, so they too abandoned the agreement in October.

The problems that persisted in the colonies' social structures and in their economies were still grave, of course, and internal political tensions were as great as ever, but the argument that British imperial reforms initiated by a more enlightened ministry might cure these internal problems again gained some credibility. To be sure, colonists could still blame the British for countless aggravations. Some of these were particular to settlers who lived on the frontier, including underrepresentation in colonial legislatures, the corruption of colonial governments, and inadequate defense against Indians. Some were shared by those merchants and land speculators who had investments in the frontier regions, the most pressing of which were the Proclamation Line of 1763 and restrictions on land grants. Some were unique to localities, such as the land-title crises in New Jersey and Maine, and the landlord-tenant conflicts in New York. And some were more widely shared among all North American colonists—rising debts, shortages of currency, a corrupt customs service, and the inflexible governors whose hands were tied by strict imperial instructions. Less logically, the colonists could imagine the empire being indirectly responsible for soil depletion, tumbling tobacco prices and escalating farmland prices, a large and growing population of propertyless immigrants, urban unemployment and crime, and the now rapid decline of fish and game.

Fixing blame on external, imperial forces in this way could still distract colonists from their own native corruption and conflicts of interest, and it could still credibly explain the major problems they faced, but not with the same unifying force as it once had. Colonists remained unflinchingly committed to the constitutional principle of "no taxation without representation" and the political position that they were not and could not be effectively represented in Parliament. Their advocacy of a principle of divided sovereignty to explain their independence within the empire had created a conflict with British officials that could not be resolved, yet they remained in denial about the insurmountable transatlantic disagreements. They could not resist the logic of their own interpretation of history, of their significance and thus leverage within the empire, and of their traditional political rights.

The colonies' perennial shortage of hard money exacerbated their other economic woes as the 1770s began. The shortage of coin affected every colony, although not all of them or each region within them to the same degree, yet the colonists came together in opposition to the empire's hard-money policy as set forth in the Currency Acts of 1751, 1764, 1770, and 1773. The British prejudice against paper currency dated back to the early years of the century, but the act of 1751 was part of the invigorated effort to administer the empire more rationally, and the next three acts concerned enforcement. Just as with taxes and customs administration, the acts did not represent new policies, but that is how the colonists perceived them—as part of a pattern of assaults on their independence during hard economic times.

In setting currency policy in 1751 and 1764, the Board of Trade had tried to balance conflicting interests but had failed to achieve a unified, enforceable policy on colonial paper money. On the one side, British merchants trading to South Carolina and New England wanted protection for sterling debts paid in local currency. They would have been happiest if all paper money were eliminated and they returned to the system of specie payments legislated by Parliament in 1708 but erratically and ineffectually enforced since then. Similarly, the major colonial merchants involved in international trade generally favored the strong money policies that Parliament endorsed. They also saw hard currency as a barrier against inflation, which increased the cost of doing business, cut their profits, and favored smaller merchants with whom they competed.

On the other side, British merchant-creditors who did most of their business with the Middle Colonies, where sterling exchange rates were much less volatile, were willing to accept paper money on the settlement of their American accounts, and they thought that outlawing colonial paper emissions would be a drag on the expansion of markets. Businessmen and land speculators in the Middle Colonies liked paper money as a source of liquidity, and farmers favored inflation to reduce their debt burdens. Those who worked in cash-poor areas, such as the backcountry, also had good cause to oppose currency regulation.

The Currency Act of 1751 had tried to bring order to the chaos of the colonial economies and to protect creditors. It aimed specifically at New England, citing the previous failures to regulate currency there. Connecticut, Rhode Island, Massachusetts, and New Hampshire had issued paper currency that could be used to pay taxes during a set period of between one and seven years; as the new act put it, "All debts of late years have been paid and satisfied with a much less value than was contracted for, which hath been a great discouragement and prejudice to trade and commerce." So as of September 29, 1751, the New England colonies were forbidden to authorize the issuance of additional bills of credit (one form of paper currency) or to extend the life span of any paper money then in circulation. The only exceptions were bills to cover current government expenditures for two years or less and currency issued in wartime; since these bills would finance only government expenditures and not payment of private debts, creditors were protected. But the policy constricted New England's economy, as it did not recognize the need for elasticity in business dealings.

The Currency Act of 1764 extended the hard-money policy that the 1751 act had imposed on New England to the rest of the American colonies, thereby reinforcing the hard-money bias of the Board of

Trade. The new law was meant to address the postwar financial crisis in Great Britain by shifting some of the burden of debt onto the colonies, so it was no wonder that British merchant-creditors had lobbied for it. But it further burdened the colonies' already depressed economies and exacerbated their currency shortages. When Parliament mandated collection of new taxes in specie and the customs collectors in Boston declared unilaterally that duties would henceforth be collected only in specie, the situation became even worse. Tobacco prices were falling and Virginia planters were more and more in debt, so the 1764 act only worsened the colony's financial challenges during Pontiac's War.

The 1764 Currency Act was also, in part, a response to Virginia's efforts to borrow its way out of insolvency in 1757 by issuing £180,000 in paper currency. It required that all debts incurred in sterling had to be paid in sterling rather than in depreciated paper money, which had responded to rapidly rising exchange rates beginning in 1762. In debating the bill before adoption, the Board of Trade called witnesses, one of whom was a London merchant doing business in Virginia who "remarked the growing independency of the Colony: the little deference paid to his Majesty's orders and even the contempt showed them," which he hoped the new currency law would help to rectify.

The American Revenue Act (Sugar Act), the Currency Act, and the Stamp Act were intended as a package that collectively addressed the British Empire's debt and revenue issues. Lord Hillsborough's recommendations on February 9, 1764, had called for a prohibition of future legal tender paper currency throughout the colonies south of New England, where the same policy was already in place. The 1764 act was a compromise, in some regards, but it was more stringent than the 1751 act in its prohibition of paper money as legal tender for any public or private transactions. Simultaneous with its adoption, bankruptcies in the colonies reached a thirty-five-year high, mercantile houses called in their American loans, and the price of flour plunged, all of which inhibited trade with the West Indies. Efforts by the London agents representing New York, Pennsylvania, and South Carolina to get the act repealed failed in 1766, 1767, and 1768. There was no sympathy in England for the colonists.

The colonies adjusted as they always did, by evasion and outright defiance of the law, while the British responded to new lobbying on the colonists' behalf in 1770 with another compromise, this time allowing new emission of treasury notes that would be viable for public debts as long as the enabling legislation made no specific reference to the paper currency as "legal tender." Any colonial law that breached this rule over the next ten years would be disallowed, which gave the ministry cover to compromise and London merchants protection from colonists using depreciated currency to pay their debts. In imperial theory, everyone should have been content, but the colonists generally were not.

Where British officials saw the administration of the Currency Act of 1764 as flexible and practical, colonists viewed it as irrational and inconsistent. "It was never imagined," said New Jersey's governor William Franklin in 1770, "that so extensive a Construction would be put upon the Act of parliament for restraining paper Currencies." The Board of Trade denied New Jersey the right to issue currency although it had approved it for years to Pennsylvania and Maryland. Lord Hillsborough's tighter enforcement of the Currency Act beginning in 1768 had created greater inconsistencies and additional burdens. Enforcement was to change yet again when Lord Dartmouth replaced Hillsborough as head of the Southern Department in 1772. In 1773, he planned a new currency law to clarify the ministry's policy, but by then the currency controversy was caught up in the empire's larger conflicts, and the colonies were simply defying the law.

In the fall of 1772, a financial panic swept Great Britain and creditors began to call in their debts. At the same time, the tobacco market collapsed and the economies of Maryland and Virginia fell into a deep recession, which was compounded by debt and a shortage of cash. Within twelve months, the price of tobacco fell by half. By the spring of 1774, one-third of the families in Pittsfield County, Virginia, had been sued for their debts and had lost the suits. From 1772 through 1774, the number of debt suits filed in Prince George's County, Maryland, doubled. Charles Yates, a Virginia planter, decided by 1774 that the price of tobacco, the commodity on which he knew his colony's economy depended, was "really too low for the Makers to live by it."

Small farmers were angry with the rich plantation owners who ran Virginia's government. They complained about the requirement that tobacco inspection fees be paid in cash, which effectively moved specie from one social class (their own) to another (the gentry who ran the business). It was feared that riots such as those in New England and New York, and bloody social strife such as in New Jersey, Pennsylvania, and North Carolina might spread to the Chesapeake region, and lead, Virginians speculated, to rebellion by the enslaved 40 percent of their colony's population. The gentry found reasons to blame external forces for the colony's internal social stress, which took some of the heat off them and restored the whites' race solidarity against slaves. No matter how far-fetched the allegations or implausible the linkages, the scapegoats were said to be British politicians and merchants on both sides of the Atlantic.

The far-flung territories of Maine, Massachusetts's northernmost district, had unique problems, but they also suffered from the travails endured by the southern tobacco farmers, the frontier settlers in the Carolinas, and the people of Boston, to which its economy was inextricably linked. Like Georgia in its relationship to Spanish Florida, Maine had until 1763 been exposed to hostile forces in Nova Scotia, and its residents still valued the protection of the Royal Navy, yet when conflict flared in Boston, colonists in Maine felt their economic and military vulnerability. But they could not agree on which paths to take and which commitments to honor. Their interests divided them: Anglican versus Congregationalist, one land-speculation company versus the others. Farmers who were not speculators competed for land both with each other and with the companies. Some of this competition played out as class conflict, and some of it pitted new settlers against well-established ones. And all these conflicts raised issues that had persisted since the seventeenth century but were raised anew by tougher enforcement and increasing pressure on resources.

One problem concerned land speculation, for the Proclamation Line of 1763 had diverted to the north and east some Massachusetts settlers who otherwise would have moved west across the Appalachian Mountains. Maine's population increased from about 23,000 in 1763 to 47,000 a decade later (about 14 percent of the Massachusetts total). Several land speculation companies, having taken swaths of forest off the market, inflated the price of available acreage in a time of increasing demand. The Kennebec Proprietors were the most politically influential within Massachusetts and in England, claiming more than three thousand square miles along the Kennebec River and with stakeholders including such power brokers as Francis Bernard, William Shirley, and Thomas Pownall, all former governors of Massachusetts. Governor Thomas Hutchinson was an investor in their chief competition, the Pejepscot Company.

Another British imperial policy that was still problematical for Maine was the one formulated in the White Pines Acts restricting its timber business and reserving the best logs for the Royal Navy. The colonists' response continued to be poaching and smuggling, which in the 1770s escalated into a war of nerves with the customs service and the Royal Navy, its enforcement arm. As the population increased and the demand for ships' masts also grew, influence peddling and politicking by land speculators were rife.

A third problem may seem unrelated, but it too was affected by Maine's rapid population growth and its distrust of the intentions of British officers with their taxes, their energetic enforcement of the Navigation Acts, and their deployment of naval force in New England's port cities. The spread of the Anglican religion in New England, and especially in Maine, made rumors about its establishment in America, and the installation of an American bishop, both credible and threatening to Maine's Dissenter majority—yet another example of the conspiracy against their independence within the empire.

To the ministry and Crown, such thinking still seemed delusional. Imperial officials perceived no pattern of oppression and believed that they had merely enforced the law more robustly, administered the colonies more rationally, and attempted more efficiently to address Britain's massive national debt by raising funds from the colonists to help cover the cost of governing them. To the extent that they considered the colonists' perspective at all, they considered that their vaunted independence claimed as a birthright was simply a response to the empire's historical pattern of weak enforcement and to defects in the imperial system that successive ministries tried to remedy in response to changed circumstances and political pressures in England and on Parliament.

Charles Dudley, collector of customs for Rhode Island, came under assault as soon as he arrived in Providence in the spring of 1768. Merchants smuggled brazenly, stole molasses he confiscated, and roughed up his agents if they interfered. No one came forward to testify and no one wanted the rewards given for informing on the thieves, smugglers, and assailants. In June 1769, a mob in Providence seized his deputy, Jesse Saville (the same men who figured in the Boston Massacre a year later), and beat him badly, the *Providence Gazette* reporting that he "was treated with more Tenderness and Lenity than is perhaps due an Informer," which suggests the general view of the situation.

In the same year, the armed customs service sloop *Liberty* seized two ships carrying goods from Connecticut to Newport, Rhode Island. Since the ships had no clearances, they were confiscated, and when the captain of one of them rowed off to avoid capture, the *Liberty*'s crew fired on him—to no avail but provoking a reprisal. A band of sailors who rowed out from shore in several small boats boarded the *Liberty*, chopped down its mast, smashed holes in its hull, and let it drift to a harbor island where it ran aground and another mob set it on fire.

The case of the Royal Navy's ship *Gaspée* and the shooting of its captain on June 9, 1772, reignited anti-British feelings and the belief that there was an imperial conspiracy against the colonists' independence. It also reinforced the British belief that the resistance was a problem of law enforcement. The *Gaspée*'s captain, William Dudingston, had been zealous in enforcing customs regulations, seizing both oceangoing vessels and small boats that ferried goods from one side of Narragansett Bay to the other. No legislator or bureaucrat had ever imagined applying customs regulations to such intracoastal trade, but Dudingston creatively saw in it a way to profit from seizures and to undercut the illegal downloading of smuggled goods from the larger ships that brought the goods into port.

On the day in question, Dudingston and the *Gaspée* were pursuing the packet boat *Hannah* across the bay. The *Hannah*'s captain, by a sly maneuver that showed his intimate knowledge of the waters and the tide, lured the *Gaspée* close to shore, where it ran aground on a sand bar near Namquit Point (later renamed Gaspée Point in commemoration of the triumph). Knowing that a rising tide would not free the

Gaspée until early the next morning, John Brown, a leading merchant of Providence, organized an attack upon it. When Captain Dudingston challenged Brown's boat as it pulled alongside with several others, one of the attackers shot him, and he fell wounded on the deck. The assault party boarded the *Gaspée*, seized its crew, including the wounded captain, loaded the men into their boat, set fire to the *Gaspée*, which eventually burned to the waterline, and then rowed to shore.

The attack on the *Gaspée* was the first in which colonists adopted the persona of Mohawks, dressing as Indians to disguise their identities, however thinly. The reasons for the choice, which later in the year was also adopted by men attacking tea-laden ships in New Jersey, New York, and Boston, are obscure, but the Sons of Liberty had identified with Indians in the past. The Mohawk, one of the tribes in the Iroquois confederacy, became for them a symbol of liberty, of resistance, and of license to break the law during the 1770s.

Captain Dudingston recovered from his wounds and filed a protest with the governor of Rhode Island and imperial officials. With much formality, the Crown appointed a commission to investigate the incident. Local people believed that the Privy Council, acting in the name of the king, had invested the commission with vast powers, but it had not. The fear that perpetrators would be identified, transported to England, and summarily tried and hanged made the investigation a cause célèbre, but the commission identified none of the culprits and the Privy Council's investigation came to naught. Still, the colonists outside Rhode Island were alarmed by how the commission appeared to fit a larger pattern, which included taxes, a military occupation, customs racketeering, and other grievances both local and widely shared. In response, they established committees of correspondence, first within Massachusetts, Rhode Island's neighboring colony, the most radicalized in response to the British occupation of Boston and the best organized for such endeavors, and eventually across the colonies, to share information about British threats to American independence. They also became virtual shadow governments, superseding formal institutions of governance. The committees made collective plans and coordinated them among the colonies, an important one being the concerted effort to lower consumption of imported commodities and make other moves to secure economic independence. They countermanded edicts issued by the governors and other royally appointed officials and ensured that those who supported British policy were identified and their influence or power neutralized. They created spy networks and organized collective action to minimize violence, while circulating propaganda that spun stories of conflict between colonies and empire that were sympathetic to the cause of independence.

In 1771, many colonists in Massachusetts, including Maine, nonetheless hoped that the relatively harmonious relations they had enjoyed with imperial officials before the Seven Years War would return, and so did settlers in other colonies. But those who would not let the coordinated efforts in support of independence die in 1772 included not only economically and politically self-interested parties such as the Virginia gentry but also all those who most distrusted the Crown, the Privy Council, and the ministries that had come and gone in London in the 1760s. Some of them continued to postulate a political conspiracy hatched in London, whose principals had simply made a tactical calculation in repealing all the Townshend Duties except the one on tea. These conspiracy theorists, who included Samuel Adams and the Sons of Liberty in Boston, predicted, accurately as it turned out, that no ministry would ever surrender the constitutional principles linked so closely to the Navigation Acts—principles about the locus of sovereignty and about representation and taxation. These had always divided the colonists from imperial officials, but the colonists' belief in divided sovereignty had become ever more hotly contested; suspicious, some say paranoid, colonial activists combed London newspapers and transatlantic correspondence for rumors and clues as to where and how the conspiracy would next rear its head.

As if on cue, the Crown offered these radicals more evidence that power in London was conspiring against liberty in the colonies when, in late 1771, the ministry decided to start paying the Massachusetts governor's salary directly from England out of funds raised by the colonial customs service. Since the governor was a royal appointment, there was a defensible logic to this plan, but an argument could be made, and was made by John Adams, that it would make the governor "independent of the people" and disrupt "that balance of power which is essential to all free governments." Writing as "Marchmont Nedham" in the *Boston Gazette*, Adams proposed that "an *INDEPENDENT ruler*, [is] a MONSTER *in a free state*."

The conspiracy theorists correctly predicted that encroachments on the colonists' independence would not end with this new arrangement for the governor's salary. On October 18, 1771, Francis Dana wrote to the Rhode Island lawyer Henry Marchant about an anticipated seizure of judicial salaries: "Here is displayed another part of that pernicious plan of government laid down for America. 'Tis open for this Province, but it will be extend[ed] thro out the Continent," and, as it spread, the plan would reduce all the colonists "to a state too humiliating and abject to be endured by a people whose ideas of Political Freedom are no better than a Hottentot's."

And indeed, reliable word reached Boston in the fall of 1772 that the Crown was, precisely, considering direct payment from customs revenue of the salaries of justices of the Superior Court of Judicature, the attorney general, and the solicitor general. Superior Court justices already served at the "pleasure" of the administration rather than "during good behavior," which was the case in England, and their independence was thus already compromised in colonists' eyes. They believed that their assembly's power to set and allocate salaries was the last remaining counterweight to the judges' self-interest in serving Crown over colony. From the perspective of the Boston town meeting, the changes would lead to the appointment of corrupt men who, "being hackneyed in the paths of deceit and avarice, will be fit tools to enslave & oppress an honest people." Alerted to the danger, the meeting resolved unanimously on October 28 "that a Committee of Correspondence be appointed to consist of twenty-one Persons—to state the Rights of the Colonists and of this Province in particular, as Men, as Christians, and as Subjects; to communicate and publish the same to the several Towns in this Province and to the World as the sense of this Town . . . Also requesting of each Town a free communication of their Sentiments on this Subject."

The unanimity was possible only because friends of the government had boycotted the meeting, which, they had hoped, would undermine its influence. Even with the absence of those opposed to it, though, the independence movement did not present a united front. Five of its wealthiest, most influential supporters, including John Hancock, publicly declined to serve on the newly created committee of correspondence.

The perceived assault on judicial independence triggered a resurgence of anger about the abuses of the customs service. As the committee wrote, "Our houses and even our Bed-Chambers, are exposed to be ransacked, our Boxes, Trunks and Chests broke open, ravaged and plundered, by Wretches whom no prudent Man would venture to employ even as menial Servants." The system was corrupt from top to bottom, with "unconstitutional Officers . . . collecting and managing this unconstitutional revenue" while protected by the Royal Navy and standing army still in Boston. On top of the existing corruption, seizure of the authority to set the salaries of judicial officials and to pay them would "compleat our slavery."

Yet the Massachusetts towns were initially not persuaded by the committee's call to vigilance. The news about the judicial salaries was still rumor, so perhaps the Bostonians were overreacting. The rumor had persisted for more than a year, and nothing had happened yet.

On the other side, Governor Hutchinson thought imperial control over salaries was essential, because the tide of resistance was coming in swiftly. On March 28, 1768, he had written to Thomas Pownall that the colonists were "more inclined to independence than they have been . . . It is a principle which spreads every day and before long will be universal." He had not changed his mind on this subject by December 8, 1772, when he wrote to the colony's agent in London, Richard Jackson, that the "doctrine of Independence upon the Parliament and the mischiefs of it every day increase." To Hutchinson, sovereignty alone was the issue. Either the colonists accepted Parliament's supremacy or they did not. If they did not, they were effectively declaring independence and seeking separation from the empire.

In 1772, Governor Hutchinson addressed the Massachusetts assembly on the subject of independence, shunning, as usual, the views of his fellow colonists.

> I know of no line that can be drawn between the supreme authority of Parliament and the total independence of the colonies: it is impossible there should be two independent Legislatures in one and the same state . . . If we might be suffered to be altogether independent of Great-Britain, could we have any Claim to the Protection of that Government of which we are no longer a Part?

Since Hutchinson believed that an independent America would be weak and vulnerable to attacks by European powers if it were not protected by the British Empire, he hoped that he was mistaken about the colonists' ambitions: "Independence I may not allow myself to think that you can possibly have in Contemplation." Or so he said. Of course Hutchinson really did allow himself to think that Massachusetts colonists were after separation from the empire.

The assembly's formal reply engaged Hutchinson's premises on his terms. "If there is no such line" between Parliament's authority and the total independence of the colonies, "the consequence is either that the colonies are the vassals of the Parliament, or that they are totally independent. As it cannot be supposed to have been the intention of the parties in the compact, that we should be reduced to a state of vassalage, the conclusion is that it was their sense, that we were thus independent." In other words, the colonists were already independent with no need for separation unless Parliament tried to impose vassalage on them 150 years after the colony's founding.

Unlike Hutchinson, the assemblymen saw no greater reason to fear "total independence" than "to dread the consequences of absolute uncontrolled power, whether of a nation or a monarch." While they had not raised the question of separation—Hutchinson had—they did not find his threats intimidating. They implied that they would consider separation only if Parliament breached the compact. Hutchinson replied that he was "glad you have hitherto avoided" drawing the same conclusion as he had and hoped they would continue to "consider the obvious and inevitable Distress and Misery of Independence upon our Mother Country, if such Independence could be allowed or maintained, and the Probability of much greater Distress, which we are not able to foresee."

Also in 1772, republished works by the famous seventeenth-century minister John Wise defended the independence of New England's churches; the Philadelphia physician Benjamin Rush wrote about financial independence; and John Witherspoon, president of the College of New Jersey (Princeton), wrote about the "spirit of liberty and independence" that the college promoted. All three men thought of independence as consistent with affiliation to British institutions and therefore did not think that dissolution of existing bonds was its implied or necessary consequence. Likewise Benjamin Church, in a speech delivered in 1773 commemorating the third anniversary of the Boston Massacre, argued that people founded societies to escape a state of eternal war and that when a nation "began to incorporate," the relationships among its constituents evolved and "subordination succeeded to independence," a higher and more stable state of governance and certainly not a threat to its existence. In various letters written by Governor Hutchinson, which Benjamin Franklin obtained and published to the embarrassment of both men in 1773, it was clear that Hutchinson had long been aware of this way of thinking about independence; he charged that in pursuing "the dark purposes of their independence," his fellow colonists accepted "no restraint of conscience, or fear, not even the guilt of threatening to excite a civil war, and revolt, if not indulged with an unlimited trade, without restraint; and British protection, without expense."

Governor Hutchinson raised the specter of independence again in a January 1773 address to the Massachusetts assembly: "Is there any thing which we have more Reason to dread than Independence?" Hutchinson was still the colonist who spoke publicly and most often about independence, by which he always meant separation from the empire, and he spoke of it in fear, in warning, as an accusation, an attribution of motive, and in his private correspondence and reports to the ministry. He had no doubt that radical colonial incendiaries, who themselves were not advocating separation publicly, were beating the drums for war behind the scenes. He was sure that the assembly's denial of the "supreme authority of Parliament" amounted "to a Declaration of total Independence." In reply, the assembly adopted the same rhetorical stance: "Independence, as your Excellency rightly judged, we have not in Contemplation. We cannot however, adopt your Principles of Government or acquiesce in all the Inferences you have drawn from them." It also expressed concern about the dangers to the "Independence as well as the Uprightness of the Judges of the Land."

As 1773 began, most of the Massachusetts colonists still shared with Hutchinson a high valuation of social order and a fear of anarchy, and they, like him, wanted to remain within the British Empire. The ideological difference between members of the resistance and Governor Hutchinson lay in their valuing liberty more highly than order, their belief that tyranny was a graver threat than anarchy, and their commitment to protecting their rights against the corruption of power they saw in the imperial ministries, the customs service, and indeed the governor himself.

The radicals interpreted events according to their theory of politics. Of course, all colonists had an ideology of some sort, however undeveloped or enthusiastically expressed. They never spoke with one voice. They held diverse beliefs, some of them inconsistently. They adhered with various degrees of dedication and success to an array of values, some of which were in utter conflict. They all acted to protect what they thought were their interests. This is not a cynical reading of their politics; many had opinions, and they tried to explain them in ways that were rational and consistent, however often they changed them and however inconsistently they behaved. In other words, they were human in all the ways that we are and, not surprisingly, were more swept up by events than successful at anticipating or orchestrating them.

Few colonists held one theoretically or theologically pure set of values to the exclusion of others. There were tensions, within individuals and across groups, among the values they held dear. Their religious beliefs furnished one of their political languages. To the extent that religious categories coincided with social classes, they were reinforcing and more predictive of allegiance than either religious affiliation or class alone. Anglicans were gentry more often than were members of some other denominations, and thus were disposed to defend the established order; evangelicals were usually lower on the social scale than Anglicans were, and hence disposed by both temperament and economic condition toward a radical position. So the judgment of political and religious moderates became decisive in the politics of the mid-1770s. But these were general tendencies and there were numerous regional, local, and personal exceptions to them.

Each of the languages that colonists used when they argued their politics had implicit and explicit contradictions, and could be as productive of dispute as of agreement. The Americans' political discourse did not cause a revolution, but it did allow them to give voice to their efforts to make sense of what they were doing and experiencing. A political language could explain spontaneous actions rationally, show the underlying logic of what might appear inconsistent or contradictory decisions, justify their interests, and idealize a political allegiance that truly was based in ideals. But to use this or that active political language did not necessarily indicate where one's loyalty lay. Nor can language alone show where and when a critical mass of colonists decided that they could secure independence only outside the British Empire in a new nation. Their words show how people made sense of the wave of events washing over them, how they sorted and explained what was happening and what they feared, and how they strove to present their ambitions in the most persuasive light.

An influential core of politically active colonists found certain ideas persuasive—what has been variously termed civic humanist, country, Whig, or republican ideas—and when these ideas were grafted onto religious principles they seemed to have even more authority. When republicans put public service on an ethical pedestal, their opponents accused them of elevating politics over religion to the detriment of their souls and as an opening move in a campaign to have a godless public sphere. The republicans claimed there were no historical examples of societies in which liberty, their highest political value, survived the corruption of powerful men, but England and America were liberty's surviving bastions against corruption in the political sphere.

Adherents of the civic humanist or republican program believed that a "mixed and balanced" constitution, such as the unwritten English one, was the best guardian of liberty. They suspected that the constitution was under assault by British officials and their political appointees in the colonies, but suspicion was not proof for most colonists in the early 1770s. After all, the ministry had rescinded all but one of the Townshend Duties in 1770, and politics was the art of compromise. The hope was that the duty on tea would be rescinded just as the stamp tax had been. On the other hand, Parliament's retention of the tea tax echoed the Declaratory Act of 1766, in which it had surrendered the point of the Stamp Act without abandoning the principle that it was sovereign, that sovereignty was indivisible, and that the authority to tax was merely a subset of its authority to legislate for the empire.

Many if not most colonists believed they could influence Parliament to repeal the duty on tea in a number of ways. They could make a conclusive case for their constitutional principles, though many knew it was unlikely at this point that they could win the constitutional argument. If Parliament considered the colonists' economic well-being and their contribution to the empire more significant than the constitutional point at stake, and if it was willing to compromise as it had with the Stamp Act, perhaps it would again restate the principle but concede the specific case. Or lobbying by English merchants holding colonial debts, acting effectively in their own self-interest, might once again save the day. Or, finally, if need be, they could resort to direct political tactics in their towns—boycotts, mob actions, and intimidation of the men whom the East India Company had designated to be its agents—which might convince the ministry that holding firm to the principle of parliamentary sovereignty came at too high a price.

Republicans believed that if Parliament understood that the colonists were united in their economic interests and unflinchingly dedicated to the two principles of divided sovereignty and no taxation without representation, the ministry would have to yield to them for practical reasons, unless there really was a conspiracy against the colonists' independence among King George and his ministers. Like a deadlocked jury, politically aware colonists could not agree on the conspiracy theory in the years between 1770, when the ministry repealed all but one of the Townshend Duties and withdrew troops from the streets of Boston, and 1774, when Parliament passed the four laws that became known as the Coercive or Intolerable Acts. But these laws finally convinced many who had wavered that there was indeed an English conspiracy against their liberty, which they had to resist by whatever means were necessary.

In February 1773, when the Virginian Arthur Lee wrote from London to his older brother Richard Henry Lee, he thought that the breakdown of the colonies' nonimportation agreement showed how moribund the coordinated efforts to defend independence had become. "The late experience of mutual faithlessness, with the disunited state which is the consequence of it, renders the probability of our harmonizing, in any mode of effectual opposition, extremely small." His pessimism may have been warranted, but the colonists were increasingly alert and capable of reviving the movement if the British offended their ideological sensitivities as they had in the 1760s.

The republican ideology espoused by the Lees and others who would become Revolutionaries had a good deal of conspiracy thinking in it, easily aroused. It was based on the liberalism expressed in such sources as John Locke's *Second Treatise of Government*, in which Locke imagined a "state of nature" that predated the formation of governments; people made compacts or contracts to form governments for their mutual protection, especially the protection of property. If a government failed to protect property rights or, as some colonists interpreted events in the 1760s and 1770s, actually attacked them, the compact was void and the people free—indeed, obliged—to create a new government to protect their property and independence.

American liberal republicans conceived of governance as being like a scale that balanced the interests of the few (the monarch, aristocrats, and wealthy gentry) and the many (the middling class and poor), that, in other words, redressed the imbalance of power between the politically influential and everyone else. To achieve such a balance, the people had to exert influence through their numbers—in town meetings, as voters, and in crowds if need be. This is why they considered representation as their best defense against the powerful, and why they adopted the most liberal suffrage requirements anywhere in the British Empire. They thought of their militias, in which most men served and that elected their own officers, as republicanism in arms and a defense against external dangers posed by the Indians and/or the French. When their liberty was threatened by imperial or domestic authority, or when authorities were deaf to warnings about such threats, the people were justified, they believed, to act against those in power—either in crowds or in militia units (sometimes the two were the same thing).

Politically aware colonists who shared this liberal republican point of view were inclined to think of the various levels of government—town, county, colony, and empire—as points on a spectrum of representation and authority. Local political institutions were close to the people, of course, representative of their interests and responsive to their needs. Here, at the local level, was the place where decisions that directly affected the lives of common people should be made—for example, the repair of roads, the building of town halls and schools, poor relief, public sanitation, and levying taxes.

Almost universally, the colonists believed they were not represented in Parliament, no matter what contrived constitutional argument defended the status quo as "virtually" representative. They disagreed about whether they could ever be represented in Parliament. "If you chuse to tax us," Benjamin Franklin wrote, "give us members in your Legislature, and let us be one people." More colonists probably agreed with Stephen Hopkins, though, that the colonists were "by distance so separated from Great Britain that they are not and cannot be represented in Parliament."

Fairly minor controversies erupting in 1773 in South Carolina, Maryland, and New York did not provide grounds for general concern. Virginia's House of Burgesses did endorse committees of correspondence, but they corresponded little that year. In Massachusetts, Governor Hutchinson kept the wounds from the 1760s open with his rigid governing hand, as did the customs service with its corruption and its eagerness to make an example of the colony. The British troops housed in Castle William were still close by, and the Royal Navy patrolling New England's shores was an irritant and a brutal reminder of Britain's past attempts to undermine their liberty. Hutchinson, impressment, customs racketeering, and the "standing army" in Boston kept the independence movement alive in Massachusetts.

Yet even there, we see little evidence before 1774 of active "contemplation of independence" in the sense of separation from the empire. Thomas Cushing, speaker of the Massachusetts assembly, wrote to Arthur Lee as late as September 1773 that although independence from the empire would likely come eventually, it was neither on the immediate horizon nor likely as a result of violent conflict. "Our natural increase in wealth and population," Cushing ruminated as other colonists had over the previous century, "will in a course of years, effectually settle this dispute in our favor." If Great Britain acted wisely, Cushing believed that the conflicts of the 1760s would "fall asleep" in the colonists' memories for the foreseeable future.

On the immediate horizon, colonial leaders such as Charles Thomson in Philadelphia thought a European war would be the next major event to affect the colonists' position in the empire. At that point, the ministry would better appreciate their importance, and it "will be the time for the American legislatures, with modesty & firmness, to recapitulate their wrongs, explain their grievances and assert their rights" effectively. One year later, in 1774, Thomson was to become the secretary of the Continental Congress, an institution he had not even anticipated in 1773, and hold that office for fifteen years. Neither Cushing nor Thomson, neither the Lees nor the Adamses, saw storm clouds or predicted a tempest in early 1773. Indeed, the general view was that if the colonies, especially Massachusetts, could avoid conflict with the British, they would soon be in a position to leverage their importance when they generously supported England in the next European war.

Still, the Massachusetts towns were becoming more open to Boston's call to vigilance, if not to resistance. Of the 260 towns that received Boston's warning about the threat posed by London's payment of judicial salaries, 144 took some action in response. Some towns agreed that the judiciary should be "as independent as possible both on the Prince and People." Some disagreed or were unwilling to assert even that moderate principle. Some favored an investigation and consideration of a possible increase in judicial salaries—albeit fixed and paid by the assembly. These conservative responses were hardly indicative of broad sympathy for anything approaching a war to separate from the British Empire. Such a mood, such outrage, such a challenge to imperial rule did not come from the towns, but the town meetings did deny Parliament's authority to tax them, and some of them even believed there were limits on its power to legislate for them as well.

The response of Concord, with its 265 families, was in the middle of the road—responsive but conservatively so. It shared a range of problems with other New England towns and looked with a similarly jaundiced eye on the outside world. In 1773, Concord was a hub of communication and trade, connected outwardly but focused inwardly on what its denizens considered a way of life superior to others but slipping away from them. In the 1760s, it had declined to join the protests that rocked Boston and other seaport cities. It was the governance of their town, not their province or the empire, that concerned them.

Seventy percent of Concord's men qualified to vote in town meetings, which meant they could also cast ballots for the town's representatives in the Massachusetts assembly. They believed in social "ranks and degrees," and most of their leaders were "substantial yeomen" and merchants who owned roughly twice as much property as the average farmer. Political office was considered a privilege and burden of social status, reserved for those who had the respect of their fellows and the leisure to govern. Traditionally, the town meeting aimed at consensus and considered its formal votes as indicative of failure, of a breakdown of the communal bonds that defined their society.

To their chagrin, the people of Concord found themselves in greater and more frequent conflict with each other than previously. They recognized that recent population increases had undermined their community—Concord was pushed to its limits of spatial growth, the townspeople were now competing for resources, the community's economic health was in decline as inequalities in wealth grew. Emigration and immigration had created a heterogeneous population. Even conflict within families and between generations, once uncommon, was now the norm. In the newly straitened circumstances, the threats and promises of prospective legacies no longer kept families intact. It saddened them that they were no longer isolated from the problems faced by other communities in decline such as Andover, Dedham, and even Boston. (Boston was no longer the North American colonies' largest city, but came in third, behind New York and Philadelphia.)

In Concord, conflict divided those who lived in the village center from the outliers living on the fringe of town. People were inclined to appeal outside the town for resolution of their disputes, which they had not done before. Part of Concord became the new village of Acton and another faction joined Lincoln, to the south. In 1765, when others had been in an uproar over the Stamp Act, Concordians had been agitated about sectional rivalries among themselves. Men jockeyed for advantage by trying to pack the town meeting with like-minded voters, and the factions eventually achieved some order by defining themselves as a confederacy of communities, but they longed nostalgically for the single community they had once been.

Concordians also fought, even more contentiously, over religion. The Great Awakening had divided them into New and Old Light factions, and they had battled over the minister, then divided into separate parishes; in 1760, a group secured town permission to form a third parish. By the 1770s, divisiveness characterized every facet of the town's governance, so it naturally also marked the way Concord responded to the entreaties of the Boston town meeting, from which they had previously remained aloof. Without the changes in their town, they would have been just as unresponsive to the imperial conflict of the 1770s as they had been to those of the 1760s. Their political beliefs had not changed, but their relationships to each other had; perhaps a common enemy could bring them back together.

In 1767, the people of Concord had been more concerned about the Massachusetts assembly's consideration of proposals to move the county courts than they were about either the Stamp Act or the Townshend

Duties. (They had thought their town should become the judicial seat of Middlesex County, but this did not happen.) For the next five years or so, they played no visible role in provincial politics and appeared to take little notice of imperial affairs. They were content to let the monarch and ministry rule the empire, and the governor, assembly, and council govern the colony with their town representative voicing their views and voting their interests.

In December 1772, a messenger from Boston delivered the news of the change in how judicial salaries would be paid. Concord appointed a committee of leading men to draft its reply to Boston's committee of correspondence. Not surprisingly, Concordians' endorsement of Boston's protest was conservative. They agreed that "Courts of Justice always Should be uninfluenced by any force but that of Law," and endorsed "an Humble Remonstrance" from the colony to the Crown about this subject, but that was it, and they returned to their shops and farms content that they had done their duty and had their say.

The ministry believed that it had compromised with the Americans as much as it could, given the pressures affecting English politics and given the principles, especially that of parliamentary sovereignty, it had to defend. The British claimed they were simply dealing with matters of colonial administration, the capacity of justices to judge impartially and of governors to govern as instructed and without constant interference from the colonial assemblies. The ministry could perceive no constitutional questions here, and the question of taxation was only tangentially related to disbursement of salaries from London. Parliament had repealed all the Townshend Duties but one, and it had mollified the East India Company with its prodigious lobbying presence in Parliament.

Most MPs were simultaneously baffled and infuriated by the American colonists' hostility to the Tea Act, because they did not think they had levied a tax on them. From London, it seemed clear that the colonists were simply resisting the belated enforcement of the law, jealously guarding their illegal profits from smuggling and couching a defense of their lawlessness in a self-serving constitutional language that was both nonsensical and incendiary, demonstrating yet again that their loyalty to the empire was minimal and their ambition for separation great and growing. To the ministers, the monarch, and a large majority in Parliament, the colonists concealed their greed in a mantle of self-interested "principles." They had no regard for the greater needs of the empire.

The larger picture, about which the ministers believed they were fully informed and the colonists largely ignorant, reached back in time and across the globe but nonetheless took full account of Anglo-American sensibilities. It was unclear whether the colonists even knew the significance of the East India Company to the empire's economy and its importance in the growth of Europe's strongest nation-state. Nor did they apparently care that the company was on the brink of bankruptcy in 1773, despite the best efforts of the ministry to infuse it with capital and regulate its business practices.

Cabinet ministers in London, as well as King George, believed that the colonists did not recognize how far they had already gone to accommodate colonial interests in the context of the empire as a whole. They guessed that the Americans were quite possibly also ignorant of hardships elsewhere in the empire and did not appreciate that Britain now had to answer in the eyes of the world for the suffering of the impoverished peoples of east India, for example, especially in Bengal.

In August 1768, there had been massive flooding in the province of Bihar, three hundred miles northwest of Calcutta. A bad drought had followed on the heels of the inundation, and there had been a disastrous rice harvest in December, which usually produced about 70 percent of the annual supply. Rice was scarce all through 1769 and prices skyrocketed, first to four and ultimately to ten times the average. The drought spread eastward, and by 1770 there were an estimated eight thousand beggars on the streets of Patua, the capital of Bihar. Fifty people died daily of starvation in Patua during January, and by March it was about 150. By April, "many thousands" had made their way to Calcutta, hoping that the English would feed them there, but instead the English took up arms to defend their supplies. The East India Company had a hundred men "carry the dead, and throw them in the river Ganges," one witness wrote. "I have counted from my bedchamber window in the morning when I got up, forty bodies lying within twenty yards of the wall, besides many hundreds lying in the agonies of death for want, bending double with their stomachs quite close contracted to their back bones." More than two-thirds of the families in the Bengali district of Rajshari disappeared, having either died or emigrated. A total of ten million Indians starved in 1770 alone.

When Lord North's ministry retained the tax on tea that year, it was with an eye to conditions in India—the horror of the greatest natural disaster of the eighteenth century—and the need to investigate and reform the East India Company. The results were the Regulatory Act and the Tea Act of 1773. The Tea Act levied no new tax but gave the East India Company a tax break: The customs service would collect the tax of three pence per pound of tea at the source, eliminating the need to collect another tax in North America. This also enabled the company to export tea directly from India to America for the first time rather than requiring its transshipment through London, which lowered the company's costs by nine pence per pound of tea even with the tax. In theory, the company could now compete successfully against both smuggled imports and tea from other sources. The consignment system that went along with this new arrangement was also supposed to reduce the risk of smuggled tea because it granted a monopoly on the sale of East India Company tea to its authorized agents in the colonies, making it easier to identify smuggled goods. It might have actually pleased the colonists, too, since it lowered the retail price of legally imported tea.

With the Regulatory Act of the same year, the British government gave the East India Company a substantial loan of £1.4 million, but it also planned to regulate its business more closely in both India and England. The goal was to keep a tighter rein on the directors, changing their terms (four years rather than one) and requiring them to rotate off the board and to be more involved in policy decisions. The act established a governor-general for Bengal—King George appointed Warren Hastings to that position, as well as three councilors—and also imposed a chief justice and a three-judge supreme court. Along with the tea tax and Tea Act, the ministry intended the Regulatory Act to return the company to a sound fiscal foundation.

But the imposition of English law was a disaster for the Bengalis, since their access to the law and understanding of it were limited. The ministry was insensitive to such collateral damage. The British saw it as a step toward governance of what had started out as a private colonial business with some similarities to the joint-stock and other ventures that had established the American colonies, another step toward global rationalization of the empire. Unlike the North American colonists, the Bengalis were not Englishmen asserting their rights, and they had no more claim on cultural privilege than did the Indians of North America or the colonists' slaves.

Authorizing the East India Company to sell through its own agents rather than through merchants who bid for its cargoes in London would help it to dump more of its surplus tea in the colonies, empty its warehouses, and achieve higher profits. Lord North and his ministry thought everyone would benefit. The company would sell more tea and enjoy higher profits, which would enable it to repay the government loan. The government would recoup its investment and collect more taxes on the higher volume of tea sold. The company's agents in the colonies, with their monopoly, would profit, and the Americans could buy legally imported tea at lower prices. If Americans were practical people, they would swallow their principles along with the cheaper tea.

As was so often the case, Lord North both misunderstood the colonists and underestimated how wide the support was for the principles they defended. He, and those around him, did not understand that the colonists believed that their provincial political systems were microcosms of the English constitutional relationship in which Parliament and the monarch acted together—"the king in Parliament"—as the legislative organ. This belief was not confined to a few die-hard radicals in Boston or even in Massachusetts's other towns. All along the east coast of North America, newspapers, pamphlets, and committees of correspondence had sprung up linking the colonists together, and they were watching closely to see if the ministry assaulted their rights yet again.

In October 1773, news of the recent passage of the Tea Act aroused Massachusetts. This time Concord responded together with several other towns; they all perceived a "crafty" plan by Lord North, the new prime minister, "to support the extravagance and vice of wretches whose vileness ought to banish them from the society of men." Included in this vile lot were the directors of the East India Company, whose fortunes the empire had saved, and the company's agents in America, city merchants who now had a monopoly on the local tea trade and could sell their product directly to customers. Massachusetts politics had changed: The towns were no longer isolated from each other or from the news and events in Boston, and the committees of correspondence had become a political force of their own.

The citizens of Concord, just like those in Boston and elsewhere, found additional evidence of a transatlantic conspiracy against their liberty in letters written by Thomas Hutchinson between 1765 and 1769, which Benjamin Franklin had obtained and leaked to the press. The letters advised imperial officials to take a strong stand against Boston even if it necessitated "an abridgment of what are called English liberties." Hutchinson knew that this publication of his views, however unfairly and out of context passages might be quoted, was the final blow to his worsening relations with his countrymen. Unbeknownst to the colonists, in June he requested a leave from his governorship at the ministry's earliest convenience. News that he had been relieved of his duties arrived in November, too late for Hutchinson and his family to arrange to sail for London in 1773, but he left the next spring and spent the rest of his life in exile. But still in 1773, there was plenty of time left for him to damage further the relationship between colonies and metropole.

The tea agents recalled clearly the fate of those who had opposed the community's will in the past. John Rowe, who was part owner of the *Eleanor*, a ship that arrived in Boston Harbor in mid-December laden with tea, had been complicit in the destruction of Thomas Hutchinson's house in August 1765. By 1770, though, he was socializing with Hutchinson and trying to play both sides against the middle in the controversy over the Tea Act. He helped to stir up crowds that gathered on the docks near the ships, but he also offered to lend Hutchinson money to pay the customs duties on the cargoes "rather then the Affair should be any longer kept up in Anger in the minds of the People."

John Singleton Copley, the portraitist and a son-in-law of Richard Clarke, one of the East India Company's agents in Boston, tried to explain to a crowd that gathered to protest landing of the tea what a tight spot those agents were in. He urged his angry fellow citizens to try to "draw the people from their unfavourable opinion" of the tea merchants. If the agents did not honor their contract to sell the tea, it would "destroy their business reputations." But according to Copley they were willing, perhaps even eager, to compromise. Although they could not be "Active instruments" in the return of the tea to London "without ruining themselves," they would "do nothing to obstruct the People" from returning it.

The closeness of the East India agents to Governor Hutchinson did not help their case with the town meeting. Two of the five of them were his sons, one was a nephew and the father-in-law of one of his daughters, and two were known supporters of his administration. To those who suspected a conspiracy against the people's liberty, such connections of blood, marriage, and insider politics reeked of corruption. The confluence of economic and political influence concentrated power in the hands of a few men with strong connections to the ministry and the East India Company—irrefutable evidence of a conspiracy, and proof that self-interest was the guiding motive of Hutchinson's governance.

One ship captain decided to take the initiative and set sail for England with the load of tea he had brought to Boston in December. Hutchinson got word of the plan, though, and declared, "That cannot be. At all events she must be stopped at the Castle." Here was the difference between the impasse in Boston and what was happening elsewhere in the colonies. In Charleston, New York, and Philadelphia, without the governor's support the agents simply resigned, which defused the conflict. Or, as in New York, where the Sons of Liberty, in the guise of "MOHAWKS," threatened an "unwelcome visit" to anyone who helped to land a tea-laden ship, the governor agreed to hold and take personal responsibility for the tea until an accommodation could be achieved. In Philadelphia, a Committee for Tarring and Feathering made a threat similar to that of New York's "Mohawks." Only in Boston was a governor insisting on literal enforcement of the law.

There were other factors that made Boston the likely place for confrontation over the Tea Act. In the South, consumers had not been drinking much smuggled tea because their tastes ran to what they believed was the higher quality of English (but still Asian) tea. But Hutchinson estimated that more than 80 percent of Bostonians drank smuggled tea, and smuggled tea cornered an even higher percentage of the market in New York and Philadelphia, where imports of legal tea had fallen to zero during the boycott of previous years. But in New England, though the sale of legal tea had fallen from a high of three hundred thousand pounds annually to eighty-six thousand pounds, there was real competition between legal and illegal tea. Only there did customers risk losing their tea of choice, and merchants the loss of profits from it, if the customs collectors could easily identify legal tea as only that sold by the East India Company agents. Only in Boston was a governor willing to back the company's agents with armed force close to hand.

On November 2, Boston's North End Caucus, a political club dominated by mechanics (tradesmen and craftsmen who repaired machinery), resolved that as long as the tea tax and East India Company monopoly remained in force, no more tea should be landed, and meanwhile it warned the company's agents of trouble if they failed to recognize the popular view of the issues. The caucus may have remembered the forced resignations of the Stamp Act distributors and hoped to replicate the intimidation and success of that effort, with riots and the burning of houses and warehouses if necessary.

The radically minded Sons of Liberty by now had about three hundred members in Boston—three times as many as the North End Caucus, which had been meeting for even longer. And they were very active: Members issued extralegal warrants for the arrest of men suspected of disloyalty to the cause of liberty, caucused before elections to nominate candidates and plan campaigns, set the programs for public demonstrations and celebrations, plotted collective action, and took charge of Boston's Liberty Tree.

Members of one or both clubs banged on the doors of East India Company agents at 1:00 a.m. on November 2, summoning them to a public meeting at the Liberty Tree the next day. Handbills posted around the city told citizens that at the meeting they could witness the consignees resign from their affiliation with the East India Company and renounce any responsibility for the tea due to arrive soon. On the morning of November 3, the town crier announced the noon meeting, and church bells summoned about five hundred people to the square in front of the Liberty Tree. But the agents did not appear.

A committee of men called on them where they had foregathered at Clarke's warehouse on King Street, site of the Boston Massacre. As Hutchinson, who watched the procession, reported, "The committee were attended by a large body of the people, many of them not of the lowest rank." The tea agents rejected out of hand the demand that they return the tea to London as soon as it arrived, indeed rejected the committee's authority to make demands of anyone. "I shall have nothing to do with you," was Clarke's reported response. William Molineaux, a committee member, merchant, and one of the Sons of Liberty, then read aloud the resolution they had just adopted at the Liberty Tree; it declared those who refused to comply with the crowd's demands to be "enemies of their country." The threat could not have been clearer, but the merchants, who believed they were protected by the governor, troops, and navy, refused again. Later, after the crowd had peacefully dispersed from the demonstration at the Liberty Tree, perhaps spontaneously, but possibly in a finale well orchestrated by the Sons of Liberty, the tea merchants composed and signed a letter to the directors of the East India Company, reporting that the crowd "consisted chiefly of people of the lowest rank; very few respectable tradesmen, as we are informed appeared amongst them. The selectmen say they were present to prevent disorder."

On November 5, John Hancock presided over a town meeting to discuss some resolutions that had been adopted by Philadelphia on October 18. The Bostonians agreed: The rights of free Englishmen included disposition of their property as they saw fit, the tea tax was a taking of their property without their consent, administration of government by fiat rendered their assembly impotent and left them subject to an arbitrary government, the plan to import East India Company tea under a special monopolistic arrangement favoring a few influential merchants illustrated systemic corruption, and anyone who aided in unloading that tea was an enemy to his country. Again, the meeting authorized a committee to wait on the consignees and demand they resign. Again, the agents refused.

The following week seemed quiet enough in Boston, although an essay signed by "Locke" appearing in the *Boston Gazette* opined, "It will be considered by Americans whether the *dernier resort*, and only asylum for their liberties, is not an American Commonwealth." Identifying colonists as "Americans" rather than Englishmen, the pseudonymous author was expressing the colonists' new sense of their collective identity. Describing separation as the last resort, he raised the stakes, at least rhetorically.

The pessimistic Hutchinson, who had long predicted that an apocalyptic imperial crisis loomed on the horizon, declared that the conflict over the tea "would prove a more difficult affair than any which has preceded it." And he refused to back off or to compromise. In a letter to Lord Dartmouth, secretary for the colonies, he reported, "At present, the spirits of the people in the town of Boston are in a great ferment." This time, he blamed the tumult on his council's collective cowardice, its unwillingness to support him in the face of popular opposition. The councilors would never "countenance a measure which shall tend to carry into execution an act of Parliament which lays taxes on the colonies," Hutchinson warned, and "The same principle prevails with by far the greater part of the merchants." He was hoping for some luck, hoping that the ships carrying tea to New York for the first time since passage of the new tea act would arrive before any cargoes of tea reached Boston, because he was confident that New York's governor Tryon would take a strong stand and thus free him from having to act alone in the hostile Boston environment. Hutchinson was stubborn, principled, and desperate, but he was not lucky.

Supporters of the independence movement in Boston also knew that the eyes of the colonists elsewhere were upon them. Five of the most prominent leaders—Samuel Adams, John Hancock, William Molineaux, Joseph Warren, and Thomas Young—wrote to counterparts in Philadelphia that "our credit is at stake; we must venture, and unless we do, we shall be discarded by the Sons of Liberty in the other colonies, whose assistance we may expect upon emergencies, in case they find us steady, resolute and faithful." Thomas Mifflin, a leader of the movement in Philadelphia, wrote to the same men: "Will you engage that the tea shall not be landed? If so, I will answer for Philadelphia." Mifflin believed from his correspondence that the colonists were in the crisis together and that the tea must not be landed anywhere no matter what the likely consequences.

On November 4, Hutchinson issued an order to John Hancock, captain of the governor's Company of Cadets, an elite militia detachment, to have his troops at the "ready, and to appear at arms at such place of parade as you think fit whensoever there may be a tumultuous assembly of the people, in violation of the laws, in order to their being aiding and assisting to the civil magistrate as occasion may require." When this order became public, it was generally assumed that Hutchinson intended the cadet corps to help with law enforcement on the Boston streets, which would free the British troops in Castle William and the naval detachment in the harbor to attend to law enforcement in the less volatile surrounding towns.

On November 17, news came that ships bearing tea were likely to arrive very shortly. The same day, a mob threw rocks at the house of Richard Clarke but dispersed when leaders of the movement told them to—but not before they had broken windows, damaged furniture, and frayed the nerves of the people inside. On November 18, the town meeting again called on a committee to demand the resignation of the agents. The reply was that the agents had "not yet received any order from the East India Company respecting the expected teas, which puts it out of our power to comply with the request of the town." Yet on the very next day, November 19, the consignees asked the governor and council for "leave to resign themselves" and permission to turn the tea over to them for storage and protection until the conflict could be resolved. This was how New York had successfully handled the problem, but it was not according to law or Hutchinson's instructions as he understood them. On November 24, he wrote to a friend summarizing his view of the situation he faced:

> When I saw the inhabitants of the town of Boston, assembled under color of law, and heard of the open declaration that we are now in a state of nature, and that we have a right to take up arms; and when in a town meeting, as I am informed, a call to arms was received with clapping and general applause . . . and, above all, when upon repeated summoning of the Council, they put off any advice to me from time to time . . . I think it time to deliberate whether his majesty's service does not call me to retire to the castle.

On November 28, the *Dartmouth*, with 114 chests of tea on board, anchored below the Castle in Boston Harbor. The captain was given permission to come into port to unload the rest of his cargo, which also enabled the townsmen to keep the ship under watch. The following day, a handbill circulated announcing another meeting: "Friends! Brethren! Countrymen! That worst of plagues, the detested tea, shipped for this port by the East India Company, is now arrived in this harbor; the hour of destruction or manly opposition to the machinations of tyranny, stares you in the face; every friend to his country, to himself, and posterity, is now called upon to meet at Faneuil Hall." About five thousand people responded to the call. The meeting resolved "that the tea should not be landed; that it should be sent back in the same bottom to the place whence it came, at all events, and that no duty should be paid on it." The meeting also assigned a twenty-four-hour rotating guard of twenty-five to thirty men to ensure that the tea would not be unloaded from the *Dartmouth*. Meanwhile, the East India Company agents had themselves and their families rowed out to the Castle to stay under the protection of the British troops there. On December 2, the *Eleanor* arrived with another load of 114 chests of tea. The *Beaver* reached Boston on December 15 with 112 chests of tea on board.

Twenty days after the *Dartmouth*'s arrival, by which time the cargo was supposed to have been unloaded and the duties paid, it would be subject to seizure for nonpayment of duties. The time period was to expire on December 17, at which point leaders of the resistance expected the navy, customs service, and army to seize the vessel. The ship's owner tried to defuse the situation by declaring on December 16 his intention to sail the *Dartmouth* back to London with the tea still on board, but Governor Hutchinson ordered the ship seized if it went past the Castle, on the grounds that to let it go would be "a direct countenancing and encouraging the violation of the acts of trade."

When the agents refused to resign, Hutchinson refused to bend, and the three ships were still at anchor in the harbor, the Boston leaders of the independence movement decided they had no choice but to escalate the conflict as they had done so effectively in the past. On December 16, more than seven thousand people gathered in the Old South Meeting House for another town meeting. When the governor's instructions and the owner's decision to abide by them were announced, Samuel Adams responded that "this meeting can do nothing more to save the country," which was apparently a signal to the "Mohawks" that it was time for them to act.

Faced with the likelihood that the next day the tea would be unloaded under the points of British soldiers' bayonets, about one hundred men boarded the three ships anchored at Griffin's Wharf in Boston Harbor. Colonists had reached such an impasse before—in Falmouth, at the Boston Massacre, when they destroyed the *Gaspée*, when the Regulator movements arose in North and South Carolina, with the impressment riots, and when they demolished Thomas Hutchinson's home and burned warehouses owned by men associated with the Stamp Act. They had always defended their independence, if not always successfully, even going back a century to Bacon's Rebellion, Coode's Rebellion, and the Glorious Revolution.

In three hours of hard work, the men hoisted and dumped all 340 chests containing forty-six tons of tea into the waters of Boston Harbor. These men were not the leaders, the plotters and the pamphleteers of the resistance, about which so much has been written. These were the men with strong arms and aching backs who led by their actions rather than by their words. Without them there would have been no riots, no massacre, no mass funeral for Christopher Seider, no burning of ships and destruction of property, and no army to fight if it came to that. They liked to fight and they had no love for the customs service, the Royal Navy, or Governor Hutchinson. Theirs was a class jealousy, a sense that wealthy men toyed with the economy, got bailed out by the government, and ignored the rampant unemployment that affected them but not the men at the top. They were angry and looking to vent their rage.

Lord North and his ministers in London—relying on information from Hutchinson, the customs collectors, and army and naval officers—were convinced that they were up against mere "rabble" and a few rabble-rousers. They did not appreciate that "Mohawks" would likely have done the same work in New York, Charleston, and Philadelphia if a stern hand like Hutchinson's, fortified by an occupying army and the support of the Royal Navy, had tried to enforce the new law in those cities. And they believed that if they could crush the opposition in Boston, making an example of the radicals there, the rest of Massachusetts and the other colonies would fall into line. On the other hand, if they failed to give a strong imperial response, the colonists would seize on what they perceived as weakness, and Lord North's ministry would forever be remembered as the one that lost the British Empire.

14

◆

INTOLERABLE EVENTS

THE CROWD ESCORTING THE TEA PARTY "Mohawks" was loud, and the governor, council, consignees, and troops stationed at Castle William heard it clearly. The night before, Rear Admiral John Montagu, commander in chief of the North American Station, had ordered the captains and officers aboard their ships, so they, too, heard the ruckus. "I had the Regiment ready to take their Arms," Lieutenant Colonel Alexander Leslie reported, "had they been called upon, [but] the Council would not agree to the Troops going to Town." Admiral Montagu wrote, "During the whole of this transaction neither the Govr[,] Magistrates, Owners or the Revenue Officers of this place ever called for my Assistance. If they had, I could easily have prevented the execution of this plan but must have endangered the Lives of many innocent People by firing upon the Town." Those in authority had hoped to avoid a sequel to the Boston Massacre, since it had been a propaganda coup for the most radical elements of the resistance to the army and the governor.

The following morning, Admiral Montagu surveyed the mess. "Who is to pay the fiddler now?" he asked a passerby. Before leaving the wharf in disgust, Montagu declared, "The Devil is in this people, for they pay no more respect to an act of the British Parliament, which can make England tremble, than to an old newspaper" (they used old newspapers in their outhouses).

A ship with 257 chests of tea on board had arrived in the harbor of Charleston, South Carolina, on December 2. Twenty days later, having heard news of the Boston Tea Party, the Charleston consignees declined to take delivery of it, having come up against the same customs regulations that had precipitated action in Boston, so the crew off-loaded the tea to a damp warehouse, where it apparently rotted. Thus did a more accommodating populace and governor make a peaceful, albeit temporary, resolution possible. South Carolina lieutenant governor William Bull believed that more decisive action might have been possible if the consignees had not been so intimidated by news of the Tea Party. According to Bull, who wrote to the Earl of Dartmouth on December 24,

> if the merchants who viewed this measure of importing tea in a commercial rather than in a political light, had shewn their disapprobation of the intended opposition to land it, by action rather than by a refusal to subscribe to a proposed association, and a contempt of the public meetings on this occasion, and the agents of the East India Company had not been so hasty in their declining to accept their trusts, all might have gone on well.

On December 24, news of the Tea Party had reached Philadelphia, too. The following evening, the ship *Polly* arrived in the Delaware River below the city carrying just under 700 (697 or 698) tea chests assigned to the shipping firm of Abel James and Henry Drinker. On December 27, a crowd estimated at upward of eight thousand Philadelphians met on the square behind Carpenters' Hall to consider the question of the *Polly* and its cargo of tea; the consignees declined to accept the tea. The captain of the *Polly*, Samuel Ayres, borrowed money from James and Drinker to purchase supplies so that he could return to London with the tea still on board. Governor John Penn took no part in these proceedings, while Ayres and the *Polly*'s owners billed the East India Company £1,168 for the round-trip transportation of the tea.

On January 6, Francis Rotch, owner of the *Dartmouth*, one of the looted ships in Boston Harbor, billed the consignees there £289 for his expenses, which included the transportation costs, payment of the ship's officers and crew, and repairs. There was also the East India Company's tally of its losses, the estimated value of the tea dumped into the harbor being £9,659. Still, there were few hints that the colonists interpreted the Tea Party or the resistance to the Tea Act shown in New York, Philadelphia, and Charleston as the first steps taken toward war and separation. Rather, they believed the Tea Party was a bold, independent, risky, but necessary and effective response to Britain's challenge to their rights as embodied in the taxes assessed without their representation, in the tightened enforcement of customs regulations, in their autocratic governor, and in the ministry that undervalued their worth to the empire. But they underestimated the ministry's response.

At a town meeting in Concord on January 10, 1774, three weeks after the Boston Tea Party, the townspeople unanimously supported a boycott of all British tea and appointed a committee to draft a statement of Concord's reaction to recent events. When the draft came back for consideration two weeks later, the town unanimously endorsed its affirmation that "these colonies have been and are still Illegaly and unconstitutionely Taxed by the British Parliament as they are not realy or Virtualy Represented therein." And the Tea Act was part of a conspiracy "to catch us in those Chains that have Long been forged." They feared that "Enemies of this as well as the Mother Country" conspired "to Rob us of our enestimable Rights," and they thanked Bostonians "for every Rational measure they have taken for the Preservation or Recovery of our Invaluable Rights and Liberty."

On January 25, a Boston crowd assaulted John Malcolm, a customs officer who worked in the port town of Falmouth, where he had seized a vessel for inadequate documentation of its cargo. Earlier in the day, Malcolm had caned a tradesman in response to what he called provocation, the tradesman had complained, and a justice of the peace had issued a warrant against Malcolm for assault. But before a sheriff could serve him, a crowd had descended on Malcolm's house in the North End. Rioting men in the street taunted Malcolm, who they saw was inside, threw rocks through the windows, and threatened to pull him from his home. In the melee, Malcolm thrust his sword through a broken window and cut one of the rioters. Enraged by this, some in the crowd broke into the house, ran upstairs and found Malcolm, seized him, and lowered him by rope from a window into a cart. They stripped, tarred, and feathered him, and dragged him down King Street to the Liberty Tree and then across Boston Neck. When they reached the city's gallows, they whipped him and beat him with sticks. The terrified customs agent believed that the mob meant to hang him. But after an hour or so of abuse, they marched him back to the North End and released him at his home.

The next day at a meeting of the assembly and council of Massachusetts, Governor Hutchinson reported on "his Majesty's disapprobation of the appointment of committees of correspondence." The assembly replied that without an explanation of the monarch's displeasure, they would not abolish the committees, which they found essential to the conduct of public business when the assembly was not in session.

A week later it ordered a declaration of loyalty from the justices of the Superior Court. The men wanted to know whether the judges intended to receive their salaries from the assembly, as they had in the past, or to accept payment from the Crown, as ordered the previous year. The four associate judges declared their loyalty to the assembly, but Chief Justice Peter Oliver affirmed his loyalty to the Crown. In response, the assembly resolved that Oliver, "having received his Salary and Reward out of the Revenue unjustly and unconstitutionally levied and extorted from the American Colonies, and being determined to continue to receive it contrary to the known Sense of the Body of the People of the Province, . . . thereby . . . rendered himself disqualified to hold his Office any longer." Governor Hutchinson declined to remove Oliver from office, however, whereupon the assembly voted to adjourn the court—which it lacked the authority to do—and began impeachment proceedings against Oliver. On February 5, it resolved, "While the common rights of the American subjects, continue to be attacked in various instances, and, at times when the several Assemblies are not sitting, it is highly necessary that they should correspond with each other, in order to unite in the most effectual means for the obtaining a redress of their grievances."

Meanwhile, in London, on January 27 a member had asked in the House of Commons whether it was proving to be worth the cost of stationing troops in North America to defend "people almost in a state of rebellion." (This was three months *before* news of what had happened in Massachusetts after the Tea Party.) Perhaps, the MP reasoned, "the sooner way to bring this people to a sense of their duty is to leave them to themselves." On February 1, George Nugent Temple

Grenville, the second son of George Grenville and the 1st Marquis of Buckingham, moved that "his Majesty should order the Boston correspondence to be laid before the House, alleging, that the question now was, not about the liberty of North America, but whether we were to be free, or slaves to our colonies."

On March 7, King George's councilors laid before the two houses of Parliament "information of the unwarrantable Practices which have been lately concerted and carried on in *North America*; and particularly of the violent and outrageous Proceedings at the Town and Port of *Boston*, in the Province of *Massachusetts Bay*, with a view to obstructing the Commerce of this Kingdom, and upon Grounds and Pretences immediately subversive of the Constitution thereof." The ministers hoped that Parliament would pass new laws that "as may be most likely to put an immediate Stop to the present Disorders, but will also take into their most serious Consideration what farther Regulations and Permanent Provisions may be necessary to be established for better securing the Execution of the Laws, and the just Dependence of the Colonies upon the Crown and Parliament of *Great Britain*."

The ensuing debate revealed a wide and strongly felt range of opinions. Some believed, as George Rice, MP from Newton Castle, Carmarthenshire, Wales, and a staunch supporter of first the Grafton and then the North administration, put it, that the "sovereign authority of this country" was under unprecedented attack "beyond all example," and the question was "nothing less than whether the colonies of America are, or are not, the colonies of Great Britain." William Augustus Montagu, an MP representing Huntington and a reflexive supporter of whichever government was in power, believed that sovereignty was the essential question Parliament was considering, and he "looked upon the unity of legislation to be as essential to the body politic, as the deity was to religion."

William Dowdeswell, representing Worcester, who had been chancellor of the exchequer in Rockingham's government and was still loyal to the Rockingham faction in Parliament, agreed that it was essential to "maintain . . . the legislative authority of this country over America," but, he claimed, Parliament's sovereignty was not under assault. Rather, he said, Parliament had gone "in search of a peppercorn"—an insignificant payment in the total scheme of things but necessary to validate an agreement between two parties—and then announced "that you would collect from peppercorn to peppercorn, and that you would establish taxes as tests of obedience." For mere peppercorns, Parliament had levied taxes "as a test to America" of its authority and its power. "We had a system," he argued, and "our system did bring quiet. The reverse of that system has brought in destruction, commotions, fruitless expedients, timidity at one time, violence at another time," and now Lord North's ministry was calling for members' "assistance to a measure the most dangerous that ever was." According to Colonel Isaac Barré (who had fought alongside General Wolfe in Canada and knew North America well), "One way to make people rebellious is to call them so too soon."

The Scottish MP and wit George Dempster gave his fellow MPs a history lesson with which John Adams would have agreed. "I do look upon all the disorder risen in America to have proceeded from our attempt to tax them contrary to the general policy of this country," he said. "Was ever [a] country more happy in her colonies? Receive [such] great benefit to the year 1764? That being the case, I look upon all disorders that have happened since to rise from that improper idea." "Keep your hands out of their pockets," advised Colonel Barré. Parliament should repeal the tea duty, and then "they will be obedient subjects . . . Repeal that tax. Satisfy the colonies. Procure eternal blessings to this country."

Solicitor General Alexander Wedderburn, a fiery Scottish lawyer, reminded MPs they had adopted the Stamp Act "to make America contribute to the common burdens of the whole, and to relieve this but too much oppressed country from an additional expense brought on it by the expensive efforts this country had made for the protection of America. It was at one time a measure met with scarce a negative." Then, in the face of resistance to the act, the members "declare[d] [t]he established rights [of Parliament to tax,] you asserted that in words . . . and you repealed the law." What happened next was predictable, he thought. The lack of resolve and the reversal in the face of opposition resulted in "ostentations of exultation" among the colonists and a sense of "triumph" that Parliament would back down again. "You must come up to this business prepared, and determined," he insisted, "whether that country shall remain, in what degree a subject to this country."

No other MP was as forward-looking as Edmund Burke, whose passionate defense of the American colonies was signaled in several memorable speeches. Not only did he anticipate that Britain's empire would become a commonwealth, with colonies such as Canada and Australia effectively becoming independent within the empire in the nineteenth century, but he went to the heart of the political crisis over the American colonies. He saw "but two ways to govern America, either to make it subservient to all your laws, or to let it govern itself by its own internal policy . . . I wish to see a new regulation and plan of a new legislation in that country, not founded upon your laws and statutes here, but grounded upon the vital principles of English liberty." To North and to most MPs, however, such a policy would surrender Parliament's sovereignty to traitors without a fight to defend the empire.

William Burke, MP for Great Bedwyn, a speculator in East Indian Company stock, and a man reputed to support any government that paid him, was frightened by what he saw as exaggerations of the colonies' resistance to law. He thought the ministry was eager to escalate the conflict, which was why it had introduced "that horrid question, whether America should belong to us or not? A question that men ought to be afraid to discuss in their closets . . . Unfortunately, brought out in every debate." He believed that the Americans were not even considering independence, and that the ministry's accusations made it more likely that the crisis would escalate to a decisive test of wills. Edmund Burke (the two men called each other "cousin" but were apparently unrelated) likewise recommended a calmer tone and hoped the debate would continue "with coolness and deliberation." The problem as Burke explained it was that "the Americans saw how incapable we were of enacting laws, and they wisely made laws of their own . . . We were in no danger of losing them, for we always had superior force to make them comply." But, he added, he was "certain they had too much good sense ever to hazard such an undertaking."

Lord George Germain, who would be appointed secretary of state for the colonies the following year, believed that the current crisis stemmed from the Declaratory Act of 1766 and its repeal of the Stamp Act. Dowdeswell agreed: "The system relative to America, has since the year 1766, been fraught with nothing but folly and inconsistency. It is a series of blundering conduct that has brought us into the present situation." Burke suggested, "You had better execute a bad plan with firmness, than a good one with hesitation."

On the other hand, Field Marshal Henry Seymour Conway, former secretary of state for the Southern Department under Rockingham, argued, "If the stamp Act had been insisted upon, you had lost America then. I do think in general that America from the earliest time, I have looked into their history with some attention, they have always held that universal language not to be taxed by Great Britain." John Sawbridge, who was a consistent opponent of the North administration, agreed: "This country has not a right to tax America. All those who have been held to write the best upon government, it has been the opinion of them all that there is no such thing as liberty where you can be taxed without your consent." Even the eloquent antislavery advocate Charles James Fox, who believed Parliament did have the authority and right to tax the colonies, said, "that is not the measure I would advise. I think the way to maintain the authority of this country over America is not to exercise it in the part of taxation."

With so many disagreements about the nature of the problem, the stakes, the appropriate responses, and the locus of blame, it is worth noting that the place where the MPs came closest to consensus was in their anger over the destruction of the East India Company tea; in this they were expressing public opinion as well as the king's fury. Parliament insisted there must be compensation, and its own honor and authority were also at stake. Rose Fuller—a rich Englishman who had spent decades in Jamaica—was one of the more moderate voices in the debate. "We all agree, that the Bostonians ought to be punished," he said, "but we differ in the mode of it." Lord North and his ministry, as well as the king, were prepared to "punish" Boston's citizens for their wanton act of "rebellion" that had challenged Parliament's authority to legislate for the empire and resulted in the destruction of almost £1,000 worth of tea.

The ministry's first proposal was the Boston Port Act, which Lord North moved in mid-March: "a Bill for the immediate Removal of the Officers concerned in the Collection and Management of His Majesty's Duties of Customs, from the Town of *Boston*, in the Province of *Massachusetts Bay*, in *North America*; and to discontinue the Landing and Discharging, Lading and Shipping, of Goods, Wares, and Merchandizes, at the said Town of *Boston*, or within the Harbour thereof." The act proposed not only to close the port to all trade but also to use the naval forces and troops stationed there to enforce the closure and to require restitution. But the bill named no specific sum and did not explain how funds could be raised by the colonists in the absence of income-producing commerce. Nor did it specify the criteria, in addition to restitution, to be met for reopening the port; it left the decision in the hands of King George. Lord North's expectation was that "the test of the Bostonians will not be the indemnification of the East India Company alone, it will remain in the breast of the King not to restore the port, until peace and obedience shall be observed in the port of Boston."

When challenged on the vagueness of the bill, Lord North replied vaguely that it was in the hands of the Bostonians to decide how long their port would be closed. But the clear goal was to show the other colonies that the empire had the power to enforce its will. By making an example of Boston, the prime minister believed he could isolate Massachusetts and keep "rebellion" from spreading:

[It was] manifest that the present disorders exist in Boston in Massachusetts Bay. In other parts of America very pernicious doctrines have been held. Very reprehensible resolutions have been come into. But it is at Boston alone that the doctrines and resolutions have been carried into effect by acts of outrages, and of violence. It is, therefore, to Boston only that I shall confine what I shall propose to submit to the House today . . . For the course of five, six or seven years the town of Boston has invariably been the ringleader and promoter of all the disorders, the discontents, and disturbances.

The mob that destroyed the tea was, to North, obviously the creature of the town meeting, so the town was responsible for the destruction.

According to him, the theory of government that informed Boston's actions went well beyond the question of taxation. "At Boston we are considered as two independent states," he explained, "but we were no more to dispute between legislation and taxation, we were now to consider only whether or not we have any authority there." Other MPs pointed out, though, that the principles Bostonians had acted on were widely shared in all the colonies. Edmund Burke blamed Governor Hutchinson for challenging the Massachusetts assembly "to a disputation upon the first principles of government." Burke argued that the ministry was responsible for the governor, and the governor had caused the resistance. Hutchinson's intransigence was, in Burke's mind, the only reason the Tea Party occurred in Boston; had Hutchinson been governor in New York, Pennsylvania, or South Carolina, the Tea Party would have taken place in whichever colony he governed.

In any event, what remained of the tea could not be sold in any of the American cities; it had been destroyed in two of them (Boston and Charleston) and shipped back to London from two others (New York and Philadelphia). North did not dispute that resistance to the tea monopoly was universal in the colonies, but he believed that Boston stood out, that the British land and naval forces there could enforce the law, and it would be necessary to make an example of only the one city for the rest to fall in line. Parliament could not "sit still and see America totally" disobey the laws of Great Britain, after all, and do nothing to prevent the colonists from becoming "totally independent of all our authority." Parliament had come "to that point that nothing that we should ordain with respect to America will be obeyed unless they think we can carry [it] into execution by force. By fair means they will not yield, unless they are sure the power of Great Britain is sufficient by other means to enforce its resolution."

Rose Fuller argued that the reaction to the Boston Port Bill in other colonies would be just the opposite of what North expected. Fuller predicted that all the colonies would rebel if Parliament enacted the punitive legislation against Massachusetts. "I am convinced from the bottom of my heart," he said on March 21, "that if this Bill passes as it now is it will ruin this country." Parliament should demand compensation. It should give Boston a chance to defend itself. "I would not destroy the port till it was known whether they would obey the law for making compensation," he said, and he was "sure" that a bill demanding compensation "would be complied with. If they did not pay it by such a day, I would have this Bill take place." On March 23, Fuller explained his expectations more fully. "I believe all North America will be dissatisfied with it," he predicted. "I believe they will look upon it as a foolish act of oppression . . . that they will be one time, or other served in the same manner . . . The next case will be a confederacy among them." If the ministry sent more troops to enforce the law, perhaps even five to six thousand more, the colonists "can crush them all to pieces. All men are armed by law in that country."

Edmund Burke was less certain than either Fuller or North. He asked Lord North directly,

Sir, can anything in the world be more uncertain than the operation of [this bill]? Whether it will increase these combinations, or lessen [them], whether it will irritate or whether it will terrify, are things in the womb of time . . . [It is] not worth risking one of the principles of justice for the sake of running the risk of procuring it . . . I beg leave to have it observed that this remedy will have an uncertain operation.

Perhaps Boston would be burned to ashes or perhaps unrest would spread. Lord North was rolling the dice with the empire at stake.

The debate left North and more than three-quarters of the MPs unswayed. To all appearances, the prime minister remained determined and confident. He believed there had to be a "firm" response to Boston, which was the "ringleader" of all resistance in the colonies. Yes, it was the first time Bostonians had destroyed a whole cargo of tea, "but during the whole seven years past there has been a series of offenses breathing throughout defiance to the authority of this House and a total independence to the laws of this country." He believed that closing the port of Boston was actually a moderate response compared to those advocated by such MPs as Charles Van, who "was of [the] opinion that the town of Boston ought to be knocked about their ears, and destroyed, *Delenda est Carthago.*"* Van had argued, "You will never meet with that proper obedience to the laws of this country, until you have destroyed that nest of locusts." Welbore Ellis, an MP for more than thirty years beginning in the mid-1750s and loyal to every administration that provided him a living, agreed: "Their conduct has been rebellion" and "Boston has acted treasonably." As North put it, Boston had made a "declaration of their own independence" and it was "the best time to assert our authority . . . Any concession at this moment, instead of effecting a reconciliation would give an air of wavering, of uncertainty, of timidity to our whole proceedings, which would defeat all the good effects which this measure," the Boston Port Bill, would otherwise have. The House of Commons voted to enact the bill on March 25. It passed the House of Lords without dissent and King George III signed it into law on March 31.

---

* Cato the Elder (234–149 B.C.E.), Roman statesman, orator, and writer, is reputed to have ended every speech he gave in the Senate with the words "*Delenda est Carthago,*" Carthage must be destroyed.

Had North stopped with the Boston Port Bill, the response in the colonies would have been shock and horror. That bill alone would have unified colonists across political boundaries. It would have seemed arbitrary, autocratic, and an unprecedented assault on commercial and thus property rights to have indicted and convicted Boston without hearing its defense. The colonists would have seen that it denied them the rights of Englishmen and made a claim of unlimited power well beyond Parliament's assertions of sovereignty in the past. And it would have transformed the mind-set of those colonists who supported the restoration of colonial independence within the empire, making them consider instead a revolution for independence from the empire. The Boston Port Bill transformed the political landscape, but Lord North was not yet done with Boston.

On April 16, he presented to Parliament a Massachusetts Government Bill. It revoked the Massachusetts Charter of 1691, which had been the colonists' great achievement after years of struggle a century earlier, and imposed an even less representative, administratively more robust charter in its place. The colonists would no longer elect the council; the governor would appoint it. The governor would now be authorized to appoint judges and sheriffs without the approval of the council. The sheriffs, in turn, would select jurors, rather than their communities choosing them, as in the past. The bill limited town meetings to one session a year for the spring elections, unless the governor called for others. This restructuring was intended to tame unruly democracy, enhance the governor's authority, and protect the judicial system's autonomy from popular politics.

There was no doubt that supporters of the bill intended to deliver a crushing blow to democracy in Massachusetts. Whether they supported or opposed it, MPs knew what it meant. William Dowdeswell spoke against the bill, noting that it "was calculated to destroy the charter of the province of Massachusetts Bay," and he predicted it would lead to the colonies becoming "separated from this country." Colonel Barré, too, believed the bill would provoke the very rebellion that Lord North claimed it was intended to prevent: The government had "been continually goading and teazing America for these ten years past. I am afraid you will, by these acts of violence, drive them to rebellion."

Barré believed the ministry's rhetoric was as provocative as its policies. "You are continually harassing and beating into their ears the word rebellion," he warned North, "till at last you will find nothing but real rebellion in it."

Colonel Constantine Phipps, recently returned from an (unsuccessful) expedition to discover a Northwest Passage, addressed a clause in the proposed bill that provided for remanding trials to England in order to protect soldiers and officers accused of unlawful violence in Massachusetts. "It would be better," he argued, "that America and England were separated entirely, than to offer to bring men here to be tried." He was prepared to "rejoice," as some other members did, "that Governor Hutchinson is removed, because he had not acted as he ought to do, either to this country or America." Hutchinson was "highly blameable" for the Tea Party, he thought, having provocatively appointed his sons as tea consignees. He could have posted guards on the anchored tea ships; he might have acted without his council; he could, as other governors did, have released the captains to return to England with their cargoes.

Solicitor General Alexander Wedderburn's position was that a rebellion had already taken place in Massachusetts, where colonists had "denied the authority of Britain generally to make laws to bind America." In the previous century, "before the time of King William, they were anarchy itself." The colonists had always sought independence, according to Wedderburn. More recently, they had disputed Parliament's authority to levy "internal taxes," then disputed "your authority to impose external taxes. Having done that, [they] did not stop short." In the dispute over the Tea Act, they had challenged the authority of the Navigation Acts to regulate trade, and their response "has been accompanied with declarations and resolutions from different parts of above one-third of the colony of Massachusetts Bay" asserting an "absolutely independent exclusive right to make laws for themselves through the charter." To Wedderburn, the North administration had no option short of revoking the colony's charter and replacing it with a new government that gave the governor more authority over the populace. "It is anarchy in Boston," the wealthy slave trader Richard Rigby declared. George Rice agreed: "If we look back to the conduct of America, we shall find that hitherto whenever we have made any concession they have made that the ground of fresh demands . . . The Americans have gone upon a system to gain step by step, to clear themselves from the control of this country." Parliament voted to adopt the Massachusetts Government Act 239–64 on May 2.

The Massachusetts Justice Bill "for the impartial administration of justice in the cases of persons questioned for any acts done by them in the execution of the law, or for the suppression of riots and tumults" received its first reading in Parliament on April 23. It stipulated that if Massachusetts courts indicted customs collectors for murder committed while carrying out their duties, the governor could order the trial to be held in England or another colony if he was convinced the accused would not receive a fair trial in Massachusetts. According to Dowdeswell, this was "as bad a Bill as ever [was] brought in Parliament." Phipps asked for evidence that Massachusetts juries had tried to "defeat the execution of the laws," because in the absence of such evidence the ministry appeared to "meddle with the local constitution" without cause. Another MP addressed Lord North's role directly: "I really am surprised at the noble lord, who said, his wish was to make their laws in America as near as possible to our own. Is this bill anything like it? No, it is quite the reverse; dragging people from one country to another to give evidence, is such a proposition as I never heard before, nor could have thought of."

Lord North replied to his critics at length, explaining the stakes, the strategy, his responsibility as prime minister, and the uncertain future of the empire. As he saw it,

> since the duty of 1766 to this day, all offence, all provocation has been on their side, none on ours . . . They have rescued your [ships] not on account of your tea, but on account of the contraband trade. They have burned the King's ships. They have entered in agreement now to [renounce] British trade. They have in this last instance plundered your merchandise. They have publicly declared they are not subject to the laws of England.

Members of Parliament disagreed about whether the colonists were already in rebellion or would be driven to it by the retributive acts proposed by the prime minister. Thomas Pownall—who had returned to England in 1760 after his five years in America—believed "they are not now in rebellion." Rigby insisted that "the Americans are justified in rebellion." Field Marshal Conway contended that the "Americans have not been to blame. England has been the aggressor." North replied in disbelief: "The Americans have tarred and feathered your subjects, plundered your merchants, burnt your ships, denied all obedience to your laws and authority; yet [s]o clement, and so long forbearing has our conduct been, that it is incumbent on us now to take a different course. *Whatever may be the consequence, we must risk something; if we do not, all is over.*"*

Richard Sutton, an avowed supporter of Lord North's American policies, read a letter from an unnamed governor to the Board of Trade, which testified firsthand that the colonists' "actions conveyed a spirit and wish for independence . . . If you ask an American who is his master, he will tell you he has none, nor any governor but Jesus Christ. I do believe it, and it is my firm opinion, that the opposition to the measures of the legislature of this country, is a determined prepossession of the idea of total independence."

Even after passage of these three punitive acts, Charles Van, an extreme anti-American, thought the ministry would be well advised to "burn and set fire to all their woods, and leave their country open, to prevent that protection they now have; and if we are likely to lose that country, I think it better lost by our own soldiers, than wrested from us by our rebellious children." Until British forces could burn the forests of North America to the ground, Van believed it would be prudent to deploy the navy to enforce the law by destroying the colonists' ships and reducing their cities to rubble.

Some MPs had favored extending an olive branch along with harsh laws enforced at the point of a sword. They believed this could be accomplished by repealing the tax on tea. Rose Fuller thought that would "gild the bitter pill" of the Port Act and "alleviate discontent." He predicted that without an olive branch, the colonists would resist the new laws in two ways: "First, an open violence, force of arms. Another by a confederacy. It is my own opinion they will resist" the Port Act and the

---

* Italics are in notes on the speech in *Proceedings and Debates of the British Parliament,* so it is unclear whether they reflect an emphasis in North's delivery or the significance attributed to the words by the note taker, but it is likely the latter.

Massachusetts Government Act by force of arms in a united effort that would be of no advantage to the empire. Another MP agreed that Parliament was about to drive the colonists into "one common cause." Charles James Fox said that Parliament was "by a most ill justice, temerity and rashness [to] give up for once, and that for no consideration at all, all the advantages, riches and prosperity which America has given to this country." Barré warned, "We have been the aggressors from the beginning, and like all other aggressors we shall never forgive them the injuries we have done them."

Others, such as General John Burgoyne (an outspoken critic of Clive and the East India Company), thought that repeal of the Tea Act would surely concede the "independence of America." Repealing the act "during the time of the resistance will make the Act not waste paper, not dead letter, but a memorial of the time and the occasion upon which . . . to date the independence of America." Wedderburn reminded them that "long before the Stamp Act, the Assemblies in America were aiming at independency." He saw no good reason to repeal the Tea Act, because the colonists would not stop short of their goal, which was "to treat with us on an independent footing." The ministry and Parliament apparently shared this interpretation of colonists' intentions and rejected such a conciliatory measure resoundingly, by a vote of 182–49, on April 19.

An amendment to the Quartering Act, which Lord North also presented to Parliament in April 1774, gave more expansive authority to military officials and governors in the colonies to house troops as necessary, even in private homes. Lord Barrington, who, despite a lisp, was long recognized as one of Parliament's best speakers and spoke most often on military matters, favored the measure, noting that keeping the four regiments stationed in Boston as they were now, quartered on a harbor island and likely "to stay there some time," undermined their mission. They could not enforce the law against mob rule when they were miles away. Pownall also spoke in favor of the bill, which he felt was likely "to prevent any blood being shed." Granting clear authority would minimize challenges to the British forces and any misunderstandings the officers had about the limits of their authority.

On May 26, an infirm Lord Chatham, William Pitt, rose in the House of Lords to speak against the Quartering Act and on the state of American affairs in general. He reminded the peers of the realm that the colonists' ancestors had fled the British Isles "rather than submit to the slavish and tyrannical principles, which prevailed at that period in their native country." With this legacy in mind, he believed no one should be surprised "if the descendants of such illustrious characters spurn, with contempt, the hand of unconstitutional power, that would snatch from them such dear-bought privileges as they now contend for." Chatham condemned, "in the severest manner, the late turbulent and unwarrantable conduct of the Americans in some instances, particularly in the late riots of Boston." Nonetheless, he believed the policies the ministry was advocating in response to the destruction of tea in Boston Harbor were mistaken, that "the mode which has been pursued to bring them back to a sense of their duty to their parent state has been so diametrically opposite to the fundamental principles of sound policy, that individuals, possessed of common understanding, must be astonished at such proceedings." But the Quartering Act, too, passed by an overwhelming margin and with little expressed concern that it might seem to threaten the colonists' sense of their liberty and independence.

Lord North presented a fifth act to Parliament in late May 1774, as the session was about to adjourn. North claimed the Quebec Act was simply an attempt to clarify the terms of the Paris peace treaty that had brought Canada into the empire, to define the colony's boundaries, and to establish a system of government and law that took into account the different religion and rights that French colonists had come to know in North America. North was not exactly clear about this: "There should be some government, and if the gentlemen will weigh the inconvenience of separate governments, they will think the least inconvenient method is to annex those spots, though few in people, great in extent of territory, better than to leave them without government at all, or make separate governments."

George Johnstone, another MP who had served in America (he was governor of Florida, 1764–1767) challenged North: "I think this bill . . . is founded almost from the beginning to the end in absurdity," he charged. "There is another and a crooked policy which is denied, that I am clear is the only design and intention of the bill: you are creating a vulture to hang over all the other colonies; you are erecting a military and despotic government as a frontier against all the other settlements." But Lord North reminded the MPs that the definitive treaty of peace had guaranteed the right of Canadians to practice the Catholic religion, and this proposed act merely made explicit the way that would be done. As for appointing a Catholic bishop in Canada, North could not imagine it was essential. Any bishop there "will see that Great Britain will not permit any papal authority whatever in that country," he explained. "It is expressly forbidden in the Act of Supremacy." North believed the Quebec Act struck a balance between governance and tolerance.

In dissent, Thomas Townshend (cousin of Charles Townshend of the infamous acts) asked how the Anglo-American colonists were likely to react. The act did not expressly outlaw the appointment of a Catholic bishop in Canada, but it did establish the Catholic religion there, which, he thought, went well beyond toleration, "my opinion of toleration not being so large" as the ministry's. Lord North rejected the idea that Britain's annexing the vast interior to Canada effectively extended Catholicism to British territories:

> Upon my word, I don't see this Act extends it further than the ancient limits of Canada, but if it should, that country is the habitation of bears, and beavers, and all these regulations which only tend to protect the trader, as far as they can protect him, undoubtedly they can't be reckoned oppressive to any of the inhabitants in that part of the world, who are very few except about the coast, at present in a very disorderly, and ungoverned state.

The act also attached the fisheries off Labrador and Newfoundland to Canada, which made sense from an administrative perspective. From the perspective of the Anglo-American colonists, however, it was a unilateral seizure of fisheries essential to the economies of New York and New England. For them, it was another in a series of imperial attacks on their sovereignty.

A second clause was meant to bring law to the interior of the continent, as settlers moved south and west, despite the Proclamation Line of 1763, to live in regions without political boundaries or government. Lord North argued for this commonsense solution to problems in a large, ungoverned region far from the towns and villages and governing institutions in the established colonies. The Quebec Act proposed to retain the existing form of government, with a governor and an appointed council, this being better, and indeed more protective of the French majority's rights, than to insist on new arrangements. Finally, Canadians would have their own body of law, which reflected their experience.

Townshend argued that the act would make the "Canadians the detestation of the English colonies." Burke wondered why it was not possible to govern Quebec in a way both sensitive to the traditions of the French inhabitants *and* in harmony with English constitutional principles: "Cannot you consistently with the happiness of the Canadians, and the policy of this country, give them a system consistent with liberty, instead of this horrid system of despotic authority?" Another MP agreed, summing up the bill as being "in every particular unconstitutional, impolitic, and unjust."

Rather than replying directly to such charges, Lord North argued on June 8 that it was time to bring the debate to a close. "There was never any Bill in this House that has been more fully, more amply debated, examined, and discussed, than this has been," he insisted. In other words, he was confident he had the votes in the House of Commons to adopt the Quebec Act. Had he been frank, he would have acknowledged that given the empire's experience with the Anglo-American colonies, its framing a government for Quebec modeled on English constitutional principles would not be the end of problems in Canada but simply the beginning of another administrative quagmire.

There was the question of who would be eligible to sit in an assembly if one were created for Quebec (as Canada was now to be called). The small Protestant minority would certainly not favor being represented by an assembly of Catholics, and the Catholics would take understandable offense if the Protestant minority ruled them. The question of Catholics' eligibility to vote and hold office was another can of worms that North preferred not to open. The bill specified that, consistent with French legal tradition, there would be no trials by jury, and this skirted a similar conflict. The ministry saw no reason to stir up trouble when the Canadians were apparently content to continue with a nonrepresentative form of government and with trials by judge, as they had all along under the French system.

John Dunning observed other problems, including the bill's annexing to Canada huge swaths of territory over which there were disputed claims—well beyond the seizure of the Labrador/Newfoundland fisheries from New York. He saw on a map drafted by the ministry that the Ohio River, which originated in Canada, "runs through the province of Virginia. That to the right [west], supposing myself walking down the river, all that country to the right, it is to this moment a part of the province of Virginia, has [been] lopped off from this part, and becomes instead a part of Canada." The new map also encroached on Pennsylvania's claims, and indeed a petition from the colony's proprietors noted that the boundaries defined in the act seized the northwest side of the Ohio River from their colony and annexed it to Canada.

Lord North replied, "It was never intended, those words should intrench upon other colonies." He meant the act to ratify existing boundaries. "Whenever any proposal is made us," he explained in a conciliatory fashion, "whatever can tend to secure Pennsylvania, and the other proprietors, shall meet with no opposition from me. The demand is so just, and so reasonable, that without hearing counsel it may be complied with." On the other hand, he was not open to extending the existing colonies farther west or creating new colonies in the interior. He apparently imagined that all the empire's existing problems with the colonies would be exacerbated by remote new colonies in the backcountry. "It is thought very improper," he maintained, "and contrary to the interests of this country, to have large thriving colonies in the interior country in North America."

The House of Commons rejected by large majorities amendments that would have extended to Canadians the rights to trial by jury, habeas corpus, and bail, but it adopted unanimously a clause extending all the British laws of trade to Canada. On June 13, 1774, the Quebec Act passed the House of Commons. On June 17, the House of Lords reconsidered the bill as amended by the Commons. Lord Chatham spoke passionately against it, since he believed it "would involve a great country in a thousand difficulties, and in the worst of despotism, and put the whole people under arbitrary power; . . . [and is] a most cruel, oppressive, and odious measure, tearing up justice and every good principle by the roots." Nonetheless, the Lords accepted the Commons' amendments to the bill they had already passed.

In early May 1774, news of the Boston Port Act arrived on the same ship as Governor Hutchinson's replacement, General Thomas Gage.

The act closed the harbor as of June 1, and this created panic along with shock. No one in North America, whether friend or foe of the Tea Party, had anticipated such a severe response. The lone exceptions to the closure were ships carrying provisions for the British troops and coastal packet boats that carried firewood and food. Never before had an American port city suffered a blockade.

Landon Carter, the wealthy Virginia planter, understood that with the Port Act Parliament had "declared war against the town of Boston." Thomas Wharton, a Quaker merchant in Philadelphia, believed that "all this Extensive Continent Considers the port Bill of Boston as striking essentially at the Liberties of all North America." Ebenezer Baldwin, the influential pastor of a Congregational church in Danbury, Connecticut, wrote that the colonists felt a "deeper Concern" about the Port Act than they had about the Stamp Act. "The present Measures tis tho[ugh]t [to] forbode something more dreadful to the Colonies than that detested Act so pregnant with Mischief."

The Massachusetts Government Act provoked an even stronger response, because it imposed a permanent structural change on the colony, nullifying as it did its fundamental institutions of governance, including the charter of 1691, the previously elected council, town meetings, and juries. The breadth of the law showed that the colonists' rights and institutions were vulnerable to the legislative whims of Parliament and a stroke of the monarch's pen. "If we suffer this," the Massachusetts lawyer Joseph Warren wrote to Samuel Adams in mid-August, "none of our charter-rights are worth naming; the charters of all the colonies are no more than blank paper."

George Washington called the Justice Act, the third of the retributive laws aimed at Massachusetts, the "Murder Act," because he thought it authorized imperial officials and soldiers to kill the colonists with impunity. As Washington read it, the clause allowing governors to decide where to hold criminal trials made it "impossible from the nature of the thing that justice can be obtained." Again, Parliament claimed unlimited authority outside the laws, procedures, traditions, and institutions of the American colonies. Just as the colonists had feared, parliamentary sovereignty meant the unlimited authority to take the colonists' property, nullify their charters, dissolve their assemblies, and render their legal system impotent. There were no limits, no rights, and no liberties guaranteed by any institution or body of laws. Parliament denied the colonists the rights of Englishmen and every protection of liberty dating back more than five hundred years to Magna Carta.

The Quartering Act was of a piece with the others, but not so threatening except as a precedent for Parliament sending an army anywhere, anytime, and requiring the colonists to feed and house it. Indeed, the Quartering Act was deemed far less serious than the Quebec Act, because, as Joseph Warren put it, "The bill for regulating the Government of Canada shows plainly that it would be very pleasing to the ministry to deprive the Americans totally of the right of representation, just as they were the Canadians." The Quebec Act's denial of a representative legislature to the colony would be a precedent for future revocation of representative government from other colonies. Likewise, should Parliament see fit, it could abolish habeas corpus, trial by jury, and the right to bail, just as it had done in the Quebec Act.

Despite Lord North's denials that the Quebec Act had any implications for the other colonies, it clearly did. If this was Britain's new or evolving vision of colonial administration, it was a shattering blow to the argument that the colonists were entitled to all the rights and liberties of Englishmen. Whether or not Lord North had meant the act as a threat to the other colonies, it was a precedent they could not ignore. Among other things, it asserted Britain's right to vast stretches of land along the frontier to which Virginia and Pennsylvania already laid claim and the Labrador/Newfoundland fisheries previously attached to New York.

Finally, allowing for the establishment of the Catholic Church in Canada could be seen as establishing a precedent for having an Anglican bishop in North America—an argument that was a stretch, but a stretch that appalled Dissenters in New England, New Jersey, and Pennsylvania could easily make. Ezra Stiles, a Dissenting minister in Rhode Island, was thunderstruck at what Parliament had done. He found it "astonishing that King, Lds., and Commons, a whole protestant Parliament should expressly establish Popery over three Quarters of their Empire." If Parliament did not intend the Canadian law as a model for the establishment of Anglicanism with an American bishop, then the only explanation that made sense to colonists was that Britain intended to use the expansion of Catholic Canada as a bulwark against the growth of the Protestant seaboard colonies. Perhaps Parliament meant to placate the Canadians in the hope of recruiting them to fight a war against the Protestant colonies, if it came to that. Wharton believed the Quebec Act was doing more to unite the colonies "from one end of this Continent to the Other" than any previous event. That was because the colonists thought it was "the greatest departure from the English Constitution of any ever yet attempted; And [they] fear that it's Meant & Intended to keep the Body of Inhabitants of that Province as Auxiliaries, to Reduce both the Laws & people of every other colony."

King George and Lord North would have agreed with Samuel Savage, of Middletown, Connecticut, who wrote in May 1774 that the whole imperial conflict was over one question: "Whether we shall or shall not be governed by a British Parliament." But the king and his ministers also believed that repeal of the Stamp Act had been the biggest error of the king's reign, and the lesson they learned from their mistake was that they must stand firm in the face of opposition and defend the sovereignty of Parliament. George Washington, who was very conservative and had been appalled by the Boston Tea Party, believed it was now, in the wake of the five Coercive Acts, "as clear as the sun in its meridian brightness, that there is a regular, systematic plan formed to fix the right and practice of a taxation upon us." The conclusion he and many others came to was that the colonists had no choice but to thwart the plan.

The watershed in frequency and usage of the word "independence" by Americans came in these vigorous responses to what they called the Intolerable Acts. Robert Carter Nicholas, a Virginia lawyer, who published *Considerations on the Present State of Virginia* in that year, framed his discussion about separation and independence clearly: "That she [the North American colonies] will be capable, some Time or other, to Establish an Independence must appear evident to every One, who is acquainted with her present Situation and growing Strength." The question was how soon "some Time or other" would come, and Carter still believed that it was in the hands of Great Britain to "govern her Colonies to their Satisfaction." He was "persuaded that she would procrastinate our Separation from her" by good governance with an eye to the happiness and well-being of the colonists, but "if she perseveres in her Rigour, and the Colonies will not relax on their Part, the Parent will probably soon be without a Child." If Great Britain persisted on its path, "I am afraid that her Independence as a State will be of very short Duration." The American colonies would seek and gain independence, the British Empire would crumble, and a greatly weakened Great Britain would lose its independence to other European powers, a sequence the North ministry had set in motion.

Pennsylvania's committee of correspondence continued to assert the colony's loyalty to the Crown when in mid-May 1774 it declared its "true and faithful allegiance." Nonetheless, in light of the news from London, the committee also declared "that as the idea of an unconstitutional independence on the parent state is utterly abhorrent to our principles, we view the unhappy differences between *Great Britain* and the Colonies with the deepest distress and anxiety of mind, as fruitless to her, grievous to us, and destructive of the best interests of both."

The Port Bill specified that Boston's harbor would remain closed to ship traffic "until such time as full satisfaction was given to the East India Company and the customs officers for the losses they had sustained" in the Tea Party. These words persuaded some merchants, who still supported the imperial administration, to initiate a private subscription to raise funds for the reparation. Sam Adams was later to recall that "the Boston Port Bill suddenly wrought a Union of the Colonies, which could not be brot about by the Industry of years of reasoning on the necessity of it for the Common Safety." It surmounted the barriers that had always made ideas such as the Albany Plan fruitless. All the colonies except Nova Scotia and Quebec had agreed before the end of May that they were ready to take measures for "preserving the Liberties and promoting the Union of the American colonies."

Tobacco planters in Maryland and Virginia received news of the Intolerable Acts with a mixture of apprehension and relief. They were an unprecedented, unwelcome challenge to the colonists' independence, but they also presented an opportunity to reinvigorate the failed trade boycott of 1769. That would surely have economic benefits and political value. A decision to join in a boycott of goods imported from Britain could both pressure the ministry into repealing the acts and help Virginians reduce their debts to British merchants. William Reynolds, a Virginia planter who was deeply in debt, wrote to the London merchant John Norton in June that he would be reducing his orders dramatically if the colonies adopted a nonimportation/nonexportation association, as he expected they would: "Indeed if the Association sho'd take place the 1ˢᵗ August next as is expected not to import any

Articles whatever from Great Britain it will prevent our troubling the Merch[an]ts and enable us to pay of[f] all old Arrears." Robert Beverly, a politically conservative planter, anticipated a potential boycott to be a "Mode of Preservation" and "a Means of extricating many People from their present Distresses."

In other words, the marketplace was already forcing Virginia and Maryland planters to cut imports when they agreed to join in a nonimportation association. And there would be a political benefit in reuniting the interests of large planters and small farmers, since it would reduce the foreclosures that inevitably occurred when economic pressures shifted down from large debtors to lesser ones. Yet another benefit, from the large planters' point of view, was that the agreement would eliminate the international slave trade, thus increasing the value of the domestic slaves they liked to sell to small planters. The 1769 agreement had failed in this regard, and there had been British vetoes of proposed bills to reduce slave imports. All this meant that the nonimportation association was an all-around economic benefit to Virginians and Marylanders whose interests the delegates from the two colonies represented. They could support, indeed lead, the political effort without cost.

Some planters had already switched from growing tobacco to producing wheat, and this had helped sustain a good tobacco price. In April 1774, William Carr, a tobacco factor in Dumfries, Virginia, had warned a merchant in London, "As the Planters in General have an aversion against shipping the Price for Tobacco being with you so Very low they will be glad of any Excuse" not to ship. The planters would soon learn that Parliament had given them just such an "excuse" in the Boston Port Bill, as London merchants recognized even before they did. A London tobacco merchant reported in a mid-April letter to traders in Annapolis, Maryland, that he and others like him expected the colonists to "enter into resolves not to have any more goods and not to ship any more tobacco until the [Boston Port] act is repealed." This expectation increased the London price for Virginia tobacco by 5 percent in two weeks.

During the summer and fall of 1774, "Tory hunts" began in Connecticut, and colonists who were considered "enemies" of the people there and elsewhere in New England had either to recant their previous loyalties or flee into exile. By early September, General Gage thought the colonists throughout the region were "as furious" as those in Boston. Delegates to a conference in Norwich declared that the towns and colonial government should prepare to fight "under the disagreeable necessity of defending our sacred and invaluable rights, sword in hand." In October, the Rhode Island assembly authorized the towns to establish independent militias, revise the militia laws, and order the distribution of arms to the local units. It also appointed one Simeon Peter of Bristol as the major general for Rhode Island's armed forces and authorized them to fight outside the colony if need be in support of its neighbors. On December 13 in New Hampshire, four hundred men seized the castle at the entrance of Portsmouth harbor and carried away one hundred barrels of powder and sixteen cannons.

Anyone back in London who assumed the empire only needed to face down some malcontents in Boston was uninformed about the wider scope of the resistance and the deeper anger the Intolerable Acts provoked. The ministry overestimated its support in the colonies and the competence of its political appointees and military commanders. It underestimated the colonists' discontent and collective sense of history and law, the ill will accumulated over the past decade, and the colonists' ability to act in concert against a common enemy. Most of all, perhaps, the ministry failed to recognize that it had seriously damaged the colonial economies and miscalculated its own military reach and ability to intimidate its opponents in North America. It thought the colonists would back down, but believed it could enforce its will against American claims and ambitions to independence in any event.

15

✦

CONTINENTAL CONGRESS

WHEN BENJAMIN FRANKLIN ARRIVED in London in 1757, he had tried and failed to arrange an introduction to William Pitt (the Elder), the celebrated "Great Commoner," then secretary of the Southern Department and leader of the House of Commons. Over the years he had abandoned his attempt to meet the great man lest he appear a nuisance or embarrass himself. But in the summer of 1774, Franklin learned that Pitt, now Lord Chatham, would like to meet him:

> [The] truly great Man lord Chatham receiv'd me with abundance of Civility, enquired particularly into the Situation of Affairs in America, spoke feelingly of the severity of the late Laws against Massachusetts, gave me some Account of his Speech in Opposing them and express'd great Regard and Esteem for the People of that country, who he hop'd would continue firm and united in defending by all peaceable and legal Means their constitutional Rights.

Franklin assured Chatham that the colonists would continue to defend their rights, and that he and they hoped for a return to the traditional policies of the empire, before "the mangling Hands of the present Set of Blundering Ministers" had bungled its governance.

As they parted, Chatham had a question for Franklin, one that was much discussed in England. The "opinion prevailing here," he said, was "that America aim'd at setting up for itself as an independent State; or at least to get rid of the Navigation Acts." Did Franklin believe that was true? "I assur'd him," Franklin wrote, "that having more than once travelled almost from one end of the Continent to the other and kept a great Variety of Company, eating drinking and conversing with them freely, I never had heard in any Conversation from any Person drunk or sober, the least Expression of a Wish for a Separation, or Hint that such a Thing would be advantageous to America." Nor, according to him, did the colonists resent those Navigation Acts that were truly meant to ensure the good of the whole empire rather than simply to profit some part of it. The requirement that Americans transship goods purchased in Europe through London was, however, an inconvenience and unwarranted expense. Chatham thanked Franklin for calling on him, and for "the Assurances I had given him that America did not aim at Independence."

In early June, the Boston committee of correspondence responded to the Boston Port Act with a Solemn League and Covenant, under which colonists vowed to cease consuming any British goods after August 31. The signatories would also pledge to stop patronizing any importers "until the port or harbour of Boston shall be opened, and we are fully restored to the free use of our constitutional and charter rights." But the Boston town meeting voted this covenant down, expressing a preference for an intercolonial boycott, which would effectively put other colonies in the same boat as the city with its closed port, and other Massachusetts towns and districts responded in much the same way. Most towns simply voted down the intercolonial boycott, but Concord, for example, endorsed a weaker version in which signers agreed to boycott only British goods sold by certain "contumacious importers."

On June 27, Concord endorsed the revised covenant and town officials went door-to-door soliciting signatures from heads of households. Eighty percent signed on, but among the 20 percent that did not were some of the most prominent men of the town. These included older men who had consistently resisted the effects of the Great Awakening in their churches and who feared the social changes that they saw as evidence of a breakdown of communal order. These conservatives were now on the outs with most of the people of Concord, and the social strains were becoming politicized.

The larger truth was that royal administration in Massachusetts was collapsing during the second half of 1774, and representative bodies at the local, county, and provincial levels were replacing Britain's appointments and official structures. Some towns created ad hoc county conventions. Political activity at the local level all across the colony made Boston less central in its politics and reduced the significance of its town meeting and committee of correspondence. The political initiative shifted to people acting in their own town meetings, where reigning theory located sovereignty. The town meetings were used as models for the county conventions, the difference being that town-meeting decisions were binding and those of county conventions advisory.

On August 30, a Middlesex County convention warned, "Life and death, or what is more, freedom and slavery, are in a peculiar sense, now before us." The delegates advocated an orderly resistance to British rule, "never degenerating into rage, passion and confusion," yet firmly in defiance of what they considered the illegal authority of government under the Intolerable Acts, which had, after all, abolished the colony's charter. They recommended suspension of the courts and the election of a provincial congress outside the sanction of the newly established government. When judges tried to open the Court of General Sessions in Concord in mid-September, the "Body of the People" resisted, and the courts remained closed for the next year.

There was also an organized effort to punish active supporters of the British-sanctioned government. Unlike in Boston, in Concord people neither tarred and feathered "Tories" nor spread excrement on anyone's door. Instead, they sought political conversions, apologies, and signed pledges to join their cause. Colonel Charles Prescott recanted his support of former Governor Hutchinson. "I am heartily sorry," he told his angry neighbors at a confrontation in his house, "for I did so in haste, and I solemnly declare, that I detest those unconstitutional Acts and would not take any Post of Honor or Profit under the Same."

On September 1, General Gage's troops seized gunpowder that the colony had stored near Cambridge. A crowd reported to be of three to four thousand men protested but disbanded peacefully by evening. A rumor circulated widely that British troops had killed civilians and bombarded Boston. Perhaps six thousand men began to march from Worcester County for Boston, while thousands more headed for Boston from even farther west, in Hampshire County, and reached Worcester before they learned that the rumor was false. Israel Putnam, a member of the Sons of Liberty and later a general in the Revolution, rushed to Philadelphia to report that militia units were marching north to Boston from Connecticut, but these, too, turned back when they discovered there had been no killings. By that time, though, the alert was unstoppable, reaching New York and then Philadelphia on September 6, just as the Continental Congress convened.

In 1773, every colony, including Massachusetts, would have considered a call for an intercolonial congress as an overreaction to the Tea Act. As late as April 1774, the most radical proposal for collaborative action among the colonies that had any chance of success was for an intercolonial post office to facilitate communication among the committees of correspondence and be a quicker and more secure means of mail delivery. But the Intolerable Acts now drove Americans to unite, and the idea of a continental congress seemed a moderate alternative to Boston's suggestion that all the colonies should close their harbors in response to the Port Bill.

By the end of June, nine colonies had endorsed a continental congress to consider collective action, and another three in the end also sent delegates to Philadelphia in September.* There was widespread talk of "union" among the colonies, and the delegates would have to decide what kind and to what end. Many still hoped the ministry in London would see the light and reverse course. More and more people believed that independence and separation from the empire were now likely the same thing, but almost all of them feared rather than welcomed the possibility.

The delegates who met in Philadelphia as the Continental Congress in early September were firm in their convictions but in a conciliatory mood. John Adams recorded toasts delivered over dinner on September 3: "A constitutional Death to Lords Bute, Mansfield and North!" "May the Collision of british Flint and American Steel, produce that

* The one holdout was Georgia. The colony was having troubles with Indians on its border and needed British military help. However, Georgia did elect Lyman Hall to the second congress, which convened on May 13, 1775.

Spark of Liberty which shall illumine the latest Posterity." "Wisdom to Britain and Firmness to the Colonies, may Britain be wise and America free." "The Unanimity to the Congress. May the Result of the Congress, answer the expectations of the People." "Union of Britain and the Colonies, on a Constitutional Foundation."

The temperament of the delegates he met at the start reassured Joseph Galloway, Speaker of the Pennsylvania assembly and a moderate who was eventually to oppose the Revolution:

> Near two Thirds of them are arrived, and I conclude all will be ready to proceed on business on *Monday*. I have not had any great Opportunity of sounding them. But so far as I have, I think they will behave with Temper and Moderation. The Boston Commissioners are warm, and I believe wish for a Non-importation Agreement, and hope that the Colonies will advise and justify them in a refusal to pay for the Tea until their Aggrievances are redressed.

When the Congress convened on Monday, September 5, it quickly made a tactical decision to confine its list of grievances to post-1763 events. Even though the Virginia delegates especially believed there were "many aggressions which had been committed by Great Britain upon her infant Colonies in the jealousies, monopolies, and prohibitions, with which she was so prodigal towards them," they opposed a "retrospect farther back than to 1763." As Richard Henry Lee, a Virginia delegate, said to John Adams, "To strike at the Navigation Acts would unite every man in Britain against us, because the Kingdom could not exist without them." If the goal was reconciliation, and it still unanimously was, the delegates had to be careful about how they framed protests and what redress they demanded.

On September 6, Thomas Cushing, of Massachusetts, moved that the Congress should open with a prayer. John Jay, of New York, and John Rutledge, of South Carolina, spoke against the motion on the grounds that the "delegates were so divided in religious Sentiments, some Episcopalians, some Quakers, some Anabaptists, some Presbyterians and some Congregationalists, so that We could not join in the same Act of Worship." Samuel Adams rose to reply. He said that he was "no Bigot, and could hear a Prayer from a Gentleman of Piety and Virtue, who was at the same Time a Friend of his Country." Although a stranger to Philadelphia, he said he had heard that Mr. Duché, an Anglican clergyman, fit that description, so he moved that Jacob Duché be invited to lead the delegates in an opening prayer the following morning. The motion carried.

That same day, an express rider interrupted the meeting. He brought news of the alleged killings in Boston on September 1 (he had left Boston before learning that the information was false). The delegates received "intelligence that the soldiers had seized the powder in one of the Towns near Boston. That a party was sent to take this; & that six of the Inhabitants had been killd in the Skirmish. That all the Country was in arms down to . . . Connecticut. That the Cannon fired upon the Town the whole Night." Silas Deane, from Connecticut, wrote to his wife that "an express arrived from N. York confirming the Acc^t of a rupture at Boston. All is in Confussion. I can not say, that all Faces, gather paleness, but they all gather indignation, & every Tongue pronounces Revenge. The Bells Toll muffled & the people run as in a Case of extremity they know not where, nor why." The delegates went on working; they formed two committees, one of twenty-four men to draft a bill of rights and another of twelve to draft a list of grievances.

The next day the session opened with a reading and prayer from the Reverend Duché, assistant rector of the united parishes of Christ's Church and St. Peter's, who, according to John Adams, "read several Prayers, in the established Form; and then read the Collect for the seventh day of September, which was the Thirty fifth Psalm. You must remember this was the next Morning after we heard the horrible Rumour, of the Cannonade of Boston. I never saw a greater Effect upon an Audience. It seemed as if Heaven had ordained that Psalm to be read on that Morning." The psalm begins, in the Book of Common Prayer translation that Duché would have used, "Plead thou my cause, O Lord, with them that strive with me: and fight thou against them that fight against me." Adams continued the description of the scene to his wife, Abigail: "After this Mr. Duché, unexpected to every Body struck out into an extemporary Prayer, which filled the Bosom of every man present. I must confess I never heard a better Prayer or one, so well pronounced."

On Thursday, September 8, Adams wrote again to Abigail: "The effect of the News We have both upon the Congress and the Inhabitants of this City, was very great—great indeed! Every Gentleman seems to consider the Bombardment of Boston, as the Bombardment, of the Capital of his own Province. Our Deliberations are grave and serious indeed." Later that night, Adams recorded in his diary that "the happy News was bro't us, from Boston, *that no Blood had been spill'd* but that Gen. Gage had taken away the Provincial Powder from the Magazine at Cambridge. The last was a disagreable Circumstance."

According to Israel Putnam, Joseph Galloway said it was Samuel Adams who had orchestrated the rumor to begin with, with multiple manufactured reports. He described Adams as "a man, who though by no means remarkable for brilliant abilities, yet is equal to most men in popular intrigue, and the management of a faction. He eats little, drinks little, sleeps little, thinks much, and is most decisive and inde-fatigable in the pursuit of his objects." The "objects" were, according to Galloway, to drive Massachusetts and the Continental Congress to-ward a war for independence from the empire. It was certainly true, as John Adams said, that the reports of civilian casualties at the hands of Gage's troops had been transformative in the Congress, although Silas Deane reported to his wife, Elizabeth, after the accurate report arrived, "The Bells of the City are Now ringing a peal of Joy on Acct. of the News of Boston's having been destroy'd being contradicted."

But the rumor had been plausible; such deeds actually could occur. So people were now thinking about how one should respond to such an event. They were overjoyed that it had not come to war, at least not yet, but they could now better imagine that it might. The colonists and the Continental Congress would have to prepare themselves to respond to the unprovoked attack on a magazine and the seizure of weapons that Massachusetts stored for the defense of its citizens, and what could happen next. According to Deane, had the rumor of civil-ian deaths been true, the local people would have attacked the British troops stationed in Philadelphia and intended to reinforce the army in Boston. "The Troops here," he wrote, "which are to assist in reducing New England, & all America amount to One Hundred & Eighty . . . It is a doubt with Me, whether the People here will let them March. Had Blood been shed by the Soldiery at Boston, there would have been No doubt at all, for these Soldiers in that Case would before this have been disarmed, & dispersed." If there was to be a war, as Deane saw it, the first shots must be fired by British troops.

Suffolk County, Massachusetts, had prepared some resolutions that were adopted by delegates from Boston and surrounding towns on September 9. They declared the Intolerable Acts unconstitutional and void, advised the establishment of an independent government until Parliament repealed the acts, suggested that taxes be dedicated to the support of the new government, called for a boycott of British goods and the creation of local militias on the authority of the towns, warned General Gage that any arrests of citizens on political charges would result in the detention and trial of the arresting officers, and asserted that subjects did not owe allegiance to a monarch who violated their rights. The delegates also resolved "that the inhabitants of those towns and districts, who are qualified, do use their utmost diligence to acquaint themselves with the art of war as soon as possible, and do, for that purpose, appear under arms at least once every week." They declared their determination "to act merely upon the defensive, so long as such conduct may be vindicated by reason and the principles of self-preservation, but no longer."

The Continental Congress received these Suffolk Resolves sympathetically and endorsed the path the people of Massachusetts were on. The members approved "the wisdom and fortitude, with which opposition to these wicked ministerial measures has hitherto been conducted, and they earnestly recommend to their brethren, a perseverance in the same firm and temperate conduct as expressed in the resolutions determined upon at a meeting of the delegates for the county of Suffolk." It also encouraged the colonists of Massachusetts to hope for a change in their fortunes, "trusting the effect of the united efforts of North America in their behalf, will carry such conviction to the British nation, of the unwise, unjust, and ruinous policy of the present administration, as quickly to introduce better men and wiser measures." Not all were in agreement, though. Galloway later referred to the Congress's response to the Suffolk Resolves as "a treasonable vote [by which] the foundation of military resistance throughout America was effectually laid."

On September 27, the Congress unanimously agreed to a total ban on the importation of British and Irish goods effective December 1. Virginians spearheaded this boycott, recognizing that the effects would be largely positive for them and cause only minor economic distress. Since the boycott association was comprehensive, leaving few loopholes, it created an equality of deprivation among the socially competitive planters, whose ability to import goods on credit was already diminished by the recession that had begun two years earlier.

On September 30, the delegates resolved unanimously to cease exports to Great Britain, Ireland, and the West Indies effective September 10, 1775. The large planters from the Chesapeake colonies, whose interests the Virginia and Maryland delegates represented in the Congress, accepted this as an economic benefit, at least in the short term. The price realized for their tobacco in Europe had been so low for consecutive years that it did not pay to sell the crop. Back in May 1773, before the political turmoil of 1774, a tobacco buyer named Harry Piper had reported from Alexandria, Virginia, that the planters would not "think of taking the low price talked of by the Merchants." The following month, James Robison, a Scottish tobacco factor, also noted that the "planters are very unwilling in various parts of the colony to part with their tobacco at the prices offered." A political boycott on exports would enable the planters to hold and store the crop until the glut on the market passed, the economy turned the corner, and prices rose. This would be possible only in an economic environment in which they were not rapidly accumulating monstrous debts, as they had been, and in which the Maryland courts froze suits for debt and Virginia courts shut down in support of the colonial cause. The Virginia House of Burgesses had engineered the closing of the courts in May 1774. All the assemblymen had to do was to resolve that Parliament's decision to close Boston's harbor was "a hostile invasion," knowing that Governor Dunmore would dissolve the assembly before it had renewed the fee act that was essential to keeping the courts open. Deprived of fees, beginning in June the courts had refused to hear debt suits.

The nonexportation element of the association featured exceptions that took into account the colonies' different economic interests. South Carolina's delegates favored a total ban on exports to Great Britain and also to Europe. Delegates from the northern colonies rejected the European ban, because they would lose the large profits they made from that trade. Philadelphia, for example, annually exported about £700,000 of goods, principally wheat, only £50,000 of which went to England. So Pennsylvania and other northern colonies would be less affected than South Carolina by a ban on exports to London, while John Rutledge, like other South Carolinians, believed his colony's economy would be "almost ruined" by such a plan, because its principal exports, rice and indigo, were enumerated articles that under the Navigation Acts could be sold *only* to England, and the Congress had agreed to break only Parliament's post-1763 economic regulations. When it came time to sign the boycott agreement in late October, all the South Carolina delegates except Christopher Gadsden, who left the Congress in protest, balked.* The convention preserved unanimity by authorizing the export of rice to Europe, which did in fact breach the Navigation Acts.

On September 28, Galloway had offered a plan for reconciliation in an effort to refocus the debate away from the boycotts. As he later wrote, he intended "to probe the ultimate design of the republicans, and to know with certainty whether any proposal, short of the absolute independence of the Colonies, would satisfy them." In his presentation, Galloway summarized the delegates' discussions during the previous month as having had two principal features: a vague call for a return to pre-1763 imperial relations, and a nonimportation/nonexportation agreement to pressure the British into accommodating them on their terms. He thought the first was "indecisive, tending to mislead both countries, and to lay a foundation for further discontent and quarrel." As for the second, it was "undutiful and illegal. It is an insult on the supreme authority of the State; it cannot fail to draw on the Colonies the united resentment of the mother Country." He said he "must therefore reject both the propositions; the first as indecisive, and the other as inadmissable upon any principle of prudence or policy."

Galloway proceeded to the gnarly question of sovereignty. He understood that the constitutional argument "for the supremacy of Parliament over the Colonies contend[s] that there must be one supreme legislative head in every civil society, whose authority must extend to the regulation and final decision of every matter susceptible of human direction." He explained that the English found this argument, based on the historical experience of the seventeenth century, unassailable and not negotiable. He supported the English argument and also agreed that any claim by the colonists to the contrary "amounts to a full and explicit declaration of independence," which he hoped his

---

* Gadsden was from the backcountry, which grew wheat and tobacco, and did not export rice and indigo. Despite this protest, Gadsden was a Revolutionary. He designed the rattlesnake "Don't Tread on Me" flag.

fellow delegates would reject as an "appeal to the sword" that would lead to "all the horrors of a civil war," a renunciation of the protection of the British Empire, and exposure of the weak and disunited colonies to the power of the French. "I am sure," Galloway declared, "no honest man can entertain wishes so ruinous to his country."

On the other hand, Galloway agreed that the colonists were not and could not be represented in Parliament, and that they could not be taxed without their consent secured through a representative assembly. He resolved, therefore, that since "the Colonies hold in abhorrence the idea of being considered independent communities on the British government," a set of new institutions was necessary to resolve the constitutional conflict that the delegates confronted. Galloway's plan proposed a president general of the colonies, to be appointed by the monarch, and a legislature or Grand Council representing all the colonies. Together, the two would hold "all the legislative rights, powers, and authorities, necessary for regulating and administering all the general police [policies] and affairs of the colonies, in which Great Britain and the colonies, or any of them, the colonies in general, or more than one colony, are in any manner concerned as well civil and criminal as commercial."

After a thorough debate of Galloway's plan, the Congress postponed further discussion. As Galloway reported, "All the men of property, and most of the ablest speakers, supported the motion, while the republican party strenuously opposed it." According to New Jersey governor William Franklin, who was also, like Galloway, to be a Loyalist in the Revolution, after the delegates devoted the day to debating the plan, "they not only refused to resume the Consideration of it, but directed both the Plan and Order to be erased from their Minutes, so that no vestige of it might appear there." Galloway nonetheless sent a copy to Benjamin Franklin in London, who showed it to Lords Chatham and Camden, and sent a copy to Lord Dartmouth, secretary of state for the colonies. Lord Gower, Lord President in North's ministry, referred to it in the House of Lords, when, according to Benjamin Franklin, "he censured the Congress severely as first resolving to reserve a plan for uniting the colonies to the mother country, and afterwards repealing it, and ordering their first resolution to be erased out of their minutes." Lord Dartmouth wrote to Governor Colden of New York on January 7, 1775: "The Idea of Union upon some general constitutional plan, is certainly very just, & I have no doubt of its being yet attainable through some channel of mutual consideration and discussion."

On October 6, Paul Revere, the post rider for the Boston committee of correspondence, arrived at the Congress with a letter, dated September 29, in which the committee reported that General Gage had taken no account of their petitions against the fortification of Boston. Apparently,

> the town and country are to be treated by the soldiery as declared enemies—that the entrenchments upon the neck are nearly completed—that cannon are mounted at the entrance of the town—that it is currently reported, that fortifications are to be erected on Corpse-Hill, Beacon-Hill, & Fort-Hill, &c. so that the fortifications, with the ships in the harbour, may absolutely command every avenue to the town both by sea & land.

On October 10, the Congress sent its own letter to Gage, reiterating the protests the Boston committee had made and asking him "to consider what a tendency this conduct must have to irritate & force a free people, however well disposed to peaceable measures, into hostilities, which may prevent the endeavours of this Congress to restore a good understanding with our parent state, & may involve us in the horrors of a civil war."

On October 12, the Congress debated the boycott agreement known as "the Plan of Association" for the nonimportation and nonexportation of goods from and to Britain. After amendment, the Congress adopted the boycott on October 18. The association avowed the colonies' allegiance to the monarch and their "affection and regard for our fellow-subjects in Great-Britain and elsewhere." The delegates blamed the problems on "a ruinous system of colony administration adopted by the British Ministry about the year 1763, evidently calculated for inslaving these Colonies, and, with them, the British Empire." The efforts to raise revenue from the colonists and the threats to trial by jury were high on their list of grievances.

The delegates sought "redress of these grievances" by the "most speedy, effectual, and peaceable measure," which they believed was the proposed boycott on trade with Britain. Their specific goals were repeal of all taxes laid by Parliament to extract revenue from them, reversal of the expanded authority of admiralty courts, restoration of the ancient right of trial by jury in all criminal cases, repeal of the customs regulations that imposed crippling restraints and damages on trade, and abolition of regulations that indemnified informers and customs agents. Finally, they would accept nothing less than repeal of the four acts adopted in Parliament's spring session, which had closed Boston's harbor, voided the colony's charter, reorganized its government and courts, and, not least, extended the boundaries of Quebec "so as to border on the western frontiers of these Colonies, establishing an arbitrary government therein, and discouraging the settlement of British subjects in that wide extended country; thus by the influence of civil principles and ancient prejudices to dispose the inhabitants to act with hostility against the free protestant Colonies, whenever a wicked Ministry shall chuse so to direct them." Once these many issues were resolved, the boycott would be abandoned.

In another address, this one "To the Inhabitants of the Colonies," adopted on October 21, the delegates acknowledged that war was one of two options before the colonists if Parliament and king did not meet their demands: "If the peaceable mode of opposition recommended by us, be broken and rendered ineffectual, as your cruel and haughty ministerial enemies, from a contemptuous opinion of your firmness, insolently predict will be the case, you must inevitably be reduced to chuse, either a more dangerous contest, or a final, ruinous, and infamous submission." The language suggests that the delegates saw no other path than war if the ministry did not offer a conciliatory response to the boycott. Independence was now on the table, although for tactical reasons the delegates chose not to make provocative predictions to the people of Great Britain at this time.

On October 22, the Congress resolved that "it will be necessary, that another Congress should be held on the tenth day of May next, unless the redress of grievances, which we have desired, be obtained before that time." It urged the colonies to choose representatives "as soon as possible," and it sent the same invitation to the maritime colonies not represented in the first Congress, along with supporting documentation of their grievances against the empire. The Second Continental Congress was also to meet in Philadelphia.

In an address "To the People of Great Britain," which the convention adopted on October 24, the delegates again explained the history of the colonies in the British Empire since 1763, their reasons for the association and what they hoped to accomplish, and their reading of the future should the ministry not comply with their demands. The only mention, or even implication, of independence came in the expressed desire that the people of Great Britain would elect a new Parliament independent of the North ministry:

> We hope that the magnanimity and justice of the British Nation will furnish a Parliament of such wisdom, independance and public spirit, as may save the violated rights of the whole empire from the devices of wicked Ministers and evil Counsellors whether in or out of office, and thereby restore that harmony, friendship and fraternal affection between all the Inhabitants of his Majesty's kingdoms and territories, so ardently wished for by every true and honest American.

The Continental Congress sent copies of this document to the colonial agents in London, asking them to circulate it in the highest government circles and to see that it was published for the British public to read. It also asked the agents to communicate to speakers of the colonial assemblies the reactions they received from friends of the colonies in England.

Shortly before the Congress adjourned on October 26, the delegates adopted a bill of rights and a list of grievances. The document listed ten rights, including an entitlement to "life, liberty, and property," which the colonies "have never ceded to any sovereign power." It also expressed the long-held belief that the colonists' ancestors had retained in perpetuity "all the rights, liberties, and immunities of free and natural born subjects, within the realm of England." The bill went on to specify their oft-stated views on representation, sovereignty, taxation, and their entitlement to the protections of the common law, which included "being tried by their peers of the vicinage," the hard-won right to peaceful assembly and to petition the king, and the freedom from a standing army "in times of peace, without the consent of the legislature of that colony in which such army is kept." They also claimed entitlement "to all the immunities and privileges granted and confirmed to them by royal charters, or secured by their several codes of provincial laws."

The list of grievances included specific breaches of the colonists' rights that Parliament had enacted in laws since 1763: Regulations imposed by governors, collectors of the customs, and admiralty courts; and attempts to collect revenue without their consent. The last straws included the standing army and the forced provision for it embodied in amendments to the Quartering Act, as well as the act "for establishing the Roman catholic religion in the province of Quebec, abolishing the equitable system of English laws, and erecting a tyranny there, to the great danger, from so total a dissimilarity of religion, law, and government to neighbouring British colonies, by the assistance of whose blood and treasure the said country was conquered from France."

Finally, in the last session of the 1774 Continental Congress, delegates addressed "A Letter to the Inhabitants of the Province of Quebec," which was published in October. In it, they invited the Quebecois to send delegates to the next session of the Congress, in May 1775. They explained their belief in representative government, trial by jury, and habeas corpus, all of which the Quebec Act denied the French colonists. Drawing heavily on the writings of the French political philosopher Montesquieu, the letter argued that the British Empire having imposed a tyrannical government on the Canadians and denied them basic rights, they should join the Anglo-American colonists and try to recover their independence. "We do not ask you by this address to commence acts of hostility against the government of our common Sovereign. We only invite you to consult your own glory and welfare, and not to suffer yourselves to be inveigled or intimidated by infamous Ministers so far, as to become the instruments of their cruelty and despotism."

General Gage's reply to the Continental Congress, dated October 20, did not reach Philadelphia before the delegates had adjourned. When Peyton Randolph received the letter on November 18, after he had returned to Virginia, he sent a copy to Charles Thomson, the Congress's secretary, for inclusion with its official records and saw to it that the letter was published in Virginia's newspapers. To begin with, General Gage denied the Congress's charges:

> There is not a single gun pointed against the town, no man's property has been seized or hurt, except the king's . . . No troops have given less cause for complaint, and greater care was never taken to prevent it;

and such care and attention was never more necessary from the insults and provocations daily given to both officers and soldiers. The communication between the town and country has been always free and unmolested, and is so still.

Gage claimed to be pleased by the Congress's stated ambitions to orchestrate "a cordial reconciliation with the mother country, which, from what has transpired, I have despaired of. Nobody wishes better success to such measures than myself." He wrote that his goal, too, was to serve as a mediator between the colonists of Massachusetts and the empire. With this in mind, he had "strongly urged" the former to pay for the tea they had destroyed and to "send a proper memorial to the king, which would be a good beginning on their side, and give their friends the opportunity they seek to move in their support." He further advised the delegates that "menaces, and unfriendly proceedings" would be counterproductive. "The spirit of the British nation was high when I left England," he reported, "and such measures will not abate it." The better approach, "decency and moderation here, would create the same disposition at home." In conclusion, he expressed hope that the disputes would end "like the quarrels of lovers, and increase the affection which they ought to bear to each other."

Charles Thomson forwarded the Congress's petition to the king, its letter to the people of England, and other papers to Benjamin Franklin in London. He included a note that expressed his own hope that "the wound may be healed & peace and love restored," and his fear that "we are on the very edge of the precipice." The Congress's intention was that Franklin and the six other colonial agents in London would present the petition directly to the king.

In early December, before the petition reached Franklin, two acquaintances approached him about opening secret peace negotiations with Lord North's ministry. David Barclay, a banker and one of the wealthiest men in London, and Dr. John Fothergill, the personal physician of both Lord Dartmouth and Franklin, were politically well-connected Quakers. Barclay had formerly been a colonial agent. Lord Hyde, a member of the Privy Council, had suggested this démarche to Barclay. Lord Richard Howe, admiral of the fleet, also became directly involved, communicating with Franklin through his sister, Caroline Howe, who offered Franklin the cover of frequent meetings to play chess. The lines of communication varied but often went from Franklin to Caroline Howe to Lord Howe to Hyde to Dartmouth and back again, although some of Franklin's communications were with Barclay and Fothergill or Lord Howe directly. The complexity reflected the fear of embarrassment if the deliberations became known publicly and the sure knowledge that if the king learned of them it would result in the fall of the ministry. King George did not trust Franklin.

Barclay first raised the possibility of negotiations with Franklin on December 1. Franklin thought there was no point, since the ministry was trying to provoke rebellion. Barclay disagreed, assured Franklin that there were men in high office who were reasonable and favored peace, and asked him to reconsider. On December 4, the three men had dinner together. Fothergill again assured Franklin that there was an opening for negotiations with the ministry and suggested that the three of them should try to agree to terms that they might forward to an unnamed contact in the ministry (Hyde). Franklin thought the timing was bad, as he expected news from the Continental Congress shortly and would not want to say or do anything to undermine its proposals. The two men pressed him: Time was short and delay would be dangerous. Boston was a powder keg, and an accidental misstep by either side could provoke an unstoppable civil war. Franklin agreed to draft some "Hints" for discussion, which he delivered to Barclay and Fothergill at their next meeting, on December 6.

Franklin's seventeen handwritten "Hints for Conversation on the Terms of Accommodation" became the basis for discussions within the ministry. Some of them he revised after discussion with Barclay and Fothergill; others he declined to change because he was sure the colonists would insist on them. He proposed that the colonists pay for the destroyed tea in return for Parliament's repeal of the Tea Act and the transfer of all duties paid under it to the colonies' treasuries from which they were collected. He recommended that the colonies reenact the Navigation Acts, which would preserve regulations the ministry considered essential, while conceding the point that only the colonists had the right to tax themselves; the Crown would appoint a naval officer to each colony who would be responsible for overseeing enforcement. Franklin proposed repeal of all other acts that restrained manufacturing in the colonies (Barclay convinced him to change the verb from "repeal" to "reconsider"). And all duties arising from regulation of trade would go to "the public use of the respective Colonies, and paid into their Treasuries." The governors would appoint the customs collectors rather than having them sent from England.

Franklin thought the colonists would be willing to provide for their own defense in return for an agreement that London would demand no financial contributions from them in times of peace. He proposed a proportional requisition system in time of war, keyed to the taxation rates imposed on English subjects. Alternatively, if Great Britain would surrender its monopoly over American trade as Parliament had legislated in the Navigation Acts, the colonists would agree to pay requisitions to the empire in times of peace as well as war. He believed they would insist that the British agree not to quarter any troops in a colony without the consent of its legislature.

The British would have to surrender Castle William in Boston Harbor to the colony of Massachusetts and build no other fortifications in the colony without the consent of its assembly. Parliament would have to agree to repeal the three Massachusetts acts and the Quebec Act passed in the spring 1774 session. Judges would be appointed by the king, but on good behavior, not for life, and the assemblies would fix and pay their salaries out of the provincial treasuries. (Franklin thought the colonists might give way on the first clause, but not on the second.) The assemblies would again pay the salaries of governors. Admiralty courts would have no greater authority in the colonies than they had in England. Parliament and the king would renounce any claim that they had sovereign authority to try colonists for treason under the harsher law of Henry VIII's reign rather than the law of treason as currently enforced in England.* Finally, "all Powers of Internal Legislation in the Colonies to be disclaim'd by Parliament."

In other words, Parliament would have to surrender on the question of sovereignty. In return, the colonies would agree to pay for the tea dumped into Boston Harbor, abide the Navigation Acts, defend themselves, affirm their allegiance to the king, accept reasonable regulations of trade applied even-handedly throughout the empire, and pay equitable requisitions in time of war. The ministry must understand,

---

* In 1768, both houses of Parliament had recommended to King George that he reverse common-law practice and subsequent legislative revisions of the law of treason in order to address challenges to imperial authority in Massachusetts.

though, that Franklin had no official standing and the Congress had not authorized him to negotiate terms. He still awaited instructions and expected the official correspondence to arrive soon.

Barclay forwarded these "Hints" to Lord Hyde on December 12. In a cover letter, he offered his view that Franklin's demands were unreasonable. Hyde, in reply, agreed that the terms had to be modified or they would go nowhere in the ministry. Barclay apparently then began to revise the "Hints." On December 18, he wrote to Franklin that he had received a response from Lord Hyde, who "intimates his hearty Wish that they may be productive of what may be practicable and advantageous for the Mother Country and the Colonies." Barclay did not mention that he and Hyde had agreed to tone down the "Hints" before passing them on to Dartmouth.

On December 19, Franklin received the anticipated package from Philadelphia with the Congress's correspondence and its order to the seven colonial agents to deliver its petition into the king's hands. This presented Franklin with two problems. First, four of the agents— Edmund Burke, Charles Garth, Thomas Life, and Paul Wentworth— declined to participate on the grounds that they had no official relationship with the Congress and no instructions from their particular assemblies on this matter. Second, for them to deliver the petition directly to the king would be a breach of protocol. The "regular Official Method," as Franklin later explained to the speakers of the colonial assemblies, was to present such a petition to the American secretary, in this case Lord Dartmouth, who would forward it to the king.

Franklin and the other two agents for Massachusetts, Arthur Lee and William Bollan, called on Lord Dartmouth with the petition on December 21. Dartmouth told them that the cabinet would first have to study the document before deciding whether to present it to the king. The cabinet met twice, deciding in the end that the petition was sufficiently significant and respectful, and only then did Dartmouth present it. He told the agents on December 23 that they could meet with him the next day to receive the king's reply. According to the agents' letter reporting the petition's progress, on December 24 Dartmouth indicated "that he had laid the same before the King, that his Majesty had been pleased to receive it very graciously, and to say, it was of so great Importance, that he should, as soon as they met, lay it before his two Houses of Parliament."

In December, Maryland's assembly approved the proceedings of the Continental Congress. It also resolved that if the British used troops to enforce the Intolerable Acts in Massachusetts or "the assumed power of Parliament to tax the colonies," Maryland would send troops to help defend it. It further recommended that militia companies be set up of all able-bodied men between the ages of sixteen and fifty, who would choose their officers and begin to drill. The county committees would raise £10,000 to purchase arms and ammunition "by subscription, or in such other voluntary manner as they may think proper," so that the militias would "be in readiness to act on any emergency."

South Carolina did little to prepare in 1774 and Pennsylvania even less. The South Carolina assembly recommended meekly that the colony's male citizens learn the use of arms and that officers train and exercise militia units at least once a fortnight. Pennsylvania's assembly deferred to the views of Quaker, Mennonite, and other pacifist delegates that there be no militias, but it did resolve that if Great Britain used force, "we hold it our indispensable duty to resist such force."

Virginia, on the other hand, made ample preparations for war, with its counties forming "independent" military units during the summer and fall of 1774. George Washington took command of the Fairfax County militia and bought supplies for it and two other units on his own account while he was in Philadelphia for the Continental Congress. In the meantime, the county voted a tax to pay for the supplies and to reimburse Washington.

Imperial relations had taken a significant turn in 1774, and the colonies were now working together more than they ever had before. Ideas about independence were evolving, but the revolution to which John Adams later referred was not yet completely in view. Most colonists still denied the ambition for it and raised the specter of independence in warning rather than in advocacy. They still said their public plans were simply attempts to avoid war and to maintain a positive approach to reconciliation with Britain.

In the first Continental Congress, the delegates from Massachusetts had been farther along the road to separation than the others. Thomas Hutchinson and officials in London were of the opinion that the Adams cousins had been angling for separation all along, but that is certainly not true of John, and it is difficult to find evidence in support of that view about Samuel; though he was among those most open to the idea of separation, he continued to claim in public as late as the fall of 1774 that he preferred to maintain the imperial connection. Despite the Intolerable Acts and the offensive military actions of Governor Gage, even the Adamses labeled the ministry as the enemy and the empire as the guardian of the colonists' rights. "Heretofore," Samuel wrote to Joseph Warren about his fellow delegates on September 25, "we [Massachusetts colonists] have been accounted by many, intemperate and rash; but now we are universally applauded as cool and judicious as well as Spirited and brave." Yet not all the delegates thought so well of the Bostonians: "There is, however, a certain Degree of Jealousy in the Minds of some that we aim at total Independency not only of the Mother Country but of the Colonies too."

As John Adams interpreted his fellow delegates in a letter of September 26, "it is the universal Sense here that the Mass. Acts and murder Act ought not to be Submitted to a Moment. But then, when you ask the Question what is to be done? They answer Stand Still. Bear, with Patience. If you come to a rupture with the Troops all is lost. Resuming the first Charter, Absolute Independency &c are Ideas which Startle People here." He evidently needed the adjective "absolute" to be clear, since the Intolerable Acts had muddied what colonists meant by "independence" five months earlier. The acts may have united colonists as never before, but they also divided them in their ambitions.

Joseph Galloway, writing retrospectively in 1780, remembered the first Continental Congress as having been split into two parties, "one intended candidly and clearly to define American rights, and explicitly and dutifully to petition for the remedy which would redress the grievances justly complained of—to form a more solid and constitutional union between the two countries, and to avoid every measure which tended to sedition, or acts of violent opposition." He himself belonged to this party of loyal subjects of the Crown. On the other side, Galloway cast the Adams cousins, the Virginian Patrick Henry, and others as "persons, whose design, from the beginning of their opposition to the Stamp Act, was to throw off all subordination and connexion with Great-Britain; who meant by every fiction, falsehood and fraud, to delude the people from their due allegiance, to throw the subsisting Governments into anarchy, to incite the ignorant and vulgar to arms, and with those arms to establish American Independence." Galloway had no doubt what "independence" meant to these revolutionaries dating back at least to 1765.

And yet, what Galloway called the republican faction at the Continental Congress included George Washington, who was no radical and who throughout 1774 opposed separation. He wrote in a letter of October 9 to Lieutenant Robert Mackenzie, who had been a captain under him in the French and Indian War and was now a lieutenant in General Gage's occupying force:

> I can announce it as a fact, that it is not the wish or interest of that Government [of Massachusetts], or any other upon this Continent, separately, or collectively, to set up for Independency; but at this you may at the same time rely on, that none of them will ever submit to the loss of those valuable rights & privileges which are essential to the happiness of every free State, and without which, Life, Liberty & property are rendered totally insecure.

Galloway's generalizations were wrong, but he was possibly correct about the small but increasing number of revolutionary delegates in the Continental Congress—Henry but not Washington, Sam but not John Adams. There would be no collective ambition for "absolute" independence until the likes of Washington and John Adams believed that separation was the only way open to recover the colonists' independence.

16

✦

INDEPENDENCE

O N THE VIRGINIA FRONTIER, Fincastle County prepared for war in January 1775, just as other Virginia counties had the previous fall. This delighted Richard Henry Lee, who wrote to his brother Arthur in England that Fincastle could field "1000 rifle men that for their number make [the] most formidable light infantry in the world." By early February he reported that Virginia's six frontier counties could provide six thousand infantrymen, who were expert marksmen. "There is not one of these men," he bragged, "who wish a distance less than 200 yards or a larger object than an orange. Every shot is fatal."

Over the winter of 1774–1775, the Massachusetts Provincial Congress had ordered the stockpiling of muskets, powder, and balls in Concord, fifteen miles from Boston. The delegates chose Concord as the location of the arsenal because it was on the main routes connecting Boston to the west and accessible only by two bridges that would be comparatively easy to defend. General Gage's seizure of powder at Cambridge the previous September had created a shortage, which a new distribution to the militia units would only partially address. In Lexington, for example, a town of 750 souls eleven miles from Boston, the militia drilled without live ammunition and took no target practice throughout the late winter and early spring.

Concord was having a hard time recruiting Minutemen, the elite corps for rapid deployment that constituted about 25 percent of the total militia force.* The provincial congress had given the town of about fifteen hundred a quota of one hundred enlistments, about a quarter of the adult males. It took until January 1775 before anyone signed up; a drill on January 12 was "unsuccessful," according to William Emerson, the minister who was there to offer a prayer for the men's safety and success. Another muster two days later brought about fifty men into the field, and by the end of the month, the officers had filled their quota, with two companies totaling 104 officers and men. More than half of these men were veterans of the Quebec and Louisbourg campaigns.

Parliamentary elections shrewdly called by Lord North for November 1774 had strengthened his hand by increasing his majority in the House of Commons. Since his ministry could now more safely disregard the lobbying of London merchants and other friends of the colonies, an economic boycott by Americans would have less impact on British politics than the Continental Congress had assumed. The delegates had worked from the premise that the British would have to make the first move toward compromise because the boycott would give North no choice. The king, North's government, and a majority in Parliament worked from the opposite presumption, that the colonists would have to bend to their will before the legislative, economic, and military pressures imposed in 1774 were relaxed. The boycott was successful as a unified commercial action, reducing imports from Europe to the Chesapeake Bay colonies of Maryland and Virginia, for example, from £690,000 in 1774 to £2,000 in 1775, and doubling the price of tobacco in Europe at the same time. But it was a political failure, having no effect on the North ministry.

Lord Howe wrote to his sister Caroline on January 2, 1775, that he was not optimistic about the negotiations between Benjamin Franklin and Lord Dartmouth: "It is with much concern that I collect, from

---

* As early as 1645, Massachusetts selected these first responders, who were generally under the age of thirty and had undergone additional training beyond that received by the local militia units, which included all able-bodied men between the ages of sixteen and sixty.

sentiments of such authority as those of our worthy friend [Franklin], that the desired accommodation, threatens to be attended with much greater difficulty than I had flattered myself in the progress of our intercourse, there would be reason to apprehend." Using his sister as a go-between, Howe asked Franklin two questions. Would the Massachusetts colonists agree to pay for the tea in return for a promise that their grievances would be redressed when their assembly petitioned for it? And was there flexibility in the position Franklin took on requisitions in the "Hints"?

Franklin dashed off a spirited, vehement response on the spot:

> The People of America conceiving that Parliament has no Right to tax them, and that there fore all that has been extorted from them by the Operation of the Duty Acts, with the assistance of an armed Force, *preceding* the Destruction of the Tea, is so much Injury, which ought in order of time to be first repair'd, before a Demand on the Tea Account can be justly made of them; are not . . . likely to approve of the Measure proposed, and pay *in the first place* the Value demanded, especially as 20 times as much Injury has since been done them by blocking up their Port, and their Castle also seiz'd before by the Crown has not been restor'd, nor any Satisfaction offered them for the same.

On January 4, between three and four hundred merchants met in the King's Arms Tavern, Cornhill, London, to discuss American affairs. The group favored making a petition to Parliament and appointed a committee to draft one by the next meeting, on January 11. About a hundred more men attended the second meeting, and they all approved the petition with little or no dissent. It explained the importance of the American trade to them and showed how disastrously the Stamp Act, Townshend Acts, and Tea Act had affected them. The interruption of trade associated with a boycott would harm not only them but also the public revenue, artisans, manufacturers, and general commerce. The ministry ignored the petition. As Franklin explained in a letter of February 5 to Charles Thomson, "Petitions are odious here." Economic arguments had no effect on the ministry or the monarch at this point.

The colonial agents, out of respect for protocol, had tried to delay publication of the Continental Congress's petition until the king's ministers delivered it to Parliament. But while they were waiting, an ambitious printer published a copy on January 16. Parliament reconvened on January 19 and received the petition among a large collection of undigested American papers. The House of Lords received it the next day. Lord Chatham rose to speak, and he tried to set the tone correctly: "America means only to have safety in property; and personal liberty. Those, and those only were her object; independency was falsely charged on her." He advocated repeal of the acts that were so obnoxious to the colonists, acts that had claimed Parliament's right "to take their money when you please," to amend or revoke their charters at will, and to lay siege to Boston.

Chatham then moved that Parliament "address the king to remove the forces from the town of Boston." Parliament had to recognize, he said, that it could not subdue three million Americans with an army of forty thousand or more. "Mal-administration has run its line" and was driving the empire into "a check mate," he declared. The Earl of Shelburne supported Chatham's principles and his plan, saying that the Boston Port Act was in any case unconstitutional. Lord Camden argued that "the natural right of mankind, and the immutable laws of justice, were clearly in favour of the Americans." The Marquis of Rockingham thought that North's avowed plan to send more troops to Boston "was a measure totally repugnant to his plan of reconciliation." He was "glad of an opportunity of resisting that mischievous and dangerous design of governing the colonies by force." The Duke of Richmond "supported Lord Chatham's motion with firmness." He later concluded, "Some nobles seem to think that regular troops will easily vanquish raw soldiers. But, my lords, discipline was intended only as a substitute for what the Americans have already: attachment to their cause; virtue to inspire; a common cause; their all, to keep them to their duty. Americans will keep to their duty without discipline."

Lord Lyttelton was one of the MPs who heartily disliked the opposition men who had spoken thus far, and he disliked Americans, too. As for the Continental Congress, "The whole of their deliberations and proceedings breathed the spirit of unconstitutional independency and open rebellion," he thought. It was "time to assert the authority of Great Britain" lest inaction "bring about that state of traitorous independency, at which it was too plain they were now aiming." Viscount

Townshend agreed. He believed the petition of the Continental Congress showed that "the views of America are not confined to the redress of grievances, real or imaginary, but are immediately directed to the total overthrow of that great Palladium [safeguard] of the British commerce, the act of navigation."

Hugh Boyd, a penniless and gifted Irish essayist who regularly attended sessions of Parliament and recorded notes of the debates from memory, paid particular attention to this one. He noted that Lord Gower addressed the House "with great sneer and contempt" and claimed to be "well informed, that the language now held by the Americans, was the language of the rabble and a few factious leaders . . . My lords, I am for *enforcing* these measures: and let the Americans sit talking about their natural and divine rights! Their rights as men and citizens! Their rights from God and nature!" The Earl of Rochford spoke, too, "for firm and decisive measures. To retreat," he insisted, was to be "vanquished."

The debate lasted all day and into the night, "till eight o'clock." Franklin reported on the outcome to Thomas Cushing, Speaker of the Massachusetts assembly, in a letter of January 28:

> Lord Chatham mov'd last Week in the House of Lords that an address be presented to his Majesty humbly beseeching him to withdraw the Troops from Boston as a Step towards opening the Way to Conciliatory Measures, &c. But after a long and warm Debate, the Motion was rejected by a Majority of 77 to 18, and open Declarations were made by the ministerial Side of the Intention to enforce the late Acts. To this End three more Regiments of Foot and one of Dragoons, seven hundred Marines, and Six Sloops of War and two Frigates are now under Orders for America.

On February 1, Lord Chatham offered himself "from a principle of duty and affection, to act the part of a mediator." He both declared the authority of Parliament and affirmed the colonies' claims to independence within the empire. The act he proposed would reassert that the colonies "have been, are, and of right ought to be, dependent upon the Imperial Crown of Great Britain, and subordinate unto the British Parliament," and that the Parliament and Crown acting in concert "had, hath, and of right ought to have, full power and authority to make laws and Statutes of sufficient force and validity to bind the people of the British Colonies in America, in all matters touching the general weal of the whole Dominion of the Imperial Crown of Great Britain."

Chatham went through the correct motions of affirming his commitment to the prevailing policy. Parliament would assert its authority "for regulating navigation and trade throughout the complicated system of British Commerce"; further, the Declaration of Rights from the Glorious Revolution made it clear that Parliament working in concert with the Crown had the "legal, constitutional, and hitherto unquestioned" right to station a standing army anywhere in the empire during peacetime, a decision that could not, therefore, "be rendered dependent upon the consent of a Provincial Assembly in the Colonies without a most dangerous innovation and derogation from the dignity of the Imperial Crown of Great Britain." Parliament would also stand fast in its insistence that the monarch appoint and pay judges.

Nonetheless, Chatham went on, Parliament would also agree, if it adopted his bill, "in order to quiet and dispel groundless jealousies and fears . . . that no Military Force, however raised, and kept according to law, can ever be lawfully employed to violate and destroy the just rights of the people." It would further stipulate that "no tax . . . shall be commanded or levied, from British freemen in America, without common consent, by Act of Provincial Assembly there, duly convened for that purpose." But Chatham also thrust obligations onto American shoulders. He thought the Second Continental Congress, scheduled for May 1775, should make "a free grant to the King, his heirs and successors, of a certain perpetual Revenue, subject to the disposition of the British parliament, to be appropriated, as they in their wisdom shall judge fit, to the alleviation of the National debt." It should also set rates and quotas for the various colonies according to their population and means.

On the contentious issue of admiralty courts, Chatham proposed to restore the traditional limits on their authority in the colonies, and also to restore the guarantee of local trials by jury; he specified that "no subject in America shall, in capital cases, be liable to be indicted and tried for the same, in any place outside the Province, wherein such offence shall be alleged to have been committed, nor be deprived of a trial of his peers of the vicinage."

All these details preceded Chatham's proposal for Parliament to repeal the Quebec Act and the acts that had revoked the Massachusetts Charter, closed its port, and altered the structure of its government and courts. More: Parliament would acknowledge the colonies' rights while extending clemency in a magnanimous act that recognized Britain's greatness and its high esteem for the colonists, for "the Colonies in America are justly entitled to the privileges, franchises, and immunities granted by their several Charters or Constitutions, and that the said Charters or Constitutions ought not to be invaded or resumed unless for misuses, or some legal ground of forfeiture."

Chatham's bill, despite its temperate nature and its defense of parliamentary right, was more shouted down than debated, and Lord Sandwich, First Lord of the Admiralty, moved that the House of Lords reject it, which they did in a decisive 61–31 vote. As accommodating as the bill had been in its effort to chart a middle path, Chatham had unintentionally demonstrated that there was no longer a middle road between the colonists and the ministry. And this was before the relationship took another turn for the worse. For now, the ministry favored tightening the screws, making no compromises or accommodations to the colonists, whom the ministers and their majority already considered rebels.

As Franklin and the two Massachusetts agents in London, Bollan and Arthur Lee, explained in a note of February 5 to the speakers of the colonial assemblies, "It was thrown out in Debate by a principal Member of Administration, that it would be proper to alter the Charters of Connecticut and Rhode Island." There were other reports of a January 27 meeting of the Privy Council at which it was "determined to take away the Charters of Rhode Island and Connecticut." Independently of these two sources, Josiah Quincy, the Boston lawyer who had worked with John Adams in the Boston Massacre trials, quoted the customs inspector John Williams as having said on January 13 that "the Connecticut charter will be snapped this session." On February 9, Thomas Hutchinson heard that the ministry intended to abolish the two colonies and absorb Connecticut into New York and Rhode Island into Massachusetts.

The Continental Congress's petition to the king, which Dartmouth had led Franklin to believe was well received in December, also failed to get a sympathetic hearing in London. As Franklin told Charles Thomson in a letter of February 5, the petition came down among a great Heap of Letters of Intelligence from Governors and Officers in America, Newspapers, Pamphlets, Handbills, &c from that Country, the last in the List and laid upon the Table with them, undistinguished by any particular Reccommendation of it to the Notice of either House, and I do not find that it has had any farther Notice taken of it as yet, than that it has been read as well as the other Papers.

The agents asked to be heard by the House of Commons on the petition, but the House denied them the privilege. "And by the Resolutions of the Committee of the whole House," Franklin reported, "which I enclose, you will see that it has made little Impression."

Franklin and his fellow agents had reached a dead end. The only remaining hope, in Franklin's opinion, was the nonconsumption agreement adopted by the Continental Congress, which was affecting the London merchants, but he might have added that this was a group whose views had no influence on the North ministry. The ministers continued to receive reports from the most conservative colonists, such as Hutchinson, that the Americans were divided on the subject of resistance and that the Continental Congress represented a radical rabble rather than the political mainstream. America's friends in Parliament and in London knew otherwise, but their influence on the government was no greater than Franklin's. As hard as it was to imagine, Chatham and Burke, the two great statesmen of their day, whom Americans and the British public revered, had no sway over the parliamentary majority. As Franklin reported, "Lord Chatham's Bill, tho' on so important a Subject, and offer'd by so great a Character, and supported by such able and learned Speakers, as Camden &c &c was treated with as much Contempt as they could have shown to a Ballad offered by a drunken Porter."

Dr. Fothergill explained to Franklin in a letter of February 6 that nothing had come of the negotiations begun in December with the "Hints." "Our difficultys arose from the American acts, the Boston Port Bill, [and] the Government of the Massachusetts and Quebec Act," he wrote. "As a concession to pay a tax was the *sine qua non* on this side, so a rescinding of those acts, or rather repealing them, is the term of reconciliation on the other." The ministry likewise decided the Continental Congress had no authorized, "authentic" standing, so it was dismissive of its petition. Fundamentally, though, a lack of willingness to compromise made negotiations "ineffectual." Dr. Fothergill thought that "was the whole of A[dministration] as cordially disposed to peace and as sensible of its advantages as Lord Dartmouth, I think there would be very little difficulty in accomplishing it; But I see and perceive so strong a current another way, that I despaer, without the interposition of Omnipotence, of any reconciliation."

On February 10, Prime Minister North introduced the New England Trade and Fishery Prohibitory Bill, which was meant to put the region's trade "under temporary restrictions" and restrain "the refractory provinces from fishing on the banks of Newfoundland." The intention was to close the fisheries "till the New Englanders should return to a sense of their duty to the mother country, and submit to her supreme authority." He observed, during the debate, that "although, the two Houses had not declared all Massachusetts Bay in rebellion, they had declared, that there is a rebellion in that Province. It was just therefore to deprive that province of its fisheries." It likewise seemed to him both fair and necessary to include New Hampshire in the reprisals, as that colony also had a weak government, and "a quantity of powder had been taken out of a Fort there by an armed mob. Besides the *vicinity* of that province to Massachusetts Bay was such, that if it were not added, the purpose of the Act would be defeated."

That was not all. Rhode Island was not "in a much better situation than Massachusetts Bay," he believed. "Several pieces of cannon had been taken there, and carried up in the country; and . . . they were arraying their militias, in order to march into any other colony in case it should be attacked." Moreover, Connecticut "had marched a large body of men into Massachusetts, on a report that the soldiery had killed some people in Boston; and though this body had returned, on finding the falsity of that report, an ill disposition had been shewn, and . . . this colony was in a State of great disorder and confusion."

Franklin met again with Barclay and Fothergill on February 16, because Barclay still did not despair of a settlement or, at least, of a negotiation with genuine potential for reconciliation. He had taken Franklin's "Hints" along with his discussions with Hyde, Howe, Dartmouth, and perhaps others in the ministry, and tried to piece together a foundation for reconciliation. He proposed that a peace commissioner be sent to America with the authority to negotiate. The three men agreed that Lord Howe was the likely candidate acceptable to both sides.

Barclay believed that a commitment from the colonial agents to reimburse the East India Company for the destroyed tea was the gesture that could get the negotiations off the ground. And he believed the ministry would in return agree to repeal the Tea Act and return Castle William to Massachusetts. The colonists could then petition the king for repeal of the Massachusetts Government Act, and in the interim the commissioner would have the authority to suspend operation of it. The colonies aggrieved by the Quebec Act could petition to withdraw from its borders to the former, traditional ones. Parliament would formally disavow the treason act of Henry VIII's reign. The colonists would agree, in times of peace, to come up with money for the requisitions deemed necessary by the ministry, and to do so by their own means and votes of their assemblies; in times of war they would raise requisitions to pay for their defense.

The ministry would agree to reexamine the Navigation Acts and see whether amendments were necessary to fit the colonies' particular needs. And, as Franklin had suggested and Chatham had recommended, the Crown would appoint a naval officer in each colony to supervise enforcement of the acts; the Crown and ministry would also reexamine acts that worked against American manufacturing. All duties produced by the acts regulating trade would go to the general treasury of the colony in which they were raised, just as Franklin had recommended. Likewise, the jurisdiction of the American admiralty courts would be revised to conform to that of the courts in England, which would mean that the courts' jurisdiction would be narrowed and the customs service could no longer bring prosecutions in Nova Scotia or even in England. All judges would receive appointments on good behavior, as the colonists had lobbied for, and colonial legislatures would pay governors and judges, though the king could supplement their salaries with imperial funds if he saw fit to do so.

On February 17, Franklin brought a number of papers with him to an evening meeting with Barclay and Dr. Fothergill. They included the draft of a note from the three Massachusetts agents—Franklin, Bollan, and Lee—to King George, which asked "to approach the Throne" to suggest the appointment of a peace negotiator. A similar note was prepared for Dartmouth, and there were notes on Franklin's replies to

Barclay's revised "Hints." Franklin thought Barclay's reliance on a petitioning process was naïve, given the disdain with which king and ministry received petitions. And he also found Barclay's revisions unbalanced: For example, "The Tea should not only be paid for on the Side of Boston, but the Damage done to Boston by the Port Act should be repair'd, because it was done contrary to the Custom of all Nations Savage as well as civiliz'd, of first demanding Satisfaction."

The colonies would never, in Franklin's opinion, agree to judges receiving any part of their salaries from the king, because that would free them from attachment to the colonial governments just as surely as if they were fully paid by the Crown. In addition, Franklin was certain that the colony "must suffer all the Hazards and Mischiefs of War, rather than admit the Alteration of their Charters and Laws by Parliament. They who can give up essential Liberty to obtain a little temporary Safety, deserve neither Liberty nor Safety."

When the three men met that night, Franklin was enthusiastic about the idea of a peace commissioner, and he suggested an amendment to Barclay's proposal that put it more in line with his idea for a plenipotentiary who would meet with delegates from all the colonies and negotiate terms for their submission to the Crown. He reiterated his view that a commitment to reimburse the East India Company must be the spur to repeal the Intolerable Acts as a preliminary to further negotiations. The two Englishmen thought this was impossible, that only the reopening of Boston Harbor was possible on those terms.

At that point, Franklin rose and gathered up the papers he had yet to discuss with the two men. Without a commitment to repeal the three hated acts of reprisal against Massachusetts in return for reimbursing the East India Company for the tea, there was no hope of reconciliation. Barclay and Fothergill promised to report his views to the ministry. Franklin found this indirect communication unsatisfactory; he wanted direct contact with the ministers. Once again, the men said they would communicate the request.

In fact, although Franklin did not know it at the time, the negotiations had already come to an end. No further communication, direct or indirect, came from the ministry. Through Howe, Franklin learned that Hyde believed that "your principles and his, or rather those of Parliament, are as yet so wide from each other, that a meeting merely to discuss them, might give you unnecessary trouble." Franklin did not disagree. Since he had "nothing to offer on the American Business in Addition to what Lord Hyde is already acquainted with from the Papers that have passed, it seems most respectful not to give his Lordship the Trouble of a Visit, since a mere Discussion of the Sentiments contained in those Papers is not . . . likely to produce any good Effect."*

On February 20, the prime minister offered what he considered a conciliatory proposal on the central issue of taxes. "Although the Parliament of Great Britain could never give up the rights, although it must always maintain the doctrine that every part of the Empire was bound to bear its share of service and burthen in the common defence," yet he was open to alternative means to raise money from the colonies. "If the Americans would propose to Parliament any mode by which they would engage themselves to raise, in their own way, and by their own grants, their share of contributions to their common defence," he was willing to entertain them, and "the quarrel on the subject of taxation was at an end." The proposals had to come from the colonial assemblies, operating under the authority of the charters and the governors, and made to king and ministry through normal channels. If, however, the dispute with America "goes to the whole of our authority, we can enter into no negotiation, we can meet no compromise." Thus did he mark "the ground on which negotiation may take place. It is explicit, and defines the terms, and specifies the persons from whom the proposals must come, and to whom they must be made."

Lord North made this pitch to his most conservative supporters in Parliament; he did not want them to think he had gone soft on enforcement of royal prerogatives and parliamentary authority. "Some gentlemen may ask the question, will you treat with rebels? I am not treating with rebels. It has never been yet said that all the Americans are rebels, or that all the Colonies are in rebellion." As far as he was concerned, it was only Massachusetts that was in rebellion, but even there, where "the people of the Province reject and oppose with force of arms, the Government, as established by the King and Parliament," he was willing to welcome them back into the fold: "The moment that they acknowledge that Government, and meet in assembly to act under it, the

---

* Nonetheless, Franklin did meet again with Howe on February 28 and March 7, and with Hyde on March 1, but nothing came of the meetings and details of the conversations are unknown.

rebellion is at an end." These were the prime minister's terms. This was his most conciliatory stance.

North continued: "It is very probable the propositions contained in this Resolution may not be acceptable to the Americans in general," since they did not address all of the colonists' claims. Still, those colonists who were "just, humane, and wise, . . . and who are serious, will, I believe, think it well worthy their attention." The House of Commons supported this endeavor to divide the Americans, separating off the "just, humane, and wise" from the rest, and voted in favor of the resolution 274–88.

On March 10, Lord North introduced another bill in the House of Commons. This one was "to restrain the trade and commerce of the colonies of New Jersey, Pennsylvania, Maryland, Virginia, and South Carolina, to Great Britain, Ireland, and the British islands in the West Indies." This was a harsh retaliation for the colonies' joint commitment to nonimportation and nonexportation agreements—though not as harsh as what Parliament had imposed on New England, and reversible once they renounced the boycott.

Franklin was in the gallery of the House of Lords on March 16 when the ministry introduced a bill to limit the trade of the New England colonies to Great Britain and its possessions alone, and to ban the same colonies from the Newfoundland fisheries until they submitted to Parliament's authority. He heard the Duke of Grafton endorse the bill as "founded on the principle of retaliation and punishment, for an outrage as daring as it was unprovoked, still further heightened and aggravated by a resistance to all lawful authority, and almost a positive avowal of a total independence on the mother country." He heard the Earl of Sandwich recall the 1758 battle for Louisbourg; General Peter Warren had told him that the New Englanders "were the greatest set of cowards and poltroons he ever knew; they were all bluster, noise, and conquest, before they got in the presence of their enemies; but then good for nothing." If it came to war, Sandwich predicted, "their numbers, and extent of country both . . . will unite with their cowardice to render their conquest the more easy; for, in the first place, it will be more difficult to assemble them, and when they are assembled, the more easy to defeat them." And Franklin heard the Duke of Grafton describe himself as a friend of America, hoping that 1775 would be the year in which the colonists reversed course and 1776 would see a return to the formerly amicable relations that governed a united empire.

> I sincerely hope . . . we may be employed in manifesting the most ample proofs of our removing all cause, or almost possibility of the return of the same evils, by ascertaining their rights, and the constitutional power of this country, on the most fair, equitable, and permanent foundations. It was my task on a former occasion: and I shall with pleasure, in the year 1776, as a strenuous friend to the just claims of America, unremittingly labour in the same cause.

Franklin left the House of Lords angry. He did not see 1775 as a year when Americans would surrender, and he would have predicted a very different significance for 1776. He was also confident that Sandwich was wrong about the Americans' willingness and capacity to fight. Only with great self-control, and at the insistent advice of a friend, did he restrain himself from aiming a parting shot at the ministers and MPs who were driving the colonists together—and perilously close to driving them out of the empire.

Franklin set sail for Philadelphia on March 20 in a sour mood. He had failed utterly to negotiate a truce in the escalating imperial conflict; the ministers were arrogant and inflexible, and they grossly underestimated the people he represented. There was also his private tragedy: His wife had died at home in December.

On March 21, the bill banning residents of the Middle and Southern colonies from the Newfoundland fisheries passed the House of Commons 73–21. The next day, Edmund Burke brought a new tone to the debate over the colonies in a speech for the ages, one that was so widely admired for its style and grace that the cynical Samuel Johnson wrote a parody of it. Parliament had already made two significant concessions, Burke noted. First, it had "declared conciliation admissible, *previous* to any submission on the part of *America*." Second, it had "admitted that the complaints of our former mode of exerting the right of taxation, were not wholly unfounded." Burke proposed to build on these by moving the debate off the subject of traditional rights and political theory and onto the firmer ground of actual conditions in the colonies. To start with, there was the size of the population, which he estimated (quite accurately) at about 2.4 million of European descent or origin. Parliament simply had to recognize that "some degree of care and caution is required in the handling such an object; it will shew that you ought not, in reason, to trifle with so large a mass of the interests and feelings of the human race. You could at no time do so without guilt. And be assured you will not be able to do it long with impunity."

Perhaps more significant was the colonists' commercial success, which was even greater than their numbers would suggest: "[Britain's] trade with *America* alone is now within less than £500,000 of being equal to what this great commercial Nation, *England*, carried on at the beginning of this century with the whole world!" At the beginning of the century the colonies accounted for one-twelfth of England's trade, but now they were "considerably more than a third of the whole." Within sixty-eight years, the life of one man, the economic relationship between England and the mainland North American colonies had been transformed: "Whatever *England* has been growing to by a progressive increase of improvement, brought in by varieties of people, by [a] succession of civilizing conquests and civilizing settlements in a series of one thousand seven hundred years, you shall see as much added to her by *America* in the course of a single life!" And that was just English transatlantic exports. Imports from the colonies had similarly transformed the English economy. "When we speak of the commerce with our Colonies," Burke continued, "fiction lags after truth, invention is unfruitful, and imagination cold and barren."

Whether considering the colonies' agricultural production, fishing industry, or lumber harvesting, "*America*, gentlemen say, is a noble object. It is an object well worth fighting for. Certainly it is, if fighting a people be the best way of gaining them." But conquest was unnecessary and the use of force counterproductive in dealing with the colonists. "I confess," Burke acknowledged, "my opinion is much more in favour of prudent management, than of force; considering force not as an odious, but a feeble instrument, for preserving a people so numerous, so active, so growing, so spirited as this, in a profitable and subordinate conexion with us."

Burke wanted the MPs to consider the colonists' culture, what made them unique, rather than agreeing to impose a system the ministry deemed universally applicable to all the empire's colonies. The North American colonists were Englishmen, after all, who valued their liberty more than any other people on earth. Their dissenting Protestantism added a stubborn edge to their resistance. They were likewise the best educated, most literate populace in the world, which completed the package of an independent-minded people who would rather die than have their rights trifled with. There was as well the geography of the problem: "Three thousand miles of Ocean lie between you and them. No contrivance can prevent the effect of this distance in weakening Government. Seas roll, and months pass, between the order and the execution: and the want of a speedy explanation of a single point, is enough to defeat a whole system."

North America was too large to be conquerable and had no single urban center. The very notion of using force to administer the colonies there was ill conceived, despite England's overwhelming military prowess, and would be impossible to execute. The policy associated with the Proclamation Line—trying to hem the settlers in from the west—was a similar folly, unenforceable and counterproductive. All in all, Burke continued, "The temper and character which prevail in our Colonies, are, I am afraid, unalterable by any human art. We cannot, I fear, falsify the pedigree of this fierce people, and persuade them that they are not sprung from a Nation, in whose veins the blood of freedom circulates . . . An *Englishman* is the unfittest person on earth to argue another *Englishman* into slavery."

Burke proposed that the MPs simply accept the "*American* spirit as necessary; or, if you please to submit to it, as a necessary evil." They had to recognize the ocean and the continent for the barriers to governance that they were. They had to see the North American population increasing beyond their capacity to contain it by drawing lines on a map. They had to reckon that force would not work, and to imagine the colonists as criminals, rebels, and traitors was counterproductive. They had to appreciate, as London merchants were telling them, that the trade relationship was significant and ever more important. And they simply had to accept that the empire could not change the colonists or subdue them, but that Britain might lose the colonies if the ministry acted tyrannically. The MPs had to be realistic.

Until now, the ministry had been trying to enforce "Revenue laws which are mischievous, in order to preserve Trade laws that are useless." But Burke made it clear that everyone knew "the publick and avowed origin of this quarrel was on taxation." To be sure, "this quarrel has . . . brought on new disputes on new questions," the "least bitter" of which concerned the Navigation Acts. With this in mind, he suggested repealing the taxes and then see "whether any controversy at all will remain." Or, as an alternative, Burke proposed that Parliament "mark the *legal competency* of the Colony Assemblies for the support of their Government in peace, and for publick aids in time of war."

He offered six propositions for conciliation with the colonies. First: a proclamation that acknowledged the colonies were not represented in Parliament. Second: an admission that the colonies had been unjustly taxed in light of the absence of such representation. Third: a further admission that "no method hath hitherto been devised for procuring a representation in Parliament for the said Colonies." Fourth: an acknowledgment that all the colonies had elected representative assemblies authorized to raise taxes. Fifth: a recognition that the colonial assemblies had in the past freely granted "large subsidies and publick aids for his Majesty's service, according to their abilities, when required thereto by Letter from one of his Majesty's principal Secretaries of State." And finally, a resolution: "That it hath been found by experience, that the manner of granting the said Supplies and Aids, by the said General Assemblies, hath been more agreeable to the said Colonies, and more beneficial and conducive to the publick service, than the mode of giving and granting Aids in Parliament, to be raised and paid in the said Colonies."

Burke believed that if Parliament adopted these six resolutions, conflict with the colonies would end. He also proposed repeal of the Intolerable Acts and recognition that Parliament considered the colonies' charters inviolable. It ought also to confirm the traditional guarantees of liberty reaching back to Magna Carta, which included trial by jury in the vicinage and habeas corpus, and which voided King Henry VIII's treason law. Parliament should guarantee the colonies an independent judiciary, the salaries for which should be set and granted by colonial assemblies. The jurisdiction of the admiralty courts should be confined to traditional limits, as in England. Burke concluded, "The Americans will have no interest contrary to the grandeur and glory of England, when they are not oppressed by the weight of it; and they will rather be inclined to respect the acts of a superintending legislature, when they see them the acts of that power which is itself the security, not the rival, of their secondary importance."

Burke's first proposition, that the colonies were not represented in Parliament, went down in the House of Commons by a vote of 270–78. The MPs rejected the five other motions as well. On March 24, the House of Commons adopted the act to restrain the trade and commerce of New England, and to prohibit the New Englanders from using the Newfoundland fisheries, by a vote of 80–12. The House of Lords had already approved the bills by majorities of 50 votes.

The second Massachusetts Provincial Congress, which convened on February 1, 1775, saw much debate but little action, though the delegates instructed a committee to prepare rules and regulations for "the constitutional army which may be raised" and authorized its committee of safety to appoint a commissary to take charge of military stores "until the constitutional army shall take the field." This was not at all the same as establishing an army, but it was a step in that direction. On February 21, committee members voted to purchase enough supplies to support an army of fifteen thousand men, and a month later sent out an order to captains of militia and Minuteman units to assemble one-fourth of their men, and to be on alert:

> Whenever the army under command of General Gage, or any part thereof to the number of five hundred, shall march out of the town of Boston, with artillery and baggage, it ought to be deemed a design to carry into execution by force the late acts of Parliament, the attempting which, by the resolve of the late honourable Continental Congress, ought to be opposed; and therefore the military force of the Province ought to be assembled, and an army of observation immediately formed, to act solely on the defensive so long as it can be justified on the principles of reason and self-preservation.

When the Massachusetts Congress reassembled on March 22, General Gage had a spy in its midst, Dr. Benjamin Church of Boston, who, as a member of the congress, the Boston committee of correspondence, and the Committee of Safety, had information to sell and an expensive mistress to support. On March 30, there was a false alarm, when British troops conducted exercises across Boston Neck. On April 1 came the news that in February Lord North had introduced the bill to ban the colony's fleet from the Newfoundland fisheries and limit its trade to Great Britain, Ireland, and the West Indies. The delegates and their fellow colonists also learned that the ministry would send four more regiments to reinforce General Gage's army and that Parliament had adopted an address to the king declaring Massachusetts to be in a state of rebellion.

On April 3, the *Boston Gazette* published a speech that John Wilkes, Lord Mayor of London, had delivered in the House of Commons on February 9 in response to Lord North's new proposals. "This I know," the newspaper quoted Wilkes as saying, "a successful resistance is a *Revolution*, not a *Rebellion*. Rebellion indeed appears on the back of a flying enemy, but revolution flames on the breast-plate of the victorious warrior. Who can say, sire, whether in consequence of this very day's violent and mad Address to his *Majesty*, the scabbard may not be thrown away by them as well as by us, and should success attend them, whether in a few years Americans may not celebrate the glorious year of 1775, as we do that of 1688?" Wilkes predicted that Great Britain lacked the military force adequate to put down a revolution in America, and that the colonists "will sooner declare themselves independent, and risk every consequence of such a contest, than submit to the yoke which Administration is preparing for them."

On April 5, the Massachusetts Provincial Congress adopted fifty-three rules and regulations "for the army that may be raised," which was still a step short of actually creating the army. The next day, it again advised the towns to be on the defensive but to avoid any actions "that our enemies might plausibly interpret as a commencement of hostilities." According to Gage's spy, "The people without doors [that is, who are not members of the Provincial Congress] are clamorous for an immediate commencement of hostilities but the moderate-thinking people within wish to ward off that period till hostilities shall commence on the part of government which would prevent their being censured for their rashness by the other colonies and that made a pretence for deserting them." The congress did finally resolve on April 8, after much debate, that it was "necessary for this colony to make preparations for their security and defence, by raising and establishing an army," and for that reason Massachusetts would send delegates to the other New England colonies asking for support.

In the first two weeks of April 1775, it would have been hard, perhaps impossible, to find a resident of Concord, Massachusetts, who favored leaving the British Empire. As the Minutemen drilled, their goal was recovery of their independence and defense of their town and its arsenal from General Gage's thirty-five hundred soldiers. And Gage was hoping to bide his time until London sent reinforcements, at which point he would consider moving more aggressively to take control of the province and enforce Parliament's new laws. In the meantime, he was isolated, sitting on a powder keg, and governing little more than Castle William. He was also taking a lot of grief from the comparatively few loyalists in Boston, who dared to complain to him and to the ministry, and from his junior officers, who mocked his orders to refrain from fighting colonists who taunted the troops.

Gage had a clear, sensible logic for trying to avoid violence: "I have been at pains to prevent anything of consequence taking its rise from trifles and idle quarrels, and when the cause of Boston became the general concern of America, endeavoured so to manage that Administration might have an opening to negotiate if anything conciliatory should present itself or be in a condition to prosecute their plans with greater advantage." His caution seemed plausible, since he also had little confidence in the ability of his troops to quash a rebellion. "If force is to be used at length, it must be a considerable one, and foreign troops must be hired, for to begin with small numbers will encourage resistance, and not terrify; and will in the end cost more blood and treasure."

On April 11, John Howe, a young man who claimed to be a gunsmith from Maine, arrived in Concord. He said he was looking to set up shop there, as he believed his skills might be of some use, and he secured an introduction to the militia's Major Jonathan Buttrick. "They said I was the very man they wanted to see," Howe wrote in his journal, "and would assist me all they could, and immediately went to hire a shop." The twenty-two-year-old Howe was actually a spy for General Gage, and he returned to Boston the next day to report what he had learned. He advised Gage against sending troops to attack the arsenal at Worcester, which he said would require a long march over hilly terrain and winding roads exposed to ambushes. As the people of the region were "generally determined to be free or die," Howe said, if Gage sent out "ten thousand regulars and a train of artillery . . . not one of them would get back alive." As to an attack on the Concord arsenal, "I stated that I thought five hundred mounted men might go to Concord in the night and destroy the stores and return safe, but to go with one thousand foot . . . the country would be so alarmed, that the greater part of them would be killed or taken."

Gage, although he had no cavalry, was under pressure to act. "There was great division among the members of the congress," according to Howe, "and great irresolution shown in the course of their debates this week." The general would have agreed with the delegates meeting at Concord that none of them wanted to start a war, but Gage now believed only force could reestablish the empire's authority. On April 16, the congress adjourned until May 10. On the same day, Gage received a letter from Lord Dartmouth that questioned his courage and judgment. "In reviewing the charter for the government of the province of Massachusetts Bay," the minister observed "that there is a clause that empowers the governor to use and exercise the law-martial in times of actual war, invasion or rebellion."

Everyone who was paying attention to events believed that the British troops would move against the Concord arsenal. Whenever soldiers crossed the Boston Neck for exercises, the aroused populace scrambled into their defensive postures. Civilian leaders feared that a shot misfired by a nervous mechanic might start a war, so they ordered citizens to stand down unless they saw a force of at least five hundred troops along with artillery and a baggage train crossing the neck. That could "be deemed a design to carry into execution by force the late Acts of Parliament," in which case the alarm should be sounded, and militia units should immediately form "an Army of Observation . . . to act solely on the defensive so long as it can be justified on the Principles of reason and Self-Preservation and [no] longer."

General Gage may have been the only man in Massachusetts who thought his troops could mount a surprise attack on the Concord arsenal. On Saturday, April 15, he relieved his grenadiers and light infantry of regular duties for the purpose, he said, of practicing new exercises, but Gage fooled no one. "This I suppose is by way of a blind," the English lieutenant John Barker wrote in his diary. When a fleet of boats launched from the warships in Boston Harbor at midnight, the Boston silversmith and Son of Liberty Paul Revere—who was part of a self-assigned "alarm and muster" group—figured out what was happening, and the next morning he rode to Lexington to warn John Hancock and Samuel Adams, who were hiding there, that the British were about to strike.

At 10:00 p.m. on April 18, Gage assembled eight hundred regular troops on Boston Common in what he still assumed was a secret operation. At about the same time, men and women were working through the night to disperse the contents of the Concord arsenal, scattering the weaponry to caches in nearby towns—Acton, Stow, Harvard—and in wooded areas outside the town. Gage had sent Lieutenant Colonel Francis Smith marching orders that afternoon, but specific details about where the troops were to go and what exactly their mission was did not come until later.

At 11:00 p.m., British troops began quietly to board transports that shuttled them and their equipment across the Charles River to Cambridge. Gage now ordered Colonel Smith to take his twenty-one companies (about one-sixth of the total), seize the military stores at Concord, including powder, balls, and muskets, and destroy any cannon they found. The soldiers should stuff their pockets with musket balls and then scatter them one handful at a time in ponds along their route back to Boston, being careful not to deposit so many in any one place that the locals could recover them easily.

As the river crossing proceeded, two lanterns appeared in the steeple of Boston's Old North Church—the prearranged signal that the British would be advancing toward Lexington by sea—and Paul Revere and William Dawes began their midnight rides to sound the alarm. As they rode, they told other patrols the news, and soon the whole countryside was aware of the British moves. Already two hours behind schedule, the British soldiers marched through the night, unnerved by the pealing of church bells and firing of signal guns that announced their progress. Colonel Smith now knew that he had lost what he had never had—the element of surprise—and he sent a messenger to Gage to request reinforcements.

At about 2:00 a.m. on April 19, about 130 Minutemen assembled on the village green in Lexington under the command of Captain John Parker, a veteran of the French and Indian War. The men, tired of standing in the dark and cold, disbanded, some to home and others to the nearby Buckman Tavern for some warming rum. At about sunrise, a scout returned with the news that the British forces were getting close. Sam Adams and Hancock rode off swiftly to a new hiding place, while about seventy men, half of the town's male populace, assembled in a double file. Parker had received word that fifteen hundred men (twice as many as Gage had actually sent off) were marching across Middlesex County with Concord as their goal, just six or seven miles down the road from Lexington. Again he gave the command to "let the troops pass by, and don't molest them, without they begin first." They were to stand as an "army of observation," witnessing the passage of the British troops but not engaging them. If Parker's men had intended to fight, they would have hidden behind walls or fired from the forest; it would be suicidal to stand on the town green and shoot at passing troops. About forty unarmed spectators were also on the common, waiting to see the soldiers parade past on their way to Concord.

Lexington was a town of one hundred families, 750 souls, 5 of whom were slaves, 200 of whom were adult white men between the ages of sixteen and sixty-five and thus obliged to serve in the militia. Jonas Parker, a cousin of John Parker and, at age sixty-two, the oldest militia-man, had fought in New England's great victory at Louisbourg in 1745. Altogether about forty of them had fought in the 1740s and 1750s at Louisbourg, at Quebec, and/or in Pontiac's War.

In the town of Lincoln, only four miles short of Concord, Colonel Smith's men managed to capture Paul Revere, and he told them to expect between five hundred and one thousand Minutemen to be waiting for them in Lexington. Revere's exaggeration, which another captive confirmed, had the British on high alert, expecting to be attacked. Major John Pitcairn ordered his advance contingent to prime their weapons before entering the town but, like the militia commander, "on no account to fire, nor even to attempt it without Orders."

When he arrived in Lexington, Major Pitcairn rode behind the American lines and ordered the militiamen to drop their weapons. No one did. But Captain Parker told his men to disperse, and some of them did. What happened next is unclear. Who fired first? Did someone actually fire at someone else, or did someone, somewhere, accidentally or in warning fire into the air? According to Parker, the British troops "made their appearance, and rushing furiously on, fired upon and killed eight of our party, without receiving any provocation therefore from us." Pitcairn insisted that he saw two hundred armed men (the actual number was seventy) and a flash from behind a wall, followed by several shots coming from the direction of the town, and only then did his soldiers fire a volley. He also maintained that no British officer ordered the men to fire.

Whether they started it or not, Pitcairn's men now panicked, lost their discipline, and were unresponsive to commands. Lieutenant Barker claimed that his men were "so wild" that "they cou'd hear no orders," continuing to reload and fire after he raised his sword as a signal to cease firing. Of the eight Americans dead, most were shot in the back. Jonas Parker, who had survived Louisbourg, was shot and then killed with a bayonet. Nine other Americans were wounded. The British then marched out of Lexington and on to Concord, giving a victory salute as they left. Later that morning, Captain Parker also marched his militia west to help in the defense of Concord.

Meanwhile, Concord had prepared for an attack, and, as the news spread that the British were on the march, other militia units converged on the town from near and far. Minutemen came from Worcester and Hampshire Counties, from as close by as Acton and Bedford, and from as far away as New Ipswich, New Hampshire. At sunrise, about 150 armed men were on Concord common. A report arrived from Lexington shortly before 7:00 a.m., but it was unclear whether there had been casualties. The decision was made for 250 militiamen to march toward Lexington and meet the British troops on the road. When they did meet, however, the Americans turned back toward Concord playing fifes and drums at the head of the eight hundred British troops, also accompanied by martial music. At about 8:00 a.m. the British finally arrived at Concord square.

The British found the town almost deserted, for the militiamen had retreated to some high ground beyond the town center, then to another hill above the North Bridge, about a mile away but "where we could see and hear what was going on." The grenadiers began their assigned tasks, breaking open and dumping sixty barrels of flour that could have been used to feed an army, throwing five hundred pounds of musket balls into the millpond, destroying the jail yard cannon the militia had left behind, and searching for any other munitions (there were none).* The soldiers ignored orders against looting, instead stealing everything from a gilt-lettered Bible to saddles, shoes, silver buttons, and an ax. They made a bonfire of Concord's liberty pole, which its citizens had constructed the previous October in imitation of Boston's Liberty Tree; from the pole they flew a flag with a pine tree emblem, a symbol of liberty New Englanders had adopted.

The four hundred men on the hill overlooking the North Bridge formed a unified brigade of militia companies from Concord, Bedford, Lincoln, Acton, and Carlisle, along with individuals from other towns, all under the command of Colonel James Barrett. When they saw the smoke rising from the bonfire on the other side of the river, they believed the British were burning down the town, so Colonel Barrett ordered them to advance to the village center. The British had only twenty-eight light infantrymen defending the North Bridge, so the militiamen were able to force them back across the river, where they joined others in a force of about one hundred total. Although it is not clear who fired first, Captain Walter Laurie, commanding the British soldiers at the bridge, gave the order to fire and believed that one of his men fired first. Two militiamen fell dead and two British soldiers died from the return fire. The British then ran back in an undisciplined retreat. By now, the smoke from the bonfire had abated and the militiamen realized that it was just the liberty pole and not the town the British had burned, so they recrossed the bridge to attend to their dead and wounded.

One out of every twelve heads of Lexington's families had died on the green that morning. The British had looted Concord, but the fighting was at the bridge rather than in the town, and before the day was over, thirty-five hundred militiamen, as individuals or in companies of between ten and forty, took positions along the fifteen-mile stretch of road that connected Concord, Lexington, and Boston, making a gantlet the British would have to run on their return march. They had accomplished little of their mission, but they did start a war.

The four hundred militiamen who had attacked the British on the North Bridge had grown to five hundred with reinforcements from

---

* Local people recovered the musket balls from the pond, and much of the flour as well, before the barrels filled with water and soaked the contents.

other towns, and now the British in Concord had to face these men when they retraced their steps to Lexington. As Amos Barrett, one late-arriving militiaman, described the scene, the British "were waylaid and a great many killed. When I got there, a great many lay dead and the road was bloody."

The British—exhausted from their march through the night and their futile efforts to find and destroy the Concord arsenal—were now fired on from the forests and behind walls, from the side and the back. Running short of ammunition, energy, and discipline, the troops panicked and left their dead and wounded where they fell. Lieutenant William Sutherland, whose command the militiamen had routed at the North Bridge, took a ball in the shoulder and later accused the militiamen who harassed the return march of "making the cowardly disposition . . . to murder us all." They were "rascals" and "Concealed villains" to him, not farmers ably defending their homes. He was right that the militiamen lacked a coordinated strategy, organized command, or traditional military discipline. As one militiaman himself described the engagements on the Concord–Lexington road, "Each sought his own place and opportunity to attack and annoy the enemy from behind trees, rocks, fences, and buildings as seemed most convenient." Lieutenant Colonel Smith took a ball in the leg, dismounted lest he be a sitting duck for the snipers, and literally limped along with his retreating men. By the time the British reached Lexington, they were totally demoralized. According to Lieutenant Barker, "We must have laid down our arms or been picked off by the rebels at their pleasure."

Twelve hours earlier, Colonel Smith's request for reinforcements had reached Gage at Castle William, so he knew that his "secret" mission had failed in its secrecy even before the troops had crossed the Charles River the previous night. Immediately, he assigned a force twice as large as Smith's, which included three regiments of infantry, a battalion of marines, and a detachment of Royal Artillery and its field pieces, to embark at 4:00 a.m. If the brigade, under the command of Lord Percy, had actually left Boston then, it would have reached Concord by 10:00 a.m., in plenty of time to play a decisive role in the day's events, including the battle at the North Bridge. Instead, after a comedy of incompetence, miscommunication, and delays, it reached Lexington at about 2:30 p.m., too late to do anything except assist in the retreat.

It was about 8:00 in the evening by the time what was left of the British force made it back to Boston. At the end of that very long night and day, 73 British soldiers were dead, another 174 wounded, and 26 missing, a loss rate of about 20 percent. Forty-nine Americans had died, thirty-nine were wounded, and five were missing—altogether about 2.5 percent of the militia who participated in the fighting. Lord Percy, at least, grasped the situation as more than a bungled mission, which it surely was:

> Whoever looks upon them as an irregular mob, will find himself much mistaken; they have men amongst them who know very well what they are about, having been employed as rangers against the Indians and Canadians, and this country being much covered with wood and hilly, is very advantageous for their method of fighting . . . You may depend upon it, that as the rebels have now had time to prepare, they are determined to go through with it, nor will the insurrection here turn out so despicable as it is perhaps imagined at home.

Percy was right all around. The colonists were now "rebels." The intercolonial movement to form a new nation was now full-grown where there had not been one before. General Gage's troops had started a war. And now many Americans would settle for nothing less than separation from the British Empire, and more were joining the ranks daily.

When Franklin arrived back in Philadelphia on May 5, he was still steaming about Lord Sandwich's speech in the House of Lords concerning the cowardice of New Englanders, but apparently he did not yet know about Parliament's votes on the fisheries and trade acts. The next day, he wrote to his friend David Hartley in London, "I arrived here last Night, and have the Pleasure to learn that there is the most perfect Unanimity throughout the Colonies; and that even N York, on whose Defection the ministry so confidently rely'd, is as hearty and zealous as any of the rest." His friend the Philadelphian Joseph Galloway had already decided to withdraw from politics, since he believed that the prominent political men of Pennsylvania no longer sought reconciliation with England. During a reunion that brought together Franklin's son William, governor of New Jersey, with William's own son William Temple Franklin and Galloway, Franklin spoke passionately about the corruption of British politics, assured them all that the colonies would prevail, and, according to Thomas Hutchinson, who heard the story from Joseph Galloway, "declared in favour of measures for attaining to Independence."

On May 8, Franklin wrote again to Hartley in London: "You will have heard before this reaches you of the Commencement of a Civil War; the End of it perhaps neither myself, nor you, who are much younger, may live to see. I find here all Ranks of People in Arms, disciplining themselves Morning and Evening, and am informed that the firmest Union prevails through North America." He did not mention that Pennsylvania had elected him on the day after his return as a delegate to the Second Continental Congress, which would convene the following week. Everything had changed over the past few months, and Franklin arrived just in time and in exactly the right mood to help lead a movement he would not have supported six months earlier.

17

✦

REVOLUTION

HE REVOLUTION THAT JOHN ADAMS DESCRIBED was over for some Americans by May 1775, and the debate was now about separation from Britain. This is not to say that the story was finished, the outcome certain, or the path forward clear—on the contrary. But there was now an open and acknowledged movement to secure independence from the empire. The description of the Americans as "rebels" who wanted separation, which is how some British politicians had characterized them collectively for more than a century, was now an accurate depiction of many, but far from all, of them. As Americans united over the next three years first in a movement and then to fight a war that had already begun, never more than 45 percent of whites actively supported the cause.

On May 10, 1775, two hundred and forty men from Connecticut and Massachusetts under the joint command of Ethan Allen, a farmer and land speculator originally from Connecticut, who had interests in the New Hampshire Grants, and Benedict Arnold, a Connecticut merchant, attacked Fort Ticonderoga while the garrison slept.* They took one hundred prisoners without a shot fired and confiscated the fortress's cache of weapons—one hundred cannons, several mortars, and

---

* The New Hampshire Grants, made by Governor Benning Wentworth between 1749 and 1764, concerned territory west of the Connecticut River claimed by both New Hampshire and New York. The dispute eventually led to the creation of the Vermont Republic in 1777, which was recognized as the fourteenth state in 1791.

a considerable quantity of shot, stores, and gunpowder. The next day the band took Crown Point, where they collected ordnance and stores, which included "two hundred pieces of cannon, three mortars, sundry howitzers, and fifty swivels, etc." From Ticonderoga on June 4, after Canadians had fired on a reconnaissance party he had sent out, Allen addressed a letter to the inhabitants of Montreal: "You are very sensible that war has already commenced between England and the Colonies. Hostilities have already begun; to fight with the King's Troops has become a necessary and incumbent duty; the colonies cannot avoid it. But pray, is it necessary that the Canadians and the inhabitants of the English Colonies should butcher one another? God forbid."

When the Second Continental Congress convened on May 10—the same day as the attack on Ticonderoga—popular enthusiasm for fighting a war against Great Britain was at a peak it would never reach again. The debate within and without the Congress was about the goals of the war—whether it would be purely defensive, an effort to recover rights and reconcile with England on the terms the first Congress had proposed, or whether it would be a war for independence from the empire. A significant body of colonists opposed both these options, but the tide had turned on the question of independence, and it left the estimated 20 percent who were Loyalists and 30 percent who were neutrals caught in the undertow. On May 16, Joseph Warren wrote to Arthur Lee in London: "The patience which I frequently told you would be at last exhausted, is no longer to be expected from us. Danger and war are become pleasing; and injured virtue is now armed to avenge herself." A committee in Tryon County, New York, wrote to the New York assembly, "It is our final resolution to support and carry into execution every thing recommended by the Continental Congress, *and to be free or die.*"

During May, General Gage's beleaguered troops in Boston received six thousand reinforcements, along with three generals new to Massachusetts: William Howe, John Burgoyne, and Henry Clinton. On June 12, Gage completed the British plans to break out of the city, now being besieged by American troops, and take the hills surrounding it. But on June 15, having learned of these plans, the Massachusetts Committee of Safety ordered men to the defense of the Charlestown peninsula directly north of the center of the city. The next day, William Prescott led twelve hundred militiamen onto the peninsula and began building a defensive position on one of its hills from which artillery fire or bombardment could reach British soldiers in Boston.

The following morning, June 17, British warships began shelling the American position. At about 3:00 p.m., General Howe led the principal assault on Bunker and Breed's Hills. After two unsuccessful charges, Howe took the two hills when the Americans ran out of ammunition. By the end of the afternoon, the British were in control of Charlestown, but they had taken heavy casualties, amounting to about one-third of the deployed forces—226 dead and 828 wounded. American casualties, mostly incurred during their retreat, were much lighter—140 dead, 271 wounded, and 30 captured. But loss of the hills was of little strategic significance to their siege of the city, and they regrouped after the retreat. The British "victory"—their capture of Bunker Hill—on the other hand, was devastating, reducing the British army in Boston to prereinforcement strength, shattering the troops' morale, and resulting in the loss of more officers than the British were to lose during the rest of the eight-year war. If belief in the invincibility of British forces was mortally wounded at Lexington and Concord in April, it died at Bunker and Breed's Hills in June. When General Gage's report on the fiasco at Lexington and Concord reached London on July 20, it hardened King George against the Americans and led him to dismiss Gage from his command three days later. News of this, and of Gage's replacement by Howe, did not arrive in Boston until October.

In Virginia, the colonists felt threatened by these aggressive British actions in Massachusetts. They had economic interests to protect, but they feared most the possibility of an insurrection, either under cover of war or actually instigated by the British, among the 180,000 Virginians who were slaves—about 40 percent of the colony's total population. There had been a slave rebellion in Georgia in December 1774, and New Yorkers had learned of a planned insurrection in March 1775. Rumors had spread for a year that Parliament was considering a slave emancipation bill to stanch the revolutionary movement among the Southern planters. In April, when Virginians discovered slaves plotting rebellion in five different counties, they assumed the worst: that the plans were a coordinated effort.

On April 21, Governor Dunmore confiscated the gunpowder from the magazine in Williamsburg and had it removed to a British ship in the James River in order to keep it from rebels. The next day, he sent a note to Peyton Randolph, the Speaker of the House of Burgesses, warning that if there were a revolt against his government, he "would declare freedom to the slaves and reduce the City of Wmsburg to ashes." Virginians quickly learned that Gage's troops were attacking the arsenal at Concord at the same time, and they diagnosed a plot hatched by the British in London that Gage and Dunmore had set in coordinated motion. The threat, the seizure of the gunpowder, the fears of slave and Indian rebellions, and the battles at Lexington and Concord—all these impelled white Virginians and others in the South toward independence.

On May 2, the Hanover County militia, under Patrick Henry, voted to attack the governor's palace in Williamsburg in order to reclaim the gunpowder, and the next day the governor issued a proclamation reminding Virginians of their vulnerability to Indian and slave uprisings—which he intended, and Virginians interpreted, as a lightly veiled threat. But as Henry's militia closed in on Williamsburg, a settlement was negotiated that paid the colonists for the seized gunpowder, which, however, remained on the *Magdalen*. Commentators at the time noted that this settlement averted the first armed attack by Virginians on the royal governor since Bacon's Rebellion a century earlier.

Relations between the House of Burgesses and Governor Dunmore did not improve, however, and on June 8, Dunmore and his family fled Williamsburg out of fear for their lives and found refuge on the gunship HMS *Fowey*, anchored in the York River. During the summer, British troops at Dunmore's direction raided plantations along the rivers that belonged to rebels, and slaves ran away in increasing numbers. Emissaries from Lord Dunmore made overtures to Ohio Valley Indians, who were still trying to organize a regional confederacy, assuring them that "the Virginians would take the whole Country if they did not all join together against them." Tensions continued to mount.

On November 14, Governor Dunmore with a force composed largely of escaped slaves defeated three hundred Princess Anne County militiamen in an engagement south of Norfolk; three men were killed, and the militiamen were scattered. The governor immediately read out a proclamation that declared "all indented Servants, Negroes, or others . . . free that are able and willing to bear Arms, they joining His Majesty's Troops as soon as may be." In response, about a thousand slaves escaped from various plantations and joined his army. At about the same time, white Virginians learned that Dunmore was negotiating with Ohio Valley Indians to organize an attack on backcountry settlers. According to Richard Henry Lee, "Lord Dunmore's unparalleled conduct in Virginia has, a few Scotch excepted, united every man in that large Colony."

By now Virginia's slaveholding gentry, so deeply involved in the efforts to oppose Lord Dunmore, were also concerned about threats to white solidarity. Smallholders and tenants were not pleased by the gentry's efforts to control the militias, in which enlisted men had always elected their own officers, and even to replace them with paid Minuteman units that had regular enlistments, conventional military discipline, and appointed officers (whose pay would be eleven times that of the enlisted men). Men who owned more than three slaves or paid more than three workers would be exempt from this military service. Naturally such plans raised questions about equity of sacrifice and the patriotism of Virginia's richest residents. There were also salt riots in early December, as the cutoff of trade had its impact on the populace. Virginia's elites began to push for independence for many reasons, one being their belief that only with a declaration of independence could they form a state government and begin negotiations to trade again with Europe; they needed arms, and they needed to relieve the considerable unrest provoked by shortages of food and other items.

During the increasingly harsh economic times brought on by the trade boycott, antagonism between Virginia's landlords and tenants also worsened, as landlords tried to keep from being paid in depreciated currency. Richard Henry Lee and George Washington were among the landlords who demanded rent payments in silver coins or enough paper money to purchase the coin that would meet rental contracts. In Loudoun County, tenants threatened with eviction went on a rent strike before the end of the year. The fear of greater disorder encouraged landlords to push for Virginia's independence from Britain, which, they hoped, would bring economic dislocation and class-based disorder to an end—even if a short war preceded it. Francis Lightfoot Lee advocated an independent government to "put a stop to the rising disorders with you, and secure internal quiet for the future."

The Second Continental Congress was not, therefore, leading an independence movement but trying to keep up with one. Its declaration that the colonists should maintain a defensive stance came after the attack on Fort Ticonderoga but before news of it reached Philadelphia; while it was meeting, colonists from Pennsylvania and Connecticut were shooting at each other over land claims in the Wyoming Valley. And at about the same time Virginia officials jailed Pennsylvanians in the dispute those two colonies had over the Fort Pitt area, while conflict among speculators in the Kentucky region continued as well.

The pace of decision making quickened. On May 25, the Continental Congress advised the New York assembly to enlist militia for an anticipated defense of New York City; two days later, it appointed a committee to purchase military supplies. On June 3, it voted to borrow £6,000 sterling to buy gunpowder. On June 14, it voted to form a "continental army" and the following day appointed George Washington its commander. It was still lagging behind events, but it did vote on June 22, when it received news of the Battle of Bunker Hill, to issue $2 million in paper money to finance the army. Washington left the next day to take up his command in Massachusetts.

Creating an army was not, in the minds of many Americans, an unalterable commitment to separating from Great Britain. In July 1775, even Thomas Paine expressed support for a "Defensive War," publishing "Thoughts" on that subject in the *Pennsylvania Magazine*: "As the union between spiritual freedom and political liberty seems nearly inseparable, it is our duty to defend both. And defence in the first instance is best. The lives of hundreds of both countries had been preserved had America been in arms a year ago. Our enemies have mistaken our peace for cowardice, and supposing us unarmed have begun the attack."

In July, white North Carolinians believed they uncovered a slave conspiracy that stretched across three Tidewater counties. They suspected that British officials had coordinated the efforts and made commitments to the conspirators; the alleged plan was for the slaves to revolt on July 8, kill their owners, then move west to the backcountry, where "they were to be received with open arms by a number of Persons there appointed and armed by [the] Government for their Protection." The rumors fit the mind-set—so familiar in the backcountry—of alienation from their richer fellow colonists and allegiance to the British. They also fit the interests of slaveholders near the frontier, who would join the independence movement and fight against loyalist neighbors, reprising the interregional conflict of the Regulator movement.

In August, New York's governor Tryon, who had abandoned his post on the same June day when Washington passed through Manhattan on his way to Massachusetts, wrote to Lord Dartmouth: "Independency is shooting from the root of the present contest," but it would be a "great injustice to America were I to hold up an idea that the bulk of its inhabitants wishes an independency." He was probably right about most New Yorkers, and many still held out hope that the Continental Congress would not declare independence before Great Britain made an offer of reconciliation. Instead, though, the ministry and the king continued with policies that drove neutrals and many conservatives in the colonies to accept the logic of war. The more people who died, the higher the stakes, and the more obvious the choice of independence became, but the debate was far from over as 1776 began.

The Continental Congress, having at first been dubious about the merits of it, had authorized the first major military operation of the Continental Army in September 1775. The objective was the conquest of Quebec, since this large British-controlled province was deemed a constant danger to the colonies, and the operation was seen as the obvious continuation of what Benedict Arnold and Ethan Allen had accomplished over the summer. There were two prongs to the invasion: One group of militiamen left Fort Ticonderoga under Major General Richard Montgomery, an immigrant Irishman and former British officer, to lay siege to Fort St. John, an old French-built fort in New Brunswick, south of Montreal and directly north of Ticonderoga; the men took it and by mid-November had conquered Montreal. The second arm of the attack, under the command of Arnold, had a more difficult time—first sailing from Newburyport to the Kennebec River in Maine and then having to march and portage north across the uncharted Maine wilderness, losing many men in the process, to reach the St. Lawrence River. The forces under Montgomery and Ethan Allen met up with Arnold's group and together they assaulted Quebec City, which eighteen hundred men defended, during a snowstorm on December 31. Montgomery died in the battle and Allen was wounded in defeat. The Americans lost 60 dead and wounded and 426 captured; the British, only 6 killed and 19 wounded. And all of this before the colonists had declared independence and while many, if not most, of them still believed they could secure independence within the empire. Many of them still fought for their rights as Englishmen rather than for their independence as Americans, and they took the battle to the water as well as fighting on land.

With only twenty-six ships, Vice Admiral Samuel Graves, who had served in the failed expedition against Cartagena and was now commander of the Royal Navy's North American squadron, was charged to patrol the entire two-thousand-mile coastline from Nova Scotia to Florida. By the fall of 1775, he was frustrated by the role his command had played in combat thus far. On May 27 and 28, ships under Graves's command had been moving livestock and hay needed to supply British troops to islands in Boston Harbor. At what became known as the Battle of Chelsea Creek, in the mudflats northeast of Boston, the British lost the schooner *Diana* to the colonists in the first naval battle of what was fast becoming a full-scale war. In June, Graves dispatched the Royal Navy schooner *Margaretta* to defend merchant ships headed to Machias, in the district of Maine, to purchase building materials and other supplies. The people of the town seized the merchant vessels and the armed schooner, killing the *Margaretta*'s captain in the battle. During July, the colonists captured two more British schooners off the coast of Maine, the *Diligent* and the *Tatamagouche*, after first capturing their officers, who were onshore near Bucks Harbor.

By early October, Graves was prepared to retaliate for the humiliations by making examples of selected seaside towns in Maine that had been supporting the rebellious colonists in their resistance to British forces over the summer. He chose Lieutenant Henry Mowat to execute his plan. Graves explained:

> My design is to chastise Marblehead, Salem, Newbury Port, Cape Anne Harbour, Porstsmouth, Ipswich, Saco, Falmouth in Casco Bay, and particularly Mechias where the *Margaretta* was taken, the Officer commanding her killed, and the People made Prisoners, and where the *Diligent* Schooner was seized and the Officers and Crew carried Prisoners up the Country, and where preparations I am informed are now making to invade the Province of Nova Scotia.

In Falmouth, whose port was just a few miles north of what is now Portland, Maine, seamen had captured several British ships carrying supplies and weaponry in the spring. These actions had largely been perpetrated by militia from Brunswick and against the locals' wishes, but Falmouth now, unfairly, bore the heaviest burden of the reprisals. On October 8, Mowat's four British vessels, which had left Boston and followed the prevailing wind "down east," sailed toward Falmouth, whose harbor they reached on October 16. He gave the townspeople two hours to evacuate; the residents, who pleaded for mercy, failed to reach an accommodation with his forces, and Mowat began to shell the town on the morning of October 18, continuing the bombardment until 6:00 p.m. A landing party was sent ashore to set fire to any buildings that were still intact, while militia units from nearby communities looted the homes of Falmouth people who had evacuated their town. What had been a community of moderates eager to chart a middle path between the radicals farther inland and the Royal Navy emerged from the ashes of Falmouth's destruction as a radicalized group that supported the independence movement. Also, reports of the injustice done them recruited others along the coast of Maine to their cause, and the region was to serve as a base of operations for anti-British invasions of Quebec and Nova Scotia in the seasons to come.

On November 9, 1775, the Pennsylvania assembly instructed its delegates to the Continental Congress to "exert your utmost endeavours to agree upon and recommend such measures as you shall judge to afford the best prospect of obtaining redress of American grievances, and restoring that union and harmony between Great Britain and the Colonies, so essential to the welfare and happiness of both Countries." For the assemblymen, the ambition for reconciliation with Britain was utterly consistent with waging war against its soldiers: "Though the oppressive measures of the British Parliament and Administration have compelled us to resist their violence by force of arms, yet we strictly enjoin you, that you, in behalf of this Colony, dissent from and utterly reject any propositions, should such be made, that may cause or lead to a separation from our Mother Country, or a change of the form of this Government." Even later, on January 5, 1776, when the assembly of New Hampshire declared itself a house of representatives and elected a council in contravention of its charter, it maintained that "we never sought to throw off our dependence upon Great Britain" and that it would "rejoice" at news of reconciliation. Delaware, New Jersey, and Maryland also instructed their delegates against independence.

Over the fall of 1775, Thomas Paine drafted *Common Sense*, which was published in January 1776. Although he allowed that "the sentiments contained in the following pages, are not *yet* sufficiently fashionable to procure them general favor," he plunged ahead with an advocacy of independence that many Americans already supported. No longer did he recommend a defensive posture to his readers; he offered those who were unsure a challenge, and he coupled it with insults: "I challenge the warmest advocate for reconciliation, to shew, a single advantage that this continent can reap, by being connected with great Britain. I repeat the challenge, not a single advantage is derived."

Paine prefaced his most incendiary attack on moderates with an assertion that he "would carefully avoid giving unnecessary offence," then he delivered the insults:

> I am inclined to believe, that all those who espouse the doctrine of reconciliation, may be included within the following descriptions. Interested men, who are not to be trusted; weak men, who *cannot* see; prejudiced men, who *will not* see; and a certain set of moderate men, who think better of the European world than it deserves; and this last class, by an ill-judged deliberation, will be the cause of more calamities to this continent, than all the other three.

Through twenty-five early printings and perhaps fifty thousand copies, Paine's *Common Sense* pushed countless thousands to see the illogic of fighting a war to reconcile with the past rather than to seize the future.* Charles Lee, a British soldier who had fought in North America during the French and Indian War and then moved to Virginia in 1773, found it "a masterly, irresistible performance" that convinced him to support American independence. From New York, Samuel Cooper reported, "It is eagerly read and greatly admired here."

---

* Harriet Beecher Stowe's *Uncle Tom's Cabin* (1852) was the first American publication to surpass *Common Sense* in sales.

Even the cynical John Adams, in assessing the pamphlet's reception, said that Paine's "Sentiments of the Abilities of America, and of the Difficulty of a Reconciliation with G.B. are generally approved."

In February 1776, the House of Commons approved treaties to hire about seventeen thousand German mercenaries to fight in "the American war," by a vote of 242–88. That same month, it rejected a motion introduced by Charles James Fox, the antislavery reformer, to appoint a parliamentary committee "for inquiring into the ill-success of the King's arms in America" by a vote of 240–104. At the same time, news of the Prohibitory Act, adopted by Parliament the previous December, reached America. Its provisions extended the Boston Port Act to all the rebellious colonies, closed off all commerce with them until the colonies submitted, and authorized the king to appoint commissions to whom the colonies could submit. All vessels and cargoes owned by Americans were forfeit to the Crown, "as if the same were the ships and effects of open enemies." John Adams called it "an act of independency."

By February 1776, Adams had committed to the idea of American independence and was frustrated by those who had not. To Abigail he wrote,

> reconciliation if practicable and Peace if attainable, you very well know would be as agreeable to my Inclinations and as advantageous to my Interest, as to any Man's. But I see no Prospect, no Probability, no Possibility. And I cannot but despise the Understanding, which sincerely expects an honourable Peace, for its Credulity, and detest the hypocritical Heart, which pretends to expect it, when in Truth it does not.

In the same month, Adams included a "Declaration of Independency" in a memorandum proposing an agenda for the Continental Congress.

In March, the British evacuated Boston, and General Washington moved his command to New York to prepare for a British invasion. In the Congress, heated debate continued on the goals of the ongoing war. "Jealousies, ill-natured observations and recriminations take [the] place of reason and argument," wrote Joseph Hewes of North Carolina, who was still opposed to independence. Charles Lee, the former British officer now stationed in New York with Washington's army, believed that "reconciliation and reunion with Great Britain is now as much of a chimera as incorporation with the people of Tibet."

In mid-April, John Adams claimed he was in no hurry for the Continental Congress to declare independence, writing to Abigail, "as to Declarations of Independency, be patient." Later that same month, though, in a letter to Joseph Warren in Massachusetts, he declared the time ripe:

> if you are so unanimous, in the Measure of Independency and wish for a Declaration of it, now is the proper Time for you to instruct your Delegates to that Effect. It would have been productive of Jealousies perhaps and Animosities, a few Months ago, but would have a contrary Tendency now. The Colonies are all at this Moment turning their Eyes, that Way. Vast Majorities in all the Colonies now see the Propriety and Necessity of taking the decisive Steps, and those who are averse to it are afraid to Say much against it.

On April 12, North Carolina's assembly voted to support independence while the Continental Congress went on debating. John Adams wrote from Philadelphia, "We continue still between hawk and buzzard. Some people yet expect commissioners, to treat with Congress, and to offer a Chart Blanc." Less than two weeks later, Franklin noted that "there is a rapid increase of the formerly small party, who were for an independent government."

On May 4, Rhode Island's assembly declared the colony independent. Virginia's convention did the same two days later. Richard Henry Lee wrote back home to Virginia that even the more politically conservative Middle Colonies "are going fast into Independency and constituting new Governmts. Convinced of the necessity of it, both for the security of internal peace and good order; and for the vigorous exertion of their whole force against the common Enemy." From Prince William County, Virginia, William Aylett wrote in late April, "The people of this County almost unanimously cry aloud for independance."

On June 14, the Connecticut assembly voted to instruct its delegates to the Continental Congress to support independence, as did New Hampshire and Delaware on June 15, a Pennsylvania conference that replaced its assembly on June 18, and New Jersey's assembly on

June 22. By June 25, only Maryland and New York had yet to act. Maryland finally joined the call for independence on June 28. On July 3, General Howe and his forces from Massachusetts landed on Staten Island. This invasion of New York left its delegates to the Continental Congress powerless to vote yes or no on independence, when the question came before it in the first days of July, so they abstained. Between April and July 4, more than ninety declarations of independence of various sorts and from various sources came to the Continental Congress, itself still lagging behind yet still eager to build a consensus that included all the colonies.

The Declaration of Independence, which some moderates had tried to block for the previous year, clarified the ambitions embodied in its name:

> When in the course of human events it becomes necessary for one people to dissolve the political bands which have connected them with another, and to assume among the powers of the earth the separate and equal station to which the laws of nature and of nature's god entitle them, a decent respect to the opinions of mankind requires that they should declare the causes which impel them to the separation.

Now, for all of the world to see, American independence was a unified effort among the colonies that could be realized only in a separation from the British Empire. John Adams's revolution was complete.

CONCLUSION

T HE TEA ACT AND THE BOSTON TEA PARTY, the arrival in America of the news of the Intolerable Acts, the responding call for the First Continental Congress, and the British seizure of gunpowder from the arsenal at Cambridge were watershed moments in the evolution of Americans' ideas about independence. The closing of the Newfoundland and Labrador fisheries, the threats made to the charters of Connecticut and Rhode Island, the decision to reinforce General Gage's troops, and the Battles of Lexington and Concord, of Bunker and Breed's Hills completed the evolution. Some of these events were larger than others—the Intolerable Acts and unprovoked killings at Lexington were decisive, but they occurred in a large context that gave them broad meanings. There could be no writing off such episodes to human error, corrupt ministers, or short-term political miscalculations. To patriotic colonists, the events of 1773–1775 were of a piece, and they saw a pattern they were powerless to reverse from within the empire.

The episodes had precursors, for the imperial relationship had a history of conflict that had bred distrust on both sides. Earlier conflicts had produced a historical record and a perceived pattern. Colonists saw a "train of abuses": the Navigation Acts, the customs racketeering, the use of admiralty courts, the White Pines Acts, the restoration of Louisbourg to France, the Proclamation Line of 1763, British policy on the international slave trade, the rumored appointment of an Anglican bishop for the colonies, the assertion of the royal prerogative, taxes, the Boston Massacre, and the suspending of rights they deemed inalienable.

Likewise, in Britain, both king and Parliament, ministers and the public knew of what they considered a sorry record in the American colonies: their seditious behavior at the time of the Glorious Revolution; a
string of isolated rebellions; their opposition to the imperial authority
of governors, indeed their armed resistance to most forms of authority;
their smuggling and poaching; their refusal to pay taxes and fees; the
violent opposition to the Stamp Act and the Townshend Duties, to
royal officials and to the British army and navy—these too painted a
consistent picture.

Resistance had not led to a war for independence during the century preceding 1775 for a number of reasons. The demography, economy, and geographical spread of the North American colonies would
not have sustained such a war or even inspired an ambition for one
among the colonists. On the other side, the British Empire was strapped
for resources, otherwise occupied by European wars, and more loosely
administered before it included India and Canada; indeed, the presence of France in Canada prior to 1763 was a brake on all parties to the
imperial conflict. Then, too, social conditions had changed fundamentally in the colonies by the mid-eighteenth century while the flash
points of conflict remained, now under new conditions that put pressure on both sides. And the inability to resolve any of the systemic tensions created an environment in which new conditions, personalities,
and ideological triggers exacerbated stress. Neither side could see its
interests as recommending compromise in 1775, but both would have
done so had they seen a clear path before 1750 or even 1770.

The American Revolution was inextricably connected to conflicts
going on within the colonies, between colonies, and among colonists.
The growth of American cities and towns, the stratification of wealth
within them as well as colony-wide competition for land, unemployment, the lack of ethnic homogeneity, conflicts with Indians, and the
reliance on slave labor—all these made for tensions and bellicose behavior. So did conflicts over natural resources between regions, between
competing interests, and over the provision of institutional resources.
And this is not to mention the realities of political corruption, debt,
and unsustainable economies. Together these made for an environment conducive to war, and one that provided enough impoverished
men to form an army, men who would risk their lives in battling for
their dreams and even in support of the interests of those who owned

property, businesses, and homes—as in all wars, those who did most of the dying had the least and had the least to gain.

Thus it was not only events in 1774 and 1775 that caused the American Revolution. There were many causes, rooted in history, economic self-interest, fear, internal conflict, and unsettling social change. There were also the fixed, inflexible ideological positions held by political elites on both sides of the Atlantic. Individuals did not cause a war, and no one led the Americans into war. Great Britain lost an empire and began to rebuild a different, perhaps more valuable one, while continuing some of its economic relationships with North America and building others.

The war for American independence promised resolution after a century that had brought none. Americans expressed what they hoped for when they took sides, much as they had in previous contests— backcountry North Carolinians versus merchants and Tidewater slave owners; squatters and tenants against landlords in western Pennsylvania, Maine, New Jersey, and the Hudson Valley; frontiersmen against Indians, the Revolution being simply an occasion to fight the Indians again. But it was not always simple, or the sides and ambitions clear. Sailors fought against the Royal Navy, slaves against masters where they dared and the opportunity presented itself, and the urban poor fought for a better life and full employment. Settlers in Concord and all the New England villages that were kin to it, and other rural villages in other colonies, fought to recover a sense of community that they felt was slipping away from them; evangelical Dissenters in Virginia and the Carolinas fought for greater religious freedom and a stronger voice in state government and local affairs.

Whichever side they were on, and for whatever reasons, the Americans who created an independent nation in 1775–1776 eventually won the war, but the more ambitious and complex social and personal goals were elusive. Some slaves became independent, but most did not; many Indians lost their independence, whichever side they fought on or whether they sat out the war; the poor remained poor for the most part, and those at the top of American society generally stayed there if they had chosen the winning Patriot side and in some cases even when they had not. America's society was already in the process of democratizing before the war and people were already moving west; independence accelerated some of these processes and set others in motion. Even women and children were becoming more independent, for the war offered them new opportunities, some of them unwelcome and some embraced gladly by wives and mothers. It was already a nation of immigrants and only became more so. Slavery had planted seeds of disunion, which the nation and racism survived.

Because General Howe failed to capture George Washington on Long Island and at Brooklyn Heights in August 1776 and the British were unable to pursue their victories, the war did not bring about an early debacle for the Revolutionaries as the British had anticipated. The Americans' victory at Trenton in December 1776 enabled them to keep an army in the field for another year, and their victory at Saratoga in 1777 soon led the French to invest in the independence movement, which made it possible for the Americans to continue the war for another five years, until the British found it impossible to sustain hostilities across an ocean and a vast continent.

Americans did not win separation from the British Empire, but they declared their independence in 1776, as they had been doing individually and collectively for the previous 170 years. The battle for hearts and minds did not end with the Declaration of Independence, nor would it with victory, the peace treaty, or the new Constitution that embodied both the new nation's principles and flaws. Americans continue to seek the independence at the core of our culture. It remains the lodestone of our politics, our ideology, and our wish for the rest of the world, and it is an anchor that inhibits our ability to define community broadly and generously. It is who we are and what we are—a link to our past, a defining feature of our present, and our legacy for the future.

SOURCES

The bibliography on the American Revolution, even the slice of it that this book is about, is endless. My interpretation is informed by reading, discussions with audiences and colleagues who share common interests, classes I took as a graduate and undergraduate student, and teaching the subject to undergraduates and graduate students over the past thirty years. During that time, I have absorbed and recast much of what I have read and discussed with others, and my intellectual debts are grand. Given the intended audience for this book, I have adopted the traditional form of a bibliography of sources that are specifically and consciously relevant to my arguments. As we know, the footnote is a beleaguered genre in our Internet world, one in which you can google keywords from a quotation to identify its source.

The grand synthesis has gone out of fashion among academic historians, as the profession has specialized just as others have. GPs are increasingly rare in every field. This trend has affected the historiography on the American Revolution in two ways. Most books by academic historians over the last three decades are either short syntheses intended for students or are unifocal. The latter include books on ideas, ideology, economics, cities, sailors, Indians, women, slavery, land speculation, immigration, the Atlantic world, *or* constitutional history. There are books on individual colonies, Loyalists, religion, riots, *or* market culture. These are good, some excellent, some even brilliant, so the fact that they are unifocal or unicausal reflects the professional trends in the larger culture.

We have monographs, building blocks for syntheses, but not so many syntheses. These topical histories have hugely enriched our understanding of the Revolutionary era, taking us well past the traditional perspectives of biographers, imperial and institutional historians, and those who write about politics narrowly construed. Again, this is not to criticize either the new or traditional history but to observe the trend and its consequences. The syntheses have tended to ignore either the new histories or the traditional perspectives.

The bibliography lists the books that have been most useful to me in my focused synthesis. The journal literature is too vast to contain in the bibliography, so I refer you to Jack P. Greene and J. R. Pole, *Companion to the American Revolution*, and Daniel Vickers, *Companion to Colonial America*, for the bibliographies and synthetic articles, and to the essay collections in my bibliography.

The primary sources on the subjects and events addressed in this book are, of course, much more numerous than the monographs and journal literature, and I have relied on the heroic work done by documentary editors over the past two centuries in addition to the digital databases of pamphlets and newspapers. These published primary sources are listed in the bibliography. The full texts of American newspapers from 1690 are available in digitized form (photographic images of the original) in *America's Historical Newspapers*, which includes *Early American Newspapers* [infoweb.newsbank.com]. Quotations from books published in England, c.1475–1661, are available in digitized form in *Early English Books Online (EEBO)* [eebo.chadwyck.com]. Books, pamphlets, sermons, and broadsides published in the Anglo-American colonies and the United States can be located by date, city, or keyword in *America's Historical Imprints*, Early American Imprints, Series I: Evans, 1639–1800, and its supplement from the Library Company of Philadelphia, 1670–1800 [www.newsbank.com]. Titles published in England during the eighteenth century are becoming available in digitized form in *Eighteenth Century Collections Online (ECCO)* [gdc.gale.com].

PUBLISHED PRIMARY SOURCES

Abbot, W. W., et al., eds. *The Papers of George Washington, Colonial Series*. Vol. 1. Charlottesville: University Press of Virginia, 1983.

Adams, Thomas R. *The American Controversy: A Bibliographical Study of the British Pamphlets About the American Disputes, 1764–1783*. Providence: Brown University Press, 1980.

American Archives: Fourth Series. 6 vols. Washington, D.C., 1837–1846.

American Weekly Mercury.

Amicus Patria [Samuel Adams?]. *An address to the Inhabitants of the Province of the Massachusetts-Bay in New-England*. Boston, 1747.

Andrews, Charles M., ed. *Narratives of the Insurrections, 1675–1690*. New York: Scribner, 1915.

An Interesting Appendix to Sir William Blackstone's Commentaries on the Laws of England. Philadelphia, 1773.

Anonymous. *An Address to His Excellency Sir Charles Hardy*. New York, 1755.

———. *A Letter to the Right Honourable the Earl of Hillsborough, on the Present Situation of Affairs in America*. Boston, 1769.

Archives of Maryland. Vol. 5, *Proceedings of the Council of Maryland, 1667–1687/8*, and Vol. 8, *Proceedings of the Council of Maryland, 1687/8–1693*. Baltimore, 1887 and 1890.

Bailyn, Bernard. *Pamphlets of the American Revolution, 1750–1776.* Vol. 1, *1750–1765.* Cambridge, MA: Harvard University Press, 1965.

Bancroft, Edward. *Remarks on the Review of the Controversy Between Great Britain and Her Colonies.* New London, CT, 1771.

Batchellor, Albert Stillman, ed. *Miscellaneous Revolutionary Documents of New Hampshire.* State and Provincial Papers, vol. 30. Manchester, NH, 1910.

Bates, William. *The Harmony of the Divine Attributes.* Wilmington, DE, 1771.

Baxter, James Phinney, ed. *Documentary History of the State of Maine.* Vol. 14, *Containing the Baxter Manuscripts.* Portland, ME, 1910.

Blackstone, William. *Commentaries on the Laws of England.* 4 vols. Philadelphia, 1771.

Bland, Richard. *A Letter to the Clergy of Virginia.* Williamsburg, 1760.

———. *An Inquiry Into the Rights of the British Colonies.* Philadelphia, 1766.

Bolingbroke, Henry St. John. *The Freeholder's Political Catechism.* Boston, 1757.

Boston Gazette.

Bowler, Charles. *Reflections on the Conduct and Principles of the Quakers in North-America.* Newport, RI, 1758.

Bradford, Alden, ed. *Speeches of the Governors of Massachusetts, 1765–1775.* New York: Da Capo, 1971 [1818].

Brock, R. A., ed. *The Official Records of Robert Dinwiddie, Lieutenant-Governor of the Colony of Virginia, 1751–1758.* Vol. 1. Richmond, VA, 1883.

[Burke, William]. *Remarks on the Letter Address'd to Two Great Men.* London, 1760.

Camm, John. *A Single and Distinct View of the Act, Vulgarly Entitled, the Two-Penny Act.* Annapolis, 1763.

———. *A Review of the Rector Detected.* Williamsburg, 1764.

———. *Critical Remarks on a Letter Ascribed to Common Sense.* Williamsburg, 1765.

Cappon, Lester J., ed. *The Adams-Jefferson Letters: the Complete Correspondence Between Thomas Jefferson and Abigail and John Adams.* Chapel Hill: University of North Carolina Press, 1959.

Carter, Landon. *A Letter to the Right Reverend Father in God the Lord-B—p of L—n.* Williamsburg, 1759.

———. *The Rector Detected.* Williamsburg, 1764.

Church, Benjamin. *An Oration; Delivered March 5th, 1773.* Boston, 1773.

Cluny, Alexander. *The American Traveller.* Philadelphia, 1770.

Darlington, William M., ed. *Christopher Gist's Journals.* Pittsburgh, 1893.

DeForest, Louis Effingham, ed. *Louisbourg Journals 1745.* New York, 1932.

Dickinson, Harry T., ed. *British Pamphlets on the American Revolution, 1763–1785.* 8 vols. London, 2007–2008.

Dickinson, John. *Letters from a Farmer in Pennsylvania, to the Inhabitants of the British Colonies.* Boston, 1768.

Dinwiddie, Robert. *The Official Records of Robert Dinwiddie: Lieutenant-Governor of the Colony of Virginia, 1751–1758.* Vol. 1. Collections of the Virginia Historical Society, New Series 3. Richmond, 1883–1884.

Douglas, John. *A Letter Addressed to Two Great Men, on the Prospect of Peace*. Boston, 1760.

Downer, Silas. *A Discourse, Delivered in Providence, in the Colony of Rhode-Island, upon the 25th. day of July, 1768*. Providence, 1768.

Drake, Francis S. *Tea Leaves: Being a Collection of Letters and Documents Relating to the Shipment of Tea to the American Colonies in the Year 1773 by the East India Tea Company*. Boston, 1884.

Dunbar, John, ed. *The Paxton Papers*. The Hague: M. Nijhoff, 1957.

Edwards, Jonathan. *Careful and Strict Enquiry into the Modern Prevailing Notions of That Freedom of the Will, Which Is Supposed to Be Essential to Moral Agency*. Boston, 1754.

Fontaine, Rev. James. *Memoirs of a Huguenot Family*. Edited by Ann Maury. New York, 1853.

Ford, Worthington C., ed. *Jasper Mauduit: Agent in London for the Province of the Massachusetts-Bay, 1762–1765*. Boston: Massachusetts Historical Society, 1918.

Franklin, Benjamin. *The Interest of Great Britain Considered: with Regard to Her Colonies and the Acquisitions of Canada and Guadaloupe*. Boston, 1760.

———. "Information to Those Who Would Remove to America." London, 1784.

Galloway, Joseph. *A Candid Examination of the Mutual Claims of Great-Britain, and the Colonies: with a Plan of Accommodation on Constitutional Principles*. New York, 1775.

Greene, Jack P., ed. *Colonies to Nation 1763–1789: A Documentary History of the American Revolution*. New York: McGraw-Hill, 1967.

Grenier, Fernand, ed. *Papiers Contecoeur et autres documents concernant le conflit anglo-français sur l'Ohio de 1745 à 1756*. Quebec: Presses Universitaires Laval, 1952.

Hall, Michael G., Lawrence H. Leder, and Michael G. Kammen, eds. *The Glorious Revolution in America: Documents on the Colonial Crisis of 1689*. Chapel Hill: University of North Carolina Press, 1964.

Hamowy, Ronald, ed. *Cato's Letters: Or Essays on Liberty, Civil and Religious, and Other Important Subjects*. 2 vols. Indianapolis: Liberty Fund, 1995.

Horsmanden, Daniel. *The New York Conspiracy*. Edited by Thomas J. Davis. Boston: Beacon Press, 1971 [1744].

Howe, John. *A Journal Kept by Mr. John Howe While He Was Employed as a British Spy During the Revolutionary War*. Concord, NH, 1827. Reprinted in *The Magazine of History* 33 (1927): 165–76.

Hutchinson, Governor Thomas. *Journal of the Honorable House of Representatives . . . Wednesday the twenty-seventh day of May . . . 1772*. Boston, 1773.

Hutson, James H., ed. *A Decent Respect to the Opinions of Mankind: Congressional State Papers, 1774–1776*. Washington, D.C.: Library of Congress, 1975.

Hyneman, Charles S., and Donald S. Lutz, eds. *American Political Writing During the Founding Era, 1760–1805*. 2 vols. Indianapolis: Liberty Press, 1983.

Jackson, Donald, ed. *The Diaries of George Washington*. Vol. 1. Charlottesville: University Press of Virginia, 1976.

James, Alfred Procter, ed. *Writings of General John Forbes Relating to His Service in North America*. Menasha, WI: Collegiate Press, 1938.

Journal of the Votes and Proceedings of the General Assembly of the Colony of New York, November 21, 1769–January 27, 1770. New York, 1770.

Journals of the Continental Congress Containing the Proceedings from Sept. 5, 1774 to Jan. 1, 1776. Philadelphia, 1777.

Kierner, Cynthia A., ed. *Revolutionary America, 1750–1815: Sources and Interpretation*. Upper Saddle River, NJ: Prentice Hall, 2003.

Kimball, Gertrude Selwyn. *Correspondence of William Pitt When Secretary of State*. 2 vols. New York: Macmillan, 1906.

Labaree, Leonard W., et al., eds. *The Papers of Benjamin Franklin*. Vols. 1–22. New Haven: Yale University Press, 1959–1982.

Labaree, Leonard Woods, ed. *Royal Instructions to British Colonial Governors, 1670–1776*. 2 vols. New York: Appleton-Century, 1935.

Leigh, Egerton. *The Man Unmasked: or, the World Undeceived*. Charlestown, SC: 1769.

Lincoln, C. H., ed. *Correspondence of William Shirley, Governor of Massachusetts*. New York: Macmillan, 1912.

Livingston, William. *The Independent Reflector*. New York, 1754.

Lloyd, Charles. *The Conduct of the Late Administration Examined*. Boston, 1767.

Martin, Howard. *A Defence of the Letter from a Gentleman at Halifax, to his Friend in Rhode-Island*. Newport, 1765.

Maury, Ann, ed. and trans. *Memoirs of a Huguenot Family*. New York: Putnam, 1852.

McDowell, William L., Jr., ed. *Colonial Records of South Carolina: Documents Relating to Indian Affairs, 1764–1765*. Columbia: South Carolina Department of Archives and History, 1970.

More, Roger. *The American Country Almanack, for the Year of Christian Account 1766*. Philadelphia, 1765.

Morgan, Edmund S., ed. *Prologue to Revolution: Sources and Documents on the Stamp Act Crisis, 1764–1766*. Chapel Hill: University of North Carolina Press, 1959.

Morison, Samuel Eliot, ed. *Sources and Documents Illustrating the American Revolution, 1764–1788, and the Formation of the Federal Constitution*. 2nd ed. Oxford: Clarendon Press,1929.

New York Weekly Journal.

Nicholas, Robert Carter. *Considerations on the Present State of Virginia*. Williamsburg, 1774.

O'Callaghan, E. B., ed. *Documents Relative to the Colonial History of the State of New-York*. Albany, 1858.

Orme, Robert. *A History of the Military Transactions of the British Nation in Indostan From the Year MDCCXLV*. 2nd ed. 2 vols. London, 1775–1778.

Otis, James. *The Rights of the British Colonies Asserted and Proved*. Boston, 1764.

Paine, Thomas. *Common Sense*. Philadelphia, 1776.

The Palladium of Conscience. Philadelphia, 1773.

Pease, Theodore C. ed. *Anglo-French Boundary Disputes in the West, 1749–1763*. Springfield: Illinois State Historical Society Collections, vol. 27 (1936).

A Pennsylvanian. *Americanus Examined*. Philadelphia, 1774.

Perry, William Stevens, ed. *Historical Collections Relating to the American Colonial Church*. Hartford, CT, 1870.

Peterson, Merrill D., ed. *The Portable Thomas Jefferson*. New York: Viking, 1975.

Ray, Nicholas. *The Importance of the Colonies of North America, and the Interest of Great Britain with Regard to them, Considered. Together with Remarks on the Stamp-Duty*. New York, 1766.

The Representations of Governor Hutchinson and Others, Contained in Certain Letters. Boston, 1773.

Rush, Benjamin. *Sermons to Gentlemen Upon Temperance and Exercise*. Philadelphia, 1772.

Sandoz, Ellis, ed. *Political Sermons of the American Founding Era, 1730–1805*. 2nd ed. 2 vols. Indianapolis: Liberty Fund, 1998.

Shaw, Samuel. *The voice of one crying in a wilderness*. Boston, 1746.

Simmons, R. C., and P. D. G. Thomas, eds. *Proceedings and Debates of the British Parliament Respecting North America, 1754–1783*. Vols. 1–6. New York: Kraus International, 1982–1987.

Smith, Paul H., ed. *English Defenders of American Freedoms, 1774–1778: Six Pamphlets Attacking British Policy*. Washington, D.C.: Library of Congress, 1972.

———. *Letters of the Delegates to Congress, 1774–1789*. 26 vols. Washington, D.C.: Library of Congress, 1976–2000.

The Speeches of His Excellency Governor Hutchinson, to the General Assembly of the Massachusetts-Bay. Boston, 1773.

Stevens, Benjamin. *A Sermon Preached at Boston*. Boston, 1761.

Stiles, Ezra. *A Discourse on the Christian Union*. Boston, 1761. *Votes and Proceeding of the Lower House of Assembly of the Province of Maryland. March Session*. Annapolis, 1774.

Votes of the House of Representatives for His Majesties Province of New-York in America. New York, 1699.

Willing, Thomas, Chairman, and Charles Thomson, Clerk. *An Essay on the Constitutional Power of Great-Britain Over the Colonies in America; with the Resolves of the Committee for the Province of Pennsylvania, and their Instructions to their representatives in Assembly*. Philadelphia, 1774.

Wise, John. *The Churches Quarrel Espoused*. New York, 1713.

Witherspoon, John. *Address to the Inhabitants of Jamaica*. Philadelphia, 1772.

Wood, Gordon S., ed. *John Adams: Revolutionary Writings*. 2 vols. New York: Library of America, 2011.

Zabin, Serena R., ed. *The New York Conspiracy Trials of 1741*. Boston: Bedford/St. Martin's, 2004.

SECONDARY SOURCES: BOOKS AND ESSAY COLLECTIONS

Adams, Thomas R. *American Independence: The Growth of an Idea*. Providence: Brown University Press, 1965.

Albion, R. G. *Forests and Sea Power: The Timber Problem of the Royal Navy, 1652–1862*. Cambridge, MA: Harvard University Press, 1926.

Alden, John R. *General Gage in America: Being Principally a History of His Role in the American Revolution*. Baton Rouge: Louisiana State University Press, 1948.

———. *A History of the American Revolution*. New York: Knopf, 1969.

Allen, Thomas B. *Tories: Fighting for the King in America's First Civil War*. New York: Harper, 2010.

Allison, Robert J. *The American Revolution: A Concise History*. New York: Oxford University Press, 2011.

Alvord, Clarence Walworth. *The Mississippi Valley in British Politics*. 2 vols. Cleveland: Arthur H. Clark, 1917.

Ammerman, David. *In the Common Cause: American Response to the Coercive Acts of 1774*. Charlottesville: University Press of Virginia, 1974.

Anderson, Fred. *Crucible of War: The Seven Years' War and the Fate of Empire in British North America, 1754–1766*. New York: Knopf, 2000.

———. *The War That Made America: A Short History of the French and Indian War*. New York: Viking, 2005.

Anderson, Virginia DeJohn. *New England's Generation: The Great Migration and the Formation of Society and Culture in the Seventeenth Century*. New York: Cambridge University Press, 1991.

Andrews, Charles M. *The Colonial Background of the American Revolution*. New Haven: Yale University Press, 1924.

———. *The Colonial Period of American History*. Vol. 2, *The Settlements*. New Haven: Yale University Press, 1936.

Archdeacon, Thomas J. *New York City, 1664–1710: Conquest and Change*. Ithaca: Cornell University Press, 1976.

Archer, Richard. *As if an Enemy's Country: The British Occupation of Boston and the Origins of Revolution*. New York: Oxford University Press, 2010.

Armitage, David. *The Ideological Origins of the British Empire*. New York: Cambridge University Press, 2000.

Bailyn, Bernard. *The Ideological Origins of the American Revolution*. Cambridge, MA: Harvard University Press, 1967.

———. *The Origins of American Politics*. New York: Knopf, 1968.

———. *The Ordeal of Thomas Hutchinson*. Cambridge, MA: Harvard University Press, 1974.

———. *Voyagers to the West: A Passage in the Peopling of America on the Eve of the Revolution*. New York: Vintage, 1986.

Bailyn, Bernard, and John B. Hench, eds. *The Press and the American Revolution*. Worcester, MA: American Antiquarian Society, 1981.

Bailyn, Bernard, and Philip D. Morgan, eds. *Strangers Within the Realm: Cultural Margins of the First British Empire*. Chapel Hill: University of North Carolina Press, 1991.

Banks, Kenneth J. *Chasing Empire Across the Sea: Communications and the State in the French Atlantic, 1713–1763*. Montreal: McGill-Queen's University Press, 2002.

Barone, Michael. *Our First Revolution: The Remarkable British Uprising That Inspired America's Founding Fathers.* New York: Crown, 2007.

Barrow, Thomas C. *Trade and Empire.* Cambridge, MA: Harvard University Press, 1967.

Bayly, C. A. *The Raj: India and the British, 1600–1947.* London: National Portrait Gallery, 1990.

Bayse, Arthur H. *The Lords Commissioners of Trade and Plantations.* New Haven: Yale University Press, 1925.

Beardsley, E. Edwards. *The History of the Episcopal Church in Connecticut.* New York, 1866.

Becker, Robert A. *Revolution, Reform, and the Politics of American Taxation, 1763–1783.* Baton Rouge: Louisiana State University Press, 1980.

Beckles, Hilary. *White Servitude and Black Slavery in Barbados, 1627–1715.* Knoxville: University of Tennessee Press, 1989.

Beeman, Richard R. *The Varieties of Political Experience in Eighteenth-Century America.* Philadelphia: University of Pennsylvania Press, 2004.

———. *Our Lives, Our Fortunes and Our Sacred Honor: The Forging of American Independence, 1774–1776.* New York: Basic Books, 2013.

Beer, George Louis. *British Colonial Policy, 1754–1765.* New York: Macmillan, 1907.

Belz, Herman, Ronald Hoffman, and Peter J. Albert, eds. *To Form a More Perfect Union: The Critical Ideas of the Constitution.* Charlottesville: University Press of Virginia, 1992.

Bence-Jones, Mark. *Clive of India.* New York: St. Martin's Press, 1975.

Berlin, Ira. *Many Thousands Gone: The First Two Centuries of Slavery in North America.* Cambridge, MA: Harvard University Press, 1998.

Berlin, Isaiah. *The Hedgehog and the Fox.* New York: Simon & Schuster, 1953.

Bobrick, Benson. *Angel in the Whirlwind: The Triumph of the American Revolution.* New York: Simon & Schuster, 1997.

Bonomi, Patricia U. *A Factious People: Politics and Society in Colonial New York.* New York: Columbia University Press, 1971.

Bonwick, Colin. *English Radicals and the American Revolution.* Chapel Hill: University of North Carolina Press, 1977.

Bradley, James E. *Religion, Revolution, and English Radicalism: Nonconformity in Eighteenth-Century Politics and Society.* New York: Cambridge University Press, 1990.

Brebner, John Bartlet. *New England's Outpost: Acadia before the Conquest of Canada.* New York: Columbia University Press, 1927.

Breen, T. H. *The Marketplace of Revolution: How Consumer Politics Shaped American Independence.* New York: Oxford University Press, 2004.

———. *American Insurgents, American Patriots: The Revolution of the People.* New York: Hill and Wang, 2010.

Brewer, John. *Party Ideology and Popular Politics at the Accession of George III.* New York: Cambridge University Press, 1976.

———. *The Sinews of Power: War, Money and the English State, 1688–1783*. New York: Knopf, 1989.

Brewer, John, and John Styles, eds. *An Ungovernable People: The English and Their Law in the Seventeenth and Eighteenth Centuries*. New Brunswick, NJ: Rutgers University Press, 1980.

Brown, Kathleen M. *Good Wives, Nasty Wenches, and Anxious Patriarchs: Gender, Race, and Power in Colonial Virginia*. Chapel Hill: University of North Carolina Press, 1996.

Brown, Richard D. *Revolutionary Politics in Massachusetts: The Boston Committee of Correspondence and the Towns, 1772–1774*. Cambridge, MA: Harvard University Press, 1970.

Brown, Richard Maxwell. *The South Carolina Regulators*. Cambridge, MA: Harvard University Press, 1963.

Brown, Weldon. *Empire or Independence: A Study in the Failure of Reconciliation, 1774–1783*. Baton Rouge: Louisiana State University Press, 1941.

Brumwell, Stephen. *Redcoats: The British Soldier and War in the Americas, 1755–1763*. New York: Cambridge University Press, 2002.

———. *Paths of Glory: The Life and Death of General James Wolfe*. Montreal: McGill-Queen's University Press, 2006.

Buel, Richard. *Dear Liberty: Connecticut's Mobilization for the Revolutionary War*. Middletown, CT: Wesleyan University Press, 1980.

Bullion, John L. *A Great and Necessary Measure: George Grenville and the Genesis of the Stamp Act, 1763–1765*. Columbia: University of Missouri Press, 1982.

Burt, Alfred LeRoy. *The Old Province of Quebec*. Minneapolis: University of Minnesota Press, 1933.

Bushman, Richard L. *From Puritan to Yankee: Character and the Social Order in Connecticut, 1690–1765*. Cambridge, MA: Harvard University Press, 1967.

———. *The Refinement of America: Persons, Houses, Cities*. New York: Knopf, 1992.

Butler, Jon. *Awash in a Sea of Faith: Christianizing the American People*. Cambridge, MA: Harvard University Press, 1990.

———. *Becoming America: The Revolution before 1776*. Cambridge, MA: Harvard University Press, 2000.

Calder, Angus. *Revolutionary Empire: The Rise of the English-Speaking Empires from the Fifteenth Century to the 1780s*. New York: Dutton, 1981.

Calloway, Colin G. *The American Revolution in Indian Country: Crisis and Diversity in Native American Communities*. New York: Cambridge University Press, 1995.

Carp, Benjamin L. *Rebels Rising: Cities and the American Revolution*. New York: Oxford University Press, 2007.

———. *Defiance of the Patriots: The Boston Tea Party and the Making of America*. New Haven: Yale University Press, 2010.

Carr, Lois Green, and David William Jordan. *Maryland's Revolution of Government, 1689–1692*. Ithaca: Cornell University Press, 1974.

Chaudhuri, Nirad C. *Clive of India: A Political and Psychological Essay*. London: Barrie & Jenkins, 1975.

Christie, Ian R. *Wars and Revolutions: Britain, 1760–1815*. Cambridge, MA: Harvard University Press, 1982.

Clark, Andrew Hill. *Acadia: The Geography of Early Nova Scotia to 1760*. Madison: University of Wisconsin Press, 1968.

Clark, J. C. D. *The Language of Liberty, 1660–1832: Political Discourse and Social Dynamics in the Anglo-American World*. New York: Cambridge University Press, 1994.

——. *English Society 1660–1832: Religion, Ideology, and Politics During the Ancien Regime*. 2nd ed. New York: Cambridge University Press, 2000.

Claydon, Tony. *Europe and the Making of England, 1660–1760*. New York: Cambridge University Press, 2007.

Clemens, Paul G. E. *The Atlantic Economy and Maryland's Colonial Eastern Shore: From Tobacco to Grain*. Ithaca: Cornell University Press, 1980.

Cogliano, Francis D. *Revolutionary America, 1763–1815: A Political History*. 2nd ed. New York: Routledge, 2000.

Colley, Linda. *Britons: Forging the Nation, 1707–1837*. New Haven: Yale University Press, 1992.

——. *Captives*. New York: Pantheon, 2002.

Conway, Stephen. *The British Isles and the War of American Independence*. New York: Oxford University Press, 2000.

Corkran, David H. *The Cherokee Frontier: Conflict and Survival, 1740–62*. Norman: University of Oklahoma Press, 1962.

Countryman, Edward. *A People in Revolution: The American Revolution and Political Society in New York, 1760–1790*. Baltimore: Johns Hopkins University Press, 1981.

——. *The American Revolution*. Rev. ed. New York: Hill and Wang, 2003.

Coupland, Sir Reginald. *The Quebec Act: A Study in Statesmanship*. Oxford: Clarendon Press, 1968 [1925].

Craven, Wesley Frank. *The Southern Colonies in the Seventeenth Century, 1607–1689*. Baton Rouge: Louisiana State University Press, 1949.

Cross, Arthur Lyon. *The Anglican Episcopate and the American Colonies*. New York: Longmans, 1902.

Cushing, Harry A. *History of the Transition from Provincial to Commonwealth Government in Massachusetts*. New York, 1896.

Davis, T. J. *A Rumor of Revolt: The "Great Negro Plot" in Colonial New York*. New York: Free Press, 1985.

Demos, John Putnam. *Entertaining Satan: Witchcraft and the Culture of Early New England*. New York: Oxford University Press, 1982.

——. *The Unredeemed Captive: A Family Story from Early America*. New York: Knopf, 1994.

Desjardin, Thomas A. *Through a Howling Wilderness: Benedict Arnold's March to Quebec, 1775*. New York: St. Martin's Press, 2006.

Dickerson, Oliver M. *The Navigation Acts and the American Revolution*. Philadelphia: University of Pennsylvania Press, 1951.

Dixon, David. *Never Come to Peace Again: Pontiac's Uprising and the Fate of the British Empire in North America*. Norman: University of Oklahoma Press, 2005.

Doerflinger, Thomas M. *A Vigorous Spirit of Enterprise: Merchants and Economic Development in Revolutionary Philadelphia*. Chapel Hill: University of North Carolina Press, 1986.

Donoughue, Bernard. *British Politics and the American Revolution: The Path to War, 1773–75*. New York: St. Martin's Press, 1965.

Doughty, Arthur G. *The Acadian Exiles; A Chronicle of the Land of Evangeline*. Toronto: Glasgow, Brook, 1916.

Dowd, Gregory Evans. *A Spirited Resistance: The North American Indian Struggle for Unity, 1745–1815*. Baltimore: Johns Hopkins University Press, 1992.

———. *War Under Heaven: Pontiac, the Indian Nations, & the British Empire*. Baltimore: Johns Hopkins University Press, 2002.

Draper, Theodore. *A Struggle for Power: The American Revolution*. New York: Times Books, 1996.

Dull, Jonathan R. *The French Navy and the Seven Years' War*. Lincoln: University of Nebraska Press, 2005.

Dunn, Richard S. *Sugar and Slaves: The Rise of the Planter Class in the English West Indies, 1624–1713*. Chapel Hill: University of North Carolina Press, 1972.

Eccles, W. J. *The Canadian Frontier, 1534–1760*. New York: Holt, 1969.

———. *France in America*. New York: Harper, 1972.

Egnal, Marc. *A Mighty Empire: The Origins of the American Revolution*. Ithaca: Cornell University Press, 1988.

Ekirch, A. Roger. *Bound for America: The Transportation of British Convicts to the Colonies, 1718–1775*. New York: Oxford University Press, 1987.

Elliott, J. H. *Empires of the Atlantic World: Britain and Spain in America, 1492–1830*. New Haven: Yale University Press, 2006.

Ellis, Joseph J. *The New England Mind in Transition: Samuel Johnson of Connecticut, 1696–1772*. New Haven: Yale University Press, 1973.

———. *Revolutionary Summer: The Birth of American Independence*. New York: Knopf, 2013.

Ernst, Joseph Albert. *Money and Politics in America, 1755–1775: A Study in the Currency Act of 1764 and the Political Economy of Revolution*. Chapel Hill: University of North Carolina Press, 1973.

Fagan, Brian. *The Little Ice Age: How Climate Made History, 1300–1850*. New York: Basic Books, 2000.

Faragher, John Mack. *A Great and Noble Scheme: The Tragic Story of the Expulsion of the French Acadians from their American Homeland*. New York: W. W. Norton, 2005.

Faught, C. Brad. *Clive: Founder of British India*. Washington, D.C.: Potomac Books, 2013.

Ferling, John. *Almost a Miracle: The American Victory in the War of Independence*. New York: Oxford University Press, 2007.

———. *Independence: The Struggle to Set America Free*. New York: Bloomsbury, 2011.

Fernández-Armesto, Felipe. *Pathfinders: A Global History of Exploration*. New York: W. W. Norton, 2006.

Fischer, David Hackett. *Albion's Seed: Four British Folkways in America*. New York: Oxford University Press, 1989.

———. *Paul Revere's Ride*. New York: Oxford University Press, 1994.

Fliegelman, Jay. *Prodigals and Pilgrims: The American Revolution Against Patriarchal Authority, 1750–1800*. New York: Cambridge University Press, 1982.

Foner, Eric. *Tom Paine and Revolutionary America*. New York: Oxford University Press, 1976.

Fowler, William M. *The Baron of Beacon Hill: A Biography of John Hancock*. Boston: Houghton Mifflin, 1980.

Fowler, William M., Jr., and Wallace Coyle, eds. *The American Revolution: Changing Perspectives*. Boston: Northeastern University Press, 1981.

French, Allen. *The Day of Concord and Lexington*. Boston: Little, Brown, 1925.

Gipson, Lawrence Henry. *The Coming of the Revolution, 1763–1775*. New York: Harper, 1954.

———. *The British Empire before the American Revolution*. Vols. 5 and 6. New York: Knopf, 1968.

Godbeer, Richard. *Escaping Salem: The Other Witch Hunt of 1692*. New York: Oxford University Press, 2005.

Gould, Eliga H. *The Persistence of Empire: British Political Culture in the Age of the American Revolution*. Chapel Hill: University of North Carolina Press, 2000.

Gould, Eliga H., and Peter S. Onuf, eds. *Empire and Nation: The American Revolution in the Atlantic World*. Baltimore: Johns Hopkins University Press, 2005.

Gray, Edward G., and Jane Kamensky, eds. *The Oxford Handbook of the American Revolution*. New York: Oxford University Press, 2013.

Greene, Jack P. *The Quest for Power: The Lower Houses of Assembly in the Southern Royal Colonies, 1689–1776*. Chapel Hill: University of North Carolina Press, 1963.

———, ed. *The Reinterpretation of the American Revolution, 1763–1789*. New York: Harper, 1968.

Greene, Jack P., Richard L. Bushman, and Michael Kammen, eds. *Society, Freedom, and Conscience: The Coming of the Revolution in Virginia, Massachusetts, and New York*. New York: W. W. Norton, 1976.

Greene, Jack P., and J. R. Pole, eds. *The Blackwell Encyclopedia of the American Revolution*. Cambridge, MA: Blackwell, 1991.

———. *A Companion to the American Revolution*. Malden, MA: Blackwell, 2000.

Greven, Philip J., Jr. *Four Generations: Population, Land, and Family in Colonial Andover, Massachusetts*. Ithaca: Cornell University Press, 1970.

———. *The Protestant Temperament: Patterns of Child-Rearing, Religious Experience, and the Self in Early America*. New York: Knopf, 1977.

Griffin, Patrick. *The People with No Name: Ireland's Ulster Scots, America's Scots Irish, and the Creation of a British Atlantic World, 1689–1764*. Princeton: Princeton University Press, 2001.

Gross, Robert A. *The Minutemen and Their World*. New York: Hill and Wang, 1976.

Gruber, Ira D. *The Howe Brothers and the American Revolution*. New York: Atheneum, 1972.

Haffenden, Philip S. *New England in the English Nation, 1689–1713*. Oxford: Clarendon Press, 1974.

Hall, David D. *Worlds of Wonder, Days of Judgment: Popular Religious Belief in Early New England*. Cambridge, MA: Harvard University Press, 1990.

Hall, David D., John M. Murrin, and Thad W. Tate, eds. *Saints and Revolutionaries: Essays on Early American History*. New York: W. W. Norton, 1984.

Harrington, Virginia D. *The New York Merchant on the Eve of the American Revolution*. New York: Columbia University Press, 1935.

Hatfield, April Lee. *Atlantic Virginia: Intercolonial Relations in the Seventeenth Century*. Philadelphia: University of Pennsylvania Press, 2004.

Henretta, James A. *"Salutary Neglect": Colonial Administration Under the Duke of Newcastle*. Princeton: Princeton University Press, 1972.

———. *The Evolution of American Society, 1700–1815: An Interdisciplinary Analysis*. Lexington, MA: Heath, 1973.

Henretta, James A., and Gregory H. Nobles. *Evolution and Revolution: American Society, 1600–1820*. Lexington, MA: Heath, 1987.

Heyrman, Christine Leigh. *Commerce and Culture: The Maritime Communities of Colonial Massachusetts, 1690–1750*. New York: W. W. Norton, 1984.

Hindus, Michael Stephen. *Prison and Plantation: Crime, Justice, and Authority in Massachusetts and South Carolina, 1767–1878*. Chapel Hill: University of North Carolina Press, 1980.

Hoerder, Dirk. *Crowd Action in Revolutionary Massachusetts, 1765–1780*. New York: Academic Press, 1977.

Hoffer, Peter Charles. *The Great New York Conspiracy of 1741: Slavery, Crime, and Colonial Law*. Lawrence: University Press of Kansas, 2003.

Hoffman, Ronald, and Peter J. Albert, eds. *The Transforming Hand of Revolution: Reconsidering the American Revolution as a Social Movement*. Charlottesville: University Press of Virginia, 1996.

Hofstadter, Richard. *America at 1750: A Social Portrait*. New York: Knopf, 1971.

Holton, Woody. *Forced Founders: Indians, Debtors, Slaves, and the Making of the American Revolution in Virginia*. Chapel Hill: University of North Carolina Press, 1999.

Horn, James. *Adapting to a New World: English Society in the Seventeenth-Century Chesapeake*. Chapel Hill: University of North Carolina Press, 1994.

Hornsby, Stephen J. *British Atlantic, American Frontier: Spaces of Power in Early Modern British America*. Hanover, NH: University Press of New England, 2005.

Hulsebosch, Daniel J. *Constituting Empire: New York and the Transformation of Constitutionalism in the Atlantic World, 1664–1830*. Chapel Hill: University of North Carolina Press, 2005.

Innes, Stephen. *Creating the Commonwealth: The Economic Culture of Puritan New England*. New York: W. W. Norton, 1995.

Isaac, Rhys. *The Transformation of Virginia, 1740–1790.* Chapel Hill: University of North Carolina Press, 1982.

Israel, Jonathan I. *The Dutch Republic: Its Rise, Greatness, and Fall, 1477–1806.* Oxford: Clarendon Press, 1995.

Jaenen, Cornelius J. *Friend and Foe: Aspects of French-Amerindian Cultural Contact in the Sixteenth and Seventeenth Centuries.* New York: Columbia University Press, 1976

———. *The French Relationship with the Native Peoples of New France and Acadia.* Ottawa: Indian and Northern Affairs Canada, 1984.

Jardine, Lisa. *Going Dutch: How England Plundered Holland's Glory.* New York: Harper, 2008.

Jennings, Francis. *The Ambiguous Iroquois Empire: The Covenant Chain Confederation of Indian Tribes With English Colonies from Its Beginnings to the Lancaster Treaty of 1744.* New York: W. W. Norton, 1984.

———. *Empire of Fortune: Crowns, Colonies, and Tribes in the Seven Years War in America.* New York: W. W. Norton, 1988.

———. *Benjamin Franklin, Politician: The Mask and the Man.* New York: W. W. Norton, 1996.

———. *The Creation of America: Through Revolution to Empire.* New York: Cambridge University Press, 2000.

Jensen, Merrill. *The Founding of a Nation: A History of the American Revolution, 1763–1776.* New York: Oxford University Press, 1968.

———. *The American Revolution Within America.* New York: New York University Press, 1974.

Johnson, Richard R. *Adjustment to Empire: The New England Colonies, 1675–1715.* New Brunswick, NJ: Rutgers University Press, 1981.

Johnston, A. J. B. *Endgame 1758: The Promise, the Glory, and the Despair of Louisbourg's Last Decade.* Lincoln: University of Nebraska Press, 2007.

Jones, J. R. *Country and Court: England, 1658–1714.* Cambridge, MA: Harvard University Press 1978.

Kammen, Michael. *A Rope of Sand: The Colonial Agents, British Politics, and the American Revolution.* Ithaca: Cornell University Press, 1968.

———. *Colonial New York: A History.* New York: Scribner, 1975.

Karlsen, Carol F. *The Devil in the Shape of a Woman: Witchcraft in Colonial New England.* New York: W. W. Norton, 1987.

Kars, Marjoleine. *Breaking Loose Together: The Regulator Rebellion in Pre-Revolutionary North Carolina.* Chapel Hill: University of North Carolina Press, 2002.

Katz, Stanley N., John M. Murrin, and Douglas Greenberg, eds. *Colonial America: Essays in Politics and Social Development.* 5th ed. Boston: McGraw-Hill, 2001.

Kenny, Kevin. *Peaceable Kingdom Lost: The Paxton Boys and the Destruction of William Penn's Holy Experiment.* New York: Oxford University Press, 2009.

Kent, Donald H. *The French Invasion of Western Pennsylvania, 1753.* Harrisburg: Pennsylvania Historical and Museum Commission, 1954.

Kerber, Linda K. *Women of the Republic: Intellect and Ideology in Revolutionary America*. Chapel Hill: University of North Carolina Press, 1980.

Klooster, Wim. *Revolutions in the Atlantic World: A Comparative History*. New York: New York University Press, 2009.

Knollenberg, Bernhard. *Origin of the American Revolution: 1759–1766*. New York: Crowell-Collier, 1961.

Knott, Sarah. *Sensibility and the American Revolution*. Chapel Hill: University of North Carolina Press, 2009.

Knouff, Gregory T. *The Soldiers' Revolution: Pennsylvanians in Arms and the Forging of Early American Identity*. University Park: Pennsylvania State University Press, 2004.

Kupperman, Karen Ordahl. *Providence Island, 1630–1641: The Other Puritan Colony*. New York: Cambridge University Press, 1993.

Kurtz, Stephen G., and James H. Hutson, eds. *Essays on the American Revolution*. Chapel Hill: University of North Carolina Press, 1973.

Labaree, Benjamin Woods. *Patriots and Partisans: The Merchants of Newburyport, 1764–1815*. Cambridge, MA: Harvard University Press, 1962.

———. *The Boston Tea Party*. New York: Oxford University Press, 1964.

———. *America's Nation-Time: 1607–1789*. Boston: Allyn and Bacon, 1972.

Lancaster, Bruce. *The American Revolution*. New York: American Heritage, 1971.

Landsman, Ned C. *Crossroads of Empire: The Middle Colonies in British North America*. Baltimore: Johns Hopkins University Press, 2010.

Lawson, Philip. *The Imperial Challenge: Quebec and Britain in the Age of the American Revolution*. Montreal: McGill-Queen's University Press, 1989.

———. *The East India Company: A History*. New York: Longman, 1993.

Leach, Douglas Edward. *Arms for Empire: A Military History of the British Colonies in North America, 1607–1763*. New York: Macmillan, 1973.

———. *Roots of Conflict: British Armed Forces and Colonial Americans, 1677–1763*. Chapel Hill: University of North Carolina Press, 1986.

Leamon, James S. *Revolution Downeast: The War for American Independence in Maine*. Amherst: University of Massachusetts Press, 1993.

Lehmann, Hartmut, Hermann Wellenreuther, and Renate Wilson, eds. *In Search of Peace and Prosperity: New German Settlements in Eighteenth-Century Europe and America*. University Park: Pennsylvania State University Press, 2000.

Lemisch, Jesse. *Jack Tar vs. John Bull: The Role of New York's Seamen in Precipitating the Revolution*. New York: Garland, 1997.

Lemon, James T. *The Best Poor Man's Country: A Geographical Study of Early Southeastern Pennsylvania*. Baltimore: Johns Hopkins University Press, 1972.

Lepore, Jill. *The Name of War: King Philip's War and the Origins of American Identity*. New York: Knopf, 1998.

———. *New York Burning: Liberty, Slavery, and Conspiracy in Eighteenth-Century Manhattan*. New York: Knopf, 2005.

Levy, Barry. *Quakers and the American Family: British Settlement in the Delaware Valley*. New York: Oxford University Press, 1988.

———. *Town Born: The Political Economy of New England from Its Founding to the Revolution*. Philadelphia: University of Pennsylvania Press, 2009.

Linebaugh, Peter, and Marcus Rediker. *The Many-Headed Hydra: Sailors, Slaves, Commoners, and the Hidden History of the Revolutionary Atlantic*. Boston: Beacon Press, 2000.

Liss, Peggy K. *Atlantic Empires: The Network of Trade and Revolution, 1713–1826*. Baltimore: Johns Hopkins University Press, 1983.

Lockhart, Paul. *The Whites of Their Eyes: Bunker Hill, the First American Army, and the Emergence of George Washington*. New York: Harper, 2011.

Lockridge, Kenneth A. *A New England Town: The First Hundred Years, Dedham, Massachusetts, 1636–1736*. New York, W. W. Norton, 1970.

———. *Literacy in Colonial New England: An Enquiry into the Social Context of Literacy in the Early Modern West*. New York: W. W. Norton, 1974.

Lossing, Benson J. *The Pictorial Field-Book of the Revolution*. 2 vols. New York: Harper, 1859–1860.

Lovejoy, David S. *Rhode Island Politics and the American Revolution, 1760–1776*. Providence: Brown University Press, 1958.

———. *The Glorious Revolution in America*. New York: Harper, 1972.

Lynn, Kenneth S. *A Divided People*. Westport, CT: Greenwood Press 1977.

Mackesy, Piers. *The War for America, 1775–1783*. Cambridge, MA: Harvard University Press, 1964.

MacNutt, W. S. *The Atlantic Provinces: The Emergence of Colonial Society, 1712–1857*. Toronto: McClelland & Stewart, 1965.

Mahaffie, Charles D. *A Land of Discord Always: Acadia from Its Beginnings to the Expulsion of Its People, 1604–1755*. Camden, ME: Down East Books, 1995.

Maier, Pauline. *From Resistance to Revolution: Colonial Radicals and the Development of American Opposition to Britain, 1765–1776*. New York: Knopf, 1972.

———. *American Scripture: Making the Declaration of Independence*. New York: Knopf, 1997.

Main, Jackson Turner. *The Social Structure of Revolutionary America*. Princeton: Princeton University Press, 1965.

———. *The Upper House in Revolutionary America, 1763–1788*. Madison: University of Wisconsin Press, 1967.

Malone, Joseph J. *Pine Trees and Politics: The Naval Stores and Forest Policy in Colonial New England, 1691–1775*. Seattle: University of Washington Press, 1964.

Mann, Bruce H. *Republic of Debtors: Bankruptcy in the Age of American Independence*. Cambridge, MA: Harvard University Press, 2002.

Mapp, Paul W. *The Elusive West and the Contest for Empire, 1713–1763*. Chapel Hill: University of North Carolina Press, 2011.

Marshall, P. J. *The Making and Unmaking of Empires: Britain, India, and America c.1750–1783*. New York: Oxford University Press, 2005.

———, ed. *The Oxford History of the British Empire*. Vol. 2, *The Eighteenth Century*. New York: Oxford University Press, 1998.

Martin, Ann Smart. *Buying into the World of Goods: Early Consumers in Backcountry Virginia*. Baltimore: Johns Hopkins University Press, 2008.

Martin, James Kirby. *Men in Rebellion: Higher Governmental Leaders and the Coming of the American Revolution*. New Brunswick, NJ: Rutgers University Press, 1973.

Martin, James Kirby, and Mark Edward Lender. *A Respectable Army: The Military Origins of the Republic, 1763–1789*. Arlington Heights, IL: H. Davidson, 1982.

Matson, Cathy, ed. *The Economy of Early America: Historical Perspectives and New Directions*. University Park: Pennsylvania State University Press, 2006.

Maurault, J. A. *Histoire des Abenakis, Depuis 1605 Jusqu'à nos Jours*. Montreal, 1866.

May, Henry F. *The Enlightenment in America*. New York: Oxford University Press, 1976.

McConnell, Michael N. *A Country Between: The Upper Ohio Valley and Its Peoples, 1724–1774*. Lincoln: University of Nebraska Press, 1992.

McConville, Brendan. *These Daring Disturbers of the Public Peace: The Struggle for Property and Power in Early New Jersey*. Ithaca: Cornell University Press, 1999.

———. *The King's Three Faces: The Rise and Fall of Royal America, 1688–1776*. Chapel Hill: University of North Carolina Press, 2006.

McCusker, John J. *Money and Exchange in Europe and America, 1600–1775: A Handbook*. Chapel Hill: University of North Carolina Press, 1978.

———. *How Much Is That in Real Money?* Worcester, MA: American Antiquarian Society, 2001.

McCusker, John J., and Russell R. Menard. *The Economy of British America, 1607–1789*. Chapel Hill: University of North Carolina Press, 1985.

McDonnell, Michael A. *The Politics of War: Race, Class, and Conflict in Revolutionary Virginia*. Chapel Hill: University of North Carolina Press, 2007.

McIlvenna, Noeleen. *A Very Mutinous People: The Struggle for North Carolina, 1660–1713*. Chapel Hill: University of North Carolina Press, 2009.

McLennan, J. S. *Louisbourg: From Its Foundation to Its Fall, 1713–1758*. London: Macmillan, 1918.

McLoughlin, William G. *Rhode Island: A Bicentennial History*. New York: W. W. Norton, 1978.

McLynn, Frank. *1759: The Year Britain Became Master of the World*. New York: Atlantic Monthly Press, 2004.

Meinig, D. W. *The Shaping of America: A Geographical Perspective on 500 Years of History*. Vol. 1, *Atlantic America, 1492–1800*. New Haven: Yale University Press, 1986.

Merrell, James H. *The Indians' New World: Catawbas and their Neighbors from European Contact Through the Era of Removal*. Chapel Hill: University of North Carolina Press, 1989.

———. *Into the American Woods: Negotiators on the Pennsylvania Frontier*. New York: W. W. Norton, 1999.

Merritt, Jane T. *At the Crossroads: Indians and Empires on a Mid-Atlantic Frontier, 1700–1763*. Chapel Hill: University of North Carolina Press, 2003.

Merwick, Donna. *Possessing Albany, 1630–1710: The Dutch and English Experiences.* New York: Cambridge University Press, 1990.

Messer, Peter C. *Stories of Independence: Identity, Ideology, and History in Eighteenth-Century America.* DeKalb: Northern Illinois University Press, 2005.

Middlekauff, Robert. *The Glorious Cause: The American Revolution, 1763–1789.* New York: Oxford University Press, 1982.

Miller, John C. *Sam Adams: Pioneer in Propaganda.* Boston: Little, Brown, 1936.

———. *Origins of the American Revolution.* Boston: Little, Brown, 1943.

Mintz, Sidney W. *Sweetness and Power: The Place of Sugar in Modern History.* New York: Viking, 1985.

Morgan, Edmund S. *American Slavery, American Freedom: The Ordeal of Colonial Virginia.* New York: W. W. Norton, 1975.

———. *The Challenge of the American Revolution.* New York: W. W. Norton, 1976.

———. *The Birth of the Republic, 1763–89.* Rev. ed. Chicago: University of Chicago Press, 1977.

Morgan, Edmund S., and Helen M. Morgan. *The Stamp Act Crisis: Prologue to Revolution.* Chapel Hill: University of North Carolina Press, 1953.

Morgan, Philip D. *Slave Counterpoint: Black Culture in the Eighteenth-Century Chesapeake & Lowcountry.* Chapel Hill: University of North Carolina Press, 1998.

Morison, Samuel Eliot. *The European Discovery of America.* 2 vols. New York: Oxford University Press, 1971–1974.

Morton, Richard L. *Colonial Virginia.* 2 vols. Chapel Hill: University of North Carolina Press, 1960.

Namier, Sir Lewis. *Personalities and Powers.* London: Hamish Hamilton, 1955.

———. *The Structure of Politics at the Accession of George III.* 2nd ed. New York: St. Martin's Press, 1957.

———. *England in the Age of the American Revolution.* 2nd ed. New York: St. Martin's Press, 1962.

Namier, Sir Lewis, and John Brooke. *Charles Townshend.* New York: St. Martin's Press, 1964.

Nash, Gary B. *Quakers and Politics: Pennsylvania, 1681–1726.* Princeton: Princeton University Press, 1968.

———. *Class and Society in Early America.* Englewood Cliffs, NJ: Prentice-Hall, 1970.

———. *The Urban Crucible: Social Change, Political Consciousness, and the Origins of the American Revolution.* Cambridge, MA: Harvard University Press, 1979.

———. *The Unknown American Revolution: The Unruly Birth of Democracy and the Struggle to Create America.* New York: Viking, 2005.

———. *Red, White, and Black: The Peoples of Early North America.* 6th ed. Boston: Prentice-Hall, 2010.

Nelson, William H. *The American Tory.* Oxford: Clarendon Press, 1961.

Nester, William R. *"Haughty Conquerors": Amherst and the Great Indian Uprising of 1763.* Westport, CT: Praeger, 2000.

Nettels, Curtis P. *George Washington and American Independence.* Boston: Little, Brown, 1951.

Newbold, Robert C. *The Albany Congress and Plan of Union of 1754.* New York: Vantage Press, 1955.

Norton, Mary Beth. *In the Devil's Snare: The Salem Witchcraft Crisis of 1692.* New York: Knopf, 2002.

Ogborn, Miles. *Global Lives: Britain and the World, 1550–1800.* New York: Cambridge University Press, 2008.

Oliphant, John. *Peace and War on the Anglo-Cherokee Frontier, 1756–63.* Baton Rouge: Louisiana State University Press, 2001.

Olson, Alison Gilbert. *Anglo-American Politics 1660–1775: The Relationship Between Parties in England and Colonial America.* New York: Oxford University Press, 1973.

———. *Making the Empire Work: London and American Interest Groups, 1690–1790.* Cambridge, MA: Harvard University Press, 1992.

Osgood, Herbert L. *The American Colonies in the Seventeenth Century.* New York: Macmillan, 1907.

———. *The American Colonies in the Eighteenth Century.* 2 vols. New York: Columbia University Press, 1924.

O'Shaughnessy, Andrew Jackson. *An Empire Divided: The American Revolution and the British Caribbean.* Philadelphia: University of Pennsylvania Press, 2000.

———. *The Men Who Lost America: British Leadership, the American Revolution, and the Fate of the Empire.* New Haven: Yale University Press, 2013.

Pagden, Anthony. *Lords of All the World: Ideologies of Empire in Spain, Britain and France c. 1500–c. 1800.* New Haven: Yale University Press, 1998.

Pares, Richard. *War and Trade in the West Indies, 1739–1763.* New York: Oxford University Press, 1936.

Parkman, Francis. *Montcalm and Wolfe.* Boston: Little, Brown, 1885.

Patterson, Stephen E. *Political Parties in Revolutionary Massachusetts.* Madison: University of Wisconsin Press, 1973.

Peckham, Howard H. *The Colonial Wars, 1689–1762.* Chicago: University of Chicago Press, 1964.

Pencak, William. *War, Politics, and Revolution in Provincial Massachusetts.* Boston: Northeastern University Press, 1981.

Pencak, William, Matthew Dennis, and Simon P. Newman, eds. *Riot and Revelry in Early America.* University Park: Pennsylvania State University Press, 2002.

Pestana, Carla Gardina. *Quakers and Baptists in Colonial Massachusetts.* New York: Cambridge University Press, 1991.

Philbrick, Nathaniel. *Bunker Hill: A City, a Siege, a Revolution.* New York: Viking, 2013.

Phillips, Kevin. *The Cousins' Wars: Religion, Politics, and the Triumph of Anglo-America.* New York: Basic Books, 1999.

———. *1775: A Good Year for Revolution.* New York: Viking, 2012.

Pincus, Steven C. A. *Protestantism and Patriotism: Ideologies and the Making of English Foreign Policy, 1650–1688.* New York: Cambridge University Press, 1996.

———. *1688: The First Modern Revolution*. New Haven: Yale University Press, 2009.

Plank, Geoffrey. *An Unsettled Conquest: The British Campaign Against the Peoples of Acadia*. Philadelphia: University of Pennsylvania Press, 2001.

Plumb, J. H. *The Growth of Political Stability in England, 1675–1725*. New York: Macmillan, 1967.

Pocock, J. G. A., ed. *Three British Revolutions: 1641, 1688, 1776*. Princeton: Princeton University Press, 1980.

Pole, J. R. *Political Representation in England and the Origins of the American Republic*. New York: St. Martin's Press, 1966.

———. *The Decision for American Independence*. Philadelphia: Lippincott, 1975.

Polishook, Irwin H. *Rhode Island and the Union, 1774–1795*. Evanston, IL: Northwestern University Press, 1969.

Pope, Peter E. *Fish into Wine: The Newfoundland Plantation in the Seventeenth Century*. Chapel Hill: University of North Carolina Press, 2004.

Porter, Roy. *English Society in the Eighteenth Century*. New York: Penguin, 1990.

Pritchard, James. *In Search of Empire: The French in the Americas, 1670–1730*. New York: Cambridge University Press, 2004.

Pulsipher, Jenny Hale. *Subjects Unto the Same King: Indians, English, and the Contest for Authority in Colonial New England*. Philadelphia: University of Pennsylvania Press, 2005.

Purcell, Sarah J. *Sealed with Blood: War, Sacrifice, and Memory in Revolutionary America*. Philadelphia: University of Pennsylvania Press, 2002.

Rakove, Jack. *The Beginnings of National Politics: An Interpretive History of the Continental Congress*. New York: Knopf, 1979.

———. *Revolutionaries: A New History of the Invention of America*. Boston: Houghton Mifflin Harcourt, 2010.

Ramsay, David. *The History of South Carolina from Its First Settlement in 1670 to the Year 1808*. Charleston, 1809.

———. *The History of the American Revolution*. 2 vols. Edited by Lester H. Cohen. Indianapolis: Liberty Classics, 1990 [1789].

Ramsey, William L. *The Yamasee War: A Study of Culture, Economy, and Conflict in the Colonial South*. Lincoln: University of Nebraska Press, 2008.

Rawlyk, George. *Nova Scotia's Massachusetts: A Study of Massachusetts–Nova Scotia Relations, 1630–1784*. Montreal: McGill-Queen's University Press, 1973.

Richter, Daniel K. *The Ordeal of the Longhouse: The Peoples of the Iroquois League in the Era of European Colonization*. Chapel Hill: University of North Carolina Press, 1992.

———. *Facing East from Indian Country: A Native History of Early America*. Cambridge, MA: Harvard University Press, 2001.

———. *Before the Revolution: America's Ancient Pasts*. Cambridge, MA: Harvard University Press, 2011.

Richter, Daniel K., and James H. Merrell, eds. *Beyond the Covenant Chain: The Iroquois and Their Neighbors in Indian North America, 1600–1800*. Syracuse: Syracuse University Press, 1987.

Ritchie, Robert C. *The Duke's Province: A Study of New York Politics and Society, 1664–1691*. Chapel Hill: University of North Carolina Press, 1977.

Robbins, Caroline. *The Eighteenth-Century Commonwealthman: Studies in the Transmission, Development, and Circumstance of English Liberal Thought from the Restoration of Charles II Until the War with the Thirteen Colonies*. Cambridge, MA: Harvard University Press, 1959.

Robson, Eric. *The American Revolution in Its Political and Military Aspects, 1763–1783*. New York: W. W. Norton, 1966.

Rogers, Alan. *Empire and Liberty: American Resistance to British Authority, 1755–1763*. Berkeley: University of California Press, 1974.

Rohrbough, Malcolm J. *The Trans-Appalachian Frontier: People, Societies, and Institutions, 1775–1850*. New York: Oxford University Press, 1978.

Rosswurm, Steven. *Arms, Country, and Class: The Philadelphia Militia and the "Lower Sort" During the American Revolution, 1775–1783*. New Brunswick, NJ: Rutgers University Press, 1987.

Roth, David M. *Connecticut: A Bicentennial History*. New York: W. W. Norton, 1979.

Rothman, Adam. *Slave Country: American Expansion and Origins of the Deep South*. Cambridge, MA: Harvard University Press, 2005.

Royster, Charles. *A Revolutionary People at War: The Continental Army and American Character, 1775–1783*. Chapel Hill: University of North Carolina Press, 1979.

——. *The Fabulous History of the Dismal Swamp Company: A Story of George Washington's Times*. New York: Knopf, 1999.

Rudé, George. *Wilkes and Liberty: A Social Study of 1763 to 1774*. Oxford: Clarendon Press, 1962.

Russell, James W. *Class and Race Formation in North America*. Toronto: University of Toronto Press, 2009.

Rutman, Darrett B. *Winthrop's Boston: Portrait of a Puritan Town, 1630–1649*. Chapel Hill: University of North Carolina Press, 1965.

——. *The Morning of America, 1603–1789*. Boston: Houghton Mifflin, 1971.

Ryerson, Richard Alan. *The Revolution Is Now Begun: The Radical Committees of Philadelphia, 1765–1776*. Philadelphia: University of Pennsylvania Press, 1978.

St. George, Robert Blair, ed. *Possible Pasts: Becoming Colonial in Early America*. Ithaca: Cornell University Press, 2000.

Sargent, Winthrop. *The History of an Expedition against Fort Du Quesne, in 1755*. Philadelphia: Historical Society of Pennsylvania, 1855.

Sarson, Steven. *British America 1500–1800: Creating Colonies, Imagining an Empire*. London: Hodder Arnold, 2005.

Schama, Simon. *Dead Certainties: (Unwarranted Speculations)*. New York: Knopf, 1991.

Schecter, Barnet. *The Battle for New York: The City at the Heart of the American Revolution*. New York: Walker, 2002.

Schiff, Stacy. *A Great Improvisation: Franklin, France, and the Birth of America*. New York: Henry Holt, 2005.

Schmidt, Benjamin. *Innocence Abroad: The Dutch Imagination and the New World, 1570–1670*. New York: Cambridge University Press, 2001.

Schultz, Ronald. *The Republic of Labor: Philadelphia Artisans and the Politics of Class, 1720–1830*. New York: Oxford University Press, 1993.

Sheehan, Bernard W. *Savagism and Civility: Indians and Englishmen in Colonial Virginia*. New York: Cambridge University Press, 1980.

Shy, John. *A People Numerous and Armed: Reflections on the Military Struggle for American Independence*. New York: Oxford University Press, 1976.

Silver, Peter. *Our Savage Neighbors: How Indian War Transformed Early America*. New York: W. W. Norton, 2008.

Simms, Brendan. *Three Victories and a Defeat: The Rise and Fall of the First British Empire, 1714–1783*. New York: Allen Lane, 2007.

Sipe, C. Hale. *The Indian Wars of Pennsylvania*. Harrisburg, PA: Telegraph Press, 1929.

Skemp, Sheila L. *The Making of a Patriot: Benjamin Franklin at the Cockpit*. New York: Oxford University Press, 2013.

Smelser, Marshall. *The Winning of Independence*. Chicago: Quadrangle, 1972.

Smith, Abbot Emerson. *Colonists in Bondage: White Servitude and Convict Labor in America, 1607–1776*. Chapel Hill: University of North Carolina Press, 1947.

Smith, Barbara Clark. *The Freedoms We Lost: Consent and Resistance in Revolutionary America*. New York: New Press, 2010.

Smith, James Morton, ed. *Seventeenth-Century America: Essays in Colonial History*. Chapel Hill: University of North Carolina Press, 1959.

Soderlund, Jean R., and Catherine S. Parzynski, eds. *Backcountry Crucibles: The Lehigh Valley from Settlement to Steel*. Bethlehem, PA: Lehigh University Press, 2008.

Sosin, Jack M. *English America and the Revolution of 1688: Royal Administration and the Structure of Provincial Government*. Lincoln: University of Nebraska Press, 1982.

Speck, W. A. *Stability and Strife: England, 1714–1760*. Cambridge, MA: Harvard University Press, 1977.

———. *The Butcher: The Duke of Cumberland and the Suppression of the 45*. Oxford: Blackwell, 1981.

Spring, Matthew H. *With Zeal and With Bayonets Only: The British Army on Campaign in North America, 1757–1783*. Norman: University of Oklahoma Press, 2008.

Stagg, Jack. *Anglo-Indian Relations in North America to 1763 and an Analysis of the Royal Proclamation of 7 October 1763*. Ottawa: Indians and Northern Affairs Ministry of Canada, 1981.

Stanley, George F. G. *New France: The Last Phase, 1744–1760*. Toronto: McClelland and Stewart, 1968.

Stanwood, Owen. *The Empire Reformed: English America in the Age of the Glorious Revolution*. Philadelphia: University of Pennsylvania Press, 2011.

Steele, Ian K. *Betrayals: Fort William Henry and the "Massacre."* New York: Oxford University Press, 1990.

———. *Warpaths: Invasions of North America*. New York: Oxford University Press, 1994.

Stone, Lawrence. *The Causes of the English Revolution, 1529–1642*. New York: Harper, 1972.

Sweet, John Wood. *Bodies Politic: Negotiating Race in the American North, 1730–1830*. Baltimore: Johns Hopkins University Press, 2003.

Sydnor, Charles S. *American Revolutionaries in the Making: Political Practices in Washington's Virginia*. New York: Free Press, 1965.

Tate, Thad W., and David L. Ammerman, eds. *The Chesapeake in the Seventeenth Century: Essays on Anglo-American Society*. Chapel Hill: University of North Carolina Press, 1979.

Taylor, Alan. *American Colonies*. New York: Viking, 2001.

Taylor, Robert J. *Colonial Connecticut, a History*. New York: KTO Press, 1979.

Thomas, P. D. G. *British Politics and the Stamp Act Crisis: The First Phase of the American Revolution, 1763–1767*. New York: Clarendon Press, 1975.

Tomlins, Christopher. *Freedom Bound: Law, Labor, and Civic Identity in Colonizing English America, 1580–1865*. New York: Cambridge University Press, 2010.

Tourtellot, Arthur B. *Lexington and Concord: The Beginning of the War of the American Revolution*. New York: W. W. Norton, 1963.

Treese, Lorett. *The Storm Gathering: The Penn Family and the American Revolution*. University Park: Pennsylvania State University Press, 1992.

Trevelyan, Sir George Otto. *The American Revolution*. 7 vols. New York: Longmans, 1899–1914.

Trumbull, Jonathan. *Jonathan Trumbull: Governor of Connecticut, 1769–1784*. Boston: Little, Brown, 1919.

Truxes, Thomas M. *Defying Empire: Trading with the Enemy in Colonial New York*. New Haven: Yale University Press, 2008.

Tucker, Robert W., and David C. Hendrickson. *The Fall of the First British Empire: Origins of the War of American Independence*. Baltimore: Johns Hopkins University Press, 1982.

Tuveson, Ernest Lee. *Redeemer Nation: the Idea of America's Millennial Role*. Chicago: University of Chicago Press, 1968.

Ubbelohde, Carl. *The American Colonies and the British Empire, 1607–1763*. 2nd ed. Arlington Heights, IL: H. Davidson, 1975.

Unger, Harlow Giles. *American Tempest: How the Boston Tea Party Sparked a Revolution*. Boston: Da Capo, 2011.

Upton, L. F. S. *Micmacs and Colonists: Indian-White Relations in the Maritimes, 1713–1867*. Vancouver: University of British Columbia Press, 1979.

Van Buskirk, Judith L. *Generous Enemies: Patriots and Loyalists in Revolutionary New York*. Philadelphia: University of Pennsylvania Press, 2002.

van der Zee, John. *Bound Over: Indentured Servitude and American Conscience*. New York: Simon & Schuster, 1985.

Ver Steeg, Clarence L. *The Formative Years, 1607–1763*. New York: Hill and Wang, 1964.

Vickers, Daniel. *Farmers and Fishermen: Two Centuries of Work in Essex County, Massachusetts, 1630–1850*. Chapel Hill: University of North Carolina Press, 1994.

———, ed. *A Companion to Colonial America*. Malden, MA: Blackwell, 2003.

Waldstreicher, David. *In the Midst of Perpetual Fetes: The Making of American Nationalism, 1776–1820*. Chapel Hill: University of North Carolina Press, 1997.

———. *Runaway America: Benjamin Franklin, Slavery, and the American Revolution*. New York: Hill and Wang, 2004.

Wallace, Anthony F. C. *The Death and Rebirth of the Seneca*. New York: Knopf, 1969.

Wallace, David Duncan. *The Life of Henry Laurens*. New York: Putnam, 1915.

Ward, Harry M. *The American Revolution: Nationhood Achieved, 1763–1788*. New York: St. Martin's Press, 1995.

Ward, Matthew C. *The Battle for Quebec: 1759*. Stroud, Gloucestershire: Tempus, 2005.

———. *Breaking the Backcountry: The Seven Years' War in Virginia and Pennsylvania, 1754–1765*. Pittsburgh: University of Pittsburgh Press, 2003.

Warren, Mercy Otis. *History of the Rise, Progress, and Termination of the American Revolution*. 2 vols. Edited by Lester H. Cohen. Indianapolis: Liberty Classics, 1988 [1805].

Washburn, Wilcomb E. *The Governor and the Rebel: A History of Bacon's Rebellion in Virginia*. Chapel Hill: University of North Carolina Press, 1957.

Webb, Stephen Saunders. *The Governors-General: The English Army and the Definition of the Empire, 1569–1681*. Chapel Hill: University of North Carolina Press, 1979.

———. *1676: The End of American Independence*. New York: Knopf, 1984.

Weintraub, Stanley. *Iron Tears: America's Battle for Freedom, Britain's Quagmire, 1775–1783*. New York: Free Press, 2005.

Wells, William V. *The Life and Public Services of Samuel Adams*. 3 vols. Boston: Little, Brown, 1865.

White, Richard. *The Middle Ground: Indians, Empires, and Republics in the Great Lakes Region, 1650–1815*. New York: Cambridge University Press, 1991.

Wilson, Kathleen. *The Sense of the People: Politics, Culture, and Imperialism in England, 1715–1785*. New York: Cambridge University Press, 1995.

Wood, Gordon S. *The Radicalism of the American Revolution*. New York: Knopf, 1992.

Wood, Peter H. *Black Majority: Negroes in Colonial South Carolina from 1670 Through the Stono Rebellion*. New York: Knopf, 1974.

Wright, Esmond. *Fabric of Freedom 1763–1800*. New York: Hill and Wang, 1961.

Wright, J. Leitch, Jr. *Britain and the American Frontier, 1783–1815*. Athens: University of Georgia Press, 1975.

———. *Florida in the American Revolution*. Gainesville: University Presses of Florida, 1975.

Wrightson, Keith. *English Society, 1580–1680*. New Brunswick, NJ: Rutgers University Press, 1982.

Young, Alfred F. *Liberty Tree: Ordinary People and the American Revolution*. New York: New York University Press, 2006.

———, ed. *The American Revolution*. DeKalb: Northern Illinois University Press, 1976.

Young, Alfred F., Gary B. Nash, and Ray Raphael, eds. *Revolutionary Founders: Rebels, Radicals, and Reformers in the Making of the Nation*. New York: Knopf, 2011.

Zabin, Serena R. *Dangerous Economies: Status and Commerce in Imperial New York*. Philadelphia: University of Pennsylvania Press, 2009.

Zobel, Hiller B. *The Boston Massacre*. New York: W. W. Norton, 1970.

Zuckerman, Michael. *Peaceable Kingdoms: New England Towns in the Eighteenth Century*. New York: Knopf, 1970.

ACKNOWLEDGMENTS

I do not know where to begin acknowledging assistance with a project that has been in motion since my undergraduate classes with Alison Gilbert Olson and Miles Bradbury at the University of Maryland, so I will begin there. Alison (proto-Namierist, neo-Imperial School) inspired me to become a historian and to see early American history as transatlantic, and Miles to take seriously the religion and ideas of early Americans (Harvard School). John McCusker (school of hard knocks) taught me to work hard at becoming a historian and to take the economy seriously, and Ronald Hoffman's seminar on the American Revolution introduced me to the historiography and one clear view of the terrain (Wisconsin School). At Princeton, in Lawrence Stone's seminars on English history, I began to learn just how much the colonists were and were not Englishmen. In seminars with John Murrin (general practitioners' school) and Douglas Greenberg (New Jersey School), I began tackling the vast history and its contentious historiography in all its breadth and depth. In Stanley Katz's (proto-Namierist/Harvard School) classes on law and American society, I engaged the constitutional and legal histories that helped me understand the political debates of the Revolutionary era. These teachers and my classmates helped me comprehend how big a project it is to explain the Revolution, its causes, roots, and consequences, fully, and how much more I had to learn. Maybe that explains why Tolstoy's views on history appeal to me so much.

I will also never forget the advice given me repeatedly by the retired gentleman who maintained an office on C-floor of Firestone Library. Wesley Frank Craven, a legendary historian of the American South during the seventeenth and eighteenth centuries, startled me any number of times while he was walking to or from his office. When I was writing, Professor Craven would tap me gently on the shoulder and ask rhetorically: "What exactly is it you are trying to prove, Mr. Slaughter?" He would then smile as he ambled away. When he passed while I was reading, the same gentle tap, but a different rhetorical question: "You know, of course, Mr. Slaughter, that research is only an excuse for not writing?"

The trajectory of this project continued at Rutgers, where I taught a course on the American Revolution to undergraduates for nineteen years and more often than any other course I taught. It was both the first and one of the last courses I taught there, always under the guiding hand of Paul Clemens (Wisconsin School) and often in conversation with Philip Greven (Harvard School) and Calvin Martin (mystical school). Since Paul read an early draft of this book, he has remained supportive of this project for many, many years, and has contributed generously to helping me see the bigger (historical geography) and smaller (teacup school) pictures. Robert Churchill, Sara Gronim, Gregory Knouff, Peter Messer, Camilla Townsend, and many other Rutgers graduate students were also critical participants in the process, as were Matthew Allison, Christopher Osborne, Matthew Salafia, and Joseph Schumaker at Notre Dame, and Mitch Gruber, Michael Read, and Serenity Sutherland at the University of Rochester.

Louis Masur (Bronx School) was with me back in the graduate colloquia at Princeton, and he and Douglas Greenberg (now Spielberg/New Jersey School) were still willing to read and help improve the manuscript thirty-five years later. Wow; thanks. Along the way I also picked up a couple more close readers with shared interests in the subject, and I am deeply grateful to Brendan McConville and David Waldstreicher for their gentle (yeah, right) and insightful (always) readings of the manuscript. Two of my colleagues at the University of Rochester also indulged me with readings of the full manuscript, and I am greatly indebted to Daniel Borus (Cardinal School) and Robert Westbrook (Colorado School) for their criticisms and suggestions, as well. I am even more grateful for their invitation to coach in the Hystoria Fantasy Baseball League.

Three research assistants have done yeoman service checking quotations, finding maps and illustrations, and otherwise following fuzzy leads, even to a few dead ends. I greatly appreciate the help of Matthew Allison, Michael Brown, and Jeffrey Ludwig at the University of Rochester, and Anna Moscatiello at Notre Dame, who chased "independence/independance" through eighteenth-century newspapers for virtual decades on end.

It has been an adventure and a thrill to work with Elisabeth Sifton, on two books now, and I am deeply grateful for her keen eye, sharp wit, and confidence in this project. Daniel Gerstle and Miranda Popkey have been unfailingly helpful, responsive, and generous. The book's production team, Abby Kagan, Lenni Wolff, Cynthia Merman, and Jonathan Lippincott, has done its usual professional job and produced a better product than what we gave them.

At home, Denise held down the fort without reinforcements when I was in the office working. When I was at home, she, Jasmine, Moses, the two furry critters (Garfield and the recently deceased and much missed Toto), and the dozens of wild feathered and little furry ones in the garden that are always demanding more seeds distracted me and helped me keep my priorities straight.

The project, by the way, was not always this book, although this book is the end of my road. I do not teach the American Revolution anymore. Instead, I teach The History of Eating and Food and The Seward Family in Peace and in War, the first a contribution to a curriculum in global history, and the second part of a digital humanities sequence and project that I collaborate in with the Rare Books and Special Collections Department in our campus library (where my office is), the Digital Humanities Center, the Seward House Museum, and our digital studies curriculum at the University of Rochester.

Things have changed. Six years ago, when I came to the University of Rochester, there wasn't a place or a need for me to teach the Revolution in what was always my global, local, transatlantic, social, economic, ideological, narrative way. How else would you teach the Revolution? Well, there are many ways, all of them valid. No, how else could *I* teach the Revolution? The project and the process were honing *my* way of telling the story—not the only way or even arguably the best of many, many ways to tell the story but the best way for me to tell the story that is true to how I see it after thirty-five years of studying, thinking, talking about, and teaching the subject. There's more to say, but this book is, at great length, all I will write.

INDEX

A NOTE ABOUT THE AUTHOR

Thomas P. Slaughter is the author of *The Beautiful Soul of John Woolman, Apostle of Abolition* (Hill and Wang, 2008) and four other books. He is the Arthur R. Miller Professor at the University of Rochester and the editor of *Reviews in American History*.